When Boston Still Had

The Babe

THE 1918 WORLD CHAMPION RED SOX

Edited by Bill Nowlin

ASSOCIATE EDITORS
Mark Armour, Len Levin, Allan Wood

Published by Rounder Books

an imprint of
Rounder Records Corp.
One Rounder Way
Burlington, MA 01803

ISBN-13: 978-1-57940-159-7
ISBN-10: 1-57940-159-7

Edited by Bill Nowlin.
Associate editors: Mark Armour, Len Levin, Allan Wood

When Boston Still Had the Babe: The 1918 World Series Champion Red Sox
1. Boston Red Sox (baseball team). 2. 1918 baseball season 3. Biography I. Nowlin, Bill.

First edition

Library of Congress Control Number: 2007909085
796.357'092

Interior design and composition by Jane Tenenbaum
Cover design by Steve Jurgensmeyer

Contents

•••

•••

1918 Red Sox — Introduction

by Allan Wood

Late into the infamous 86-year championship drought of the Boston Red Sox — from 1918 to 2004 — it became nearly taboo to talk seriously about the 1918 team.

One reason for that reluctance was the sullied reputation of the team's then-owner, Harry Frazee — the man who sold Boston's beloved superstar, Babe Ruth, to the New York Yankees. Then there were the four World Series losses — 1946, 1967, 1975, and 1986 — each loss coming in the seventh and final game, reinforcing the image of the Red Sox as a team unable to win when it truly counted.

Over the last decade, the national sports media became obsessed with the idea that this chronic futility was caused by a beyond-the-grave curse. Indeed, media often reported with a straight face that the Boston franchise was cursed. The very year "1918" became a taunt at Yankee Stadium.

Taken together, one can well understand why many Red Sox fans wanted to forget the year 1918 altogether.

But winning a World Series championship is nothing to be ashamed of, and nothing to be brushed under history's rug. 1918 was a fascinating season — not only for the Red Sox, but for major league baseball in general.

The United States had entered Europe's Great War in April 1917, but few players enlisted that summer and the war had very little direct impact on the national sport. During the winter of 1917–18, however, dozens of major league players left their teams. They either enlisted in the military or accepted jobs in war-related industries, such as shipyards or munitions factories.

Some of the players the Red Sox lost were: manager/second baseman Jack Barry, left fielder Duffy Lewis (who led the team in batting and slugging in 1917), pitcher Ernie Shore, and utility infielders Hal Janvrin, Mike McNally, Del Gainer, and Chick Shorten.

As 1918's spring training loomed, most owners bided their time, deciding to wait until the beginning of the season was closer and their needs became more certain. The one owner who was the most pro-active, who took the biggest and quickest steps to rebuild his team's roster, was Red Sox president Harry Frazee. In December 1917 and January 1918, Frazee made two headline-grabbing deals with Connie Mack of the Philadelphia Athletics, sending a handful of players and the sizeable sum of $60,000 to Mack for pitcher Joe Bush, catcher Wally Schang, infielder Stuffy McInnis, and outfielder Amos Strunk.

In the wake of this wheeling-and-dealing, a January editorial in the *New York Times* expressed disgust at the "disorganizing effect" that Frazee and Chicago Cubs president Charlie Weeghman were having on the national game by "offering all sorts of money for star ballplayers." (Weeghman had spent a small fortune to acquire the superb battery of pitcher Grover Alexander and catcher Bill Killefer from the Philadelphia Phillies.) The *Times* wrote: "The club owners are not content to wait for a few seasons while their managers develop a pennant winner, but have undertaken to accomplish in one year what other clubs have waited years to achieve."

In other words, the *Times* was accusing Harry Frazee of trying to buy the American League pennant.

This view of Frazee as a free-spending, win-at-all-costs magnate clashes with his modern-day image. If baseball fans know Frazee's name at all, it's because he was the man responsible for selling Babe Ruth to the Yankees after the 1919 season. But in 1918, Frazee was intent on bringing another World Series title to Boston. The Red Sox won the championship in 1912, their first year at Fenway Park, then won back-to-back titles in 1915 and 1916. (The cross-town Boston Braves had swept the 1914 series.) After a second-place showing in 1917 — Boston won 90 games, but finished 10 games behind the eventual World Series champion Chicago White Sox — Frazee was determined to put the Red Sox back on top.

Boston was also fortunate in that most of its war-related personnel losses came well before spring training. Many other clubs started 1918 strong, but saw their line-ups decimated as the summer went on.

In addition to the two deals with the Athletics, Frazee hired former International League president Ed Barrow to manage the team. Barrow had previously managed the Detroit Tigers in 1903 and part of 1904 (for a combined record of 97–117). Next, Frazee signed George Whiteman, a 35-year-old outfielder, to replace Lewis. Whiteman was a career minor-leaguer, though he did have cups of coffee with both the Red Sox (1907) and Yankees (1913). And a few weeks before Opening Day, Frazee traded for Cincinnati's 34-year-old second baseman Dave Shean. Whiteman and Shean were both out of the draft's age range (21–31).

Of the eight regulars in Boston's Opening Day lineup, only two were holdovers from the previous year: right fielder Harry Hooper and shortstop Everett Scott.

The great Red Sox teams of the 1910s were built around excellent pitching and air-tight fielding. The team's offense had been below league average in 1916 and 1917 (and would be again in 1918), so it was fortunate that the 1918 pitching staff remained largely intact. Anchoring the rotation were Babe Ruth and Carl Mays, a left-right tandem that had combined for 41 wins in 1916 and 46 wins in 1917. Dutch Leonard was another lefty and newcomer Joe Bush would take Shore's spot as the fourth starter. After Leonard took a shipyard job in mid-season, right-hander Sam Jones took over. Those five pitchers — Mays, Ruth, Bush, Leonard, and Jones — would start all but six of Boston's 126 games.

The roster upheaval caused by the war also gave plenty of marginal players the opportunity, however brief, to play in the major leagues. In Boston, a handful of players counted their time with the 1918 Red Sox as their only big league experience: Eusebio Gonzalez (seven plate appearances over three games) Red Bluhm (one at-bat as a pinch-hitter), George Cochran (.117 average), and Jack Stansbury (who *slugged* .149 in 20 games).

In 1918, a summer-long soap opera played out over whether the remaining players would receive a blanket exemption from the draft, as other entertainers such as stage actors enjoyed. At first, the National Commission — the sport's ruling body, comprised of American League president Ban Johnson, National League president John Tener, and Cincinnati Reds owner August Herrmann — simply assumed that an exemption would be granted. When baseball was deemed "not essential," the Commission scrambled to file requests for extensions, desperately hoping to finish the regular season.

The Commission bumbled its way through the summer, insisting to sportswriters that it would be happy to cancel the season because winning the war was the highest priority, then begging the War Department for a further extension, so owners wouldn't lose as much money. The government finally set September 1, 1918 as the absolute deadline. The owners decided against continuing the season past that point with players either under or over draft age.

Not only did the regular season come to an early close, the World Series almost did, too. The 1918 World Series, played in early September, was nearly derailed by a furious off-field battle between the Red Sox and Chicago Cubs players, on one side, and the National Commission on the other, over what percentage of the gate receipts would be awarded to the winners and losers of the series.

In the three previous years, 1915–17, the shares were almost $4,000 for each player on the winning team and $2,500 for each player on the losing side. In some cases, those amounts were as much as a player's annual salary.

Ticket prices for the 1918 World Series were reduced with the hope of boosting attendance. In 1917, box seats were $5.00, grandstand seats were $3.00, pavilions were $2.00, and bleachers were $1.00. For the 1918 series, box seats were reduced to $3.00 and the other ticket prices were cut in half.

The plan did not work. The crowds for the first three games at Comiskey Park were 19,274, 20,040 and 27,054 (the third game was on a Saturday afternoon thanks only to the rainout of Game One). The first two games of the

1917 World Series, also played at Comiskey, drew over 32,000 each.

The National Commission had also decided, for the first time, that players on the second-, third- and fourth-place teams in each league would get a cut of the World Series dough. The Commission also "volunteered" to donate some of the players' shares to charity — without consulting the players. The players learned about all of this as the Series began. It looked like the shares could be cut by as much as 75%.

The Commission refused to meet with the players. The two teams, led by Red Sox captain Harry Hooper, decided to not take the field at Fenway Park for Game Five until the matter was resolved.

When Ban Johnson arrived at the park drunk, and with no intentions — or ability — to seriously discuss finances, and with nearly 25,000 fans waiting for the start of the game, the players reluctantly agreed to play that afternoon, and to finish the Series. A teary-eyed Johnson assured Hooper the players would not be punished for their one-hour delay of Game Five. One month later, Johnson broke his promise, as the Commission refused to award championship emblems, the equivalent of World Series rings, to the Red Sox. (The individual shares ended up being $1,100 for the Red Sox and $670 for the Cubs.)

1918 was also the summer that a young man from Baltimore, Maryland, began his unprecedented transition from ace pitcher to the greatest hitter in baseball history.

Babe Ruth had been one of baseball's best pitchers in 1916 and 1917, but three weeks into the 1918 season, faced with a depleted roster, no reinforcements, and a need for more offense, Ed Barrow moved Ruth into the regular lineup, eventually playing him at first base and in left field.

Although Ruth's potential as an everyday player had been an occasional topic in the sports pages since his rookie season of 1915, when he was actually out there, there was plenty of debate. Would Ruth's weaknesses at the plate be quickly discovered and exploited by opposing pitchers? Would he ruin his arm making long throws from the outfield? Could he play every day *and* continuing pitching?

On May 6, 1918, in a game against the Yankees at the Polo Grounds, Ruth debuted at first base and batted sixth. He went 2-for-4, including a two-run home run. The next day, in Washington, Ruth was moved up to the #4 spot in the lineup — and celebrated the promotion with another home run, off Senators ace Walter Johnson. In the final game of the Senators series, on May 9, Ruth lost a 10-inning complete game on the mound, but also went 5-for-5 with three doubles, a triple, and a single. (That is still the major league record for extra-base hits by a pitcher in an extra-inning game.)

Oddly enough, Boston lost their first six games with Ruth in the field and slipped out of first place. Melville

Ruth's spring training clouts attracted attention from the start. March 22, 1918 *Boston Post*.

Webb Jr. of the *Boston Globe* was not impressed: "Putting a pitcher in as an everyday man, no matter how he likes it or how he may hit, is not the sign of strength for a club that aspires to be a real contender."

As Ruth's hitting began drawing more attention, his desire to pitch dwindled. This didn't sit well with Barrow, especially after Dutch Leonard's departure left the team without a left-handed starter. Ruth insisted his left wrist was sore; he and Barrow argued throughout June. After a dugout confrontation in Washington on July 2, Ruth quit the team, fleeing to his father's house in Baltimore.

Babe considered joining a shipyard and playing for the company team, but quickly learned that the shipyard would also want him to pitch. He'd also be taking a huge cut in pay. Ruth returned to the Red Sox a couple of days later, patching up his differences with Barrow. As the Red Sox got hot in the month of July, Ruth turned in what was arguably the greatest nine- or ten-week stretch of play the game has ever seen.

In one 10-game period (July 6–22) during a Fenway homestand, Ruth batted .469 (15-for-32) with four singles, six doubles, and five triples. Although he did not hit any home runs in July or August, Ruth was feared as a batter all year long. He was walked intentionally in the first inning as often as he was in the ninth inning. In mid-June, the St. Louis Browns gave him a free pass in five consecutive plate appearances over two games. As far as can be determined, that remains a major league record (Barry Bonds was also walked intentionally five straight times on September 22–23, 2004).

After returning from his Fourth of July defection, Babe took his turn on the mound every fourth day and proved that he was still one of the game's top pitchers.

Ruth made 11 starts and won nine of them (all complete games), including the pennant-clincher against Philadelphia. In his last 10 starts of the season, he allowed more than two runs only once.

Of the many nicknames Ruth earned during his Red Sox career — the Big Fellow, Tarzan, the Caveman, the Colossus — one was particularly apt. As the Colossus of Rhodes was believed to have straddled the entrance to the harbor of ancient Greece, his New England namesake towered over the national sport in 1918, one huge foot planted on either side of baseball's pitching and hitting camps.

Imagine Johan Santana playing first base or DH-ing in every game he didn't pitch. Then imagine Santana remaining a dominant pitcher while putting up a batting line to rival Barry Bonds or Albert Pujols. *That* was Babe Ruth in 1918.

Ruth wasn't the first major leaguer to pull double duty, but almost all of the players who pitched and played the field in the early 1900s either had very short careers or their performances were unexceptional.

In contrast, Babe led both leagues in slugging average by a wide margin in 1918 — his .555 topped Ty Cobb's second place finish of .515 in the AL and Edd Roush's NL-best .455. His 11 home runs were more than the totals of five other AL teams. Ruth finished second in doubles, third in RBI, fifth in triples, and eighth in walks — all accomplished in 100 to 175 fewer plate appearances than his American League peers.

Ruth's 2.22 ERA was eighth best in the AL. He allowed an average of only 9.52 hits and walks per nine innings, second only to the Senators' Walter Johnson. Ruth had the third lowest opponents' on-base average and fourth lowest opponents' batting average.

In the World Series, Ruth beat the Cubs in Games One and Four, setting a new World Series record of 29.2 consecutive scoreless innings, a streak he began in 1916. Ruth set many records during his career, but that accomplishment was the one of which he was most proud. It would stand until the Yankees' Whitey Ford broke it in 1961.

When lists are made of baseball's top dynasties, the Red Sox teams of the 1910s are rarely mentioned. While they are not in the upper echelon of the 1906–12 Chicago Cubs (713–356, .667) or the 1936–42 New York Yankees (701–371, .654), their seven-year winning percentage from 1912–18 (632–406, .609) is better than the seven-year run of the 1996–2002 Yankees (685–445, .606).

In this book, 28 members of the Society for American Baseball Research have compiled the most in-depth look at the 1918 Red Sox. They have unearthed a wealth of information — much of it never seen before — about every one of the 32 players who suited up that year, from Harry Hooper and Everett Scott, who played in all 126 games, to Red Bluhm, who had one pinch-hitting opportunity.

For Red Sox fans, the life-changing events of October 2004 should forever remove any stigma attached to the 1918 club. And for all baseball fans, it will be a chance to travel back to a time when the Boston Red Sox were the kings of the diamond.

The 1917 Red Sox—An "Off-year"

by Bill Nowlin

The Red Sox were coming off back-to-back World Championships in 1915 and 1916. From 1910 through 1916, the American League pennant had either been won by Philadelphia or Boston. No one else.

Early in January 1917, and after several entreaties that he stay, manager Bill Carrigan reaffirmed his earlier announcement that he would not be back as manager of the Red Sox. President Harry Frazee, who'd purchased the team right after the 1916 World Series, had earlier traveled to Lewiston, Maine to try and sign the popular Carrigan for another season, but it was not to be. Tim Murnane of the *Boston Globe* noted that second baseman Jack Barry and right fielder Harry Hooper had been mentioned as possible skippers, but added that Frazee probably hadn't given the matter much thought, so determined was he to re-sign Carrigan.

Renowned sportswriter Grantland Rice said Boston would be "as hard to beat in 1917 as they were in 1915 and 1916." He foresaw another Giants/Red Sox World Series, reprising their classic from 1912.

On January 4, though, Carrigan definitively declared he would remain in Maine and not return to skipper the Sox.

Frazee was ready with a replacement and on January 5, he named Jack Barry to manage, and continue as the team's second baseman. Barry accepted the job, saying, "I know that no cleaner living, more loyal fellows ever put on spikes and I am sure I will have hearty support from every man on the Red Sox team." Murnane predicted that the White Sox could give Boston a run for its money. The Red Sox, though, planned to bring back pretty much the same team that had done so well the previous two years—and that was a good thing.

Pitcher Smoky Joe Wood wouldn't be back, though. On February 24, Frazee sold him to Cleveland for $15,000. There was some wrangling over pay between Frazee and some of the players. Though Dave Fultz was trying to organize the Players' Fraternity—an early attempt at what might be called unionization—Frazee succeeded in signing most of the players in early February. Carl Mays balked at signing and was informed that he could pay his own way to spring training if he had not signed before the time to report.

Anticipating U. S. entry into the World War, Frazee said he would have his players drill for a full hour each day, starting in spring training. On March 3, the Red Sox party left Boston for Hot Springs, Arkansas, departing from Track 13. On March 6, the players had a light workout and took a hike over a mountain trail. Some of

the holdouts came into camp one at a time over the next week or two. On May 18, the Sox played their first opponent, the Brooklyn Robins, losing 7–2. The team got in their games, despite a few rainouts, and closed out March with a beauty, keyed by Jack Barry pulling a squeeze play to beat Brooklyn. The exhibition schedule brought the Red Sox north through Davenport, Indianapolis, Toledo, and other cities, arriving in New York on April 9, ready to play the Yankees on Opening Day.

The season began with Babe Ruth pitching Boston to a 10–3 win over New York. Dutch Leonard beat the Yankees, 6–1, the following afternoon. After playing their first seven games on the road, the Red Sox came home for Opening Day with a 5–2 record. They beat the Yankees 6–4 in the Fenway Park opener but lost the next two, one of them a 2–1 loss in a no-hitter thrown by George Mogridge. Nonetheless, when Babe Ruth won his fifth start in a row on April 30, they closed out the month sporting a 9–4 record. They were in first place, a half-game ahead of the White Sox.

Ruth ran his record to 7–0 with a two-hit 1–0 shutout against Washington and Walter Johnson on May 7 and a 2–1 win over Detroit on May 11. The Red Sox lost consecutive games to the White Sox on May 18 and 19, and actually dropped to third in the standings, percentage points behind the Yankees and White Sox. A 2–1 win by Carl Mays the next day put the Red Sox back in first, but Jack Barry suffered a serious knee injury during the game.

The Red Sox continued to play well, sweeping the Senators in back-to-back doubleheaders on May 29 and 30. They ended the month in first place, a game and a half ahead of the White Sox, with a record of 27–10. At this point the Red Sox had won 10 games in a row (there was one tie game in the midst of the stretch) and were, in the words of a *Globe* headline, "not stopping to tie their shoelaces."

Oops. On June 1, the Indians shut them out, on only one hit—the first time the Sox had been shutout in 1917. Then Cleveland shut them out again the next day. The Red Sox hit a stretch where they were shut out four more times and lost seven out of eight games, dropping to second place, a full 3½ games behind Chicago. The bats had gone quiet, hitting below .200 as a team during most of the first half of June. On the year, they were hitting .236 as of Bunker Hill Day.

They took two from Chicago on June 18th to close the gap. Two days later, Babe Ruth won his 12th game of the year. In his next start, against the Senators, Ruth walked the first batter of the game on four pitches but disagreed with umpire Owens about two of the calls. Ruth punched the umpire and was thrown out of the game, dragged off the field by a few policemen; Ernie Shore came in and retired 27 consecutive men — the first one being the runner on first who was cut down trying to steal second. Retiring 27 in a row is a perfect game, regardless of how Major League Baseball might choose to define it. When June ended, the Red Sox remained in second, 1½ games behind Chicago.

After winning the final five games of three back-to-back-to-back doubleheaders from the visiting Athletics, Boston was a half-game out of first, briefly taking first place on July 7. They then balanced the scales by dropping five of their next six. Visiting Chicago was a disaster. Boston won one, tied a game that ran 15 innings, but lost four, and left Comiskey Park for home with their tails between their legs, 4½ games behind the White Sox as of July 23.

Back in Boston, the Red Sox reeled off seven wins in a row, the last two against the visiting White Sox and worked their way into a tie atop the standings as of July 31. It was too good to last; they dropped the next two games to Chicago. Things went wrong. Rube Foster threw a one-hitter against the Indians, and lost 2–0. The following day, the Sox made five errors and lost that one, too. The two Sox teams kept pace with each other. August 17 saw the Red Sox up by percentage points over the White Sox, but the Chicagoans picked up the pace and won 13 of 15; by month's end, they had restored their 4½ game lead.

The White Sox didn't cool down; they kicked off September taking 12 of their first 14 games. That 25–4 run was a torrid pace that the Red Sox couldn't match. By September 10, Boston was seven games behind. By the 20th, they were 9½ games out. The very next day, September 21, Chicago took a 2–1 game from the Red Sox after 10 innings at Fenway, clinching the 1917 pennant. The Red Sox would not repeat as World Champions.

Frazee sent a telegram of congratulations to Chicago's Comiskey. Several days later, he declined to play the Braves in a postseason exhibition City Series, saying that the fans just weren't interested. That was an understatement. On September 28, the *Boston Globe* reported that only 356 fans came out to watch the Red Sox drop a game to the St. Louis Browns. Boston finished the season with a very good 90–62 record, but were nine games behind the White Sox. Red Sox pitchers allowed the fewest runs of any team in the league, but Chicago batters scored the most runs of any team. The White Sox won the World Series, defeating the New York Giants in six games.

On November 1, Jack Barry reported for duty in the Navy, as did Duffy Lewis, Ernie Shore, Chick Shorten, and Mike McNally. The war in Europe was on in earnest and would greatly impact the coming 1918 season. Hal Janvrin enlisted in the Signal Corps on December 1. More than 50 major league ballplayers had enlisted in military service, and 11 of those were from the Red Sox — clearly the team most affected. In the Navy were: Lore Bader, Jack Barry, Del Gainer, Duffy Lewis, Mike McNally, Herb Pennock, Ernie Shore, and Chick Shorten. Jack Bentley, Jim Cooney, and Hal Janvrin were serving elsewhere. Sam Jones had been accepted for service and awaiting orders, and Dick Hoblitzell was working to get into the Dental Reserve Corps. Another draft was expected to follow, which would scoop up more players. Harry Hooper, for one, was ready to go.

On at least two occasions, Harry Frazee denied he was planning to sell the team. On the contrary, he was hoping the war would be wrapped up by Opening Day and vowed to have a strong team when it did. On December 14, he pulled off a major trade with the Athletics, sending them Pinch Thomas, Vean Gregg, Manny Kopp, and a reported $60,000 in cash (yes, Frazee spent some serious bucks on at least one occasion), acquiring pitcher Bullet Joe Bush, catcher Wally Schang, and outfielder Amos Strunk. The *Globe* called it "one of the biggest baseball deals that has been pulled off in years." The newspaper expected it would make the Red Sox a very strong contender in 1918. He hoped to have Jack Barry back as manager and to add Ed Barrow to his executive staff. As events transpired, the war would continue and contribute to a shortened season.

1918 — Spring Training

by Bill Nowlin

Frazee kicked off the new year making another move, again with Connie Mack's Athletics, trading players to be named later for first baseman Stuffy McInnis. Mack termed the deal a "near-gift," letting McInnis go to the team where he wanted to play even though he could have sold him for more than $25,000. Mack later selected Larry Gardner, Tillie Walker, and Hick Cady. The first player to sign with the Red Sox for 1918 was pitcher Babe Ruth. He inked a contract for $7,000 and talked about the possibility of winning 30 games (he was 23–12 in 1916).

Towards the end of January, the Red Sox received word that Jack Barry would not be relieved from Navy duties for at least several months and was effectively lost for the season. Frazee again approached Bill Carrigan, with no success. On February 11, Ed Barrow was named as Jack Barry's replacement as manager of the Red Sox. One of Barrow's first pronouncements was that players would be prohibited from bringing their wives to spring training. Former Cubs star infielder Johnny Evers was hired as a coach, possible second baseman, and a "general strategy man."

Assembling a team was far more difficult than usual, given the number of players who were either gone to service or likely to be called. Barrow and Frazee had to constantly consider the depth of their roster and the replacements that could be brought to bear if this player or that player left for war-related work or to enlist in one of the service branches. Hanging over it all was the question as to whether the season itself might be curtailed at some point. Even as late as early March, the Sox roster was — to put it mildly — a little unsettled. It wasn't exactly clear who might play second base and Barrow was considering playing first baseman Stuffy McInnis at third base. Other teams faced similar situations.

On March 8, the Red Sox left for spring training in

Spring training in Hot Springs, Arkansas, 1917. Front row l-r: Tilly Walker, Larry Gardner, Chick Shorten, Dick McCabe, Ernie Shore, Everett Scott, Fred Thomas. Back row: Unknown, Tyson, Kelleher, Walsh, Pennock, Jenkins, Devine. Courtesy of Michael Mumby.

the Ozarks, returning again to Hot Springs, Arkansas. A snow storm caused a delay of several hours in the trainyard outside Buffalo, and the Sox party missed their connection, costing them the first full day of practice. Soldiers on board the train sought out conversations with a gregarious Babe Ruth. The party heading south also included team secretary Larry Graver, attorney Thomas Barry, trainer Dr. Martin Lawler, and scout Billy Murray.

On March 11, Barrow met with his charges and "made it plain to them in a 15-minute talk that discipline more rigid than has ever been exercised before" would be a feature of the camp and throughout the season. No player was to be seen in the breakfast room after 9:30 in the morning. Moreover, poker was too be "confined strictly to the 10-cent variety and all games must end promptly each night at 11 o'clock." The same rules applied to newspapermen, rooters, and others associated with the team. Not one player failed to conform the first day; two who worked out so intently they had to be told to end their day were Johnny Evers and Babe Ruth. After three hours of working out, the players walked the two miles back to the hotel. "Barrow refused to allow his men the luxury of a ride either to or from the park." [*Boston Post*] As for Barrow, he had cut a bit of a stern image sitting in the bleachers and watching the men work out without saying a word. Harry Frazee was in town and finalized contracts with Sam Agnew and Carl Mays. A couple of days later, Barrow decided to drop mountain climbing from the exercise program; only if it was too wet to work out on the ballfield would the players be compelled to take mountain hikes.

Early in camp, a strange thing happened: despite some initial nervousness, 18-year-old prospect Mimos Ellenberg of Chuckey, Tennessee (some accounts say Mosheim), who Ed Barrow had proclaimed "may be another Hornsby," impressed the Red Sox so much that they wanted to sign him. They couldn't find him; he simply disappeared. It was later determined he'd become quite ill and, come March 17, he was sent home.

On March 16, several more of the squad turned up in town: Everett Scott, Amos Strunk, Fred Thomas, George Whiteman, and Paul Smith. Dick Hoblitzell arrived on the 19th — and four days later Ed Barrow named him as team captain. Dutch Leonard turned up on the 21st. McInnis was working out at third base, fielding bunt after bunt, while Fred Thomas "ostensibly recruited as a third sacker, is developing into a likely second baseman." Pitcher Rube Foster said he wanted more money, then found Frazee telling him not to bother coming to Hot Springs unless he was to pay his own way, and was ultimately traded (on April 1) to Cincinnati for Dave Shean.

The first exhibition game came on Sunday, March 17 and Red Sox batters bombed Brooklyn pitching for 16 hits at Majestic Park, and won 11–1. Babe Ruth hit two home runs for the 2,500 assembled, matching his total

for the entire 1917 regular season. It was one of only two games the Red Sox played in their Hot Springs home. As it happened, both the Brooklyn Robins and the Red Sox trained at Hot Springs in 1918, Brooklyn working out at Whittington Park. The two teams played 11 games, with Boston winning seven. After six days of workouts in the "Valley of the Vapors," the two teams played another couple of games and then took their show on the road and proceeded to play five games at Little Rock, before heading on to three cities in Texas, as well as New Orleans, Mobile, and Birmingham.

Just a few days after the first game, however, there was a bizarre incident that could have ended the team's pennant hopes before they had even really begun. Hooper, Ruth, Schang, Joe Bush, and Everett Scott had hired a car to take them from the race track back to the Hotel Marion. The driver tried to let them off short of the hotel, demanding payment, so he could run back to the track and pick up another fare. The Sox quintet called a policeman who ordered the driver to continue on to the hotel. The enraged driver shouted, "I will tip you all out first" and then tore off at such speed that he "banged a jitney aside, knocked a horse down and busted up a wagon." Hooper's threat regarding the chauffeur's nose brought an end to the affair. [*Boston Globe*, March 21, 1918]

After the March 17 opener, the two teams didn't play another game for a week. Nevertheless, despite being a war-shortened season, the number of exhibition games was not diminished. The spring season comprised 14 games, more than any year since 1911. (During the season, they added three more. None of them were fundraisers for the war effort; this became widespread practice during the Second World War. The Red Sox hadn't played postseason games since 1910, though some of the players toured after the World Series — and paid a stiff price for doing so.)

The weather failed to cooperate. Several players developed colds, and there were almost no intrasquad scrimmages. The Sox and Dodgers finally got in another game on the 24th, and Babe Ruth hit a grand slam home run as part of a six-run third inning that sank the Trolley Dodgers, 7–1. Mays and Ruth pitched; both Ruth and Dutch Leonard played right field. With two outs and the bases loaded in the third, Ruth swung at the first pitch and the ball "cleared the fence by about 200 feet and dropped in the pond by the alligator farm." In Little Rock, the second-string Boston Yannigans clobbered the Brooklyn Rookies, 18–8.

The following day, too many players were under the weather, so Barrow had the men work on signals, leads off first base, sacrifice bunts, and a number of fundamentals. Too many lame arms among the pitchers resulted in the following day being one devoted to batting practice.

On March 27, the two teams matched off for two games in Little Rock. The games were held at Fort Pike;

the first was played in front of 700 or 800 soldiers who saw the Brooklyn regulars beat the Red Sox, 3–2. The *Post*'s Paul Shannon noted several situations where Red Sox players didn't seem to have their heads in the game, and lost opportunities as a result. Thomas was charged with two errors. The Red Sox regulars beat the "Agnews" the following day, 2–1. Prospect Lona Jaynes threw a complete game three-hitter for the Regulars and Dick McCabe allowed the first stringers only six hits.

On March 29, the Red Sox learned that Majestic Park would be demolished later in the year so that railroad tracks could be laid through the property. The Sox signed a five-year option on Fordyce Park in Hot Springs as their new spring home, but it was a revocable deal and Frazee commented that he might move the team to another location, one that did not have a racetrack. He felt the ballplayers sometimes seemed a little too ready to end practice early and head out to the track.

Sam Jones arrived in camp at this point; the Red Sox had thought he was due to be inducted at Camp Sherman, and had placed him on voluntary leave, but he had instead been placed in Class B and was hurriedly offered a 1918 contract. Frazee said he might seek an extra infielder but otherwise believed he had the men he needed.

On March 30, the Red Sox beat the Dodgers at Little Rock, 4–3, scoring twice in the eighth and twice in the ninth — on Ruth's home run. It was his fourth home run in four games against Brooklyn.

On the last day of March, the Red Sox again won the game in the ninth inning, scoring five times to come from behind and take the honors, 7–4. On the first day of April, the Sox did it yet again, scoring the run that broke a 2–2 tie with one out in the bottom of the ninth. Strunk walked, stole second, took third on McInnis's sacrifice. After Hoblitzell was walked intentionally, Whiteman singled Strunk in with the game-winner.

The two teams traveled to Texas and played their first game on April 2, a dramatic 16-inning affair in Dallas that began with the Red Sox scoring four times in the top of the first. Tied 4–4 after nine, both teams scored twice in the 15th, the tilt going in Boston's favor in the 16th when newly-arrived Dave Shean doubled and then took third on a bad pickoff peg. He scored on Strunk's sacrifice fly for a 7–6 Boston victory. Ruth was so angry at striking out his first time up that he flung his bat "half way to right

Detail from March 22, 1918, *Boston Post* cartoon, which appeared under headline "Babe Ruth Is Hard Worker and He Is A Considerable Hitter".

field" and then batted right-handed his second time up (he whiffed again). The teams traveled to Waco on April 3 and the Dodgers won 2–1, but not without some ninth-inning suspense, as Shean, the potential tying run, was stranded at second to end the game.

And for the third game in a row, Shean shone. Playing in Austin at the University of Texas (most of the crowd being military aviation students), Boston beat Brooklyn, 10–4. Shean had himself a 5-for-5 day. Harry Hooper had three hits, including a triple and a home run. Boston lost in Houston on the 5th, 5–3, with two McInnis errors proving very costly. Shean drove in two runs. It might have been spring training, but the *Boston Herald* reported that the Sox manager gave the men a "merciless tongue-lashing...a full hour of the ruthless criticism that big Ed Barrow knows how to hand out."

The two teams squared off for 13 innings in New Orleans on April 7. Some 5,000 fans saw the Dodgers' Jim Hickman triple, then score on Clarence Mitchell's single for a 4–3 Brooklyn win. Moving on to Mobile, the teams played 13 innings again, but this time darkness brought an end to a game knotted 6–6. Each team scored once in the 14th frame. Playing the following day in Birmingham, the temperature dropped 50 degrees and Brooklyn beat Boston, 3–1, the game called after seven innings due to darkness.

There was an odd twist on the two Alabama dates in that men from both teams joined together to play as the "Supersox" (derived by combining the old Brooklyn Superbas name with the Red Sox) for a couple of extra games. On April 7, the "Brooklyn-Boston" team (as it was shown in box scores) played the Southern Association team at Mobile and suffered a 2–0 one-hit shutout. The combined team was composed of "second team" players, by and large. On April 9, at Birmingham, the Barons beat the combined team by, again, a score of 2–0 in another "Supersox" game. The regular game was played in frigid conditions and both teams rushed through the work, completing the entire seven-inning game in 35 minutes.

The game scheduled for Chattanooga on April 10 was called off due to cold weather after both teams arrived at the ballpark. Several of the players visited a nearby internment camp for German prisoners of war. Earlier hopes to play in Louisville and Pittsburgh, or Richmond, on the way north had come to naught. That evening, the Red Sox took the 10:30 train out of town and headed for

Boston with a three-hour layover in Cincinnati. The Red Sox had won the series of games, 8–5, with one tie. There was also the game the Red Sox second team crushed Brooklyn's Yannigans. Scott, Strunk, and Hoblitzell were all hobbled with foot and ankle injuries and, in general, as Paul Shannon wrote in the *Post*, "The Red Sox did not put up the brand of ball toward the end of the series that they did at first. There is a lot of room for improvement in their work."

The team arrived home on April 12. Groundskeeper Jerome Kelley was to have had Fenway ready for an afternoon workout on Saturday the 13th, but the city was blanketed with snow. Those who boarded at Put's (a hotel where many players dwelled) checked in there; the others made their way to their various apartments/abodes.

Coach Hugh Duffy arranged for the use of the Harvard cage — the first time major leaguers had worked out there — and after four days of inactivity the ballplayers "raced around the cage like a lot of colts let out to pasture." [*Boston Herald*] Harry Frazee told the *Herald*, "You can say that I am well pleased with the club's prospects for the coming season."

The *Boston Post*'s Paul Shannon wrote a long piece the day before the season opened, headlined "Red Sox Feel All Set to Go After Another World's Title This Season." He began the article, "Barring the absence of a strong utility string, hitherto one of the traditional features of a Boston Red Sox team, the newly constructed American League outfit, an organization that hovered on the verge of disruption only to be rebuilt with marvelous rapidity will take the field . . . Monday."

The war had taken many, Carrigan was no longer manager, others had been traded away . . . all told, it was "practically a new team." Shannon gave new manager Barrow credit for having "moulded a team well worthy of supporting Red Sox tradition and repeating Red Sox triumphs."

And triumph was, of course, the tradition for the Boston Americans who had won the pennant in five of the preceding 15 years. Credit must go, of course, to Harry Frazee, who hired Barrow and funded the acquisitions that seemed to Shannon to set the team up for a strong season. Frazee was not an absentee owner but, despite his other responsibilities in the theater world, an engaged and energetic owner.

Shannon detailed the various positions. Even at this late date, two players that he expected to make strong contributions never did: Johnny Evers and Paul Smith. But all in all he saw "an array of congenial, hard-working players with confidence in their own ability and supreme confidence in the judgment and ability of their new manager. A brainy, well-behaved set of players who will pull hard for victory all the time, because they see the vision of another pennant and regard their amalgamation that union of veterans with newly purchased stars as a remodeling, which may assure them of first honors for more than one year. No jealousy mars their good fellowship and harmony is the keynote of this crowd. Small wonder that Barrow is contented."

No team can go through an entire season in harmony, however, but the Red Sox did begin the 1918 season on April 15 with a 7–1 win over the Philadelphia Athletics.

The 1918 Team

1918 Boston Red Sox. Back row l-r: Trainer Dr. Martin Lawler, Hack Miller, Sam Jones, Fred Thomas, Babe Ruth, Harry Hooper, Carl Mays, Dave Shean, Walt Kinney, Amos Strunk, Stuffy McInnis, Edward Barrow. Front row l-r: Everett Scott, Jean Dubuc, Joe Bush, George Whiteman, Wally Schang, Wally Mayer, Heinie Wagner, Sam Agnew, Jack Coffey. Mascot and batboy in front.

SAM AGNEW *by John McMurray*

G	AB	R	H	2B	3B	HR	RBI	BB	SO	BA	OBP	SLG	SB	HBP
72	199	11	33	8	0	0	6	11	26	.166	.221	.206	0	3

Sam Agnew is best remembered for being the catcher for both of Babe Ruth's pitching victories in the 1918 World Series. Although Agnew did not get a hit in the four Series games in which he played, he caught Ruth's complete game shutout in Game One and eight innings of Ruth's pitching in the tightly-contested Game Four before being removed for pinch-hitter Wally Schang in the bottom of the eighth; Schang singled and scored the game-winning run. A *Hartford Courant* subhead in mid-September, when a number of players appeared in a postseason exhibition game in Connecticut's capital, read, "Ruth and Agnew Regarded as One of Strongest Batteries in Majors."

Sam Agnew, Red Sox catcher 1916–1918.

Agnew shared the catching duties with Schang and Wally Mayer in 1918, catching the most games of the trio. He was known for taking risks trying to throw out baserunners, which contributed to his leading the league in errors twice in three years while with the St. Louis Browns, with 28 errors in 1913; 25 in 1914; and 39 in 1915. In 1918, however, Agnew made only 13 errors, one of the lowest totals of his career, albeit in fewer games.

As a major leaguer, Agnew was never known for his hitting. Playing in 72 games in 1918, the right-handed batting Agnew got only 33 hits in 199 at-bats, finishing the year with a .166 average, no home runs, and six runs batted in. In fact, Agnew never hit better than .235 or drove in more than 24 runs in any of his seven major league seasons.

Samuel Lester Agnew's first professional baseball experience came in California with Vernon of the Pacific Coast League in 1912. There, the Farmington, Missouri, native had a strong offensive season, hitting .283 with five home runs. His performance caught the eye of the St. Louis Browns, who selected Agnew in the day's equivalent of the Rule 5 draft. One thing impressed them: He was reportedly the only catcher in the United States who had caught more than 100 games without a passed ball.

Agnew made his major league debut with the Browns two days before his 25th birthday, on Opening Day, April 10, 1913, in a 3–1 St. Louis victory over Detroit.

Agnew's rookie season was his best offensively: The 5-foot-11, 185-pound backstop had career highs with nine doubles and five triples and 11 stolen bases. Agnew also hit the only two home runs of his career in 1913, the first a three-run homer off Boardwalk Brown on June 11 in Philadelphia and the second a solo homer served up by Russ Ford on July 13 at home in Sportsman's Park.

Agnew's rookie success was short-lived. On July 25, 1913, in a game against the Washington Senators, Agnew suffered a broken jaw after being hit by a Joe Engel fastball. During that game, which ended in an 8–8 tie after 15 innings, Johnson struck out 15 batters in the last 11 innings. Agnew was hospitalized for a week, until August 1; he began work again with the Browns on August 20. He completed the year appearing in 103 games, hitting .208 with the two homers and 24 RBIs. After the regular season was over, Agnew took part in a spirited city championship series in which the Browns beat the Cardinals, the final double-header apparently degenerating, as reported in the *New York Times* to a "fist fight between players, numerous verbal battles between the managers, the desertion of the umpires, and many other exciting features."

Agnew also caught more than 100 games in both 1914 and 1915 for the Browns, but the team languished, finishing in seventh place in both seasons. In 1914, he caught 115 games and hit .212, driving in only 16 runs. The following year, he hit .203 in 104 games with 19 RBIs. Incidentally, he led the league in passed balls both years, with 18 and 17 respectively. Once more, the Browns won the St. Louis city series. Agnew made one headline after a bizarre moment on August 18, 1914, when he was called out by the umpire while sitting in the Browns dugout. With two runners on base, when Tillie Walker came up to bat in place of Doc Lavan, umpire Evans noticed that, according to the lineup card, the Browns had been batting out of order. Agnew was supposed to be batting, not Lavan. Agnew was called out and Wallace, who had singled, was removed from first base.

On December 16, 1915, Agnew was sold to the Boston Red Sox, who wanted him to serve as a backup to

Agnew getting loose before a ballgame.

incumbent catcher Pinch Thomas. He had impressed Boston with his ability to cut down base stealers; in 1915, Agnew had thrown out Harry Hooper six times. Despite his anemic batting average, the *Boston Globe* termed the new acquisition "a fine all-around player" and asserted that "he is a pretty good batter." The price was apparently $10,000. League president Ban Johnson announced that the deal would not be allowed to go through, but he was soon forced to back down.

Although Agnew played in only 40 games in 1916 with Boston, he was involved in one of the most dramatic incidents of that season. On June 30, Senators shortstop George McBride threw his bat at Boston pitcher Carl Mays, who had hit McBride with a pitch. In the ensuing brawl, Agnew reportedly punched Washington manager Clark Griffith in the face. The outcry was so great that Agnew was arrested on the field, and Boston manager Bill Carrigan had to bail him out of jail. Fortunately for Agnew, all charges were ultimately dropped.

Agnew and Hick Cady both backed up Thomas throughout the 1916 season. Thomas, Cady, and Carrigan all saw action in the World Series, but Agnew did not. He was, however, the first player to report to Hot Springs for spring training in 1917.

Now 30 years of age, Agnew caught more games than any other Boston catcher in 1917 and again in 1918. Appearing in 85 games to Thomas's 83 in 1917, he hit .208

and drove in 16 runs. In 1918, after a brief holdout in spring training, Agnew appeared in 72 of the season's 126 games, batting just .166.

Agnew did have his moments in the 1918 World Series: Though hitless in nine at-bats, he threw out three of the four Chicago Cubs baserunners who tried to steal against him and played errorless defense.

As noted above, Agnew and Babe Ruth were among those who played in a three-game exhibition series in Hartford. In the rubber game on September 15, Ruth outpitched Dutch Leonard, 1–0, and Agnew singled in the winning run in the ninth inning.

In March 1919, Agnew was purchased by the Washington Senators. The move was surprising in that the Senators were still managed by Clark Griffith, with whom Agnew had brawled three years earlier. The *Washington Post* headline read: "Griff Will Have Real Scrapper. Claims Agnew, Red Sox Catcher, Who Punched Him in 1916." As one contemporary article noted, "Griff is likely to have a little difficulty in getting [Agnew's] signature to a contract. [Lest] we forget, a couple of years ago, Griff and Sam had a punching match at Fenway Park, which resulted in Sam being grabbed by a man who wears a blue coat and brass buttons."

The six-year veteran was a known quantity at the time, but it was his work behind the plate — rather than at it — that presented value. The *Post* noted, "When it comes to slugging, as we know it in baseball, Sam is in the never-was class. Anything over a .200 batting average is as found money to him. But Sam can catch." His defensive work had improved remarkably during his years in Boston.

With the Senators, Agnew played behind catcher Val Picinich. He caught only 36 games for the seventh-place Senators, appearing in six other games, and batting a career-high .235, with 10 RBIs. But he often served as the preferred catcher for Walter Johnson, because, according to the *Post*'s J.V. Fitz Gerald, "he puts plenty of life and ginger in his work, something Johnson likes in a batterymate."

Agnew's major league career was over following the 1919 season. In addition to the eventual Hall of Famers who Agnew played with in Boston, Agnew in his career had also been a teammate of Walter Johnson, Branch Rickey, and George Sisler.

Agnew's career actually got a boost after the left the major leagues. He was purchased by the San Francisco Seals of the Pacific Coast League for the 1920 season, where he became, according to his obituary in the August 1, 1951, issue of *The Sporting News*, "a favorite with the fans in the Bay Area" over what would become almost an eight-year stay with the team. There was a hitch at the start of the long relationship, though, when he balked at the pay he was offered. The *Washington Post* said he "shocked" the team with his salary demands. The Coast

League played a longer season, and Agnew said he would need more than he was paid in the major leagues for that very reason, since he "must hire a man to run his farm for a longer period."

In four of those seasons with the Seals, Agnew batted over .300, and he hit more than 10 home runs in a season five times. Agnew was a key contributor to the 1925 Seals team that went 128–71, hitting 20 home runs, driving in 85 runs, and batting .326.

With the Seals, Agnew had the chance to catch Lefty O'Doul, Ernie Shore, and Walter Mails, among others. In the Coast League, Agnew also formed a strong friendship with Seals teammate Archie Yelle, a major leaguer with the Detroit Tigers from 1917 to 1919. Agnew's obituary in *The Sporting News* recounted the following incident, as told by Agnew's good friend, sportswriter Abe Kemp:

> One day, Agnew suspected that Yelle was injured in a close play at the plate. Archie brushed Sam aside when he offered to catch the remainder of the game. After the game Yelle dressed beside [Charley] Graham [the manager of the Seals]. As he took off his right shoe, blood splattered over the floor.
> "When did you get cut, Arch?" said Graham.
> "In the second inning," replied Yelle.
> "Why didn't you mention the accident when it took place?"
> "Sam has been working too hard," was Yelle's laconic answer.

Agnew was ambitious. In late 1922, while playing some winter ball with San Bernardino's Santa Fe team, he partnered with two area men and organized the San Bernardino Baseball and Amusement Association, which planned to build a ballpark and launch a new Class B or Class C league in Southern California. In January 1923, backed by "unlimited financial interests" (*Los Angeles Times*), he shifted to trying to purchase the Salt Lake City Bees ballclub and move it to San Bernardino. The move never happened and Agnew kept on playing.

Agnew finished his playing career with Hollywood of the PCL, playing for the Stars at the end of the 1927

"Sam Agnew, the Red Sox' Husky Catcher."
Boston Post, March 28, 1918.

season and throughout 1928. At age 41, Agnew finished his playing career and opened a gas station in Boyes Springs, California.

Sam Agnew's brother was Troy Agnew, who had an accomplished minor league career and was the player-manager for the 1924 Okmulgee Drillers team that had a 110–48 record in the National Association. Troy went on to run the Augusta franchise of the Sally League in the 1930s, and Sam managed. Troy later bought the Palatka Azaleas in the Florida State League.

Troy hired Sam to manage the Azaleas to start the 1937 season. However, according to a July 29, 1937, newspaper account, the Agnew brothers had several run-ins with the local community, "including a report that the city had refused water to [the team] to sprinkle the diamond and police to patrol the park. Now Mayor J.W. Campbell is rallying the citizens to the support of the club as a civic enterprise to show the Agnews the city is behind the team." Sam Agnew soon left to become the manager of the team in Augusta, under his brother Troy.

In December 1939, Sam Agnew purchased the Meridian, Mississippi, team in the Southeastern League, where "he will be in complete charge next season," according to one newspaper report. With experience managing minor league teams in San Diego, Augusta, and Palatka under his belt, Sam had taken the next step. The team had been known as the Scrappers since 1937, but fans argued for a name change to something more robust. Sam approved a contest run by the local *Meridian Star* newspaper to pick a new name, and the team became the Bears for the 1940 season. But the Mississippi team struggled to be economically viable from the start, and Sam publicly proposed relocating the team to Florida, making his tenure as owner a rocky one.

Agnew battled a severe heart condition in his later years. He slipped into what his obituary called a "semicoma" for months before having a "miraculous" recovery in November 1950. His heart trouble caught up with him, however, and Sam Agnew died on July 19, 1951, at a hospital in Sonoma, California, at the age of 63. He was survived by his wife, Dorothy. Agnew is buried at Chapel of the Chimes Cemetery in Santa Rosa, California.

LORE VERNE "KING" BADER *by Rob Edelman*

G	ERA	W	L	SV	GS	GF	CG	SHO	IP	H	R	ER	BB	SO	HR	HBP	WP	BFP
5	3.33	1	3	0	4	1	2	1	27	26	13	10	12	10	1	3	0	116

G	AB	R	H	2B	3B	HR	RBI	BB	SO	BA	OBP	SLG	SB	HBP
5	9	0	1	0	0	0	0	0	3	.111	.111	.111	0	0

Lore Verne "King" Bader was a lesser member of the 1918 Boston Red Sox. A right-handed hurler, he pitched in just five games, starting four and compiling an unexceptional 1–3 record. All told, Bader appeared in a modest 22 games over three major league campaigns, in 1912 (with the New York Giants) and 1917–18 (with the Red Sox), winning five and losing three. His ERA was an impressive 2.51 in 75$\frac{1}{3}$ innings, and he pitched memorable games against future Hall of Famers Grover Cleveland Alexander and Walter Johnson. Bader's top professional seasons came between his years of major league service, when he hurled for the Texas League Dallas Giants and International League Buffalo Bisons, and in 1920, when he was a leader on the Ill. Toronto Maple Leafs mound staff. His latter minor league and semipro careers were tainted, however, as he was accused of unfairly baffling batters with emery balls, shine balls, and spitballs.

Bader was born on April 27, 1888, in Bader, Illinois, a small railroad town. Some sources list his hometown as Astoria, Illinois, but the Bader birthplace was confirmed by his wife, Lura, in a 1973 letter to the Baseball Hall of Fame. Lura described it as "a small town very near Astoria" that was "settled by the Bader clan. An old uncle was in the logging and lumber business and through him a [railroad] spur was built. . . ."

Bader grew to be 6'0" tall. During his career, his average weight was 175 pounds. Although a right hander on the mound, he batted left-handed. How he earned the nickname "King" is unknown, but his fondness for playing cards won him a second moniker: "Two Pairs."

During his childhood, Bader moved with his parents to LeRoy, Kansas. Starting in 1908, he began playing for a town team. He originally was a first baseman, but one day the LeRoy hurler failed to appear for an important game. Bader volunteered to replace him. Despite his wildness, he emerged victorious — and decided to become a pitcher.

Bader went to work as an assistant cashier in banks in Lenora and Avard, Oklahoma. "But I was too much

King Bader in 1912, with the New York Giants. Courtesy of Chicago History Museum.

in love with baseball to settle down to any such business," Bader told sportswriter during one of his Red Sox tryouts. "My head would fairly swim after poring over account books all day and I actually dreamed of figures at night." By August 1909, he was pitching for a town team in Lenora. An item from an unidentified newspaper, published that month, noted, "Bader who pitched a good game in the morning against Cestos, was in the box again for the afternoon game, and the way he made the Mooreland salaried players fan the air was great."

Bader was eager to become a "salaried player." On January 5, 1911, he signed his first professional contract, with the Independence Packers in the Western Association, a C-level minor league, and, as he recalled to O'Rourke, he "quit the bank clerking business [forever]." When the league broke up prior to the season's end he signed with Dallas, where he compiled a 1–1 record in eight games and 45 innings.

Nineteen-twelve was a momentous year for Bader. He returned to Dallas, compiling a 16–14 record in 41 games. He surrendered 215 hits in 273 innings while walking 71 and striking out 123. The *LeRoy Reporter* noted that Bader had married Lura Brutchin in Dallas on June 19. Then on July 31, New York Giants manager John McGraw announced that the team had purchased the contracts of two hurlers, Al Demaree from Mobile of the Southern Association and Bader of Dallas. In reporting the deal, *The Sporting News* referred to the hurler as "'Iron Man' Bader, the best right-handed pitcher Dallas has this year and one of the best in the Texas League. . . ." On August 15, the Giants played the Cubs in Chicago. "Pitcher Bader of Dallas, Texas, joined the Giants to-day, and warmed up in a Cub traveling uniform," reported the *New York Times*. "He is a big, husky athlete, and showed plenty of speed."

Bader's big league debut came on September 30, several days after the Giants clinched the NL pennant. It could not have been much more impressive. The 24-year-old tossed a nine-hit, complete game 4–2 victory over the Philadelphia Phillies, besting Grover Cleveland Alexander, who had been vying for his 20th victory. The *Boston*

Globe reported, "Another of McGraw's recruits showed big league class today at the Polo Grounds.... While Bader was hit hard, he always tightened in the pinches, and was at his best with men on bases." Added the *New York Times,* under the headline "Giants Try New Pitcher and Win, "Lou [sic] Bader of Dallas, Texas... went to the rubber and showed that he had a backbone of steel under fire." Damon Runyon described Bader as "a loose-jointed right-hander, who devotes himself to old-fashioned pitching. He appeared to have the limber curves expected of a young man of his occupation, and he also has quite some vapor on the baseball when he drives it through."

Bader got into one final game that season, pitching a scoreless inning in relief on October 3 against Brooklyn, in one of the final games at Washington Park prior to the christening of Ebbets Field. His major league introduction augured well for Bader. In 10 innings pitched, he allowed just one earned run. His ERA was a snazzy 0.90. The one smudge on his record was his walk-to-strikeout ratio. He struck out three, but handed out six passes.

On December 31, the Giants announced that Bader was one of nine young pitchers invited to the team's Marlin, Texas, spring training camp. On January 19, 1913, the *New York Times* ran his picture (along with those of Ferdie Schupp, La Rue Kirby, and Ted Goulait) under the headline "Young Pitchers for the Giants." "From these four youngsters, and also Al Demaree," the *Times* reported, "Manager McGraw expects to be able to pick out a couple of promising additions to his pitching staff next season."

The Giants received Bader's signed contract on January 18. Spring training commenced in mid-February and Bader promptly reported to Marlin, where he and his fellow rookies were tutored by Wilbert Robinson, McGraw's assistant. On March 2, Bader pitched four shutout innings against Dallas. But his chance to make the team faded when he contracted measles and left training camp for two weeks. He was back by the end of the month; on March 30, he surrendered five hits in four innings' work against Dallas. Despite his impressive debut the previous season, Bader never again pitched for the Giants. On April 9, as major league teams were finalizing their opening day rosters, McGraw announced that Bader had been released to Dallas. He was the workhorse of the Texas club's staff that 1913 season, appearing in 46 games, tossing 308 innings, and compiling a 22–12 record. He surrendered 238 hits while walking 90 and striking out 170.

From 1914 to 1916, Bader was a leader on the pitching staff of the International League's Buffalo Bisons, compiling records of 16–7, 20–18, and 23–8 while taking the mound for, respectively, 30, 48, and 37 games and 224, 334, and 294 innings. During his first season in Buffalo, he likely was tutored on how to toss the soon-to-be illegal emery ball. One of his teammates was Russ Ford, who is credited with perfecting the pitch in 1910.

Bader's only opportunity to face major league batters in 1914 was in exhibition games. On March 27, he was one of three pitchers who toiled for Buffalo against the New York Yankees in Charlotte, North Carolina. Surely the highlight of his season came on opening day, when he pitched a 13-inning, complete game victory, besting the Baltimore Orioles (then an International League club), 1–0. Then on October 15, he hooked up with no less a personage than Walter Johnson. The Big Train, a native of Humboldt, Kansas, suited up with the Coffeyville nine — described in newspaper reports as "the hometown team" — and faced Bader, pitching for an Independence nine. Not only did Bader win the 1–0 contest, but he singled and scored the lone run on a three-bagger.

Despite these heroics, no big-league club selected Bader for a roster spot. But he was proving to be a steady performer at Buffalo. In an April 28, 1915, preseason game, he spun a four-hit, 3–0 victory against the Providence Grays. Similar successes followed as the season progressed, with newspaper reports citing Bader as one of the International League's premier hurlers.

In 1916, the hurler might have returned to the majors with the Red Sox. On January 12, Bill Carrigan, manager of the then-world champs, announced that Bader had been picked up by the team on the recommendation of Patsy Donovan, the Bisons' skipper. The following day, the *Boston Globe* reported that "the chances are that [Bader] will get a good try out at Hot Springs [Arkansas]." On February 6, the day after the Bosox received Bader's signed contract, the *Globe* ran a photo of the hurler under the headline, "'King' Bader, Latest Addition to the Red Sox Pitching Staff."

Given his record in Buffalo, much was expected of Bader in 1916. "Manager Carrigan has confidence that Bader will show big league form this season and plans to give him a regular berth from the start," the *Globe* noted. *Boston Herald* scribe Burt Whitman reported, "He's a rookie here in the Red Sox camp... but [he] has the appearance and the self-possession and evidently the self-confidence of the seasoned veteran..." The headline of Whitman's article described Bader as the "Hercules of the 1915 International league."

But inconsistency and an injury-plagued spring training doomed his chances to stick with the big club. While warming up in the outfield prior to a March 18 exhibition, Bader severely twisted his knee. Three days later he was back on the field, pitching for the Boston regulars in a six-inning exhibition with the intrasquad "yannigans," and the *Globe* noted that he "was effective with a slow, dreamy delivery...." On March 26, the paper ran a photo under the headline "This Eleven Comprises the Pitching Staff of the Red Sox, One of the Best in Baseball." Bader was pictured between two future Hall of Famers, Babe Ruth and Herb Pennock. But on March 29, Bader fared miserably in a six-inning contest pitting the

Bosox regulars against the second-stringers. His failure was emphasized in the following day's *Boston Globe* game report, which was headlined "Red Sox Jump on 'King' Bader." Bader and Babe Ruth pitched for the second team. Ruth started, and limited the regulars to two hits in three innings. He was relieved by Bader, who promptly was pummeled. He also committed two errors, on a Dick Hoblitzell grounder and a Marty McHale squeeze play. "Bader's showing was a disappointment," the *Globe* wrote, "but a lame arm was undoubtedly responsible. Yesterday he showed signs of having overcome the 'tied up' feeling that has characterized his delivery, but today that old kink made its reappearance."

Bader rebounded on April 11, when he and Herb Pennock combined to five-hit Boston College in a 9–1 victory. At the time, four hurlers were battling for the final spot on the Bosox pitching staff — and he was one of the odd men out. On April 19, just as the regular season started, he was dispatched to Buffalo.

In 1916, Bader topped the IL with an exemplary 2.05 ERA. He pitched brilliantly that year, with a typical newspaper account of his heroics appearing in the May 4 *Boston Globe*, which reported that Providence "was almost helpless before Bader" in the previous day's 3–2 Bisons victory.

In 1917, Bader finally stuck with the Red Sox. That season, with the permission of Jack Barry, the new Red Sox skipper, Bader came to Hot Springs to work out for 10 days before reporting to the Bisons' Norfolk, Virginia, training camp. On March 23, the *Boston Globe* reported from Hot Springs, "Bader is here now and is looking fine," and Barry became interested in securing the pitcher's contract. Bader was scheduled to leave for Norfolk on March 28, but instead accompanied the Red Sox to Little Rock. Two days later, he was traded to Boston for pitcher Vean Gregg and a player or players to be named. These turned out to be infielder Bob Gill and outfielder Manny Kopp.

1917 was Bader's busiest major league campaign. He started one game, pitched in relief in 14 others, and compiled a 2–0 record with a 2.35 ERA in 38 1/3 innings. As in 1912, his major debit was his walk-to-strikeout ratio; he gave free passes to 18 batters while striking out 14.

Bader saw his first action on May 17, when he followed Ernie Shore and Herb Pennock in a 7–1 loss to the Indians in Cleveland. The following day, he appeared in one of his more memorable major league games — if only because of the pitcher he replaced, and the streak that was halted. The Red Sox played the White Sox in Chicago. Babe Ruth, the Boston starter, had won eight straight games, but was fated to be the losing pitcher. The Babe surrendered three runs in the second inning. After he gave up two more in the third, Bader replaced him and surrendered three more runs in the sixth in the 8–2 loss.

Bader played in both games of a May 30 doubleheader against the Nationals in Washington. It arguably was his finest day in the majors. In the first game, the Nationals knocked out starter Ernie Shore in the eighth inning. Bader relieved with runners on second and third, retired the side, and earned the save (retroactively calculated — saves were not a statistic in 1917) in the 4–3 victory. Then he started the nightcap, surrendering six hits and eight walks in seven innings before handing the ball over to Herb Pennock in a 3–2 win. Yet again, Bader smashed a single off Walter Johnson.

Notwithstanding, Bader pitched sparingly for Boston. On August 11, the *Globe* reported that he had been traded to the Providence Grays for catcher Walter Mayer, but Bader remained in Boston. He was in the headlines again 10 days later. In the fourth inning of an August 21 game against the Chicago White Sox, Red Sox first sacker Del Gainer was doubled off first base. He slid back into the base with one of his spikes too high off the ground to suit Chick Gandil, the White Sox first baseman. The two began jawing, with the argument continuing in the ninth when Gandil unnecessarily slid into first base. After the game, Bader and several teammates approached Gandil. Bader and Gandil began fighting and, according to the *New York Times*, Gandil "disposed of Lore Bader ... in one round of [an] encounter on the way to the rival shower baths." The paper added, "All accounts agree that one punch settled the argument for the rest of the season and Bader was the recipient of the punch." He emerged with a split lip and claimed that Gandil had a ball in his right hand when he threw his punch.

During the 1917 season, Bader's plate appearances also were infrequent. He may have hit .300 on the nose, but he accomplished this in just 10 at-bats. In his three seasons in the majors he amassed a total of four base hits, and sported a measly .182 batting average.

Back in April, the United States had declared war on Germany and entered World War I. On December 14, 1917, Bader and Herb Pennock enlisted as yeomen in the Naval Reserve. Bader immediately reported for duty at the Charlestown Navy Yard and eventually found himself pitching for the Charlestown ball club, primarily composed of big leaguers from the Red Sox, the Boston Braves, and the Philadelphia Athletics. On May 4, 1918, Bader tossed a 12–0 shutout against the Harvard University varsity nine. His three hits were one more than he surrendered to Harvard, one a bunt single and the other a clean single. Bader's teammates included Pennock, Rabbit Maranville, Ernie Shore, Whitey Witt, and Jack Barry, the team's manager. On June 2 he allowed three hits in a 5–0 shutout of the Newport Naval Reserves. On June 18, he beat Holy Cross, 3–2. However, he was discharged from the Navy two days later because of a loose ligament in his knee.

Bader immediately rejoined the Red Sox, but was used sparingly. His Red Sox tenure may be summed up

King Bader throwing at Chicago's West Side Grounds, 1912. Courtesy of Chicago History Museum.

by the sub-heading of a *Globe* report on a June 28 game against Washington, which he lost, 3–1: "Pass By Bader Spells Trouble." According to the *Washington Post*, "Bader walked Nationals at bad times. His wildness in the fourth helped the Griffs to a run and a walk in the eighth handed them another." For the season, he had a 1–3 record, surrendering 26 hits in 27 innings while walking 12 and striking out 10 and compiling a 3.33 ERA.

On July 18, 1918, Bader played his final game for the Red Sox — and in the majors. It was a less-than-auspicious end to his big-league career. The St. Louis Browns bested Boston, 6–3, with the *Globe* reporting that the Brownies "found King Bader's offerings soft picking, [as they] slammed him for 11 blows...." The game was not without some minor fireworks. In the fifth inning, Bader unintentionally hit George Sisler. The *Globe* reported that "the Michigan marvel before trotting to first strutted out toward the box and addressed some objectionable remarks, it is alleged, to the Boston pitcher."

Bader then was quietly dropped from the Boston roster. He was not a part of the team during its pennant run and World Series victory over the Chicago Cubs.

In 1919, Bader was out of professional baseball, but various *Boston Globe* game reports in June and July recorded his pitching exploits for a local semipro team in Quincy, Mass. On July 8, in the paper's "Live Tips and Topics" column, it was noted that Bader "turned a neat

trick last Saturday down at Danielson, Conn., where he pitched against one of the mill teams. 'King' not only pitched a no-hit, no-run game, but fanned 22 batters...." On July 21, the *Globe* printed the following notice: "Quincy Baseball Club, with King Bader in the box and a record of victories over the [top] semiprofessional clubs in New England...wishes to book games away or at home in August." Being a team's marquee player and spinning a no-hitter is an accomplishment for any ballplayer. Only for Bader, who so recently had pitched in the big leagues, such exploits must have been bittersweet.

In 1920, Bader returned to pro baseball, playing for the International League Toronto Maple Leafs and compiling a 19–9 record with a 2.91 ERA. He appeared in 39 games, in which he tossed 229 innings, walked 77, and struck out 94. That season, a question emerged regarding Bader: Was he employing the emery ball in game situations? This issue was subtly referenced in a June 17, 1920, *New York Times* game report, which referred to the "failure to solve the puzzling delivery of Pitcher Bader by the Jersey City bat wielders...." Skepticism over the pitcher's on-field ethics resulted in his being placed on Toronto's "voluntarily retired list" for 1921–22.

Bader returned to the Boston area in 1921, where he worked in the mercantile business while pitching for the twilight league Haverhill Professionals. At this level, his walk-to-strikeout ratio was more than satisfactory. On

August 4, he relieved in the third inning against Norton's South Boston All Stars, fanning nine and surrendering no walks and one hit in an 8–7 defeat. Two days later, he struck out 12 while walking two as he bested Dorchester Town, 1–0, holding them to four scattered singles. His season was not without incident. On September 25, Bader led Haverhill to a 5–2, 10-inning victory over the North Cambridge Knights. He pitched the entire game, surrendering five hits and striking out 16. The *Boston Globe* reported, "The Cambridge players protested Bader's pitching several times, claiming that he was roughing the ball. Some balls were withdrawn from the game by umpire [and former Red Sox flychaser] Olaf Henriksen."

Bader again played ball in Massachusetts during the summer of 1922, spending May and June pitching for the twilight league St. Andrew's A.A. of Forest Hills. By July, he had switched back to Haverhill. On July 8, in one of his best games of the season, he struck out 12 while spinning a one-hit, complete-game victory against Dorchester. Then in August, he was back with St. Andrew's — and courting controversy. On August 15, he fanned 11 while shutting out Dorchester, 1–0. Reported the *Globe,* "Whether or not the contest will count in the league standings is a question, as [Dorchester] Manager Dan Leahy . . . protested the game in the eighth inning, declaring that King Bader, St. Andrew's fadeaway slabster, was 'roughing' the ball." Before the end of the month, he briefly pitched for Haverhill before signing on with the Sacred Hearts of Woonsocket, Rhode Island — and he must have savored the victory he earned on August 27. In an exhibition game against the Red Sox, played in Woonsocket, he bested his former team, 5–3, in a rain-soaked seven-inning complete game victory. The *Boston Globe* game report noted that, "although the Red Sox hit the ball often, it usually went right at the infielders."

On September 17, Bader hurled a complete game for the Sacred Hearts in an exhibition against the Boston Braves, also in Woonsocket. While he was the losing pitcher, the final 2–0 score was more than respectable. But again, the *Globe* report of Bader's effort was less than complimentary: "King Bader, although allowing the Braves but seven hits, was wild in the early innings, but pulled out of several bad holes."

In 1923, Bader "unretired" and rejoined the Toronto Maple Leafs, compiling a 3–1 record in seven games and 47 innings. Throughout his minor league career, his walk totals were high but never more than his number of strikeouts. Now, the aging hurler — he was 35 years old — walked 20 while striking out 13.

His tenure in Toronto ended in controversy. During his time with the Maple Leafs, newspaper reports hinted that he was doctoring his pitches. On June 2, he pitched against the Rochester Tribe, and the *Chicago Tribune* reported that manager George Stallings had complained about Bader's "alleged 'shine ball' delivery." The skipper even promised to protest any future game in which Bader pitched against his team. As proof, Stallings produced several of the balls he claimed Bader had used; reports vary as to whether Bader employed them only in this game or in several recent contests.

While the matter was under investigation by International League officials, Bader abruptly quit the Maple Leafs and returned to Boston. On June 6, the *Syracuse Herald* noted that the constant skepticism by rival teams "may have been the reason he decided to quit organized ball after only having been reinstated this year." Bader finished the summer playing twilight league ball for the Sacred Hearts — and his reputation preceded him. He was dubbed a "Shine Ball Outlaw" and "Shine Ball Artist" in the headlines of articles appearing in June issues of the *Fitchburg Sentinel*. On June 15, the paper claimed that Bader "is barred out of the big leagues because of a freakish delivery and whose shine ball only recently caused a wrangle in the International league. . . ." Ten days later, the *Sentinel* reported that "Speed" Shea, a St. Andrew's pitcher, was a Bader protégé — and the veteran "is teaching the youngster how to get away with the spitter and the shine ball."

In 1924–25, Bader continued pitching in the Boston area and coached a semipro team in East Douglas, Massachusetts. A February 17, 1930, *New York Times* article cited him as the mentor of Bump Hadley, then an up-and-coming major league hurler who played in East Douglas prior to his 1926 debut with Washington. There was no mention of Bader counseling Hadley on how to scuff his pitches.

In March 1926, Bader was hired as a coach for the Boston Braves. After spring training, he was offered a job as pitcher-manager of the New England League Lynn Papooses. He hurled 102 innings, compiling a 6–3 record and 2.64 ERA. On June 30, the *Daily Kennebec Journal* of Augusta, Maine, described Bader as the "hurling ace of the Lynn team," but quickly added that the 38-year-old "is not so young and spry as he was ten years ago." The paper also reported that Bader "is said to be resorting to nicking the ball and this fad has resulted in the throwing out of a few horsehides in Lewiston and other places."

Bader then became a Boston Braves scout. His assignment was to scrutinize promising minor leaguers from New York to the Midwest and Texas. In 1928–29 he returned to the field, managing the Providence Grays (which had become an Eastern League franchise). He also concluded his playing career as he pitched briefly during these seasons, appearing in seven games and winning one without a loss. As a minor league hurler, Bader compiled a respectable 124–72 record. At the end of the 1928 season, Providence scribe Frank Wakefield described him as "still a better twirler than one or two of the moundsmen collecting wages here. . . ."

In 1930, Bader managed the Eastern League Hartford

Senators. He was out of professional baseball the following year but returned in 1932 for one final fling as a coach for the American Association Milwaukee Brewers.

Starting in the mid-1930s, Bader was employed as a WPA manager in Coffey County, Kansas. (The WPA, or Works Project Administration, was a Depression-era jobs program.) According to a 1938 report in *The Sporting News,* he also operated a baseball school in Emporia, Kansas. Primarily, he spent the rest of his working life as a farmer. He and Lura purchased a farm near LeRoy, where they remained until 1955 before moving into a new house in town. For decades, Bader was active in LeRoy's Neosho Masonic Lodge No. 27, and served as district deputy grand master and grand marshal of the Grand Lodge of Kansas A.F. & A.M. Masonic Temple.

A June 22, 1962 news item in the *LeRoy Reporter* noted that Lore and Lura Bader were about to celebrate their golden wedding anniversary. "Modern players," exclaimed the old hurler, "are on the 'sissy side' when they protest that pitchers are throwing at them." Six years later, prior to yet another wedding anniversary, Bader lovingly cited his wife while observing, "We sure have had a wonderful life together."

During the early months of 1973, Bader began preparing his baseball mementoes for donation to the Baseball Hall of Fame. They included a ball autographed by Babe Ruth and Lou Gehrig and a scrapbook, loaded with newspaper clippings charting his career, which had been presented to him by *Providence Evening Bulletin* sportswriter Bill Perrin. The scrapbook was inscribed, "To my friend Lore V. 'King' Bader . . . with whom I passed many pleasant moments during the Eastern League campaign of 1928."

On March 22, Lee Anthony of LeRoy penned a letter in which he solicited the Hall of Fame's interest in Bader's memorabilia. Anthony noted that the aged pitcher suffered from glaucoma and was totally blind, and reported that he had once roomed with Babe Ruth. In a follow-up note, dated April 17, Lura Bader observed that the scrapbook "can tell you more about L.V.'s . . . baseball days than I can." The book and the ball arrived in Cooperstown on May 14.

Bader died quietly in his sleep just over two weeks later, on June 2. He was 85 years old, and was survived by his wife; a brother, Max; and a sister, Ethel; he was predeceased by a brother, Dr. Jesse Moren Bader, the first president and general secretary of the World Convention of Churches of Christ, an evangelical organization. The Baders had no children.

During his later years, Bader savored reminiscing about his baseball career. In his obituary, published in the *LeRoy Reporter*, it was noted that from him "came a rich store of experiences which have made joyful listening for his friends over the past half century."

Bader was buried in LeRoy Cemetery. It is a shame that the old pitcher played for the Giants and Red Sox, rather than Yankees. His funeral service was held at LeRoy's Mattingly Funeral Home. Its proprietor was named Don E. Mattingly.

WALTER BARBARE *by John McMurray*

G	AB	R	H	2B	3B	HR	RBI	BB	SO	BA	OBP	SLG	SB	HBP
13	29	2	5	3	0	0	2	0	1	.172	.172	.276	1	0

While he would have a more substantial role playing for three other teams during his eight-season major league career, Walter Barbare appeared in only 13 games for the 1918 Boston Red Sox. He joined the Red Sox in June after playing the first part of the season with New Orleans of the Southern League, and he finished the season with Jersey City of the International League. As a consequence, Barbare did not play in the 1918 World Series.

That 1918 season was Barbare's least productive in the major leagues. He batted only .172 with five hits in 29 at-bats, no home runs, two runs batted in, and one stolen base. Barbare played 11 games at third base, where he joined George Cochran, Jack Coffey, Jack Stansbury, and Fred Thomas as players who attempted to fill the position for the 1918 Red Sox.

Barbare had been out of baseball in 1917, but he was able to land a spot in the major leagues the next year in part because so many regular major leaguers were serving in the military or working in the defense industry during World War I.

Walter Lawrence Barbare was born on August 11, 1891, in Greenville, South Carolina, and began his professional career with the Greenville Spinners, playing third base, accumulating 413 at-bats and batting .230 with its Carolina Association team in 1912. In 1913, he played third for Asheville in the North Carolina League, batting .273. He made his major league debut at the age of 23 on September 17, 1914, with the Cleveland Naps, and he soon established himself as a versatile utility infielder. He had begun the year with the New Orleans Pelicans, playing exclusively at shortstop, and building up a .296 average in 150 games. As soon as the Southern Association season was completed, Barbare joined Cleveland, playing short and tripling in the only run in the Naps' 8–1 loss to the Red Sox in his very first game. "Dinty" Barbare hit .308 in the 15 major league games he played in 1914, a season limited by the broken jaw he suffered at some point during the year.

He was courted by the Chicago Federal League team, but was under contract to Cleveland and didn't receive an offer sufficient to bolt. Barbare, who batted and threw right-handed, struggled during the 1915 and 1916 seasons with the Cleveland team, which was renamed the Indians in 1915. In 77 games in 1915, he batted only .191. In the two seasons, he drove in a total of 14 runs while playing in 90 games. He initiated a triple play with a spectacular catch on July 24. After playing half his team's games at third in 1915, Barbare was a backup to Bill Wambsganss in 1916, and saw action in only 13 late-season games, with a .229 average.

At 6-feet even, weighing 185 pounds, and with very long arms, Barbare could

Left: Walter Barbare, with the Boston Braves. Courtesy of Chicago History Museum. Right: with the Pittsburgh Pirates. George Brace photo.

be described as lanky. While he did bat .260 and accumulate 462 hits in his 500-game major league career, Barbare never hit for power. The only home run of his career came off Lee Meadows on September 11, 1919. Barbare batted in more than 30 runs in a season only three times as a major leaguer, and he never stole more than 11 bases in a season.

In a letter dated December 8, 1915, Franklin Rostock of the *Cincinnati Post* recommended Barbare to August Herrmann, president of the Cincinnati Reds:

> I received your analysis of Walter Barbare's playing record," said Rostock. "You say that I will notice that his percentage is very low and that he also appears to be a slow man, having stolen only three bases in 77 games [in 1915]. That is the very reason I recommend this player to you, paradoxical as it may seem.
>
> I saw Barbare play and know he is a real ball player, and, because of the poor record he made last season, I figured the Cleveland club might ask waivers on him and send him to a lower league. Of course, if Barbare had batted .280 last season, this matter would not be considered....
>
> Barbare can be used at either third or short, and that is why I recommend him.
>
> Barbare is only a kid and, with proper handling, should develop into a high class ball player.

> His habits are absolutely clean, and, if he is given a chance, I feel he will surely make good.

Despite Rostock's efforts, the Reds never did acquire Barbare, and his offensive struggles led him back to the minor leagues. Barbare played in 122 games with Little Rock of the Southern Association in 1916 in addition to the 13 September games at the major league level with Cleveland. The next year, he began the season playing 21 games with Milwaukee of the American Association, hitting just .163, but the New Orleans Pelicans of the Southern Association traded for him in early May to bolster their defense at shortstop; he played in 123 games with New Orleans, (batting .246).

In 1918, Barbare played short for the Pels again, batting a solid .283 in 70 games before the Southern Association closed its season in late June during the war-shortened campaign. After clinching the pennant, New Orleans announced on June 25 the sale of Barbare, along with infielders Jack Stansbury and Harvey "Red" Bluhm, to the Boston Red Sox.

When the Red Sox left for Chicago on a road trip on July 24, Barbare wasn't with them. Suffering from a "stone bruise," he'd been left behind in Boston and the Sox picked up Eusebio Gonzalez as they passed through Springfield on their way west. It was the end of Barbare's season.

New Orleans still held his contract, but in a late September draft Barbare was selected by the Pittsburgh

Pirates. He got his first extended playing time in Pittsburgh, and batted better than .270 in each of his two seasons there, hitting .273 in 1919 and .274 in 1920 while playing three infield positions. After two fairly productive years in Pittsburgh, Barbare was traded on February 23, 1921, by the Pirates to the Boston Braves along with Fred Nicholson, Billy Southworth, and $15,000 in return for future Hall of Famer Rabbit Maranville.

As he turned 30, Barbare enjoyed his greatest success in the major leagues as a member of the Braves. He set career highs in almost every offensive category in 1921 while playing as the team's regular shortstop: Barbare batted .302 with 166 hits and 49 runs batted in. A solid bunter, Barbare also had 26 sacrifice hits during that season. One of his career highlights took place on April 26, 1921. In a game at Philadelphia, Barbare went 5-for-5 and scored two runs while batting second in the lineup during a 10–6 Braves win. The next year, which would be Barbare's last in the major leagues, he played part time with the Braves and collected 86 hits while batting in 40 runs. He had a hit in his final major league game, getting a single at the Polo Grounds on October 1, 1922, against the New York Giants. On December 14, 1922, Barbare was purchased by Toledo of the American Association for a reported $7,500, and he never played again in the major leagues.

For the 1923 Mudhens, Barbare played third base and second base, batting .288. He was sold to the Memphis Chicks in April 1924, and appeared in 74 games, batting .319. Come 1925, he began the season playing for Memphis but was sold to Knoxville of the Sally (South Atlantic) League in mid-June after batting .315 in 51 games. Barbare served as player-manager for the Smokies, appearing in another 51 games and hitting .317.

He managed Jackson in the Cotton States League in 1926, hitting .296 while playing 65 games at second base, then was out of organized baseball from 1927 through 1929. By early 1930, he was found umpiring college baseball in Clemson, South Carolina. He was hired to manage Talladega of the Georgia-Alabama League that year, and put himself into 19 games, batting .277. They were his last in organized ball.

Barbare went on to play extensively in the industrial leagues of his native South Carolina, including some postseason play for Judson Mills in 1924; Lyman in 1926; and Brandon in 1928.

In his post-professional years, Barbare umpired in the Piedmont League, the Mississippi Valley League, and the South Atlantic League, where he was umpire-in-chief in 1939 according to the plaque installed in the Greenville Baseball Hall of Fame at the time of his September 7, 1993 induction. He coached high school baseball and basketball. Barbare lived in Traveler's Rest, South Carolina, before moving to a nursing home in his birthplace of Greenville, where he died on October 28, 1965, at the age of 74 after a five-month illness. He is buried at Graceland Cemetery in Greenville, South Carolina.

HARVEY "RED" BLUHM *by Maurice Bouchard*

G	AB	R	H	2B	3B	HR	RBI	BB	SO	BA	OBP	SLG	SB	HBP
1	1	0	0	0	0	0	0	0	0	.000	.000	.000	0	0

It was to be Harvey Bluhm's big day, his first major league start. Regular Red Sox first baseman John "Stuffy" McInnis had been suffering from a bad case of boils on his neck and was going to miss at least one game. Boston manager Ed Barrow called on the recently acquired Bluhm to start at first. Barrow would not have been concerned about a weakening of his defense, because Red Bluhm was known to be a slick fielding first sacker. Cleveland Indians scout and former big leaguer Bob Gilks once said, "Bluhm is the best fielding first baseman I have ever laid my eyes on." Bluhm, for his part, must have been anxious to play. He'd gotten close with Cleveland in 1915. He had been practicing with the Sox regulars in this 1918 season and, other than one pinch-hitting assignment on July 3, he had yet to see major league action. On the morning of July 9, Barrow convened a meeting of his team while the day's opponent, the Cleveland Indians, took infield practice. Barrow read the starting lineup, including Bluhm playing first base. Babe Ruth wanted to know what was wrong with Stuffy. When Barrow told him about McInnis's medical problems, Ruth said he would play first. Ruth proceeded to convince Barrow and Bluhm sat on the bench. Harvey Bluhm never got his chance to start and never played in another major league game.

According to official baseball records, Harvey Fred Frank Bluhm was born in Cleveland, Ohio, on June 27, 1894. The year of his birth is in doubt, however. Bluhm's draft registration card from 1917 records his birthdate as June 27, 1891. Census records from 1920 and 1930 have his birth year as 1892 and 1895 respectively. Earlier census records indicate he could have been born as early as 1889. Not much is known for certain of Bluhm's early life. His parents were John Bluhm and the former Mary Saas. John was likely born in Germany. Mary was born in New York state. Harvey Bluhm may have had as many as 11 siblings and half-siblings. Sometime in 1915 or 1916,

Harvey Bluhm married. His wife, Margaret Ann, came to the United States from Ireland in 1913 at 17 or 18 and was a naturalized citizen by 1916. The two had a son, Richard James (born in 1917) and a daughter, Mae Irene (1920).

How Harvey Bluhm got his early baseball education is not known. By 1912[1], the right-handed hitting and throwing first baseman was playing for the Duluth (Minnesota) White Sox of the Central International League. It was the inaugural year for the four-team Class C circuit. Duluth won the league title in 1912 with a 58–41 record. Statistics are incomplete but Bluhm played in at least 30 games, achieving a .223 batting average while playing first base. The following year, the 5-foot-11, 165-pound Bluhm was secured for the Toledo Mud Hens of the American Association, a very high minor league at that time. The Mud Hens were owned by Charles Somers, who also owned the Cleveland Indians. It is possible the Indians secured Bluhm for the Mud Hens. Bluhm had 478 at-bats in 132 games for Toledo in 1913, batting .220 with one home run, six triples, 17 doubles, and 17 stolen bases. The Mud Hens, managed by 14-year major league veteran Topsy Hartsel, finished sixth in the eight-team league.

In 1914, Bluhm was transferred to the New Orleans Pelicans of the Southern Association, a very good minor league, equivalent to the modern Double A level. The Pelicans, owned in large part by Somers, were a powerhouse in the second decade of the 20th century. Managed by former major leaguer Johnny Dobbs, the Pels finished no lower than third in the eight-team league between 1914 and 1922. Bluhm was with the team for most of those years, playing five seasons for the Pelicans.

In 1914, Bluhm played in 131 games, batting .229, with one homer, four triples, 13 doubles, and seven stolen bases in 449 at-bats. The following season, 1915, Bluhm had his finest season as a professional, hitting .293 (second highest on the team) with two home runs, 11 triples, 17 doubles, and 10 stolen bases. He set career highs in batting average, triples, total bases (184), runs (61), at-bats (475), games (137), and hits (139). Bluhm produced a .987 fielding percentage in 1915, third best among Southern Association regular first basemen. He was an integral part of the Pelicans' success on their way to a 91–63 record and the 1915 Southern Association crown. In fact, Bluhm's season was good enough to arouse the notice of the Cleveland Indians. Thanks to Indians scout Bob Gilks, who later told Cleveland sports reporter Henry P. Edwards that Bluhm would be "a sensation in the American League," the Indians purchased the contract of native son Red Bluhm on August 24, 1915.

Because the Pelicans were involved in a pennant race, Bluhm could not join the Indians until the end of the Southern Association season. He played for New Orleans until at least September 26. Bluhm apparently did join the Cleveland club (photos show him wearing a 1915 vintage Indians uniform), but did not appear in a major

league game in 1915. Cleveland manager Lee Fohl decided Bluhm would not hit major league pitching and released him in January, 1916. Bluhm, who had been touted by *The Sporting News* as "just the thing to round out the Indian infield," was back with the Pelicans at the start of the next season. Bluhm tailed off in 1916 as did the Pelicans (they finished second in 1916 and 1917). Bluhm again played in 137 games but hit only .224. In 1917, he bounced back a little, hitting .266 with four home runs, eight triples, and 17 stolen bases in 121 games. In 1918, Bluhm was starting his fifth season for the Pelicans.

He had played in more than 500 Pelicans games and his spectacular play at first base and his shy demeanor made him popular with the Crescent City fans. A three-run, inside-the-park home run to break a 3–3 tie at the home ballyard, Heinemann Park, only increased his popularity with the locals. According to a New Orleans newspaper account, with the score tied 3–3 in the eighth inning, Birmingham Barons pitcher Perryman intentionally walked Pelicans outfielder Brittle to pitch to Bluhm. Bluhm responded with "perhaps the hardest hit ball of the season at Heinemann Park." The report went on to say it was "the cleanest home-run ever hit inside the park — and doubtless the best hit Bluhm ever made."

Red Bluhm was so popular that on June 20, 1918, Pelicans president A.J. Heinemann declared the following Sunday (June 22) to be Red Bluhm Day. Bluhm was likely the first Pelicans player so recognized. One newspaper report discussed at length Bluhm's bashfulness and his reluctance to be in the limelight, and wondered whether the red blooms the lady fans would be wearing would come closer to matching the shade of Bluhm's carrot top locks or his sure-to-be red face. The Pelicans beat the Atlanta Crackers, 4–1, on Bluhm's Day, but the honoree went 0–3 against Crackers hurler Joe Thorburn.

Bluhm hit .267 in 69 games (the Pelicans played only 70 games in 1918) with one home run, three triples, nine doubles, and 12 stolen bases. The Pelicans finished with a 49–21 record, good enough for first place in the shortened season.

The 1918 season was an unusual one throughout professional baseball. The nation was at war. A "work or fight" order was in effect, and draft-age men either had to enlist in the armed forces or show they were working in an essential industry. Was playing professional baseball essential work? That was an open question during most of the season. With no firm federal guidance, local draft boards were left to their own devices. Between players voluntarily enlisting and various draft boards ruling baseball was not essential (and consequently enforcing the "work or fight" rule), major league rosters were in tatters. Big league teams looked to the minors for players to fill their depleted dugouts. Further, attendance was down throughout professional baseball. With their demographic mainstays in the service or working long hours, baseball teams could not keep their turnstiles turning. Most of the minor leagues decided to end their seasons early. The Southern Association was no exception. The league voted to cease operations on June 28. On June 25, president Heinemann announced the sale of three in-fielders to the Boston Red Sox: Bluhm, Walter Barbare, and Jack Stansbury. The three players would join the Sox when the Southern Association ended the following Friday. Bluhm was about to get a second chance at playing in the big leagues.

Bluhm joined the Boston club, likely on June 29 or 30, while the Red Sox were on the road in Washington. His chance to play came against the last-place Philadelphia Athletics on July 3. The Red Sox were in a statistical first place tie with New York and Cleveland, but the team could be excused for look-ing past the lowly Athletics because Boston's big star, Babe Ruth, had quit the team after an argument with man-ager Barrow. The Red Sox sent Lore "King" Bader to the mound at Shibe Park that day. The Athletics countered with southpaw Vean Gregg. The Ath-letics got to Bader in the second, third, and fifth innings but the Sox could do nothing with Gregg. With the Mackmen leading 5–0 in the eighth inning, Bluhm got his opportunity.

Red Bluhm. Detail from a New Orleans newspaper.

The July 4, 1918 edition of the *Boston Globe* described the visitors' half of the eighth this way: "...McInnis and Whiteman both hit safely. Gregg disposing of the next man [Everett Scott], made short work of pinch hitters Barbare and Bluhm, Southern recruits." Bluhm had been sent into the game to hit for the pitcher Bader and popped up to make the final out of the inning. The Athletics went on to win the game, 6–0. That was it, Bluhm's only major league appearance.

Other than playing in some exhibition games on offdays, Bluhm never got in another game with the Red Sox or with any other major league club. After the Red Sox beat Detroit at Fenway Park on July 19, 1918, team president Harry Frazee announced he had optioned first baseman Bluhm to Jersey City of the International League. Bluhm played in 53 games for the Skeeters in 1918, hitting .291 with two homers, four triples, 10 dou-bles, and nine stolen bases. In 1919, Bluhm apparently played for the St. Paul Apostles. His contract was sold to New Orleans for the 1920 season but Bluhm refused to report.

The Bluhms were renting a flat on White Avenue in Cleveland in 1920. They moved to Flint, Michigan, in 1927, and Bluhm went to work for Buick. While employed at the automaker, he played for the highly regarded Buick Majors. He was considered one of the finest first base-men to ever play on a Flint diamond. By 1930 the Bluhms owned their own home at 2840 Begole Street in Flint. Bluhm went to work for Fisher Body in 1930 and played on the factory's baseball team for four or five seasons. After his playing days were over, Bluhm remained actively involved in Flint baseball. He helped or-ganize the City League in the mid-1930s and managed teams from Fisher Body and Citizens Bank.

Bluhm succumbed to a heart attack while watching the Chuck Davey-Chico Vejar welterweight fight, shortly before 10 P.M. on May 7, 1952. He is buried in Sunset Hills Cemetery in Flint. He was survived by his wife, two children, and a grandson, James Edward Bluhm.

Interestingly, Bluhm's participation in the July 3, 1918, contest was lost to of-ficial records for 44 years. While at least three Boston papers had Bluhm in the text of the account of the game and in the box score (additionally, the *New York Times* showed Bluhm's name in the box score for that game), the official score-card of the game sent to the American League did not include his pinch-hitting appearance. In the November 17, 1962, issue of *The Sport-ing News*, sportswriter Lee Allen titled his "Cooperstown Corner" column "Mystery Man Bluhm — Phantom of the '18 Hub Hose." He posed the question about Bluhm's participation in the form of a limerick:

There once was a player named Bluhm.
To pitchers he symbolized doom.
Record-keepers insist
He belongs on the list.
But just when did he play, and for whom?

The question was answered by Bostonian Paul Do-herty. Doherty went to the library, did the research, and reported to Lee Allen (Doherty's letter is in Bluhm's folder at the A. Bartlett Giamatti Research Center, National Baseball Hall of Fame). In the December 15, 1962, issue of *The Sporting News*, Allen reported Doherty's findings and declared the mystery solved.

Note

1. Two small articles about Bluhm in *The Sporting News* (November 25, 1915, page 1, and July 25, 1918, page 4) claim Bluhm had his first professional experience with Youngstown in 1911. If true, the team was probably the Youngstown Steelmen of the Ohio-Pennsylvania League. More research is necessary to verify this claim.

BULLET JOE BUSH *by Ron Anderson*

G	ERA	W	L	SV	GS	GF	CG	SHO	IP	H	R	ER	BB	SO	HR	HBP	WP	BFP
36	2.11	15	15	2	31	4	26	7	272²/₃	241	88	64	91	125	3	3	5	1119

G	AB	R	H	2B	3B	HR	RBI	BB	SO	BA	OBP	SLG	SB	HBP
36	98	8	27	3	2	0	14	6	11	.276	.317	.347	0	0

"Giants Slain By Mere Boy" was the headline of the October 10, 1913 edition of the *Boston Globe*, reporting on 20-year old Joe Bush's defeat of John McGraw's New York Giants and their 22-game winner, Jeff Tesreau, that paved the way for the Philadelphia Athletics' World Championship that year. Bush, known as "Bullet Joe," became an instant hero of the 1913 Series, described by the media as the "Little Boy" who had slain "Goliath."[1]

Leslie Ambrose (Joe) Bush was born on November 27, 1892, in Cass County, Minnesota in an area known as Gull River — possibly a village or township — several miles west of Brainerd. He was the third of seven children of John William "William" Bush and Margaretha "Maggie" (Wieshalla). John William, originally from Ohio, was a conductor with the Northern Pacific Railroad. Mother Maggie was from Dziekanstwo, Poland. Joe's formative years were largely spent in the nearby town of Brainerd, where his family resided in a tiny frame house on Fir Street that still stands, and where he attended high school starring in football and baseball.[2] It is noteworthy that Hall of Famer Chief Bender — Bullet Joe's teammate with Connie Mack's Athletics — was also a Brainerd native.

A November, 1974 article in the *Crow Wing County Review* by Brainerd historian Dr. Carl A. Zapffe described Brainerd as a "baseball-conscious town," erecting a ball park in the very center of the village before many of the city streets were formed. He tells the story, as told to him by a former Joe Bush Brainerd teammate, Louis Imgrund, how Joe would practice his pitching in an old orchard by throwing "exceedingly-fast rotten apples" at the crescent-shaped hole of a neighboring outhouse. A direct

Joe Bush, St. Louis Browns 1925.
Courtesy of Chicago History Museum.

hit meant considerable spray spattered throughout its interior, particularly annoying to anyone seated there. According to Imgrund, Joe "rarely missed."

Brainerd was at the geographical center of Minnesota, populated by railway centers and mills, and was a gateway to numerous lakes and deep forests ideal for sportsmen's pursuits. This lifestyle was influential on young Joe Bush — an avid hunter and outdoorsman — who was later a regular participant in sharpshooting events and hunting excursions, often with such gun-toting baseball cronies as Eddie Collins, Mickey Cochrane, Eddie Plank, Walt Huntzinger, and Sad Sam Jones.

The heretofore earliest known account of Joe Bush's background was described by Joe, himself, to journalist, Carroll Slick, who wrote about Joe's baseball exploits in a series of *Saturday Evening Post* articles in 1929 and 1930. In 1906 — at age 13 — Bush played some third base for the Brainerd town team — recognized as the Brainerd Baseball Club — then named the Brewsters. It is unclear the extent to which he played for them at that young age, although he remained with the club until he turned pro.[3]

In 1910 — at age 17 — Joe began to do some pitching for the town team when the captain, Herb Payne, became impressed with the speed he had on his throws across the diamond. "He was knocking the mitt off the first baseman's hand with his speed," said Payne.[4]

Bush's first important game as a pitcher was in 1911. "I won my spurs as a pitcher," said Joe, in relief against a St. Cloud team. Bush said that he had relieved "an Indian pitcher" who had been hired by Brainerd to play professionally for them.[5] He struck out 11 men that day, won all of his starts that summer, and never looked back.

Joe Bush, detail from *Boston Post* cartoon
depicting action from the July 22 ballgame.

Hugh Campbell, president of the Missoula, Montana, club of the Union Association (Class D) — upon advice of a friend who spotted the young Brainerd phenom — signed Joe to a contract for the 1912 season for $125 per month plus expenses. Cliff Blankenship, an ex-major leaguer, then catcher-manager for Missoula, Montana, of the Union Association (Class D), discovered Joe and signed him to a contract for the 1912 season. Blankenship had discovered and signed the great Walter Johnson to a contract after a scouting mission for the Washington Senators.

An April 1914 article in the *Philadelphia Inquirer* reported in great detail Bullet Joe's experiences hunting and trapping deep in the woods of northern Minnesota in the fall of 1913, following the World Series that year. His guide and companion was Henry Thunderclap of the Red Lake reservation, who was Bush's teammate on a "little team" at Cass Lake, Minnesota when — it is likely — Bush first started in organized ball. As the article describes, young Bush, with the help of his Indian teammate, "put it over their opponents in good style."

Most baseball record books regularly list Bullet Joe at 5-feet-9 inches tall. However, photographs of him standing next to players who, with more than a degree of certainty, were known to be 6-feet or taller is persuasive that Joe's height was probably closer to 6'0". He is, in fact, listed on the Philadelphia A's 1928 roster as 6-feet tall and 185 pounds.

Bush threw with great velocity and was generally compared with the best speed-ball pitchers of the day, second only to Christy Mathewson according to Connie Mack. He had a very good curve ball, and would later develop a forkball when arm trouble made throwing the curve more difficult. Although not the first to throw the unusual flutter ball, Bush would be credited as one of the earliest major leaguers to popularize the delivery, throwing the pitch with consistency and effectiveness. Some say he "invented" it, including Joe himself.[6] Others are usually credited with that distinction.

Bush had a few idiosyncrasies, as well, in his pitching delivery: he threw every pitched ball with such intensity that he emitted a "grunt" sound "that could be heard in the bleachers."[7] He had a pirouette style of delivery called the "Joe Bush twist-around" pitch that Babe Ruth considered quite effective. Ruth encouraged other young Yankees pitchers to mimic the style.

In the articles written with Carroll Slick for the *Saturday Evening Post*, Bush described his pitching style when he first arrived in Missoula as "depending on speed alone to win." Blankenship took him under his wing and taught him how to pitch. It was effective. Missoula won the Gladsome Rug, emblematic of the Union Association championship, with an 83–51 record. Bush posted a league-leading 29–12 record, a winning percentage of .707.

The nickname "Bullet Joe" took hold in Missoula. The club president, Hughie Campbell, began to call him Joe Bush after a former local bronco buster. Later, the local media began to call him Joe Bullet, because of the speed of his fastball. Bush credits the nickname — Bullet Joe — to teammate Eddie Collins, who applied the label after observing a letter in the clubhouse that was addressed to "Joe Bullet" Bush. The nickname stuck for the rest of his baseball career.

Upon the advice of Blankenship — who worked with A's scout Mike Drennan — and Hughie Campbell, Connie Mack, distinguished gentleman, part-owner and manager of the Philadelphia Athletics, purchased Bullet Joe from the Missoula team on August 20, 1912. He made his debut with the A's on September 30 against the New York Highlanders, a game the A's won in 11 innings, 11–10. Bush pitched eight innings, yielding all 10 runs and giving way to future Hall of Famer Stan Coveleski, who got the win in relief. This was Bush's only appearance in 1912.

Mack's ace pitcher, Jack Coombs, fell ill in 1913 and missed most of that season. This unfortunate turn of events for the A's proved fortuitous for Joe Bush, who was called on to be an "added starter" for Mack, and he fulfilled the role nicely, winning 15 of 21 decisions in the regular season.

"Bullet Joe Had Meteoric Rise," proclaimed *The Sporting News* describing his rapid ascent from an obscure minor league team to sudden fame, in 1913, after Bush shut down the New York Giants in the third game of the World Series.[8] At 20, he was but a lad, one of the youngest to play in a World Series at that time, but he stemmed the momentum of a New York team that had soundly defeated the Mackmen, 3–0, at the hands of

Christy Mathewson the day before. That loss seemed to rattle McGraw and his Giants and the A's went on to win that Series, four games to one.

Though he had an illustrious 17-year major league career, young Joe's victory over the Giants in 1913 — early in his career — would be one of only two victories in his seven World Series' decisions. He would long share the dubious distinction of five World Series losses with future Hall of Famers Christy Mathewson, Rube Marquard, and Eddie Plank, a record eventually surpassed by Whitey Ford of the Yankees in 1963. Ford would lose eight Series games, along with his ten victories. But Bullet Joe's World Series losses are distinguishable from the others; his five losses were consecutive, a record that still stands.

Bush had another fine year with the Athletics in 1914, winning 17 games and losing 13, with a 3.06 ERA. A strong staff of Chief Bender, Eddie Plank, Bob Shawkey, and Joe Bush led the team into the 1914 World Series against the "Miracle Braves" from Boston, who rose from last to first place in little more than seven weeks, passing the New York Giants for keeps on September 8.

If the 1913 World Series was a crowning achievement for Bullet Joe, it was the opposite for him in the Series of 1914. Once again he was given the pitching assignment for Game Three, but this time the result was different. The A's lost the first two games in Philadelphia. The third and fourth games were played at Fenway Park — the home of the Red Sox — due to the run-down condition of the Braves' home field, the South End Grounds.

Bullet Joe's pitching heroics in the 1913 World Series had buoyed his team to a championship. But his misplay in the 1914 Series helped lead to their downfall. Bush had pitched well and was locked in a duel with Lefty Tyler through nine innings, knotted at 2–2. Both teams scored two runs in the 10th. Then, in the 12th inning, Hank Gowdy, a .243 hitter during the regular season, but a .545 hitter in the Series, stroked a double. After an intentional walk to Larry Gilbert, the next play was a sacrifice bunt by Herbie Moran that Bush threw past third baseman Home Run Baker, allowing the winning run to score. The A's were crushed. The Braves won the fourth and final game by a score of 3–1, and made a clean sweep of Connie Mack's nine.

The next day's October 13 edition of the *New York Times* reported that both starting pitchers that day had pitched with aplomb and neither team would give an inch, but the mood changed suddenly for the A's when Bush made the errant throw, ending the game in defeat. The

Bullet Joe with the Yankees. Courtesy of the *Boston Herald*.

Times described the misplay as "fraught with tragedy" and it went on: "Then, by one tragic throw, he had knocked the foundation from under the Mackian machine and it came tumbling down in ruins." Bush was inconsolable as he slinked away under the stands toward the clubhouse with tears in his eyes as the crowd roared its approval of the Braves' victory. Not even Connie Mack could comfort him.

The *Philadelphia Athletics Historical Society* reported in a 2003 article that Joe Bush had an opportunity to join the upstart Federal League, for more money, after the 1914 season, but he passed it up. Phil Ball, owner of St. Louis' Federal League club offered him a two-year contract for $18,000, to be paid up-front. Bush stayed with Philadelphia, and his reward for such loyalty was membership on a team that went into a precipitous decline.[9]

In 1914 Connie Mack began to dismantle his club selling off star players rather than compete in a bidding war with the "outlaw" Federal League. Future Hall of Famers Eddie Plank, Chief Bender, Eddie Collins, and Frank "Home Run" Baker were not with the Athletics in 1915. Former ace pitcher Jack Coombs signed on with the Brooklyn Nationals for the 1915 season. Other prominent players like Bob Shawkey, Boardwalk Brown, and Jack Barry of Mack's "$100,000 infield" fame would soon follow, through trades to other clubs.

Joe Bush would find little support from the fractured ranks of a team that bore no resemblance to the great Athletics teams of years past. The A's were woeful, plummeting from first place in 1914 to last in 1915, finishing 58½ games behind the American League leader, the Boston Red Sox. Bush won five games and lost 15 with a 4.14 ERA that year.

The same ineptness that characterized the A's in 1915 continued in both 1916 and 1917. The A's lost more than 100 games in 1915 and 1916, and nearly as many in 1917, dropping 98 and finishing 44½ games behind the leader, the Chicago White Sox. In 1916, the A's lost 117 games and, astonishingly, they finished 40 games behind the seventh-place finisher, Washington. The A's held the record for most losses in a single season by an AL club for 87 years, until 2003, when the Detroit Tigers dropped 119 games.

Despite little run support and a poor defense behind him, in 1916 Bush still won 15 games, while losing 24. He put together a remarkable 2.57 ERA, striking out a career-high 157 batters, yielding only 222 hits in 286⅔ innings pitched, including eight shutouts and 25 complete games. He shares the distinction with several notable pitchers of having the highest percentage — 41.7

percent — of team wins in a single season, winning nearly half of the 36 games won by Philadelphia that year. In 1917, he improved his ERA to 2.47, despite an 11–17 won-loss record.

Although the A's faithful had little to cheer about in 1916, a highlight of that year was a near-perfect game no-hitter thrown by Bush at Shibe Park on August 26. He beat the Cleveland Indians, and their future Hall of Famer Stan Coveleski, 5–0, walking only one batter, the first he faced. As the *Washington Post* described the occasion, "When Graney ended the game by putting up a fly to McInnes, after O'Neill and Coleman had fanned, the crowd broke onto the field to congratulate Bush, and the latter was so excited that he pulled off his cap and joined in the cheering."[10]

What made Bullet Joe's feat more remarkable was that he had pitched against the same Cleveland team the previous day, and was soundly beaten. He was disconsolate over the loss and his poor performance, and persuaded manager Mack to let him pitch the next day to redeem himself. Mack had few options besides Bush, so he agreed to the proposal.

Another hallmark event that day: It was the last major league game played by future Hall of Famer Nap Lajoie, Connie Mack's second baseman that year.

Cash-strapped Connie Mack dispensed with three more members of his once-great teams on December 14, 1917. He dealt Bush, Wally Schang, and Amos Strunk to the Boston Red Sox for three undistinguished players, and $60,000. All three ex-Athletics would contribute to the Boston ballclub in their run for the pennant in 1918, especially Joe Bush.

Bullet Joe managed a 15–15 won-loss record in 1918, but with a career-best — and team best — 2.11 ERA, a career-high 26 complete games, including seven shutouts and a team-high 125 strikeouts. Bush, Babe Ruth, Carl Mays, Sad Sam Jones, and Dutch Leonard formed a strong pitching corps that led the Red Sox into the 1918 World Series, which the Sox took in six games from the Chicago Cubs.

Bush appeared in two games in the 1918 Series. He lost Game Two, a well-pitched 3–1 contest, and saved Game Four's win in relief of starting pitcher Babe Ruth.

The following year was a difficult one for Bullet Joe, who developed arm trouble and remained out of action most of the season, throwing just nine innings. It was also not a good year for the Red Sox. They finished sixth.

It appeared that Bullet Joe was all but washed up due to the injury, but his toughness and indefatigable spirit sustained him and pushed him to a comeback with the Red Sox in 1920. Essentially, he reinvented himself, coming up with a new pitch — the forkball — that enabled him to pitch another nine years in the big leagues.

In the *Saturday Evening Post* series, Bush described his "invention" this way: "Probably one of the most bewildering balls ever pitched was my own invention — the fork ball, which I discovered in 1920 when I was essaying a comeback with the Boston Red Sox after I had hurt my arm several years before and was forced to stop throwing curve balls."[11] Though Bush claimed arm trouble of "several years" duration, there is no indication in the record that it pre-dated the 1919 season.

1920 was a comeback year for Joe, and he put together another 15–15 won-loss record. But the Red Sox bore no resemblance to the champions of 1918. Owner Harry Frazee had begun to dismantle his championship team at the end of the 1918 season. Once again Bush found himself on a team in the process of being sold off.

The Red Sox were now mired in mediocrity, finishing 1921 in fifth place once again. Bullet Joe had a good year, however, with a 16–9 won-loss record and a 3.50 ERA, second-best on the team. He struck out 96 batters, second to Sam Jones, who had 98. He also hit .325 with 39 base hits in 120 plate appearances.

On December 20, 1921, the Red Sox traded their two ace pitchers, Sam Jones and Joe Bush, along with short-stop Everett Scott, to the Yankees. It was a trade made in heaven for Bullet Joe, who expressed delight at the move. "It's the greatest Christmas present imaginable," said Bush. He added, "Then another good point is that I will have Babe Ruth with me instead of against me. That always makes a pitcher's life a happier one."[12]

Bush joined a strong Yankees club that had won the American League pennant in 1921, and would go on to win two more pennants and a World Series during his stay with them.

Joe had a career year in 1922 with a team-high 26 victories, losing only seven, for the best winning percentage in the American League. The Yankees won the pennant with a 94–60 record, but then were swept in the World Series, four games to none, with a controversial tie, by McGraw's New York Giants. Bullet Joe started the opening and final games, losing both, by 3–2 and 5–3 scores. He had little run support from the team which had a combined .203 batting average. Babe Ruth hit an anemic .118 without a home run in the Series.

Joe was embroiled in controversy after the Giants' Series-ending fourth victory. In the final contest, Bush and the Yankees were leading 3–2 in the eighth, but the Giants had men on second and third with two outs. Yankees' skipper Miller Huggins ordered Bush to walk future Hall of Famer Ross Youngs and pitch to High Pockets George Kelly. Bush became enraged at the proposal, shouting audibly at Huggins, but he complied with his manager's order, walking Youngs. Kelly then singled to center, scoring two runs. The Giants went on to win the game and the Series the next inning.

Bush further distinguished himself in 1922 by halting the consecutive game hitting streak of future Hall of Famer, George Sisler, who had hit safely in 41 straight games. Bush stopped the streak on September 18. Sisler's record stood for 19 years until Joe DiMaggio eclipsed it in 1941, hitting safely in 56 consecutive games.

The Yankees had another strong year in 1923, finishing in first place by 16½ games over second-place Detroit. Joe Bush did not match his 1922 performance, but had a good year nevertheless, with a 19–15 won-loss record, a 3.43 ERA, and 125 strikeouts. The Yanks beat the Giants in the World Series this time, four games to two.

Game One of the 1923 World Series was the first Series game to be played in Yankee Stadium and the first to be broadcast nationally. Bullet Joe pitched well in relief that day, but his World Series jinx continued; he lost to the McGraw nine, 5–4, when Casey Stengel hit an inside-the-park home run off him in the ninth. He came back in a crucial fifth contest with the teams locked at two wins apiece, however, pitching a masterful game and shutting down the Giants, 8–1. The *Atlanta Constitution* reported, "'Bullet Joe' Bush Baffles Sluggers of the McGraw Clan With Slow Fork Ball." It broke the back of the Giants team, which lost the next and final game, 6–4.

The Yankees would not repeat in 1924, finishing second to Walter Johnson's Washington Senators, who won the World Series that year over the Giants, four games to three.

Joe posted a 17–16 record with a 3.57 ERA, striking out 80 batters, a decline from previous years. He batted .339 with 42 base hits in 124 at-bats. "He is…one of the best hitting pitchers in the American League," said a 1924 *Washington Post* article.[13]

On December 17, 1924, the Yankees traded Bush and two other players to the St. Louis Browns, obtaining spitballer Urban Shocker. This was a major disappointment for Bush, who had had three solid years with the Bronx-based team.

The Yankees finished a dismal seventh in the American League in 1925, while the Browns finished third, though 15 games behind the leader, Washington.

Bullet Joe compiled a 14–14 record that year, with 63 strikeouts, but had an unimpressive 5.09 ERA. He pitched two shutouts, one of them a splendid one-hitter on August 27 over Walter Johnson of the American League champion Washington Senators, 5–0. Johnson got the only hit off Bush, a double in the sixth inning.

It must have seemed to some that Bullet Joe had a certain knack for transitioning to good teams in the course of his career. Others would say it was merely his good fortune. On February 1, 1926, the Browns traded Joe to the Senators. The Senators had won the World Series in 1924, and the AL pennant in 1925. Manager Bucky Harris was counting on him as the key player in the deal, in which pitchers Tom Zachary and Win Ballou went to St. Louis. The *Washington Post* quoted Harris stating that the addition of Bush "assured his team of a third American League pennant."[14]

Harris's predictions for Bush did not play out. On April 18, Joe was hit on the knee by a vicious drive off the bat of New York's Earl Combs. Bush had pitched one-hit ball — a double by Lou Gehrig in the sixth — before he was struck by Combs' shot in the top of the ninth. He was slow to recover, and was never able to regain form with Washington, posting a 1–8 won-loss record.

The Senators gave Bush his unconditional release on June 24, 1926. Bucky Harris would later say, "If I had to name the most disappointing event in the race, I'd probably say it was the failure of Joe Bush to win for us. I banked heavily for him to come through for us, but lost."[15]

Ever a man of action, Bush immediately made arrangements with a semipro club — the East Douglas, Massachusetts team of the so-called "Millionaire League" — to play for them. He did play — one game. On June 29, 1926, Bush pitched a shutout over a local Worcester team. The next day, he signed to play for another contender, the reigning World Champion Pittsburgh Pirates. He was back in the majors.

Joe's performance with Pittsburgh was more than respectable. The Pirates were in a pennant race and Bullet Joe was being counted on to bolster the staff. He was a contributor, as a pitcher and with his bat. Although his won-loss record was a mere 6–6, he finished with a 3.01 ERA, fanning 38 batters in 110⅔ innings pitched, with two impressive shutouts, the second a two-hitter on September 20 against the Phillies. The Pirates were inconsistent as a team, however, and finished third, 4½ games behind the first-place Cardinals.

Bush was on the Pittsburgh roster at the outset of the 1927 campaign, but his tenure with them was short-lived. New Pirates manager, Donie Bush, a take-charge guy, sensed a pennant was possible, but knew he would need to shore up his pitching staff if he was going to win. Joe Bush was not in his plans and received his unconditional release from the Bucs on June 15.

The Pirates won the AL pennant that year, but lost to the Yankees juggernaut, led by Ruth and Gehrig, in four straight games.

Bullet Joe appeared in seven games for Pittsburgh in '27, used as a pitcher and pinch-hitter. He was the starting pitcher in three games, won one and lost two, with an unimpressive 13.50 ERA.

Once again Joe was on the outside looking in. But an old opponent, John McGraw — the victim of Bush's heroics in the memorable 1913 World Series — was in need of pitching; he threw Bullet Joe another lifeline, signing him to a contract with the Giants on June 29. But Joe lasted barely long enough to dirty his uniform. He pitched in three games — starting two — beating the Boston Braves on July 2, 4–1, with an impressive seven-hitter; but getting bombed by the Brooklyn Robins on July 9, giving up seven hits and four runs in the first inning.

He was released by the Giants on July 19.

Wasting little time, in late August, Bush joined the Toledo Mud Hens of the Double-A American Association, led by manager Casey Stengel. Stengel put together an assemblage of major league cast-offs for a stretch run at Toledo's first pennant. Bullet Joe "turned in four important victories," according to the *New York Times*.[16] Toledo won the pennant and went on to win the Little World Series championship, five games to one, over the International League's Buffalo Bisons. Bush pitched and took the one Toledo loss.

On December 7, Toledo released Bullet Joe and, later, its other veterans, Irish Meusel and Everett Scott.

Joe's resiliency in always landing on his feet emerged again when, in late December 1927, Connie Mack signed the 35-year old veteran to a contract with the Philadelphia Athletics. Bush joined a star-studded team that included Ty Cobb, Mickey Cochrane, Lefty Grove, Al Simmons, and Jimmie Foxx. They finished second to a strong Yankees team that swept the St. Louis Cardinals in the 1928 World Series.

Bullet Joe was used sparingly by Mack, finishing with a 2–1 won-loss mark. Sportswriter Frank Young of the *Washington Post* reported that Bush's role on the A's was largely one of fungo hitter most of the season. Joe was waived — along with Ty Cobb and Tris Speaker — by the A's on November 3, 1928, and later released. It was the end of his major league career.

In 1929, Bush signed on with the Portland Beavers of the Pacific Coast League as an outfielder. He was released on May 25, and promptly went back to the East Coast, joining player-manager Tris Speaker and his Newark Bears of the International League, on June 17. There he was used in utility roles and pitched, finishing with a 3–3 won-loss record.

On October 23, 1929, the stock market collapsed, leading to the Great Depression. Baseball was affected, especially the minor leagues, which lost three leagues almost immediately following the crash, and others later.

But Joe Bush once again demonstrated the adaptability that was becoming legendary when he surfaced again,

Joe Bush, 1927, at the Pasa Robles, Cal., Pirates spring training site. George Outland photograph. Courtesy of John Outland.

in 1930, by getting a player-manager position with the Eastern League's Allentown team. Frank Young of the *Washington Post* described Bush as "a high powered salesman" because of his ability to secure desirable posts when none appeared likely.

Allentown won the 1930 Eastern League championship on September 22, beating Bridgeport, four games to one. Bush stayed with the team for the 1931 season but it finished a mediocre fifth, 34 games out of first.

Bullet Joe finished his baseball career in 1932 pitching for the Kentucky Colonels of New York City, a semipro club.

Leslie Ambrose "Bullet Joe" Bush was in organized baseball from 1906, it is believed, through 1932. He played 17 years in the big leagues, from 1912 until 1928. During his major league career he won 196 games, lost 184, struck out 1,319 batters, and posted a quite respectable 3.51 lifetime ERA. He pitched 35 shutouts, including a no-hitter.

Bush was also a well-respected batsman and was used often as a pinch-hitter. He once pinch-hit for future Hall of Famer Joe Cronin in a 1926 game with Pittsburgh. Bush's lifetime major league batting average was a solid .253 with 313 base hits in 1,239 at-bats.

Aside from Joe's well-known baseball talents, he was a man of some creative expression as well. As was true with many ballplayers of the period, on occasion Joe would participate in vaudeville skits — usually with other ballplayers. He was described as having an "excellent baritone voice."

Joe also was a ventriloquist. On one occasion when he was with the Red Sox, traveling north from spring training with the Giants, Joe got himself into some trouble with the locals in the small town of Morristown, Tennessee. While in a restaurant there, he began to mimic animal sounds that could be heard coming from different parts of the room, alarming the restaurant staff. They called the local constable, who arrested Joe. As the story goes, Joe then mimicked the sound of a vicious barking dog projecting his voice behind the constable, and while the officer turned to protect himself, Joe broke free.

Describing Joe's good nature, a sports journalist once

Bush as a parimutuel clerk in Atlantic City, N.J., September 1946. Courtesy of the *Boston Herald*.

characterized him as "the proverbial boy that never grew up." He added, "Joe Bush has been a character as well as a great pitcher. Joe has a peculiar smile. It is one of great friendliness. It is a guileless one, a disarming one, and many a rookie has discovered that Joe Bush is the greatest kidder and practical joker in the world and yet has lived to forgive Joe because of that smile."[17]

Bullet Joe credits himself with discovering Pie Traynor. Bush described his find — as well as disappointment in Red Sox manager Ed Barrow — to a reporter in a 1967 interview. Bush worked with Traynor who was working out with the team. He liked his hands and told Barrow to "get him a job and be sure and keep a string on him." Barrow was not interested in the future Hall of Famer, but relented and "got him a job." Barrow, however, "forgot to keep the string on him," said Joe. Pittsburgh acquired Traynor in 1920.[18]

Bush's draft registration card, signed by him in April, 1942, lists an employer, the A. Overholt & Company of Philadelphia, PA. It is believed they were in the bituminous coal business. And then, a footnote in the March 11, 1943 edition of *The Sporting News* found Joe working as a timekeeper in a Philadelphia shipyard. Later, while attending a Yankees 25th reunion in June, 1948, Bush informed *New York World-Telegram* reporter, Lester Bromberg, that for the previous five years he had been working "a politician's job" for the Bureau of Recreation in Philadelphia.

In his later years Joe Bush and his wife, Alice Marie

Wray Bush, whom he married November 6, 1937, had a home in Fort Lauderdale, Florida, where they resided only part of the time. Beginning in 1946, Joe kept active from 11 A.M. to 7 P.M. as a pari-mutuel clerk working at New Jersey and Florida race tracks, notably the Garden State, Atlantic City and Hialeah, Florida. "I'd rather have too much rather than not enough to do," he once said to a sportswriter. According to his obituary he worked at the tracks "well into his seventies."

Joe remained active throughout his life participating in numerous recreational pursuits. In September, 1958, Joe informed sportswriter Tom O'Reilly of the *New York Morning Telegraph* that he had sustained a heart attack the previous year causing him to give up bowling, a favorite pastime.

During an interview in 1967 with sportswriter Bill Duncan of the *Courier-Post*, a Cherry Hill, N.J. paper, Bush described his "biggest kick" in baseball was picking off Ty Cobb at second base with the bases loaded. "Man, but he was furious! He pawed and kicked and howled at the umpire. It is a picture I'll never forget," said Bullet Joe.

Leslie Ambrose (Bullet Joe) Bush died in Fort Lauderdale, Florida on November 1, 1974 at the age of 81. He was survived by his wife, Alice, and three brothers. Joe Bush had no children.[19]

Notes

1. Murnane, T. H. "Giants Slain By Mere Boy." *The Sporting News*, October 10, 1913, p. 1.

2. From records of: Crow Wing County Treasurer, Brainerd, MN, and Cass County Treasurer, Walker, MN, *Cass County Birth Record Book*, Book D, p. 259, Line # 424; Lane, F.C., "The Yankees' Pitching Ace." *Baseball Magazine*, February 1923, p. 395–396. Bush was popularly known as "the Brainerd Boy" — referencing the town of Brainerd, MN — where he played high school and semipro ball; According to the 1901–1902 Brainerd city directory, the Bush family resided at 907 Fir Street in Brainerd (Crow Wing County). Thus Brainerd was Joe Bush's actual place of residence during his formative years. Evidence is persuasive, however, that Joe Bush was born in Cass County in an area known as Gull River — possibly a village or township — contiguous to Brainerd.

3. 1910–1911 *Brainerd City Directory*, shows Leslie Bush employed as a "driver" for Hutchins Laundry on 719 Broadway in Brainerd. He would have been somewhere between age 17–19 at the time, when he was also playing ball for the local semipro town team.

4. Nasium, Jim. "Lloyd Waner, the Rookie: And Other First-Year Stars." *The Sporting News*, November 17, 1927, p. 3.

5. Bush, Bullet Joe, with Carroll S. Slick. "On The Mound." *Saturday Evening Post*, June 8, 1929, p. 10; SABR member Robert Tholkes, from his extensive research of local paper the *Brainerd Dispatch*, on the game played in St. Cloud, MN on July 30, 1911; paper mentioned the Native-American player by his surname, Roy. It is believed this was Charlie Roy, a Minnesotan, who went on to play briefly in the major leagues, in 1906, for the Philadelphia Phillies. Brainerd finished the 1911 season 20-4.

6. Bush, Bullet Joe, with Slick, Carroll S. Slick. "On The Mound." *Saturday Evening Post*, June 8, 1929, p. 152.

7. Kieran, John. "Sports Of The Times: Faultless Pitcher." *New York Times*, January 23, 1934, p. 24.

8. Nasium, Jim. "Lloyd Waner, the Rookie: And Other First-Year Stars." *The Sporting News*, November 17, 1927, p. 3.

9. Smith, Dale B. "The Unsinkable Bullet Joe Bush." *Along The Elephant Trail*. Philadelphia Athletics Historical Society. 2003.

10. Unsigned article. "Bush Slabs No-Hit Game; Detroit Defeats Red Sox." *Washington Post*, August 27, 1916, p. S1.

11. Bush, Bullet Joe, with Carroll S. Slick. "On The Mound." *Saturday Evening Post*, June 8, 1929, p. 152.

12. Unsigned article. ""Bullet Joe" Bush Satisfied With Transfer To New York." *Washington Post*, December 23, 1921, p.16.

13. Unsigned article. "Yanks Get Shocker In Trade For Bush And Pair Of Rookies." *Washington Post*, December 18, 1924, p.1.

14. Unsigned article. "Old Master To Oppose A's Today." *Washington Post*, May 27, 1926, p. 17.

15. Unsigned article. "Peck To Pilot Browns, Is Report." *Washington Post*, July 31, 1926, p. 17.

16. Unsigned article. "Joe Bush Returns To The Athletics." *New York Times*, December 20, 1927, p. 36.

17. Unsigned article. "Bush, Nemesis of Giants at 20, Now With Clan McGraw at 35." *New York Times*, July 4, 1927, p. 11.

18. Duncan, Bill. "Bullet Joe: At 74, He's a Go-Go Guy." *The Sporting News*, January 28, 1967, p. 23.

19. Obituary from *Brainerd Dispatch*, November 1, 1974; Censuses for: Brainerd, Minnesota, Crow Wing County, 1900 and 1910; Abington Lower District, Pennsylvania, Montgomery County, 1900. Moreland Township, Pennsylvania, Montgomery County, 1910; Philadelphia, Pennsylvania, 1920 and 1930. Unsigned article. "Cupid Strikes Out 'Bullet Joe' Bush." *The Philadelphia Inquirer*, October 11, 1914, p. 3. Bush was to have married 18-year old Sylvia McMahon, a "remarkably pretty girl," described *The Philadelphia Inquirer*, on October 14, 1914. That was two days after he pitched in Game Three of the WS against the Boston Braves. Various censuses support that Bush was married to Sylvia until at least 1930. There is no information on wife Sylvia after 1930. Bullet Joe married Alice Marie Wray on November 6, 1937.

GEORGE COCHRAN *by Craig Lammers*

G	AB	R	H	2B	3B	HR	RBI	BB	SO	BA	OBP	SLG	SB	HBP
24	60	7	7	0	0	0	3	10	6	.117	.264	.117	3	2

After Fred Thomas left the Boston Red Sox for the Navy in July 1918, third base was a tough position for manager Ed Barrow to fill. Catcher Wally Schang played for a few games, but the hot corner was mostly played by a succession of career minor leaguers. All had strengths and weaknesses as players. George Cochran — acquired after the American Association suspended operations that summer — was noted for a strong arm and solid defense. Cochran was also a very streaky hitter throughout his minor league career. Unfortunately for the veteran infielder he was in the midst of a batting slump during his five-week major league career.

George Leslie Cochran was born in Rusk, Texas, on February 12, 1889. His father was a Missouri native. His mother, the former Mary Guinly, was born in Pennsylvania, but the family moved to Missouri settling in the village of Steelville on the northern edge of Missouri's Ozark region. Mary's father was an ironworker imported from Missouri to work at a foundry near the prison at Rusk. George's father's name is not known, but he may well have been an ironworker as well.

George Cochran.
George Brace photo.

Reasons are unclear, but by 1900, George and his older brother James were living with their elderly maternal grandparents Peter and Elizabeth in Steelville. Within a few years, the widowed Mary Cochran and her two sons were reunited and moved further west.

Mary Cochran and her sons were living in Carthage by 1905 at 502 Budlong Street, a working class neighborhood. Carthage, Missouri is located in the southwest part of the state, near the Oklahoma and Kansas borders. It was mostly a farming community with some industry at the time the Cochrans moved there. Baseball Hall of Famer Carl Hubbell and future television host Marlin Perkins were born in Carthage during George's early years in the city. George Cochran attended Carthage High School, starring on the baseball team as a pitcher and infielder. After graduating in 1909, he worked as a driver for the McCormick Grocery located at Second and Main Streets. He played ball when not working, and the following season began his professional baseball career.

Bartlesville, Oklahoma is about 120 miles southwest

of Carthage. In 1910, the city had a team in the Class C Western Association. The Western Association had once been a strong minor league. After losing Topeka and Wichita to the Western League, and Oklahoma City to the Texas League following the 1908 season, the Association was struggling. Playing in Bartlesville was a great opportunity for Cochran, and manager Jake Beckley took advantage of the 21-year-old infielder's strong arm, using him mostly at shortstop. Unfortunately, even a great hitter like Beckley couldn't help George at the plate. He managed to hit just .165 playing in all 102 Bartlesville games before the team disbanded on July 31. He stole 27 bases.

Despite his weak offense, Cochran received a tryout the following spring with the Class B Three I League. One source said Cochran almost won the starting short-stop job with Springfield, Illinois, but was beaten out by future major league star Heinie Groh. A Decatur, Illinois newspaper places him on the Bloomington, Illinois roster. After receiving his release, Cochran chose to play independent ball in 1911.

Independent teams with a Native American makeup (either real or imagined) were common in the Deadball Era. Perhaps the most famous was the Nebraska Indians, but the Cheyenne Wyoming Indians were apparently a very talented team as well. In 1910, pitcher Claude Hendrix jumped his contract with Salina of the Central Kansas League to play with Cheyenne. The next season George Cochran joined the team. His 1911 season was soon ended by a broken leg, but he returned to Cheyenne in 1912. That season, he developed a reputation "of being a heavy hitter." By the middle of 1912, the Cheyenne team was losing money and George Cochran received an opportunity to return to organized ball.

Since joining the Class A Western League in 1909, the Topeka club had been at or near the bottom of the standings, 1912 being no exception. Manager Dale Gear's team was buried so deeply in the cellar that *Topeka Daily Capital* columnist Jay House later wrote, "Announcement has been made that the Western league season ends next Monday. The Western league season appears to have been detained along the route. It ended here in early June."

Gear was an excellent judge of young talent, sending at least five members of that 1912 club to the major leagues — Ross Reynolds, Harry Chapman, Josh Billings, Gene Cocreham, and Cochran. On July 16, it was announced he'd purchased Cochran from Cheyenne. George debuted that afternoon in a home game against St Joseph (Missouri) and House was impressed with the new switch-hitting infielder. "Cochran is a big fellow, very fast on his feet and has what appears to be the most wonderful throwing arm in the Western league. He shoots them across with a half arm motion and apparently with as little effort as the average man would employ in driving a fly from the bridge of his nose. His work on ground

Cochran with the 1918 team. Detail from *1919 Spalding's Official Base Ball Guide.*

balls looked as strong as his arm. He hits from the right side of the plate and [also] increases by one Manager Gear's long string of left handed hitters."

Though very talented, Cochran's inexperience was a problem in a Class A league. In one early game, he made three errors. In another game, he made two errors, though one was a throwing error blamed on the ball still being moist from the pitch by a Topeka spitball pitcher. House said of the young infielder: "Cochran who showed finely in his first few games has aviated. [He is a] promising youngster but the class is, as yet, too fast for him." Soon benched, Cochran might have been released or sent to a lower classification league, except for some quick thinking on his part. "He opined he might be able to pitch. Manager Gear told him to pick out a nice round ball and get busy. That was three or four days ago. With only that brief period intervening between his third basing and his pitching he was sent in to face Omaha, the shiftiest hitting team in the league. But Cochran looks like a thousand dollar bill. He made the mistake of most young slabsters and pitched his head off in the opening innings." That was the first of three tie games Cochran pitched during the last two months of the 1912 season. He won his first game over Sioux City a few days later. Lack of endurance and control were noted as his weaknesses on the mound.

The remainder of the season, Cochran was the most versatile member of the Topeka Kaws. Between pitching assignments, he was used at second, third, shortstop, and in the outfield. A highlight was a 4–2 win over first-place Denver. In that game, "Cochran went over into foul territory and took a pop fly for the last out. Cochran began pitching so recently that he has not yet learned that the average pitcher considers it against the law to stir out of his tracks for a pop fly." Future 1918 Red Sox teammate Jack Coffey went 0-for-4 against Cochran that afternoon. His control was gradually improving as well. He threw nine straight strikes to Denver's Lee Quillan in one at-bat.

That was Cochran's last win of the season. In consecutive September starts, he surrendered a total of five hits but lost both games. In one of those games, House wrote, "Cochran looked like a million dollars, except in the fourth. What happened in that round was enough and aplenty. Both the hits made by the [Des Moines] Boosters were plucked in this inning, and two walks and two errors by Cochran's support and two stolen bases occurred during this spasm." George Cochran finished 1912 with a 3–8 pitching record for a team that finished 51-109. He hit .276 in 48 games.

Offseason plans were to keep Cochran as a member of the Topeka pitching staff for 1913, but plans have a way of changing. When he reported to the Kaws spring camp in Denison, Texas, Cochran was a pitcher. When the team arrived back in Topeka, he started an exhibition game against Kansas City of the American Association. Cochran wasn't particularly effective that afternoon, and began to be used at second base in later exhibitions.

When Topeka opened the 1913 season at home versus Denver, Cochran was the leadoff hitter, and tripled in his first at-bat of the season, scoring the team's only run against former Red Sox pitcher Casey Hageman. He also made two errors that day. Another second baseman was soon signed, and Gear moved Cochran back to the mound. George made just one start allowing seven runs in five innings at Wichita on May 1.

The next day was a key day in Cochran's career. Gear told the *Topeka Daily Capital*: "We used Cochran at third base yesterday, and he worked like an old hand at the station, besides getting two hits, stealing a base and scoring two runs." Except for an occasional mop up relief stint, that was the end of George's career as a pitcher. Cochran played 13 straight games without an error and hit .328 in that span but still couldn't escape fan criticism. House said, "He booted a couple of hard chances and the hammer and anvil crowd fell upon his neck. What by the way, does the hammer and anvil crowd wish in the way of third basing?" House also believed "the Kaw infield as presently constituted is the fastest ever foregathered on this circuit."

Cochran slumped at the plate, but continued his excellent defense. Only an injury kept him out of the lineup. While making a tag, "Cochran's hand connected with Neff's shinbone with such force as to fracture a small bone in the hand. The bone snapped with a pop which was heard all over the diamond." Expected to miss a month, he was back at third in just two weeks.

In mid-August, he demonstrated another talent. The *Capital* noted: "Cochran was up twice in the seventh, was plunked in the slats on each occasion and scored two runs in the inning." George was hit by a pitch three times in the game. Incredibly he was again hit three times in a game the following season. A few days later, George led off a game against Sioux City with a home run against former major leaguer Kirby White.

During Topeka's last homestand in 1913, Cochran's performance was "the finest ever given by a Western League third bagster at the local park. He has starred throughout the series, and has contributed one or more feature plays in every game." Cochran finished 1913 with a .263 average and 22 steals. House predicted "Cochran should be among the top line of Western league third basemen next season."

For the first half of the 1914 season, it looked like that prediction would come true. In late June he was batting .325 and was third in the league with 18 stolen bases. Chicago White Sox scout Jack Doyle was looking for a third baseman that summer, and in late June he was closely watching George Cochran. Doyle was looking for a player "who can smite the ball frequently." Other clubs expressed interest as well and it was predicted Cochran would receive a promotion in 1915. A prolonged second-half slump resulted in 1914 stats quite similar to his 1913 numbers. Cochran's final batting average was .261 and his stolen base total increased to 34.

On May 12, 1914, Cochran left the team after a series at Wichita to return to Carthage for a day. Jay House said: "George Cochran, who subscribed to a permanent lecture course in Carthage Monday, was back on the job. And George has fixed himself so that is where he will have to stay. The only chance a married man ever has to loaf is when the works shut down." On his off day, he had married Wilma Ford, described "as the daughter of a mine operator at Carthage." There were several lead and zinc mines west of Carthage, and the operators (including the Ford family) generally lived in Carthage, the nearest sizable town.

Dale Gear resigned as Topeka manager during the 1914 season. Gear was clearly an important figure in George Cochran's career and life. The Cochrans named their son Dale. Cochran evidently didn't get along with Jim Jackson, Topeka's 1915 manager. Jackson was a veteran, apparently very critical of his players. 1915 was Cochran's worst season at the plate since 1910. Playing in just 125 of the team's 154 games, he hit .242.

The 1916 season presented challenges for players throughout the upper levels of the minor leagues. With the demise of the Federal League, there was an influx of players onto Western League rosters. One of those facing a challenge was George Cochran. Topeka signed a pair of former Federal League infielders. First baseman Joe Agler wasn't a concern, but the other newcomer Pep Goodwin was a third baseman. New manager Ralph Lattimore was also an infielder.

Cochran was initially shifted to shortstop, and Topeka owner John Savage felt Cochran "was too fast to play the hot corner." Savage had wanted to use Cochran at short in 1915, but Jackson was opposed to the idea. House was impressed with the change. "Cochran again played dazzling ball at short. If he keeps going he will have a lot of them eating their words." His offense had improved so much that a photo was captioned identifying Cochran as a "heavy hitting shortstop."

A game at Sioux City in late May was a highlight of his season. "The Savages robbed the home club of runs in the third frame with a lightning double play by Cochran unassisted. With Watson on third and Metz on first, Livingston, on a hit and run play, sent a liner to short. Cochran leaped two feet in the air to pull down the ball and then tagged Metz as he was sliding into second." Later in the game, Cochran scored the winning run. The next day, he doubled twice in an 18-inning tie. One of those doubles was probably the most unusual hit of his career. "Cochran sent one to right and the ball stuck in the chickenwire and he was allowed two bases on the hit."

The team wasn't playing as well, and Cochran was shifted back to third base. Even that didn't help, and manager Lattimore was fired and replaced by former Red Sox player Clyde Engle. The new manager meant changes for George Cochran. Always in the lineup, he was shuttled between short, third and the outfield. He even pitched in a game showing "a fast ball, a curve, and a change of pace, but as a pitcher he still ranks as one of the most brilliant third basemen in the league." No matter where he played, he showed a consistency at the plate lacking in his previous seasons in the Western League. He also hit a career-high six home runs in 1916.

Cochran's 1916 season ended early. On August 15, he was injured in a collision with catcher Lawrence Spahr of Des Moines. Expected to make a quick return, Cochran was unable to play the rest of the year. On the season, he hit .305 with 25 stolen bases. The team suffered a succession of injuries the latter part of 1916, worsening an existing attendance problem. In the offseason, owner Savage transferred the team to Joplin, Missouri.

The Western League was hit hard by World War I and worsening economic conditions. In a cost-cutting move, Savage became manager of the Joplin team during the second half of the league's split season. There was also a pair of midseason franchise shifts. The St. Joseph, Missouri team moved to Hutchinson, Kansas. Two weeks later, the Sioux City, Iowa team moved to St. Joseph. Despite the confusion, George Cochran was one of the struggling league's stars. He led the league with 55 stolen bases and was chosen by the league president as the All-Star third baseman. He also hit .301 with six home runs.

The 1917 Joplin team was Cochran's opportunity to play postseason baseball. Pitcher Roy Sanders shut out Hutchinson in both games of a season-ending doubleheader to force a playoff series between the two teams for the right to meet first-half champion Des Moines. Just two weeks before, the Miners were in sixth place. Joplin

Cochran. Detail from the 1919 Spalding's Guide.

lost the best of five series, 3–0, but Cochran contributed three hits including a double and stole a base in the series. After the 1917 season, Savage sold his third baseman to Kansas City of the Double-A American Association.

The American Association was one of the top minor leagues in 1918. Affected somewhat by wartime personnel losses, the league was a mixture of veterans like Napoleon Lajoie and Roger Bresnahan, minor league stars like Joe Riggert, and young prospects. The Kansas City Blues were managed by John Ganzel, a former major league third baseman. Ganzel had confidence in his new third baseman. George Cochran likely resembled one of those veterans. His hair was prematurely gray, his eyes blue, and he was described as being of medium height and build. He was the leadoff hitter for the Blues and was a key to the team's success. Contending from the beginning, the Blues took over first place in the middle of June. Many of the league's younger players were being inducted into the armed forces, but Cochran was deferred due to a wife and two-year-old son.

Secretary of War Newton Baker issued his work or fight order in July, and almost immediately, the American Association suspended operations for the duration. In fact the International League was the only minor league to complete its season in 1918. Kansas City held a two-game lead over Columbus when the American Association ceased play after the games of July 21. George Cochran was hitting .284 with 11 stolen bases, playing in 67 of the Blues 74 games. Thanks in part to Baker, George Cochran would receive an opportunity to play major league baseball.

Third base was a revolving door for the 1918 Red Sox. Stuffy McInnis began the season at third before moving to his accustomed station at first. Fred Thomas played the hot corner for most of May and June before joining the United States Navy. Wally Schang and coach Heinie Wagner also filled in at third base for a few games. After Thomas left, Ed Barrow tried Jack Stansbury, Walter Barbare, and Eusebio Gonzalez in quick succession.

The Red Sox were in St. Louis when George Cochran was signed. Even before the team left St. Louis, there was indication that his major league career would be short. American Association President Thomas Hickey said that since his league didn't disband for financial reasons, players not purchased would revert to their teams when the league resumed operations. This included Cochran.

Cochran made his debut against the Browns on July 29. The Red Sox pitcher that afternoon was Babe Ruth. Cochran batted second and in his first major league at-bat against the Browns' Allan Sothoron, he fouled out to third. He went 0-for-4 in a 3–2 Boston win. Boston won the next afternoon, 11–4, and Cochran got his first major league hit off Dave Davenport, beating out a ball hit to first baseman George Sisler. Cochran made two errors that afternoon, the only miscues of his major league career. Overshadowing Cochran's play and even the win, was the arrest of an estimated 20 gamblers at Sportsman's Park by the St. Louis police.

July 31 was Cochran's best day as a major leaguer. The *Boston Globe* said: "Cochran was a busy boy at bat. He got on four out of five times. The hustling third sacker singled in the second, was hit in the third, walked in the fifth, was called out on a doubtful third strike in the seventh, and again got his ribs in the way of the ball in the ninth." Cochran scored two runs, stole a base, and advanced two bases on an error. The next day, Cochran scored the winning run after catcher Hank Severeid's throwing error. It looked like Boston had found the answer to its third-base problem.

From St. Louis, the Red Sox went to Cleveland dropping three of the four games, and Cochran was dropped in the batting order. He went hitless in three of the four games, but managed two hits and stole a base and scored the only run in a 5–1 loss to Jim Bagby. He managed just one hit in a series at Detroit, but walked twice scoring a pair of runs in one of the games. That hit on August 8 would be his last for almost three weeks.

The Red Sox returned home on August 10, and on the return, there was bad news for George Cochran. The *Globe* reported the signing of Cochran's former Western League rival Jack Coffey. Coffey's managerial experience and a stint earlier in the season with Detroit made him a desirable addition. George made his Fenway Park debut in that afternoon's doubleheader against the Yankees. He again went hitless, dropping his batting average to .143 but fielded well and was part of an unusual 4-3-5 double play in the second game.

On August 14, Coffey joined the team and made his first start at third. Except for an exhibition game in New Haven, Connecticut, Cochran started just once in the next two weeks. Apparently considered the superior defensive player, he sometimes replaced Coffey in the late innings. As the Red Sox came close to clinching the pennant, Cochran began to play more. He started against Detroit on August 27 and 28 and started in both games of an August 30 doubleheader against Philadelphia. The weak hitting continued in those games. He was a combined 0–11 dropping his average to .091.

George Cochran was in the lineup batting seventh in the first game of the August 31 doubleheader against the Athletics. Boston beat rookie Jack Watson 6–1 in the opener. In what would be the last pennant clincher by a Boston team for almost three decades, Cochran broke out of his slump going 1-for-3. He replaced Everett Scott at shortstop in the latter innings of the second game. Watson returned to the mound for Philadelphia in that second game, shutting out the American League champs, 1–0.

What turned out to be George Cochran's final major league game was Boston's last regular season game in New York. Cochran managed a hit in four at-bats against George Mogridge, and fielded flawlessly starting a double play. In an article comparing the relative strength of the Red Sox and Cubs infields, Cochran's defense was praised. The article also mentioned the possibility of Fred Thomas receiving a furlough from the Great Lakes Naval training station.

George Cochran traveled with the Red Sox to Chicago for the opening of the World Series. When the team arrived in Chicago, Thomas was waiting for them. Cochran sat on the Red Sox bench but didn't appear in the Series. Cochran was one of six late-season acquisitions to receive a $300 share of the World Series proceeds. George spent that offseason working in the Oklahoma oil fields.

As American Association President Hickey predicted, Cochran and other players who went elsewhere after the league suspended operations were returned to their prior teams. That development, and the suspension of the major league draft, ended any chance of Cochran returning to the major leagues. George batted .311 for Kansas City in 1919. After sitting out the 1920 season, he returned and batted .322 for the Blues in 1921, his final professional season.

Cochran used his baseball earnings to move his family, which included Wilma, his mother, a son Dale G. (born in 1916), and daughter Marian (born 1919), to a newer home. He also opened a combination confectionery, cigar store, and newsstand with partner L.H. Dillard. The store was located on Carthage's town square. He also owned and operated a ballpark on West Fairview Avenue in Carthage later in the 1920s.

The Great Depression effected Missouri even before the stock market crash of 1929. Sometime near the end of that decade, George Cochran moved his family to California. Settling in Los Angeles, the family rented a home on East Rennington Road, and George opened another cigar stand. By the time George Cochran died on May 21, 1960, he was living in the Harbor City community located in the southern part of Los Angeles. He was working as a grocery clerk at the time of his death.

JOHN FRANCIS COFFEY *by Maurice Bouchard*

G	AB	R	H	2B	3B	HR	RBI	BB	SO	BA	OBP	SLG	SB	HBP
15	44	5	7	1	0	1	2	3	2	.159	.213	.250	2	0

"Atta-boy, Frank,"[1] the slick-fielding Fordham University shortstop shouted to the diminutive second baseman with every successful double play turned on the practice field at Rose Hill. The oft-repeated ritual helped propel the shortstop to a major league contract before college graduation. More than 50 years later, when the shortstop-turned-baseball-coach-turned-Fordham institution had to retire, the keystone partner gave the keynote address. Of course, by then, the shortstop, Jack Coffey, referred to the second baseman in more deferential tones, because the second baseman had become the Archbishop of New York, Francis Cardinal Spellman. There are not many professional baseball players who have to list their stint in the major leagues among the least of their accomplishments, but such is the case for Jack Coffey. His greatest accomplishment was the positive impact he had on the lives of the numberless throng of undergraduates. Yes, Coffey was a coach at Fordham, but he was also a teacher, friend, advisor, cheerleader, and confidant to many, many young men in his 54-year association with Fordham. While his milieu was athletics, his influence was much wider. As sportswriter Caswell Adams wrote, "There hasn't been a Fordham man, bookworm, crapshooter, or athlete who hasn't felt the influence of Jack."[2]

John Francis "Jack" Coffey, the son of immigrants, was born January 28, 1887, in New York City. Jack's mother was born in England; his father, Michael, in Ireland. Jack attended Morris High in the Morris Heights section of the Bronx, playing baseball and football. In the fall of 1905, Jack entered St. John's College at Rose Hill in the Bronx

Jack Coffey with the Boston Doves, 1909.
Courtesy of Chicago History Museum.

(in 1907, St. John's College became Fordham University), and excelled at academics and sports. He won eight varsity letters at Fordham, four each in baseball and football.[3] His first game for the Maroon was a football game against Rutgers in the fall of 1905. Left tackle Coffey would drop off the line into the backfield to take the pitchout; the play, which became known as the "Coffey-Over," worked for three touchdowns in that initial contest. While Coffey was quite adept at football, baseball was destined to become his career. The speedy Coffey was the star shortstop for four years and was the Rams' team captain in 1909. During his playing career at Fordham, he was a teammate of three future major league players: pitcher Dick Rudolph, who won two World Series games with the 1914 "Miracle Braves," and infielders Dick Egan and Dave Shean.

After the 1909 Fordham baseball season ended, Coffey signed a major league contract with the Boston National League franchise (the team was known then as the Doves, after team owner George Dovey but Coffey later joked the name derived from "their pacifistic tendencies.")[4] The 5'11", 178-pound Coffey joined the Doves on June 23 at the Polo Grounds in New York City for a doubleheader against the Giants. The Doves were a very bad team, 13–35 as the day started, on their way to a 45–108, last-place finish. Luckily for Coffey, the Doves were desperate for help. Coffey entered the first game in the bottom of the eighth after starting shortstop Bill Dahlen was ejected for arguing a close play at third base. In the top of the ninth, with the score tied, 4–4, Coffey had his first major league at-bat. It came against future Hall of Famer

Christy Mathewson, who had entered the game in the ninth in relief of starter Rube Marquard. The right-handed-hitting Coffey, who later recalled fouling off about a dozen pitches, struck out. In the bottom of the ninth, with the score still tied, Coffey made an error that gave the Giants an opening to win the game, 5–4. Between games, Coffey was honored with a ceremony on the field by "his young Westchester County friends."[5] He was given a gold watch and a floral horseshoe. Coffey started the second game at short. He got his first major league hit, a single, off Doc Crandall. Coffey also scored a run and made another error as the Doves were drubbed, 11–1.

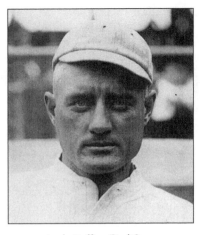

Jack Coffey, Red Sox, August 11, 1918. Courtesy of the *Boston Herald*.

Coffey became the everyday shortstop for the 1909 Doves, playing in 73 of 80 games between June 23 and September 9. He had a difficult time in the field, making at least one error in five of his first six games. He would go on to make 40 errors in 73 games for an .896 fielding percentage, well under the league average. He acquitted himself better at the plate for a while, reaching .268 (on a team that hit .223 for the season) before settling at .187. He had a 3-for-5 day on July 8 against St. Louis while playing errorless ball in the field. The *Boston Globe* enthused: "Coffey made it plain to all that he is a high class ball player."[6] Arthur D. Cooper wrote, "The Fordham shortstop has partially braced up an infield which as yet is a little wobbly. Coffey has certainly made good."[7] Coffey was moved up in the batting order from seventh to fifth and even batted in the third spot on occasion.

On July 16, Coffey was reunited with fellow Fordham alum Dave Shean, whom the Doves had acquired from the Phillies. By July 27, the *Boston Globe* noted, Coffey seemed to play better when the "Arlington boy [Shean]"[8] was playing second. On July 26, the Doves were playing the Giants at the South End Grounds; Boston started Al Mattern. The Giants went with Leon Ames. Coffey, batting third, hit a long line drive to right center field with one on in the first inning. Giants center fielder Bill O'Hara cut in front of right fielder Moose McCormick, attempting to make the catch. The ball went off O'Hara's glove deep into the right-field corner, allowing Coffey to circle the bases. The *Globe* gave Coffey credit for a home run. No error was given to O'Hara or McCormick. Although the *Boston Herald and Journal* described Coffey's hit as a "long liner to right center and under almost any circumstances would have been an out,"[9] the box score shows a home run for Coffey. The *Boston Post* gave Coffey credit for a triple but no error to O'Hara or McCormick. There is no further explanation of how Coffey scored. The *New York Times* credited Coffey with a home run in the box

score and noted only that "O'Hara made an error of judgment" in the account of the game. The game was suspended because of darkness after 17 innings with the score tied, 3–3. Coffey reminisced about this home run to Arthur Daley[10] and was proud of hitting a home run in each major league. He has not, however, been given official credit for the four-bagger.

After a forgettable August, Coffey went back to Fordham in early September to finish his bachelor's degree and to coach the freshman football team. In late December, the Indianapolis Indians of the Class A American Association announced they had obtained Coffey from the Boston Nationals. His amateur eligibility exhausted, Coffey could not play for his college baseball team so, in 1910, he coached the Fordham nine to an 18–2 record.

With his degree in hand and the college season over, Coffey played for the 1910 Indians. Managed by former major leaguer Charlie Carr, the Indianapolis team finished fourth (83–85) in the eight-team league. Coffey, playing shortstop, hit .226 with six triples, four doubles, and 16 stolen bases in 93 games. In 1911, Coffey's contract was purchased by the Denver Grizzlies of the Western League (Class A). The 1911 Grizzlies, managed by Jack Hendricks, were arguably the best team Denver ever fielded in the Western League and one of the finest minor league teams ever. Pitcher Buck O'Brien was 26–7 with the Grizzlies and, after a September call-up, was 5–1 with a 0.38 ERA for the Boston Red Sox. The Grizzlies reached first place in June and never let up, winning 111 and losing only 54, leaving the second place St. Joseph (Missouri) Drummers 18 games behind. Coffey had an excellent year for the Grizzlies, playing in 168 of the 169 scheduled games and hitting .278 with five homers, nine triples, 31 doubles, and a Western League record 68 stolen bases. He fielded .923, fourth in the league among everyday shortstops. An article in *Baseball Magazine* about the 1911 Grizzlies said, "The shortstop position had for several seasons been the weakest place on the Denver infield. Jack Coffey was bought from Indianapolis and took care of the position so well that the other shortstops in the league were forgotten."[11]

The Grizzlies also finished in first in 1912 and 1913 although in not so dominating a fashion as the 1911 squad. Coffey raised his batting average to .293 in 1912. He hit a career-high nine home runs along with 11 triples and 23 doubles over 147 games and stole 43 bases. For the 1913 Bears, as they were now known, Coffey's power numbers were down from the previous year but he still hit .291 with 39 stolen bases while playing 154 games at shortstop.

Coffey's August 21 home run. Detail of *Boston Post* cartoon, August 22, 1918.

In addition to his work with the Bears, Coffey was a co-manager of the Fordham varsity baseball team in 1912 and 1913. He was instrumental in the Rams' early season workouts and with the team selection before leaving to join the Western League in April.

After the 1913 season and three successive Western League crowns, Denver team owner and president James C. McGill asked skipper Jack Hendricks to manage another of his baseball properties, the Indianapolis Indians. McGill then named Jack Coffey to succeed Hendricks. This was Coffey's first foray into the ranks of player-management, a role that would last until the end of his minor league career. The pressure of management, apparently, had a salutary effect on Coffey's playing. In 1914, he had the finest season of his professional career. Coffey achieved career highs in at-bats (628), batting average (.330), total bases (287), hits (207), triples (15), and runs (116) while playing in 165 games. The Bears finished second, however, winning 96 and losing 72.

In August of 1914, Coffey signed a contract extension, at an increased salary, to manage the Bears in 1915. In September 1914, though, the Pittsburgh Pirates purchased Coffey's contract for $1,500. On September 21, the *New York Times* declared: "Coffey to Succeed Hans Wagner."[12] The story that followed, however, dampened the grandiose claim somewhat. Coffey had not yet signed a contract with the Pirates. Pittsburgh scout Chick Frazer was dispatched to Denver to induce Coffey to sign. Coffey was balking at the idea, though. If he was going to move east, he wanted to be well compensated. Coffey was using the newly-formed Federal League as a bargaining ploy. Federal League teams in Indianapolis and Chicago were interested in Coffey. In the end, Pirates owner Barney Dreyfuss would not pay Coffey what he wanted and Coffey was back with Denver as a player-manager in 1915. Coffey's numbers tailed off that season, as they were bound to after his stellar 1914. He played in only 105 games but stole 34 bases and hit a respectable .282. He also saw some time at third base for the first time in his professional career. As a manager, he guided the Bears to another second-place finish at 82–55, three games behind Des Moines. After the season, St. Joseph owner Jack Holland tried to pry Coffey loose from Denver. Coffey told Holland he was under contract with the Denver club for 1916. McGill, miffed because of the attempted backdoor deal, set the price for Coffey's contract very high. Holland declined to pay it and the popular Coffey appeared set to play and manage another year in Denver.[13] It was not to be, however. Before the start of the 1916 season, Coffey's contract was sold to the San Francisco Seals of the Class AA Pacific Coast League.

Jack Coffey was joining another very good team. The Seals won the PCL crown in 1915, posting 118 victories against 89 defeats under manager Harry "Fighting Harry" Wolverton, a nine-year major league veteran and one-time New York Yankees manager. Wolverton remained the manager for 1916 and Coffey was relegated to player-only status. The Seals played 206 games in 1916 (the PCL typically played the most games of any professional circuit). After briefly attaining first place in the league, the Seals fell to third before finishing in fourth place at 104–102. Their new shortstop had an off-year as well. Coffey hit only .223 in the tougher league, managing just two triples and 13 doubles in 135 games. Coffey had another good year in the field though. The shortstop fielded at a .948 clip in 135 games.

Coffey, now 30, was back in the Western League in 1917, this time as player-manager for the Des Moines Boosters. Coffey guided the Boosters, including future major league star Lefty O'Doul, to a 55–35 first-place finish for the first half of the season and a 29–27 fourth-place finish in the second half. The Boosters beat the Hutchinson (Kansas) Wheatshockers four games to two in the league playoff, winning the Western League crown. Coffey, playing second base, had a better year at the plate. He hit .289 over 142 games with four homers, eight triples, 19 doubles, 71 runs, and 28 stolen bases.

Coffey was back to manage the Des Moines club in 1918 but it was destined to be an abbreviated season. Larger forces than professional baseball were at work. World War I and the concomitant "work or fight" order was wreaking havoc with minor league rosters and with attendance. Most minor leagues decided to truncate their seasons. The Western League ceased operations on July 7. The Boosters were 36–31, in third place, and Coffey was hitting .267 when the season ended. The major leagues were having their own difficulties with the "work or fight" order. All of the big league teams had lost players to the draft or to jobs in "essential" industries. They were looking for players to fill their depleted squads. Coffey, at the age of 31, was unlikely to be drafted so the Detroit Tigers signed him to a contract on July 10.[14] When Tigers second baseman Pep Young was out with an injury, Coffey filled in.

Coffey's first game with the Tigers came on July 13 in Washington against the Senators. He went 0-for-3 in the Tigers 1–0 victory. Coffey's last game for the Tigers came on August 3, also against the Senators. Overall, Coffey played in 22 games for the Tigers and hit .209 with two triples, four RBIs, and two stolen bases. He played well in the field, making five errors in 116 chances for a .957 fielding percentage. When Pep Young came back, however, Coffey became expendable.

Old friend Dave Shean came to the rescue, indirectly. The 34-year-old Shean was the everyday second baseman for the first-place Boston Red Sox. He had rheumatism in his foot bad enough to cause doubt he would finish the season. Red Sox owner Harry Frazee had Eusebio Gonzalez on the bench but wanted a bit more insurance. When the Red Sox came to Detroit for a three-game set on August 6, a deal was made for Coffey.[15] On August 10, Edward F. Martin of the *Boston Globe* reported that Coffey would join the Red Sox that day. He went on to say Coffey "played second base capably for the Tigers in the absence of Pep Young."[16]

It was not at second base, but at third base, however, that Coffey would contribute to the Red Sox. He played 14 games at third and only one at second for the eventual AL champions. He hit a lowly .159 with a homer and a double in 44 at-bats. He made two errors in 49 chances for a .959 fielding average. His best game at the plate came on August 21 against the St. Louis Browns at Fenway Park. Spitballer Allen "Dixie" Sothoron held the Sox to two hits through the first seven innings but one of the hits was a home run by Coffey in the fifth. Coffey hit what the *Herald and Journal's* Burt Whitman called "a funny home run…a whack which ordinarily would have been good for three bases and which Hooper or Speaker either would have caught or held to a double."[17] The speedy Coffey, however, turned it into an inside-the-park home run, only the second home run hit at Fenway Park during the entire 1918 season.

Coffey played his last games as a major leaguer on September 2, 1918. (Due to the war, both the American and National League had agreed to end the season by September 2 and start the World Series on September 4.) Coffey played in both games of a doubleheader in New York against the Yankees. He played third in the first game, going 1–for-3 and second base in the second game, going 2-for-4. Coffey was on the roster for the World Series and it looked as though he might get to play when Dave Shean injured his hand fielding a ball during practice. A rainout on September 4, however, allowed Shean time to heal. Fred Thomas, who had played 44 games for the Sox in 1918, was on leave from the Great Lakes Naval Training Station and held down the hot corner during the Series. Consequently, Coffey did not appear in the World Series but was voted a $300 share of the victors' prize money.[18]

It was back to the Western League and the Des Moines Boosters for Coffey in 1919. The player-manager played 123 games at second base and led his team to a fourth-place finish, just four games over .500 (71–67). Coffey bounced back at the plate, however, hitting .306 with three homers, seven triples, 29 doubles, and 32 stolen bases. In 1920, Coffey became a part-owner of the Des Moines franchise and, U.S. Census records show, by 1920 he was a married man. He was renting a home in Des Moines with his wife, Lorraine, a Missouri native, who was five years his junior. No other information is known about Lorraine Coffey.

It was a disappointing season for the Des Moines club. The Boosters finished in last place, 33 games behind the league-leading Tulsa Oilers. Coffey did his part, however. The 33-year-old played in 137 of the team's 151 ball games. He was leading the team in hitting at .385 in mid-June[19] before settling at .290 with four homers, four triples, and 25 doubles. He could still steal a base, garnering 26 more thefts that year. The next year, in what would be his final season in Des Moines, Coffey could improve his team's fortunes by only one place as the Boosters finished seventh in the eight-team circuit. Coffey hit .300 but played in only 95 games, his lowest total in the minors since 1910 (the shortened 1918 season excepted). He hit 23 doubles but no home runs, only two triples, and only five stolen bases.

At the end of the 1921 season, Coffey announced that he would not be back for 1922. *The Sporting News* reported, "Folk all over the circuit [the Western League] view the passing of Coffey with much regret for there never was a more popular man in the league than the prematurely-gray boss of the Des Moines outfit."[20] Coffey was very popular with the players and the fans wherever he managed or played. After playing most of the previous 12 years in the West, Coffey was heading home.

On February 18, 1922, Fordham named Coffey and Billy Keane (Fordham Class of 1904) co-managers of the varsity baseball team.[21] It was understood Coffey would manage the Rams only part of the time because he had also taken a player-manager position with the Hartford Senators of the Eastern League. Coffey was taking over a Hartford club that finished fifth in 1921, five games below .500 at 71–78. The veteran manager could coax only two more wins out of the Senators in 1922. They finished in sixth place at 73–76. In 1922 Coffey had his worst year in minor league ball. He hit only .231 and played in only 50 games.

As the Hartford skipper, Jack Coffey has the distinction of being Jim Thorpe's last manager. Thorpe, 35, was signed by Hartford during the 1922 season. The aging star could still hit but his off-field activities became on-field problems. Coffey was forced to dismiss Thorpe for "indifferent play." Coffey himself spent only one year in Hartford. The next year, Coffey again co-managed the Fordham baseball team but also was the player-manager for the Macon Peaches in the Class B South Atlantic League. The Peaches, who had started the 1923 season as the Charleston Pals, had won the Sally League championship in 1922. Coffey did not have much to work with, however, since most of the players were sold before the start of the 1923 season.[22] It did not get any better as the seasoned progressed. Attendance dropped dramatically in Charleston and manager Coffey was "much handicapped by lack of funds."[23] The Pals had won only seven of 28 games when they moved to Macon. Coffey rebounded nicely at the plate, at least partly due, no doubt, to the lesser quality pitchers in this league. The 36-year-old Coffey played in 114 games, hitting .294 (on the worst hitting team in the league[24]) with 11 home runs (a career best), three triples, 30 doubles, and 53 RBIs. He also stole nine bases. Again, he lasted only one year with his team. In 1924, Coffey, who continued his co-managing duties at Fordham, was the player-manager for two teams in the Three-I League. He started the season with the Peoria (Illinois) Tractors and finished with the Decatur (Illinois) Commodores. He hit .270 in just 38 games for the two teams.

On New Year's Day 1925, *The Sporting News* reported, "Jack Coffey, worthiest of managers and grandest of men in baseball, has made it positive he will not return."[25] It was his last season of professional baseball. Coffey had

Jack Coffey with Fordham.
Courtesy of the *Boston Herald*.

played for 11 teams in eight leagues over the course of 16 seasons. The scholarly Coffey referred to his baseball sojourn as "a prolonged series of peregrinations to points provincial."[26]

In 1925, Jack Coffey returned to Fordham University to stay. He earned his law degree and was now the full-time, sole manager of the baseball team. During the summer of 1925, Coffey worked as a scout for old friend Jack Hendricks, who was now managing the Cincinnati Reds. Coffey scouted in the Eastern League as well as in the Pacific Coast League. In 1926, Coffey succeeded Frank Gargan as Graduate Manager of Athletics at Fordham. Coach Coffey held both positions until he retired in 1958.

While Coffey was in charge of athletics at Fordham, the University became a national sports powerhouse. The baseball team won five Eastern Collegiate Conference championships and 14 Metropolitan Conference titles. Coffey's career winning percentage as a Fordham manager is above the .700 mark.[27] So popular was the baseball team it could draw 12,000 people to the Polo Grounds for games against Manhattan or Columbia. During the 1920s, 1930s, and into the 1940s, Fordham was a perennial football power. Fordham football games were extremely popular as well. Games against New York University would be played before more than 70,000 people at Yankee Stadium. Two Fordham teams, 1929 and 1937, went undefeated. The once-beaten teams of '35 and '36 included Vince Lombardi, whom Coffey had persuaded to come to Fordham in the fall of 1932.[28] Lombardi's first brush with fame came as one of the "Seven Blocks of Granite," as the '36 Rams football line was called. Fordham football teams also made two bowl appearances, the 1941 Cotton Bowl and the 1942 Sugar Bowl (back when an invitation to a bowl game was a rare event). Fordham also produced quality basketball teams and track stars during Coffey's tenure.

By the 1950s the awards and accolades started to accumulate. In 1953, Coffey received a citation for "long and meritorious service to sports" from the Sports Broadcasters Association. In 1954, he was elected to the Collegiate Baseball Hall of Fame. On April 3, 1954, Fordham

University renamed its baseball field Jack Coffey Field, which it remains to this day. Also in 1954, Coffey was named to the Helms Foundation Collegiate Baseball Hall of Fame. In 1958 the Eastern College Athletic Conference awarded Coffey its annual James Lynch Memorial Award for outstanding service over a long period. By 1958, though, Coffey had passed the mandatory retirement age at Fordham and the 71-year-old made plans to retire at the end of the spring semester. May 17, 1958, was Jack Coffey Day at Fordham (it was actually the second Jack Coffey Day; Fordham had honored him with a day on May 17, 1947, for his 25 years as manager of the baseball team). The The 1958 Day's events began with a baseball game against Manhattan College at Jack Coffey Field. The Rams prevailed, 14–7. A reception followed the game and a dinner was held that night. Among the 500 guests were Frank "The Fordham Flash" Frisch, Hank Borowy, Johnny Murphy, and sportswriter Tom Meany. The president of Fordham, the Very Rev. Laurence J. McGinley, SJ, announced the creation of the John F. Coffey Award, a medal given each year to the Fordham varsity athlete who achieves the highest academic standing. Father McGinley also announced that the title Graduate Manager of Athletics would be Coffey's forever and would be retired in his honor. In 1966, Coffey was elected to the American Baseball Coaches Association Hall of Fame.[29] In 1970, he was in the inaugural class of inductees in the Fordham Hall of Fame.

Jack Coffey had been associated with Fordham for more than 50 years. He was an institution at the university. He mentored countless baseball players at Fordham, teaching them not only the technical aspects of the game but also how to play the game with class. At least 23 of his baseball charges made it to the major leagues, among them Hank Borowy, who won World Series games with the Yankees and the Cubs; Johnny Murphy; Babe Young; and Sam Zoldak. To his friends and associates he was Genial Jack, Mr. Fordham, or Mr. Birthday, the latter sobriquet given to honor Coffey's prodigious memory. Sportswriters at the time claimed Coffey could remember the birthdays of 3,000 people. He was in the habit of addressing people by their birthday instead of by name, as in "Hello, Mr. July 30." Coffey, an autodidact in foreign languages, was fluent in French (he wrote a sports column, in French, for "Fordham France"[30]), Spanish, Italian, and German. From at least 1929 until his retirement, Coffey traveled widely with his second wife, Anastasia. The two traveled to France, Italy, Spain, Germany, Alaska, Australia, and South America, among other places where Coffey would hone his language skills. At the end of his life, Coffey was suffering from arteriosclerosis and was confined to a nursing home. He succumbed to a heart attack on February 14, 1966. He was survived by his wife, Anastasia. The couple had no children. Coffey is buried at Calvary Cemetery, Queens, New York.

At Jack Coffey Field at Fordham a bronze plaque, placed there April 3, 1954, is inscribed:

To John F. "Jack" Coffey, A true sportsman, scholar and Christian gentleman.

These are fitting words and a lasting testament to an exemplary person, baseball player, coach, and teacher.

Notes

1. Daley, Arthur. "Sports of The Times," *New York Times*, May 12, 1958, p. 34.

2. Adams, Caswell. "Through the Years . . . ," *Fordham Ram*, May 17, 1947, p. 2.

3. Gilleran, Ed. "Looking Them Over," *Fordham Ram*, May 17, 1947, p. 3.

4. Daley, op. cit.

5. *Boston Globe*, June 23, 1909, p. 5.

6. *Boston Globe*, July 9, 1909, p. 5.

7. Cooper, Arthur D. *Boston Post*, July 8, 1909, p. 10.

8. "Doves Showing a Much Better Frame of Mind," *Boston Globe*, July 27, 1909, p. 4.

9. *Boston Herald and Journal*, July 27, 1909, p. 4.

10. Daley, op. cit.

11. Norton, Russell, F. "Baseball Above the Clouds," *Baseball Magazine*, February 1912, Vol. VIII, No. 4, pp. 27–33.

12. Coffey to Succeed Hans Wagner," *New York Times*, September 21, 1914, p. 8.

13. Niely. "Coffey Remains with Denver," *The Sporting News*, October 21, 1915, p. 8.

14. *Boston Globe*, July 11, 1918, p. 4.

15. Wood, Allan. *Babe Ruth and the 1918 Red Sox* (Lincoln, NE: Writers Club Press, 2000), p. 210.

16. Martin, Edward, F. *Boston Globe*, August 10, 1918, p. 4.

17. Whitman, Burt, *Boston Herald and Journal*, August 22, 1918, p. 4.

18. A full share was $1,108.45, the smallest amount ever awarded to a World Series winner. Wood, op. cit., p. 342.

19. *The Sporting News*, June 17, 1920, p. 3

20. *The Sporting News*, November 17, 1921, p. 2

21. "To Coach Fordham Nine," *New York Times*, February 18, 1922, p. 16.

22. *The Sporting News*, December 21, 1922, p. 8.

23. *The Sporting News*, May 10, 1923, p. 2.

24. *The Sporting News*, November 8, 1923 p. 6.

25. *The Sporting News*, January 1, 1925, p. 3.

26. Daley, op. cit.

27. Solomon, Burt, Fordham University Press Release, May 19, 1958.

28. Cohane, Tim. *Bypaths of Glory: A Sportswriter Looks Back*, New York: Harper and Row, 1963, p. 4.

29. www.abca.org/downloads/pdf/ABCA_HallOfFamers.pdf

30. www.fordham-tradition.org/SEP96.HTM

JEAN DUBUC *by Tom Simon & Guy Waterman*

G	ERA	W	L	SV	GS	GF	CG	SHO	IP	H	R	ER	BB	SO	HR	HBP	WP	BFP
2	4.22	0	1	0	1	1	1	0	10⅔	11	5	5	5	1	1	0	0	46

G	AB	R	H	2B	3B	HR	RBI	BB	SO	BA	OBP	SLG	SB	HBP
5	6	0	1	0	0	0	0	1	2	.167	.286	.167	0	0

For 77 years, the 198-foot Gothic spire of Notre Dame des Victoires Church dominated the St. Johnsbury skyline. Standing on Prospect Street, just around the corner from the Fairbanks Museum of Natural History, the church was a familiar landmark to most residents of "St. Jay" until it burned in 1966. But probably no one knew that it was the reason that Jean Dubuc—a pitcher with an 85–76 lifetime record, 3.04 ERA, and a solid .230 batting average in nine major league seasons—was born in the chief city of Vermont's remote Northeast Kingdom.

Before the turn of the century, the Dubuc family owned Granite Construction Company, an itinerant firm that specialized in building churches throughout the northeast. In the spring of 1887, Napoleon Dubuc relocated to Railroad Street in St. Johnsbury to start work on Notre Dame Church. That first summer, 150 carloads of Concord granite and thirty carloads of Isle la Motte stone were used to build the church's exterior. In the summer of 1888, the interior was finished in ash, frescoed, and lighted with stained-glass windows—St. Patrick on one side for the Irish parishioners and St. John the Baptist on the other for the French-Canadians.

Later that summer—on September 15, 1888, to be exact—Napoleon and Mathilde Dubuc had a son (one of six she bore) whose given name at birth is variously reported as Jean Arthur, John Joseph, Jean Baptiste Arthur, and Jean Joseph Octave Arthur. As if those weren't enough, somewhere along the line he picked up the nickname "Chauncey." Despite his French-Canadian heritage, his first name was pronounced "Gene," at least in American baseball circles, while his last name was pronounced like Dubuque, the city in Iowa.

When Jean was four, the Dubucs moved to Montpelier.

Jean Dubuc, New York Giants, 1919.
Courtesy of Bob O'Leary.

The future major leaguer lived in Vermont's capital city for seven years before his parents sent him to the Seminary of St. Theresa in Montreal, where he studied for the priesthood. There, the *Rutland Herald* reported, Jean "was undefeated in high school games pitched in Canada." As he entered adolescence, the family re-located yet again, this time to Fall River, Massachusetts, where Napoleon was the contractor in charge of building St. Ann's Church. Dubuc relative Bob O'Leary recalls a story from his childhood about how the 15-year-old Jean first learned to control his pitches in Fall River: "Behind home plate at the sandlot was the exterior wall of a drug store. Jean was throwing so hard and wild that the catcher could not always catch the ball. When it struck the outside of the pharmacy, all the items displayed on the inside of that wall fell to the ground and broke. Jean learned to control his great arm so that they could keep playing."

Jean attended the prep program at the College of the Holy Cross in Worcester for one year, 1904–05, studying electrical engineering. He went out for varsity baseball, but on the second day of practice school authorities informed the 15-year-old that he was too young to play. For the 1905–06 school year, Dubuc enrolled at St. Michael's College in Winooski Park, Vermont. In only its second year of existence, St. Mike's already had a winning baseball team. Jean pitched every game that season, compiling a 13–4 record and recording double-digit strikeouts routinely. His exploits at the plate were even more impressive. Batting third in the order, he hit .528 with an .843 slugging average. To put that in perspective, subtracting Dubuc's contributions, the team's batting average falls from .300 to .271, and its slugging average plummets from .375 to .316. A century later, Dubuc, a three-sport athlete, was inducted into the college's Athletics Hall of Fame in September 2006.

The following fall, Jean headed west to South Bend, Indiana, and enrolled at the University of Notre Dame. Though his first athletic participation on campus was as starting forward on the varsity basketball team, Dubuc showcased his true athletic brilliance on the baseball diamond. In the spring of 1907, the 18-year-old Vermonter posted a 5–1 record as the Fighting Irish amassed 21 victories against only two losses. Notre Dame was 20–1 the following season, with Jean upping his contribution to 9–1. Aside from Dubuc, the 1908 squad featured no less than four future major leaguers: second baseman George Cutshaw, who played regularly for 11 seasons with Brooklyn, Pittsburgh, and Detroit; first baseman Bert Daniels, who patrolled the outfield with the New York Highlanders for four seasons; catcher Ed McDonough, who backstopped for the Phillies for a couple of years; and pitcher Frank Scanlan, who had a cup of coffee with the Phils.

Even in that fast company, Chauncey Dubuc glistened. His nine wins in 1908 stood as a school record until 1989, though later Notre Dame teams played much longer schedules. Of his 14 wins over two seasons, seven were shutouts, and even his two defeats were glorious. In 1907's only loss, Dubuc gave up just one hit and one walk while striking out 16 — and getting three hits of his own. And his 1908 defeat was one of the most interesting games in the annals of Vermont baseball history.

When Jean Dubuc pitched against UVM at Centennial Field during Notre Dame's 1908 eastern trip, Vermont baseball enjoyed a banner day. The game featured three of history's most distinguished Green Mountain Boys of Summer: Dubuc on the mound for the visitors, Ray Collins for the home nine, and Larry Gardner at shortstop.

In a hard-fought game in which Collins struck out 13, UVM handed the Fighting Irish — and Dubuc — their only loss of the season, 6–3. "[Notre Dame], the much heralded champions of the Middle West, came to Burlington with a series of 12 victories," bragged UVM's yearbook, *The Ariel*, "yet even with the far famed Dubuc in the box, they were unable to keep us from scoring six runs."

Jean Dubuc intended to return to Notre Dame in the fall of 1908 but was forced to change plans when a semipro game in Chicago cost him his amateur status. Adopting the alias of "Williams," Dubuc pitched a lackluster team called the White Rocks to a 2–1 victory over the powerful Gunthers, but the ruse was detected and reported in the *Chicago Tribune*. Without hesitation, Notre Dame authorities ruled their best pitcher ineligible for further collegiate competition.

Jean barely had time to peel off his White Rocks uniform before receiving offers from seven major league teams. He signed with the Cincinnati Reds, with whom the 19-year-old made his major league debut on June 25, 1908. In his first big league game, he was pulled in the fourth inning after severely wrenching his knee, an injury that plagued him for the rest of his career. He pitched only once more until September, when he returned to action as a regular starter. Dubuc ended up 5–6 with a solid 2.74 ERA. One of his victories was a two-hit shutout over the world-champion Chicago Cubs.

That fall, Jean won three of his four decisions on Cincinnati's barnstorming tour of Cuba. It looked like 1909 might be a big year for the young Vermonter. But in spring training he contracted malaria, causing him to miss most of the season and reportedly still affecting his play badly the following year. In 1910, Reds manager Clark Griffith sent Dubuc to Buffalo of the Eastern League, but when the pitcher continued to struggle (his record was 0–6), Buffalo released him. Jean went home to Montreal, where his father had moved after Jean's mother's death.

For the French-speaking Dubuc, Montreal was the perfect place to turn around his sagging baseball fortunes. Jean joined the Royals, the local Eastern League club, and rebounded to 21–11 in 1911, thanks mainly to an effective change-up reportedly learned from his catcher, major league veteran Frank Roth. Jean was no slouch at the plate, either. The Dubuc scrapbooks reveal that in 26 pinch-hit at-bats in Montreal, Jean had an astounding 22 hits. Dubuc also opened a successful business, The Palace Bowling Alley and Pool Room at 282 St. Catherine Street, and bought stock in the Montreal Wanderers, one of two local National Hockey Association franchises. Of course, with 21 wins to his credit, Dubuc was eagerly wanted back in the majors — it was said that 15 big league scouts were in the stands for one of his starts. Montreal's asking price was reportedly $10,000 and a couple of players, but in September the Royals accidentally exposed him to the major league draft. Ten of the 16 clubs put in claims, with the Detroit Tigers finally obtaining him for the bargain price of $1,500.

Detroit offered Dubuc a salary of $2,250 for 1912. Sitting pretty in Montreal, Jean played coy. In a letter to Tigers owner Frank Navin, he pointed out that $2,250 for seven months' work contrasted poorly with his 1911 salary of $2,196.68 for five months, not to mention the need to hire a manager to run his business if he left Montreal. Dubuc countered with two options: Navin could raise him to $2,800 or allow him to buy out his own contract for $1,500. While that response may seem brazen for an unproven youngster, Dubuc's letter, preserved to this day in his file at the National Baseball Library, is a model of courtesy.

Somehow the differences were resolved, and in 1912 Jean Dubuc began a five-year stint in Detroit (rooming with Ty Cobb on road trips) with a spectacular first season, beginning with a win in the first game ever played at Tiger (Navin/Briggs) Stadium. Though overshadowed by Walter Johnson's and Smoky Joe Wood's record 16-game winning streaks, Dubuc compiled an 11–game streak of his own en route to a 17–10 record, with two shutouts and an ERA of 2.77. In a feature article in *Baseball Magazine*, F. C. Lane called Dubuc "The Slow Ball Wizard." Lane wrote that it was Roth who taught him the slow ball in Montreal in 1911, though others claim that Clark Griffith had shown it to him two years earlier. Another sportswriter dubbed him the "best pitching find of the season." Hall of Fame umpire Billy Evans pronounced his change-up the best in the American League.

Over the next four seasons, amid repeated salary wrangles, Dubuc showed flashes of his original glitter but never put together an entire season of distinction. In 1914, for example, he started off in a blaze, winning his first five decisions — despite hurting his knee again on April 15 — and bringing forth headlines like "Looks Better Than Ever." According to one newspaper, "Some of the diamond critics believe that he is destined to become the best pitcher in baseball." But for the rest of that year his won-lost record was only 8–14, his ERA for the season escalating to 3.46. He came back in 1915 with a 17–12 record, including a career-high five shutouts (one of them a one-hit, 1–0 triumph over the great Walter Johnson). But when his knee injury resurfaced in 1916, causing him to tail off to 10–10, the Tigers figured he wasn't worth a big salary and sold him to Chattanooga.

Dubuc went 22–16 games for the Salt Lake City Bees in the Pacific Coast League in 1917, playing outfield often and pinch-hitting with some frequency. He suffered a serious automobile accident in late March 1918 but again pitched well for Salt Lake that season. In July he was one of 10 Bees ordered to show cause why they should not be designated 1–A in the draft. Dubuc told the Salt Lake papers that he wanted to join the war effort as a French interpreter, but when he was granted a deferment due to his bad knee, his appeal increased to major league teams seeking to restore depleted rosters. The Boston Red Sox purchased his contract and on July 25 he reported to the Red Sox on the road at Comiskey Park.

With the Red Sox Dubuc appeared in five games, but

Dubuc with Detroit. *George Brace photo.*

pitched in only two. The first was his debut on July 28; he allowed one run, throwing the last two innings of an 8–0 loss to Chicago, and was 1-for-1 with a single in his only at-bat. His second appearance was his only start, the second game of a double header in New York, which he lost in the bottom of the ninth, 4–3. Dubuc was 1-for-6 at the plate during the regular season. His only appearance in the World Series came when Barrow wanted a right-handed pinch hitter in the ninth inning of Game Two. The Red Sox were down 3–1 with men on first and third and one out. Dubuc struck out, then Schang popped up to end the game.

John McGraw's New York Giants acquired Dubuc before the 1919 season. In an era when relief specialists were unheard of — Firpo Marberry, often credited for launching that role, didn't appear until five seasons later — Dubuc pitched in 36 games, only five of them starts, leading the N.L. with 31 relief appearances. He won six, lost four, saved three (tied for second in the league in that category), and led the league in games finished (22), an early example of the "closer" in baseball. Dubuc compiled a 2.66 ERA and allowed only 119 hits in 132 innings as the Giants finished in second place. He seemed to have found a niche.

Based on his stellar 1919 performance, Jean Dubuc appeared to have earned another shot at the majors. "He doubtless will festoon the Giant staff for some time to come," was how one writer put it. But after the fall barnstorming tour, McGraw unexpectedly released Dubuc. The 31-year-old veteran hooked on with the Toledo Mud Hens, for whom he played all positions except catcher and middle infield in 1920. In the American Association, Dubuc proved his value by winning nine games on the mound with a 2.72 ERA, batting .292, serving as field captain, and even replacing Roger Bresnahan as manager at midseason.

Why did the sage McGraw exile Dubuc to Toledo, and why did he never again pitch in the major leagues? The answers to those questions became apparent only as the details of the Black Sox scandal unfolded. On September 24, 1920, pitcher Rube Benton, a former teammate of Dubuc's with the Giants, testified before a grand jury in Chicago that he'd seen a telegram disclosing that the

Series was fixed. "I don't know who sent it," Benton said, "but it came to Jean Dubuc, who was barnstorming with us. It simply said: 'Bet on the Cincinnati team today.' I suppose it came from Bill Burns, who had been close to Dubuc a few weeks before the Series when both were living at the Ansonia Hotel in New York City." Benton didn't mention another possible source: Chick Gandil, with whom Dubuc had been good friends since they played together in 1911.

Having his name come up in the baseball bribery investigation wasn't a positive development for Dubuc, to say the least. In the aftermath of Benton's testimony, *The Sporting News* published a piece in its issue of November 11, 1920, entitled "Why Dubuc Was Dropped." The article quoted McGraw as saying that he released Dubuc because he "constantly associated" with Burns, a gambler who'd played with Jean on the 1912 Tigers. According to *The Sporting News*, McGraw suspected that Burns and Hal Chase, who'd also been mentioned in the Chicago hearings, might have caused the Giants to lose out to the Reds in the 1919 pennant race.

While Commissioner Landis was handing out banishments from baseball, Dubuc wisely made himself unobtrusive by leaving the country for the entire 1921 season. Others who were no more implicated in the scandal than Dubuc were banned for life, but Landis failed to notice the newly obscure pitcher in Montreal's Atwater Park Twilight League. By 1922, Jean was back in the United States, pitching in the minors for the Syracuse Stars. *The Sporting News* lifted an offended eyebrow: "The astounding news comes from Syracuse that President Ernest Landgraf plans to take on Jean Dubuc, former major leaguer and later with Toledo, from which club he drew his walking papers because he was supposed to know too much about the throwing of the 1919 World's

Jean Dubuc in a Chicago courtroom, 1920. Courtesy of Chicago History Museum.

Series." Still Landis looked the other way, and Dubuc was allowed to carve out a modest living in the minors for the next several years.

Dubuc played for Syracuse again in 1923, and was a player-manager for both Ottawa and Hull in 1924. He played for Manchester in 1926 and Nashua in 1929, where his brother Arthur owned the team. In 1927 Jean moved to Providence, Rhode Island, where he coached the Brown University baseball and hockey teams and founded the Rhode Island Reds of the American Hockey League. While in Rhode Island he scouted for the Detroit Tigers, signing Josh Billings, Gene Desautels, Birdie Tebbetts, and the great Hank Greenberg among others. New York Yankees scout Paul Krichell recalled spending the better part of a year visiting the Greenberg family and manfully eating Yiddish food, only to watch with dismay as "in stepped Jean Dubuc...who called at the Greenberg house, bringing along his own ham sandwich, and signed up Hank right under the very shadow of Yankee Stadium."

In 1936 Dubuc returned to his native state as manager of the Northern League's Burlington Cardinals, but the following year he left sports altogether. For the next two decades he worked as a printer's ink salesman for the Braden-Sutphin Ink Co., eventually retiring to Florida. His wife, Lu, died in 1956. The couple had no children. Bob O'Leary's grandmother cared for her uncle Jean after a stroke robbed him of mobility and speech; she reported that for the last months of his life, the only word he could say was "merde." Following a three-year illness, Jean Dubuc passed away in Fort Myers on August 28, 1958. "He was a very dear friend of mine up to the time of his death, was a very fine baseball man, an excellent baseball instructor, and a fine gentleman," said Birdie Tebbetts.

EUSEBIO GONZALEZ *by Bill Nowlin*

G	AB	R	H	2B	3B	HR	RBI	BB	SO	BA	OBP	SLG	SB	HBP
3	5	2	2	0	1	0	0	1	1	.400	.571	.800	0	1

One of the more obscure players in Red Sox history, Eusebio Gonzalez was the first foreign-born Latino to play for the Bosox. Eusebio Miguel Gonzalez Lopez was born in Havana, Cuba on July 13, 1892. Batting right and throwing right, he was an infielder listed as 5'10" with a playing weight of 165 pounds.

It appears that he hailed from the Cayo Hueso district of Havana and first began playing ball with a local club named "Libertad." A perusal of the Havana newspaper *Diario de la Marina* indicates that the first professional game for the 17-year-old Gonzalez appears to have begun as shortstop with Havana's Fe team on February

10, 1910. On February 13, he recorded his first base hit, going 1-for-4 during a tough day in the field: he committed three errors. Jorge S. Figueredo shows Gonzalez hitting .109, with seven hits in 46 at-bats during 16 games. Spotty records show he played on and off for a number of Havana-area semipro teams from 1910–1913 such as La Discusion and the Vedado Tennis Club. Rafael Figarola, with whom he'd played on the Fe team, included Gonzalez on a team he assembled to play a series of exhibition games in Mexico City.

On his return, Gonzalez spent some time in the ranks of the Cuban Army and in 1912 was sent to help forcefully suppress unrest among a number of Afro-Cubans in Oriente province. Even then, a newspaper article noted that he was given a special furlough to play ball for the topnotch Vedado team.

Gonzalez came to the attention of Brooklyn Dodgers captain Jake Daubert while the Dodgers were playing a series of games in Cuba in early November, 1913 against Havana, Almendares, and Fe. An early profile in *Carteles* magazine suggests that it was Cuban baseball promoter Abel Linares who may have made the introduction.

Bozeman Bulger of the *New York World* wrote, "A young fellow, Gonzalez by name, has been doing such wonderful work for the Havanas that Daubert has offered $3,000 for his release to Brooklyn. He believes the young Cuban will make one of the greatest infielders in the world. During the season, which is now at its height in Havana, Gonzalez has batted better than .400."

Instead, Gonzalez began his U.S. career with the Troy (New York State League) Trojans in March 1914. The April 10 *Troy Times* wrote that Gonzalez "was tried at shortstop and surprised the rest of the squad with his speed and the amount of ground he covers." Nowhere in Troy newspaper coverage did there appear any sense of controversy noted regarding the inclusion of a player from Cuba on the hometown team.

"Papo" Gonzalez was signed as a utility infielder, and before the season was more than a month underway, he had played at each of the infield positions. His first big game came on May 10, when he was 2-for-4 with a double. The *Times* noted, "Notwithstanding the fact that Gonzalez is unable to speak English, the opponents of the Troy team do not put much over on the Cuban. Baseball is the same no matter what language the players speak and Gonzalez knows the game. Apparently he does not have much trouble knowing when he had three strikes or four balls."

Gonzalez was an immediate hit with observers of the game, and the May 21 *Times* stated, "Gonzalez adds to his popularity every game he plays." A month later, the paper

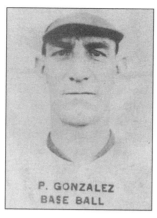

Eusebio Gonzalez on a 1924–25 Aguilitas Segundas baseball card. Courtesy of Cesar Lopez.

wrote, "The Cuban always has his mind on the game."

Gonzalez finished 1914 with a flourish, 3-for-5 with a double and a triple in the first game, and 1-for-3 with a double in the second. The right-handed Gonzalez played a full 126 games, batting .264 and (with 41 errors) a .947 fielding average. Many games in this era had a high number of errors, both due to the much smaller gloves used by fielders and the less than immaculate field conditions.

Eusebio Gonzalez returned to Cuba after the season was over. In winter ball, Gonzalez played for Havana, batting .180 in an even 100 at-bats over 33 games, but he had made an impression on a team with deeper pockets. Manager John C. Calhoun signed Gonzalez to play for Binghamton (New York State League) and signed him as a free agent, apparently possible given the Troy club's failure to pay him his full 1914 salary.

1915 into 1917 — the Binghamton Bingos

The Binghamton Bingos operated, as did the league as a whole, under a salary cap of sorts — $2,500 per month for the total team player payroll.

Even though the *Binghamton Press* was prone to some of the casual ethnic slurs of the day (one headline about a pitcher from Hawaii read "Chink Flipper to Join Redlegs"), it never exhibited any sense of animosity to Gonzalez or any of his compatriots who may have played for the Bingos. Coverage typically referred to him simply as "Gonzalez" or "the Cuban" but never pejoratively.

Gonzalez finished the 1915 season with 40 errors and a .899 fielding average. He batted .258 on the year, according to the *Press*, which also ascribed him 21 doubles, 12 triples, and one home run. Speedy on the basepaths, he had 35 stolen bases. Handwritten statistics found in Hall of Fame files are similar, but not identical, indicating fewer errors (36) and a higher batting average (.268.) Binghamton won the pennant. Gonzalez played with Havana again that winter and had a terrific Cuban League season, batting .349 in 32 games, with 37 hits in 106 at-bats — and showing more power, with seven doubles and four triples.

Gonzalez played virtually every game of Binghamton's 1916 season until suffering a season-ending injury while blocking second base during the August 24 game against Harrisburg. In his second year with Binghamton, Gonzalez played in 111 games, with 360 at-bats, hitting .272 with 34 stolen bases.

Again, Gonzalez played winter ball in Cuba, this time — as though foreshadowing later developments — for the Red Sox! Not the Boston Red Sox. Author Roberto Gonzalez Echeverria explains that the year was an unusual one; while the new Almendares Park was being built, there was a short-lived one-year competition between three teams known as the Orientals, White Sox, and Red Sox from January into March. Gonzalez hit .226 in 14 games.

In 1917, Gonzalez left management wondering about his whereabouts but finally showed up, quite late, for spring training. He was in great shape and hopped into the April 28 game without seeming to miss a beat. On May 2 — opening day — he was 1-for-4, with a double, and stole third, scoring on a single a few moments later. One of the best days he had in a Bingos uniform came on May 25. Gonzalez was 4-for-5 with a solo home run in the ninth inning over the left-field fence in Scranton. As of June 7, he was batting .267, pretty much in line with his record for the three previous seasons in New York State League play.

The World War was heating up, conscription was implemented, and baseball owners were uncertain as to whether they would be able to continue to field teams. At midpoint in the season, in July, they called off the season, but then reversed course somewhat, scheduling a "second season" beginning with a new set of games. As part of the retrenchment, the salaries for Binghamton players were cut by $53.37 per month, or they were offered their outright release. The final game for the first season was July 8 and the Binghamton papers show Gonzalez finished the season playing third base, batting an even .260. Other records show him as 61-for-224 in 66 games, with the same .272 average he had posted in 1916.

Mid-season 1917 to Mid-season 1918 — with the Springfield Green Sox

When the second season started on July 11, Eusebio was no longer with Binghamton. The July 23 Springfield (MA) Daily Republican headlined his signing with the Springfield Green Sox. He'd been let go, and the Green Sox pounced. They'd been after him for a while.

Gonzalez quickly became a local favorite. His first day saw him go 1-for-2, and he scored the winning run in the top of the 10th inning. After his first full week in the Eastern League, he had gone 8-for-21 and scored four runs. The July 30 paper declared, "Gonzalez has proved why he was popular up in the New York State league." Springfield went on a tear, winning 17 of 25 games, and the August 25 Republican wrote, "'Eb' Gonzalez keeps the old head up there all the time. He pulls down some mighty hard hits and difficult chances during an afternoon." On the 27th, it was noted that "Gonzy" had come to the attention of some big league scouts.

The season ended on September 8, with Springfield in seventh place. Despite the various encomiums accorded him, in the time he was with Springfield during the second half of 1917, he committed 22 errors and had a fielding average of .873. His average was fourth highest on the team, though, and the local paper concluded, "Gonzalez was a big addition to the club and played good ball here all the way, in spite of his fielding average. He was particularly strong in the pinches, both as a fielder and sticker."

Gonzalez spent the winter months in Cuba, and was in good shape for the May 22, 1918 Opening Day game. He played during Paddy Green's no-hitter on June 4 and continued to earn recognition for spectacular fielding plays; the June 9 paper praised a play that "belonged in the big leagues. Gonzy is the third baseman of the Eastern League." After the first 27 games, he was hitting .365, second on the team.

On July 2, another Gonzalez joined the Springfield Green Sox. Ramon Gonzalez, Eusebio's brother, was signed and played second base. He had only played a handful of games when the Eastern League held discussions about suspending the rest of the season. Attendance was down dramatically. The Providence Greys were hit the hardest, only drawing about 200 fans to each game. The Republican mentioned the two brothers in its July 16 edition: "Eb Gonzalez spent a busy day at third, handling five chances without trouble, and came through with two solid smashes which totaled three bases. Both Eb and his brother, Ramon, limped badly during the game. Each has a lame pedal extremity." Ramon played shortstop, Freddy Parent moving to second base.

Making the major leagues — with the Boston Red Sox

On July 19, U. S. Secretary of War Newton D. Baker announced that baseball was "non-essential" to the war effort and the Eastern League decided to close up shop. The Springfield paper headlined a sports page story "Gonzy Local Star; Majors Spotted Him; Chance Probably Lost." The gist of the story was that the Green Sox had received a couple of offers for Gonzalez — a prime commodity of sorts, because being a Cuban national he was not subject to the U. S. military draft. But since the major leagues were also talking about terminating their season as well, the opportunity might have passed. The paper concluded, "Fans would have liked to have seen the Cuban given a trial. He has played remarkable ball for Springfield and has been the real life and hope of the club all season."

It was good news, then, when the July 24 edition could report: "Eusebio Gonzalez, the crack third baseman of the Springfield Green Sox, was sold yesterday by Magnate Bill Carey to the Boston Red Sox...all who seen him perform have realized all along the speedy Cuban was major league timber" and added that Gonzy "should have been there long ago." As for Carey, he said, "Gonzalez is the fastest and hardest working baseball player I have ever had on my club and I have never seen any in the Eastern league that could touch him." The paper said that "all of Springfield wishes Gonzy the best of luck in his new undertaking." He was due to join the Red Sox as their train passed through Springfield at 12:25 pm en route to Detroit to play a series with the Tigers.

Gonzalez debuted for the Red Sox in Chicago on July 26, entering in the late innings for Everett Scott at short in a game Boston was losing to the White Sox, 7–1. Gonzalez got his first major league at-bat in the eighth and he tripled. Jack Stansbury singled, driving in "recruit Gonzalez" and bringing the score to 7–2.

Back home in Havana, there was a brief acknowledgement of Gonzalez' debut. *Diario de la Marina* offered a modest sports page headline reading, "Papo Gonzalez debuto con gran suerte en el Boston Americano pegando un triple en su unica excursion al bate." There was no particular attention accorded the native Cuban upon his debut, nor was there in the weeks to come — no feature, no player profile, no photograph. The *Springfield Republican* was far more interested in Gonzalez than Havana's *Diario do la Marina*.

Two days later, Gonzalez again filled in for Scott in the later innings. Facing Reb Russell, who had an 8–0 shutout going in the top of the ninth, Gonzalez made an out in his one at-bat. His average was cut in half, from 1.000 down to .500. Paul Shannon of the *Boston Post* commented on Gonzalez's work in the eighth inning: "Gonzalez made two pretty plays in the inning."

At least one other baseball man had his eye on Gonzalez. A story out of St. Louis on August 3 in the *Ft. Wayne News and Sentinel* said that Branch Rickey of the Cardinals was reported interested in the Gonzalez brothers, both Eusebio and Ramon.

Eusebio's third appearance in a Red Sox game came in Detroit, on August 6, and he played a full game at the hot corner. He was 1-for-3 in a game that was tied 4–4 after nine innings. Gonzalez led off the 10th and drew a walk. Carl Mays walked, too, and Wally Schang got on due to a Detroit error. Bases loaded. Tigers pitcher Rudy Kallio fielded Hooper's grounder and threw home to cut down Eusebio and start a double play, but the throw went all the way to the backstop and two runs scored as the Red Sox took the lead when Gonzalez crossed the plate. Dave Shean drove in a third run. Mays gave up one run to the Tigers in the bottom of the 10th, but the Red Sox won, 7–5.

All told, after three games for Boston, Eusebio Gonzalez had played error-free ball in the field, batted .400 with a triple, and scored two runs — but he never got another chance to play in the big leagues.

The Red Sox played two more games on the road trip, August 7 and 8 in Detroit, then headed home to host the Yankees. Gonzalez was exempt from U.S. military service,

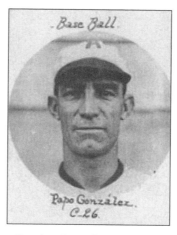

Eusebio Gonzalez with Almendares, 1923–24 Nacionales. Courtesy of Cesar Lopez.

but the Sox also had Dave Shean (too old for the draft) and manager Ed Barrow was bringing in a number of other players. George Cochran debuted on July 29 and played most of the games at third. Everett Scott stuck at short, playing out the games, which were mostly relatively close ones. Gonzalez did return to Boston with the team and presumably was fitted with a home uniform, but never wore it in Fenway competition.

Boston Post sportswriter Arthur Duffey seemed to connect with Gonzalez, even though he managed to misspell both first and last names. As far as Duffey knew, Gonzalez was likely to be around for a while. In the August 8 *Post*, Duffey wrote, "Ensevio Gonzales, the new recruit corralled by the Red Sox, is pining to figure in a world's series if only to run for someone else. Of the several Cuban players who have come to this country within a decade Ensevio is the only one who has had any chance to compete in baseball's big classic. He states that if he gets this opportunity he will be a bigger man than the governor of Havana when he returns home in October." The *Boston Traveler* called him "Eusebo Gonzales" and the *Boston Herald* announced him as "Octavio Gonzales."

Why didn't Gonzalez play more than the three games for Boston? In his book *Early Latino Ballplayers in the United States*, Nick C. Wilson points out, "During the course of that season the Red Sox field-tested five utility players at shortstop; Gonzalez was the only man who lasted more than one game. It may seem strange that a rookie who hit a triple off one of the best hurlers in the American League in his first at-bat was treated so indifferently." Wilson then raises a couple of questions: "Was he too dark-complected to bring back to Boston? Did his previous minor league club demand too high a payment for his services?" Asked about the conjecture, Wilson replied that he was just guessing, trying to figure some reason why the Red Sox let the draft-exempt Gonzalez go. The compensation answer seems unlikely, given what we know of his departure from Springfield, and the fact that he finished 1918 with Toronto. The Red Sox were the last major league club to sign an African American player, so it's not surprising the question of color comes to mind. These weren't the Yawkey years, though. There was different ownership at the time — Harry Frazee. During the first 20 years of the Red Sox franchise, the team had previously signed two Mexican-American ballplayers (Frank Arellanes and Charlie Hall) and also a full-blooded Native American (Louis Leroy.) There was no indication in the Boston press that Gonzalez or any of these other Red Sox players were controversial signings due to their ethnicity.

When the Red Sox returned home from a 15-game road trip, the title was still very much up for grabs, and Paul Shannon of the *Post* foreshadowed their arrival, writing how much the Boston fans were looking forward to return of a reanimated Babe Ruth and also the opportunity to see George Cochran, "a brilliant fielder, a clever base runner and the best man that the Red Sox have had at third base since Fred Thomas was called by the draft. Cochran is a heady base runner, a fair hitter and a good run getter." Cochran was apparently an improvement over Gonzalez in Ed Barrow's estimation. As it happened, as soon as Cochran hit Fenway, he began to slump seriously, so Barrow brought in former Boston Brave Jack Coffey (he'd last played in the majors in 1909) from the Tigers, to take over third base duties. All evidence seems to point to Barrow ranking Gonzalez third amongst his choices for third base.

Gonzalez did play for the Red Sox during one game in New England, an August 18 exhibition game against the New Haven Colonials in Connecticut. He played shortstop and batted second, but was 0-for-4 at the plate (with one sacrifice hit). Two days later, he was in a Toronto Maple Leafs uniform.

Because of the World War, it had been agreed that the 1918 major league season would end early, around September 1, and that a World Series would be played, to finish by the 15th. The *Boston Globe* reported on August 20 that Everett Scott, Stuffy McInnis, Harry Hooper, and Amos Strunk had each heard from their draft boards that they would not be called before September 15. The talent needs of the organization were becoming clearer, and apparently the first-place Red Sox didn't need Gonzalez that badly and Barrow looked to see if he could cut a deal elsewhere. The *Toronto World* reported that Barrow had wired Toronto manager Dan Howley "asking if he could use Infielder Gonzalez. Dan wired back to hurry him along. Shortstop Joe Wagner was unexpectedly called to report to his draft board in New York, and it looked like Gonzalez could fill the bill.

1918 — 1923 with the Toronto Maple Leafs

The *Toronto World* acknowledged his August 20 arrival: "He came via the Boston Red Sox route, and the gentleman from the warm isle is very acceptable. He displayed all the earmarks of a real ball player. He is fast, knows how to run bases, and is a good fielder." Gonzalez singled in the first inning, stole second, took third on an error, and scored easily on a drive that rattled around in front of the left-field bleachers. The *Toronto Star* praised his "right-smart performance," saying he "fielded cleverly, showed a strong whip, and hit and ran the bases as if he knew how." The *Star* mistakenly gave him the name Ramon Gonzales.

Even after he'd gone to the Red Sox, the *Springfield Daily Republican* followed Gonzy's play. After his debut, the paper reported his "brilliant start," wrapping up the brief account with an exhortation: "Keep it up Gonzy." An August 7 headline read "Gonzy Is There" and said, "Gonzy performed brilliantly." After Gonzalez had moved on to Toronto, *Republican* coverage waned.

On August 22, the Leafs took first place in the International League race. Eusebio singled and scored the tying run in a six-run bottom of the eighth inning that lifted them to a 6–4 lead. Rochester failed to score in the ninth and Eusebio joined in the celebration. Two stories in the *World* said that "pandemonium broke loose" and the Toronto players "danced like a lot of crazy kids." The *World* noted that "Gonzalez turned handsprings in the joy of the moment," a dozen in all.

Playing second base and batting second, he scored the first run in the next game, and on August 24, he was involved in one of those kinds of plays that champions seem to turn: the ball was hit to him, he "reached for it with his gloved hand, the ball deflecting off the glove to Dolan, who made a grab for it, but couldn't hold it, he knocking the ball in the air about three feet, and Gonzalez, swinging around, grabbed it with his bare hand, and threw the runner out at first." The Maple Leafs played excellent ball and held on as the race came down to the wire.

On September 2, as the Toronto game went into extra innings, word came that Binghamton had lost; a win would give the Leafs the flag. Gonzalez already had two hits on the day and two stolen bases, had executed a sacrifice perfectly, and "pulled sparkling work on ground balls." He also played a crucial role in the final frame, the 12th inning. The Leafs' Heck popped up to the second baseman, ranging deep, but the Buffalo right fielder bumped his teammate just after he got his glove on the ball, dislodging it. Dolan sacrificed Heck to second and Gonzalez was up once more. He drove a single to left field, putting Heck on third base. Gonzalez ratcheted up the pressure, with a steal of second. Buffalo walked Callahan on purpose, and the fielders all moved in. Lear slammed the first pitch he saw far over the center fielder's head for "one of the longest hits of the season" — and for the International League pennant.

Even if he were no longer with the Red Sox, Gonzalez had still helped to secure a pennant in 1918 — and apparently enjoyed the experience immensely. The Maple Leafs barnstormed a bit around Ontario in the following week, beating city teams in St. Catherine's, Brantford, and Ingersoll, and eventually Gonzalez set sail for home.

In fact, Papo Gonzalez played with *three* pennant winning teams in 1918, in three different countries, appearing for Boston, Toronto, and Havana.

Gonzalez played for Havana (with his brother Kakin) and they won the 1918–1919 Cuban League championship. "Papo" was the nickname accorded Eusebio and "Kakin" that given Ramon. Roberto Gonzalez Echevarria reports that Havana (Papo was joined by his old teammate Lujan, who'd played in 1915 preseason exhibition games with Binghamton) also won a 1919 Campeonato Oriental in September 1919.

1919

Papo was a little late arriving for spring training 1919, due to passport problems, but he was in such good shape from winter ball that it didn't cost him any playing time. His first big game of 1919 came on May 15. He reached base all five times he was up, stole two bases, and scored four times. His defense won acclaim as well.

Gonzalez was still remembered fondly by fans in Binghamton, and when he first appeared there for Toronto, on June 19, he "was given a great ovation when he stepped to the plate in the first inning." For much of the year, Gonzalez was the Maple Leafs' leadoff batter. He played shortstop all year, off to a spectacular start, hitting as high as .377 by May 24. He slipped into a prolonged slump, though, and wound up batting .247 in a full 146-game season, with 127 hits in 515 at-bats, with 22 doubles and 36 stolen bases.

In the 1919–20 Cuban season, playing for Habana, he hit a much lighter .181 in 72 at-bats.

1920 — 1922

Returning to Toronto in 1920, Gonzalez had an excellent year, batting .297 in 160 games playing second and third base. He hit 16 doubles and four triples and his highest total yet in stolen bases: 38. He often earned praise for other parts of his game, too, helping turn four double plays on May 26 against the Rochester Colts and scoring from second on a sacrifice on June 24. On August 20, he "showed the fans an honest-to-goodness Ty Cobb slide when he scored in the sixth by throwing his body way to the back of the plate and getting the rubber with his toe." (*Toronto Star*)

Back in the Cuba, he played for Almendares in the 1920–21 season, batting .257 and leading into his best year in the International League.

In 1921, Gonzalez had an exceptionally good season for Toronto, playing in 160 games, with 581 at-bats, and hitting .301 with 60 stolen bases, six triples, and 28 doubles. Why the Boston Red Sox didn't purchase him and give him another try (Boston finished in fifth place in 1921 and in last place in 1922) remains an open question.

The next day, there was some concern that Gonzalez might be "ball shy" as a result of being hit on the head, but his first time he laid down a beautiful bunt and his second time up he hit a "slashing double to right, effectively laying that shy idea at rest." (*Telegram*)

His play suffered badly, though, and the papers got on his case. The truth of the matter came out shortly afterward. Gonzalez had a broken bone in his hand. He had indeed been hit by a pitch on the 26th. He shouldn't have been shown up by his own manager. He shouldn't have

been asked to play in the later games. The *Star* apologized more or less, allowing, "His poor showing against Detroit is thus accounted for. Many players would not have attempted to go on the field at all with an injury of this nature." His season was over. He was unable to grip a bat or throw a baseball. There was some fear that he would be permanently disabled.

He played second, third, and short for Toronto in 1922, his average dipping to .274, appearing in 118 games. This winter, he chose to stay in Canada rather than return to Cuba.

Marriage

A big reason he stayed in Ontario became clear on November 25, 1922. The *Toronto Star* headlined a story "Gonzy's New Contract" that told readers Gonzalez was "making the greatest double play of his life . . . signing a life contact this morning in Barrie."

The *Barrie Examiner* explained, "Congratulations to Miss Audrey Jary and Mr. Eosebeo Gonzales who were married here on Saturday. Mr. Gonzales is a famous baseball player." Yet another spelling for Sr. Gonzalez. They got his name right on the marriage license, though. Recorded on November 30, the license reflects the November 25 marriage between the 22-year-old stenographer Audrey Redverse Jary (daughter of Arthur Jary and the former Martha Ellis) and the 28-year-old Eusebio Gonzalez.

1923 — from the Maple Leafs to the Brasscos

As 1923 began, the Leafs added Eusebio's brother Ramon to the mix; he'd played shortstop for Springfield since 1918. Asked how he'd deal with two Gonzalezes in the same infield, manager Howley told the *Globe & Mail*, "I'm going to simplify this thing by calling one of them 'Pat' and the other 'Mike.'" The newspaper explained that Ramon had been playing winter ball for the Santa Clara team in Cuba. However, "Eusebio ('Mike') Gonzalez is wintering in Toronto and district, and has gained sixteen pounds in weight since the season closed last fall." No baseball and maybe a little home cooking?

Ramon had come off back-to-back years of .313 and .314 with Springfield and was looking to cash in a bit. He was slow to arrive for the season, happy enough with the salary he'd been offered, but holding out for a percentage of the purchase price paid to Springfield, which he claimed he'd been promised. Something was worked out and the "swarthy third baseman" (*Toronto Star*) soon turned up. Howley had said he was thinking of alternating the Gonzalez brothers at third, but room was found for both of them.

"Mike" wasn't the player he'd been, maybe a bit out of shape, and reporting a sore arm in late March. The hand seemed to have healed but one speculates that a little of the fire may had dimmed, perhaps in part due to the unfair treatment he'd suffered at the end of the 1922 campaign. There was one incident early in the year when Eusebio didn't run out a grounder, and Howley read him the riot act, "told him if he intended to keep his place on the team he had to run out every time." He was fined $50 and benched.

Three weeks later, on May 12, Ramon was hitting at a .296 clip, but Eusebio was only 20-for-79, a .253 average. On June 20, he had tonsilitis and lost a few more days. Finally, at the very end of June, Eusebio was sold to the Eastern League's Waterbury Brasscos in Waterbury, Connecticut. The *Globe & Mail* said he was "anxious to get away from Toronto...the Cuban is a good player when he cares to hustle, but his heart was not in his work here."

In his sixth season with the Maple Leafs, he appeared in 26 games at second and third, before being sent to Waterbury, where he played exclusively at shortstop. For Toronto, he hit .249; for Waterbury, he hit .254 in 70 games.

By mid-August, Gonzalez was batting .307. He tailed off sharply, though, and finished the season with a .254 average in 252 at-bats for Waterbury, just a little higher than the .249 he'd hit with Toronto. Gonzalez was seventh from the bottom of the list of league hitters published in the *Republican* at year's end.

Shot by a sportswriter

A January report in the *Toronto Star* predicted he'd return to the International League in 1924, playing for Rochester. He'd apparently been released by Waterbury and signed by the Rochester club. Ramon was playing winter ball and "going great guns" but Eusebio was said to be taking the rest of the winter off and "spending his time and money trying to pick winners at Oriental Park."

Speaking of guns, when "Mike" reported to Rochester spring training at Haddock, Georgia (near Savannah) to prepare for another season of International League play, he brought a shocking story with him: Gonzalez had been shot — by a sportswriter (!) — in Havana. Shot in the hand.

A dispatch in the *Rochester Democract and Chronicle* informed readers that he was "late in reporting to the Rochester Club, because of a bullet wound in his wrist.... The bullet fired by a Havana sporting editor has left its mark and it is a question how long it will be before the Cuban is able to play with the Tribe." He required a bit of surgery in New York City when the wrist failed to heal promptly.

How had Gonzalez been shot? González was playing for the Habana Leones (also known as the Rojos) in the Gran Premio of 1924. Come the aftermath of the March 9, 1924 game, in which Habana had beaten Santa Clara, and per David Skinner's translation of the March 10 article in *Diario de la Marina*: "As the fans were exiting Almendares Park following the game, three gunshots rang out behind the main grandstand. This attracted the reporters, and when they arrived on the scene they saw Habana third baseman Manuel Cueto and backup catcher Eugenio Morín trying unsuccessfully to protect a teammate with a wounded hand from apprehension by several policemen led by a Sgt. Ortega. That player turned out to be Rojo second baseman Papo González, who was taken into custody by the lawmen, to the dismay of [*Marina* reporter] Peter, who referred to him as one of the most admired players for his modesty and gentlemanliness."

Sportswriter Pepe Conte was charged with the shooting and released on $200 bail.

W. A. Phelon's column in the March 20, 1924 issue of *The Sporting News* provided a fuller description of the incident and its protagonists. It is worth reprinting here in its entirety:

> Here in Cuba, they sure take their baseball seriously — and in the old-time way. If a sporting writer pans a player, good night! He has to whale the athlete, hand to hand, or be disqualified forever. A few days ago, Pepe Conte — well known to all American writers — penciled a paragraph that hurt the proud spirit of one Gonzales (not the noble Miguel) second baseman of the Almendares Club. Senor Gonzales sought out Señor Conte during the eighth inning, and smote him on the nose, proboscis, or snoot, so that Señor Conte fell extremely prone.
>
> Señor Gonzales trumpeted in triumph, but not for long. Señor Conte uprose, and with him came a dark blue automatic, and, one instant later, Señor Gonzales lay upon the reddened soil. Then all Cuba went to war; and the strife between the partisans of Señor Conte and Señor Gonzales endured, with many casualties, until the police charged from several directions and bore everybody to the hoosegow. The doctors say that Señor Gonzales will recover. The judge says Señor Conte is out on bail. And, as might be expected, in the tumult and confusion, somebody took a darn good kick at the umpire. Isn't it a wonderful world?

What transpired with Pepe Conte after the shooting? The *Toronto Star* provided a little more information, recounting the story told their reporter by Emilia Zarzo, a catcher for another ballclub who was "a cousin of the brothers Gonzalez." Zarzo said that Eusebio was not seriously hurt but had been shot in the hand by Havana sportswriter Conte during an altercation on the field. "Zarzo maintains that Gonzalez was protecting himself against an attack by Conte when a bullet penetrated his left hand, inflicting a minor flesh wound. Ramon, according to the story told by Zarzo to the Canadian press, was involved in the dispute and summoned to court as a witness."

There was one oddity, dating back to May, though, the game against Newark in which he was sent in as a pinch runner, but "the Cuban...did not have on the same uniform as his teammates and the Bears objected." Stallings sent him to the clubhouse to change. The Bears complained that the game shouldn't be held up waiting for him to put on the right uniform, but the umpires allowed the change.

The May 28 *Globe & Mail* said that Eusebio "has been playing great baseball since the injury to his hand mended. For some time it was feared that Gonzalez would not be able to play again after he was shot in the hand by one of those remarkable sporting writers in Havana. The gunman was bonded over to keep the peace, and escaped a jail sentence. Gonzalez stated that there is no lack of excitement when the Cuban teams, all the players being armed, swing into action. Half the spectators are also armed."

By season's end, Gonzalez had quite a good season for Rochester, batting .278 with seven triples and 21 doubles, driving in 57 runs in an even 500 at-bats spread over 133 games.

Perhaps not surprisingly, given the gunshot wound, early 1924 had proven to be his last season playing winter ball in Cuba.

1925 — 1928

Gonzalez played three more seasons in U.S. ball, and just a bit of a fourth. He surfaced in the Texas League, playing for San Antonio in both 1925 and 1926. Ramon joined him there in 1925. (Ramon had joined New Haven in 1924, playing in 76 games and batting .253.)

Eusebio had a full 1925 season — perhaps his best one ever — batting .306 with six home runs and 58 RBIs. Both were career highs; the home runs were his first recorded. His 180 hits, his 36 doubles, and 238 total bases were all career highs, too. Ramon played less than 10 games for San Antonio.

Eusebio's 1926 production was off from the highs of '25, but nonetheless a good year at the middle two infield slots, getting in another 445 at-bats, batting .258 with 39 RBIs. He was homerless again, but struck 25 doubles.

In 1927, Eusebio Gonzalez turns up back in New England once more, playing for the Eastern League's Hartford Senators. He first turns up in a lineup on April 22, playing right field.

The *Hartford Daily Courant* referred to him as "Mike" Gonzalez, never using the name Eusebio and never mentioning his time with Boston in 1918. Gonzales played regularly at second base or shortstop in May and June but suffered an injury in June; once Hartford signed Jiggs Donahue, Gonzales never appeared again in the Hartford paper. There was no mention of his leaving Hartford and nothing on his subsequent signing with Amarillo within the week.

In 25 games (94 at-bats), without ever playing one game at home, Gonzalez had hit .245 with one double and one triple and hadn't stolen even one base.

Gonzalez played the second half of the 1927 season in west Texas. For the Western League's Amarillo Texans, he played shortstop and part of one game at third base, batting an even .250 in 85 games.

Slumping soon afterward, Eusebio had another exceptional day on July 17. Batting leadoff against Wichita, he was 2-for-5 in the first game of the day's doubleheader with a single and a triple, scoring twice in a 10–3 win for the Texans. Wielding a "bloody bat" according to *Daily News* writer Charles M. Hall, the shortstop "just about made absolute believers of all who have been chiding him about the blanks he has been drawing in the hits column. He just got two singles, a walk, a triple, and a home run. Otherwise all he did was to figure in two double plays." The home run was an inside-the-park two-run homer in the bottom of the seventh, his last home run in American pro baseball. Amarillo won the nightcap, 10–4, and Gonzalez had himself a 6-for-9 day, with five runs scored — hitting for the cycle during the doubleheader.

In 1928, Gonzalez returned to the Texas League, playing a final few games for San Antonio. He began the year playing with semipro teams, but when the Bears second baseman Frank Philbin was "indefinitely suspended because of insubordination" (*San Antonio Express*), Gonzalez earned a headline in the June 28 newspaper: "Mike Gonzales Back in Game at Second Bag." The San Antonio *Light* reported that Gonzalez "manages a West Side team now." The *San Antonio Evening News* wrote, "Mike had been in San Antonio all year, managing a local semipro team. He stepped into uniform Wednesday and played his game of old, getting one hit, being robbed of another, sacrificing once and handling four chances without a bobble at second." His replacement arrived in time for the next day's doubleheader but was injured in the second and Gonzalez once more stepped in to fill the void, picking up two more at-bats and one hit, with four more plays in the field. The two appearances appear to be the last two of Gonzalez's professional baseball career.

Nearly a half-century of mystery

What happened from this point on has been difficult to determine. We've not yet learned what team he managed on San Antonio's West Side, nor how long he might have done so. At some point between 1928 and the 1970s, he returned to Cuba. It may have been right away. It may have been years later. Older ballplayers and aficionados of the game in Cuba recall Papo being around, but they don't have much detail to their memories. Connie Marrero, for instance, told Kit Krieger that he only met him once and has no idea what he did after his baseball career ended. He allowed that Papo had a reputation as a bit of a "joker." Krieger talked to several older Cuban ballplayers, but came to the conclusion: "It seems that he did not travel in baseball circles later in life. Most revealing is that Marrero does not know him as it appears that Marrero knew every figure in Cuban baseball over the last sixty years." For whatever reasons, Papo may have just decided to keep to himself, perhaps even disassociating himself from the game.

Cuban broadcaster Eddy Martin Sanchez graciously broadcast an appeal for information about Eusebio Gonzalez over his national broadcast, within a couple of weeks after the conclusion of 2006's World Baseball Classic. No one came forward.

The only contact we've yet been able to turn up came in an exchange of letters, when Gonzalez responded on May 4, 1974 to a note sent in March by Cliff Kachline of the Hall of Fame as part of a survey of former Latin ballplayers. In a formally constructed but touching note (possible typed out for him, but to which he appended his signature), Papo thanked Kachline for reaching out to him, adding that he was "enfermo y casi olvidado" (unwell and nearly forgotten), but concluding "pero sentiendo siempre el mismo entuasiasmo y devocion por el

Base Ball" (but I always feel the same enthusiasm and devotion to baseball).

What happened to Audrey is unknown. Attempts to trace the Jary family in Canada have proven fruitless. Whether Audrey and Eusebio had any children is unknown, just as it remains unknown how long their marriage may have lasted.

From 1928 to the date of his death in 1976 represents almost a half-century and yet we know virtually nothing of how Eusebio lived, what work he may have done, how he felt about his time in the game. He survived the Batista years. He saw the Cuban Revolution come and lived through more than a decade and a half afterward. His note to Kachline is gracious and appreciative of the interest shown in him, and rather touching.

We may never learn more.

DICK HOBLITZELL *by Tom Simon*

G	AB	R	H	2B	3B	HR	RBI	BB	SO	BA	OBP	SLG	SB	HBP
25	69	4	11	1	0	0	4	8	3	.159	.266	.174	3	2

An intelligent player whom both teammates and opponents respected, 29-year-old first baseman Dick Hoblitzell opened the 1918 season as the Red Sox' captain and cleanup hitter, but an early-season slump and his June induction into the Army Dental Corps marked an inglorious end to an otherwise distinguished 11-year career in the major leagues. Though he spent the more productive early part of his career with the Cincinnati Reds, "Hobby" looked back most fondly on his time with three World Champion teams in Boston, and in later years he kept in touch with Red Sox teammates Larry Gardner, Harry Hooper, Herb Pennock, and Tris Speaker.

The middle of three sons, Richard Carleton Hoblitzell was born on October 26, 1888. His mother, the former Laura Alcock, was of English descent, while his father, Henry Hoblitzell, whose ancestors hailed from the oft-disputed Alsace-Lorraine region, was part German, Swiss, and French. The Hoblitzell surname was a source of confusion throughout Dick's baseball career; Dick himself, however, consistently spelled it with two l's. Dick's older brother, William, and his younger brother, Clinton, both had blue eyes and light-colored hair, but Dick had dark brown hair, brown eyes, and a darker complexion than his brothers.

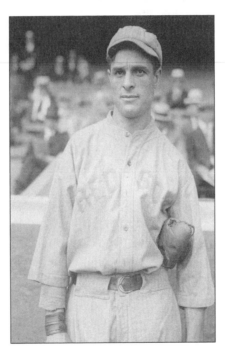

Dick Hoblitzell with the Red Sox.

The Hoblitzell boys were born in the Ohio River village of Waverly, in West Virginia's oil region, and the family owed its middle-class existence to Henry's work in the oil fields. When Dick was eight years old his mother died and the family moved a short distance downriver to Parkersburg, West Virginia. Dick captained the Parkersburg High School football team during his freshman and sophomore years, and it was around that time that he gained his first professional baseball experience. As Dick told the story, Henry Hoblitzell had remarried a woman from France and Dick was not getting along with his stepmother, so he accepted an invitation to join a barnstorming Bloomer Girls team to get away from her. Henry ended up having to retrieve him somewhere in Pennsylvania.

For his last two years of high school, Dick attended prep school at Marietta Academy on the Ohio side of the Ohio River. There he met and fell in love with Constance Henderson, a fellow West Virginian whom he later married in 1912 after he had established himself with the Reds and she had graduated from Hollins College. Dick starred at halfback for the 1905–06 Marietta College football teams and in the fall of 1907 enrolled at the Western University of Pennsylvania, which became known as the University of

Pittsburg the following year. He played end for the famous WUP football team. Earlier that year Dick had played professional baseball with Clarksburg, West Virginia, of the Pennsylvania and West Virginia League, assuming the alias of "Hollister" to protect his amateur status. After playing shortstop for two weeks, the 6-footer was pressed into duty at the initial sack when Clarksburg's regular first baseman got injured. Though Dick had never played the position before, it became the one that he manned for 1,284 contests in the majors.

A note about Hoblitzell's "handedness": All of the standard reference works list him as a left-handed hitter and thrower, and I describe him as such in my biography that appears in *Deadball Stars of the National League*. In my research for this project, however, I interviewed Dick's daughter, Connie (Hoblitzell) Michael, who commented on how strange it was that her father was a left-handed thrower when he did everything else (except bat) right-handed. My curiosity piqued, I checked out images of Hoblitzell on the Internet and am now convinced that the reference works are wrong, and that he was in fact a right-handed thrower. His T-206 tobacco card, for example, depicts him with a first baseman's mitt on his left hand, but even more convincing are the four photographs from the *Chicago Daily News* collection on the Library of Congress's web site, all taken during different seasons, showing him in the act of throwing right-handed. This also helps to explain Hobby's start as a shortstop and the seven games he played at second base for Cincinnati in 1910.

When the 1908 school year ended, Dick jumped his contract with Clarksburg to join Reading, Pennsylvania, of the outlaw Union League. When that league folded after only six weeks, he accepted an offer from Newark of the Eastern League. Before Hobby appeared in any official games, however, the National Association informed Newark that its new first baseman still belonged to Clarksburg. Dick remained in Newark for two weeks, awaiting settlement of his case. On June 30 he was informed that Clarksburg had sold him to Wheeling of the Central League. Returning to his native state, Hoblitzell appeared in 53 games and attracted attention by batting .357.

On August 4, 1908, the Home Furniture Co., which owned the Clarksburg team, wrote the following letter to Frank Bancroft, business manager of the Cincinnati Reds: "We understand that your people are looking over young Hoblitzel [sic] now with Wheeling, Central League. This man belongs to us and we have had three offers for him, but have been trying to get more money for him. He is a very promising player with good habits and enough brains to do as he is told. If you want this man we will sell him to you for $1000, we can get this from other parties but would rather do business with you as our dealings with you in the past have been very satisfactory."

The Reds purchased Hoblitzell from Clarksburg on August 21. In the interim between the letter and his purchase, however, St. Louis Cardinals manager John McCloskey had made a special trip to watch Hoblitzell play and had taken the young first baseman with him to St. Louis. When word reached Cincinnati, the National Commission (through Cincinnati owner Garry Herrmann, no doubt) immediately notified the Cardinals that Hoblitzell couldn't play until title to him was resolved. Not surprisingly, the Commission ruled in Cincinnati's favor, finding that Clarksburg had allowed Hoblitzell to play for Wheeling on condition that it retained the right to sell him to another club.

Making his debut with the Reds on September 5, 1908, Dick took over at first base for player-manager John Ganzel and batted .254 over the last 32 games of the season. In 1909 he appeared in 142 games and batted a career-best .308, third highest in the National League behind only Honus Wagner and teammate Mike Mitchell. When the 1909 season was complete, having shaved a year off his true age, Hoblitzell was considered a 19-year-old phenom whose "rise in baseball has been of the meteoric variety." Commentators mentioned him in the same breath as Ed Konetchy and Kitty Bransfield as one of the NL's greatest first basemen. Over the five-year period 1909–13, the left-handed-hitting slugger batted in the heart of the Cincinnati order and was the top run producer in the Reds' strong offensive attack. During the offseason, Dick continued his education at the Ohio College of Dental Surgery and shared an office with his older brother, Bill, who had established a dental practice in Cincinnati.

During the first half of 1914, the 25-year-old Hoblitzell mysteriously lost his ability to hit, slumping all the way to .210 after 78 games. He cleared waivers, a trade with the New York Yankees fell through, and on July 16 the Boston Red Sox claimed him off the waiver wire for a mere $1,500. Hobby rebounded during the second half of 1914 to hit .319 in 69 games, plugging a hole in the Boston lineup and turning the Sox into pennant contenders. Assigned to share a room on the road with Babe Ruth (Connie remembers that her father would never tell Ruth stories in her presence), the steady and gentlemanly Hoblitzell remained Boston's regular first baseman throughout the start of the 1918 season, usually batting third or cleanup in the batting order and performing well. In successive years, he hit .283, .259, and .257 in 1915 through 1917. He also performed admirably in the World Series of 1915 and 1916, playing in every game. He hit .313 in 1915 while six walks boosted his on-base percentage to .435 in the 1916 Series.

Declared eligible for the military draft, Dick took and passed an examination for the U.S. Army Dental Corps in March 1918. After reporting late to spring training, he opened the regular season with only one hit in his first 25 at-bats and was eventually benched with an injured finger on May 6. His replacement at first base that day was none other than his old roommate Ruth, making his first major league appearance at a position other than pitcher. Hoblitzell received his commission as a first lieutenant on June 6 and left the Red Sox three days later, his teammates presenting him with a gold wristwatch as a going-away present. Stuffy McInnis moved over from third base to fill the vacancy at first, Harry Hooper took over the captaincy, and the Red Sox went on to win another World Series, awarding Hobby a partial share of $300 from the proceeds. Dick never played another game in the majors, retiring with a lifetime batting average of .278.

While stationed in El Paso, Texas, Dick contracted influenza and nearly died during the 1918 pandemic. When he recovered, he was assigned to join his old Reds teammate Hans Lobert as a baseball coach at the U.S. Military Academy, West Point, where Douglas MacArthur was serving as superintendent. After his discharge from the Army in 1920, Hoblitzell played for and managed the Charlotte Hornets of the Sally League for five seasons, leading the team to a pennant in 1923, and his daughter still uses a silver tea service he received from the Charlotte fans on "Hobby Day" in 1922. Around the time that Constance first became pregnant—the Hoblitzells eventually had two children that they named after themselves: Richard was born in 1925 and Constance was born in 1929—Dick gave up baseball to work full time in the real estate business with his partner, Lee Kinney, though he eventually returned to the Hornets dugout in 1929–30 for the highest salary ever paid to that point to a Sally League manager.

Living in one of their own apartment buildings on Lamar Street, the Hoblitzells loved Charlotte and intended to make it their permanent home, but at the height of the Great Depression they were forced to return—temporarily, they thought—to Constance's hometown of Williamstown, West Virginia, just across the Ohio River from Marietta, Ohio, where the couple had met, to save her family's 540-acre farm. The Hendersons were among that area's earliest settlers, tracing their roots to an ancestor

Hobby throws right-handed in a 1914 photograph, Comiskey Park. Courtesy of Chicago History Museum.

from Alexandria, Virginia, who served in the Virginia House of Burgesses and who bought the property on the recommendation of its original surveyor, George Washington. But Constance's father had died in 1926 and her mother couldn't manage the farm on her own. Dick and his family moved into the 13-room farmhouse, which was built in 1875 on a hill overlooking the B&O Railroad and the Ohio River, and they never did make it back to North Carolina. Dick's daughter, Connie, still lives on the farm in Williamstown to this day, though the property has been reduced to about 125 acres.

During the Depression many unemployed—the children called them "hoboes"—hitched rides on the railroad, looking for jobs, and Dick put them to work on the farm in exchange for a home-cooked meal and a place to sleep. There was an abundance of quail on the property, and Dick was an exceptional marksman. On one occasion he accumulated so many birds that he invited his fellow members of the Sons of the American Revolution to a quail dinner. The Hoblitzells expected eight to 10 guests, but every member in the valley showed up, filling the yard with cars, so Constance cut up what was intended to be a bird each into small pieces and somehow made do.

In addition to raising cattle and growing produce, Dick hosted a sports radio show on WPAR, wrote a column on sports and other topics for the *Parkersburg News*, and umpired youth baseball. He was active in Republican politics, serving as county treasurer and being elected sheriff. Dick also served as superintendent of the Sunday school at the Episcopal church. He never "officially" practiced dentistry, but he did set up a dental chair in his home and filled many a cavity for his neighbors, no charge, though without Novocaine. "It was not a pleasant experience having those big ol' baseball hands stuck in your mouth," recalls Connie. The former ballplayer kept himself in excellent shape, his weight never much exceeding his playing weight of 172 pounds, and he managed to avoid illness until he contracted the colon cancer that killed him on November 14, 1962.

HARRY HOOPER *by Paul J. Zingg and Elizabeth A. Reed*

G	AB	R	H	2B	3B	HR	RBI	BB	SO	BA	OBP	SLG	SB	HBP
126	474	81	137	26	13	1	44	75	25	.289	.391	.405	24	4

One of the best defensive right fielders in baseball history and one of the top leadoff hitters of the Deadball Era, Harry Hooper was also a team leader, superb practitioner of the inside game, and clutch hitter who played a key role in four Boston Red Sox world championships. As a product of rural California, but a college man who earned a degree in engineering, Hooper also symbolized baseball's transition, ongoing during the Deadball Era, from a game rooted in the eastern cities and played by professionals who were largely uneducated and illiterate, to a game that broadened its geographical horizons and expanded its social appeal through players like Hooper.

Although his play at times achieved the spectacular, Hooper eschewed flamboyance for simplicity, exaggeration for modesty. Possessing neither the crafted appeal of Christy Mathewson nor the raw excitement of Babe Ruth, Hooper practiced his profession quietly, skillfully, and confidently. More Everyman than Superman, he is a mirror of the game and its human touches in ways that his myth-encrusted contemporaries never can be. Though he never led the American League in any major statistical category, Hooper crafted a solid statistical resume that included 2,466 hits, 1,429 runs and 1,136 career walks, good for a lifetime .281 batting average and .368 on base percentage. In 92 career World Series at-bats, Hooper batted a solid .293; in the 1915 Fall Classic he batted .350 with two home runs.

Harry Bartholomew Hooper was born on August 24, 1887 in California's Santa Clara Valley, the fourth and youngest child of Joseph and Mary Katherine Keller Hooper. In 1876, Joseph had left Canada's Prince Edward Island, slowly working his way westward through a series of jobs before landing in California, where he met Mary Keller, a German immigrant working as a housekeeper, and married her in 1878. Growing up on the family ranch, Harry first honed his athletic skills by tossing fresh eggs against the side of the family's barn. This merited little reaction from his parents, and Harry spent more time throwing various objects, challenging himself in distance and accuracy.

His first formal exposure to nine-man-a-side baseball came during a trip East with his mother. While visiting her family in Central Pennsylvania, Harry watched with great interest the Lock Haven team play. He capped the

Harry Hooper. Detail from 1919 *Spalding's Official Base Ball Guide.*

trip with a visit to relatives living in New York City, and a chance to see his first Major League game. The Brooklyn Bridegrooms played the Louisville Colonels, and although the home team lost, Hooper's dedication and love of the game solidified. Just before he and his mother began the long journey back to California, he received from his uncle something he later called "the best of all" his boyhood treasures: a bat, ball, and well-worn fielder's glove.

Harry Hooper's formal baseball career began when he left the family's farm in August, 1902, for the high school attached to Saint Mary's College of California, then located in Oakland. Although Hooper originally arrived for a two-year secondary program, the Christian Brothers who ran the school quickly recognized his mathematical aptitude, and encouraged his parents to consider allowing him to complete the full baccalaureate program, which would stretch his time at the school from two years to five. Consistent with the emerging sense of education as a means to economic opportunity, Harry's parents agreed to the school's request. At roughly the same time, he earned a place on the secondary school's new baseball team.

Working his way up through the four teams at the school, Hooper earned a place as a starting pitcher on the junior varsity as a collegiate sophomore, but his stature — he stood slightly over five feet tall at the time — and pitching velocity limited his chance to earn a spot on the varsity squad. The top team's head coach suggested a switch to an outfield position, which Hooper accepted. It assured him the starting left-field spot on the College's varsity nine at the start of the 1907 season, a team regarded by many as one of collegiate baseball's finest in the pre-World War I era. With a roster that contained six future big leaguers, Hooper played alongside catcher Eddie Burns, third baseman Joe Hamilton, pitcher Harry Krause, plus outfielders Charlie Enwright and Mickey Thompson, on a team that completed a 27 game season with a perfect record. Among that year's victims were Stanford University, the University of California, a Pacific Coast League all-star team, and the Chicago White Sox who the Phoenix faced in an exhibition game prior to the start of the major league season.

Hitting for a .371 average during his senior season, Hooper drew the attention of several organized ball representatives, and signed his first contract — for 10 days — to play with the Alameda club of the California League, where he teamed with Duffy Lewis for the first time; the two had been schoolmates but not teammates at St. Mary's. Ironically, the short length of the contract was Hooper's idea. Focused primarily on his engineering career, he agreed to play only for the time between the end of the Phoenix's season and his graduation date. His strong play during the short stretch earned Hooper a contract with the Sacramento club, which he agreed to accept with the proviso that Sacramento's owner arrange a surveying position for him, which was done.

Late in the 1908 season, after hitting .347, scoring 39 runs, and stealing 34 bases in 68 games, Hooper earned the tag, "Ty Cobb of the State League," and an offer from his manager, Charlie Graham, who also served as a scout for the Boston Red Sox. Initially when approached about the possibility Hooper recalled saying he thought baseball "was a sideline to engineering to make enough money for a living." Graham persisted and Hooper agreed to meet with Red Sox owner John Taylor, who soon would be in the area to observe several prospects for his team. At their meeting at a Sacramento saloon, the two agreed to a contract that would pay the 21-year-old Hooper $2,800 for the 1909 season, approximately $1,000 more than he would have made combined through his California baseball play and his job with the Western Pacific Railroad.

Harry Hooper's career with the Boston Red Sox began on March 4, 1909 when he arrived in Hot Springs, Arkansas for the team's training camp. The Red Sox of 1909 represented a team in transition. Following the demise of the championship clubs of 1903 and 1904, owner Taylor aspired to build a pennant contender with young pitchers, power hitting, and speed on the bases. The rotation included Joe Wood, Eddie Cicotte, and Frank Arellanes. Other than Heinie Wagner (shortstop), no member of the squad had two complete seasons with the team.

Harry Hooper's major league debut came on April 16, in Washington, D.C., during the team's second series of the season. Called upon to start in left field and bat seventh, Hooper lined a single in his first at-bat that also notched his first RBI. That day he went 2-for-3 at the plate, with

Harry Hooper.

"a clever steal in the ninth," three flies caught including "a superb running back catch" that saved a triple, and one assist when he threw out Gabby Street at home. During the first month of the season, he played occasionally, always fielding well.

A natural right-handed hitter and fielder while at Saint Mary's, the 5'10" 168-pound Hooper experimented with switch hitting. Playing in an era when manufacturing runs one at a time mattered more than sheer power, Hooper decided to take advantage of his abilities and reduce one step from the batter's box to first base by making the move to full-time left-handed hitting. His hard work and dependable play, especially in the field, made personnel decisions easier for the club's management. By the season's midpoint, Hooper firmly held the fourth outfield position, and often entered games in the late innings because of his defensive skills. The squad finished the year in third place, 9½ games behind Detroit, but also 25 games over .500. Hooper recorded a .282 average in 81 games, while completing the transition from one side of the plate to the other.

The Red Sox that assembled in Hot Springs, Arkansas in March, 1910 had reason to be optimistic about the coming season. Most of the lineup returned, with Hooper virtually assured one outfield spot. With Tris Speaker secure in center, the only question was whether it would be right or left on a day-to-day basis. The arrival of another veteran of the Saint Mary's Phoenix in camp, George "Duffy" Lewis, largely settled the issue. The outfield trio of Tris Speaker, Harry Hooper in right, and Duffy Lewis in left made its debut on April 27. Through the course of that season — when they hit a combined .296 — and the next five, the "Million Dollar Outfield" played more than 90 percent of Boston's games. After batting .267 in 1910, Hooper improved to an impressive .311 average in 1911, scored 93 runs, and posted a .399 on-base percentage. The club, however, failed to finish better than fourth in either season.

Despite his .242 batting average, Hooper was an integral piece of the 1912 pennant-winners, ranking second on the team with 98 runs scored, 66 walks, 29 stolen bases, and 12 triples. In that year's World Series against the New York Giants, Hooper elevated his play, batting

.290 for the Series and making several crucial plays at bat and in the field. In Game One, Hooper rapped a game-tying double in the seventh inning to secure a 4–3 Boston victory. After taking a three-games-to-one lead in the Series, the Red Sox saw the Giants even things at three games each. There was one tie game.

Despite numerous baserunners for both teams, the Giants held a slim 1–0 lead in the seventh inning of the deciding Game Eight, which would have been greater if not for Hooper's catch of Larry Doyle's drive to the right-field fence, robbing him of a home run. The game was tied 1–1 after nine. In the 10th inning, after Clyde Engle reached second when Fred Snodgrass muffed a fly ball, Hooper followed with "a sure triple" that Snodgrass caught, but it advanced Engle to third. After a walk to Yerkes, Speaker singled in Engle with the tying run. Yerkes took third on the play, Speaker took second on the throw home, and Larry Gardner's sacrifice fly won the World Series for the Red Sox.

Hooper's "paralyzing catch" in the final game earned him accolades in the press, but John McGraw paid an even higher compliment when he labeled the Californian, "one of the most dangerous hitters in a pinch the game has ever known." In the next day's *Boston Globe*, Speaker called Hooper's catch "the greatest, I believe, that I ever saw."

Coming off the championship year, Hooper married Esther Henchy, a 20-year-old banker's daughter from nearby Capitola, California, but remained dedicated to his offseason training. Although the Red Sox struggled as a team in 1913 and 1914, Hooper personally improved his offensive output, hitting .288 in 1913 and scoring 100 runs, and batting .258 with 85 runs scored in 1914. On May 30, 1913, Hooper hit home runs to lead off both games of a double-header, a feat not equaled until Rickey

Walter Johnson and Harry Hooper.
Courtesy of John Hooper, Baytown, Texas.

War Sports 25 Years Ago
(In Boston Herald, May 2, 1918)
Walter Johnson pitches four-hit game as Washington blanks Red Sox, 5 to 0. Harry Hooper, always a nemesis of Johnson's, makes three of the four hits off the speed ball artist. Washington scores all its runs in the fourth inning off Carl Mays.

Henderson did it 80 years later.

In 1915 the Red Sox returned to championship form and began a stretch of success where the team played the best, and most consistent, baseball in the major leagues. Between 1915 and 1917, the team won at least 90 games each season, and likely would have done so again in 1918 if World War I had not shortened the season. The successes came through the team's effective use of the strategies of the era. Rather than power hitting and home runs, the Red Sox won by manufacturing runs, playing strong defense, and, most of all, getting solid pitching. In fact, during the four-year stretch, the team never featured more than one hitter with an average of .300 or higher. As Hooper wrote, "With the best pitching staff and the best defensive outfield . . . we played for one run — tried to get on the scoreboard first and then increase our lead."

In 1915, Hooper's average dipped to .235, but he compensated by collecting 89 walks, fifth best in the league, and posting a respectable .342 on-base percentage. Once again, he saved his best work for the World Series, when he helped Boston finish off Philadelphia in five games with a .350 batting average and two home runs, both of which came in the final game of the Series, making Hooper only the second player in World Series history to homer twice in the same game. (Both homers bounced into Baker Bowl's temporary stands; today they would be considered ground-rule doubles.)

After another championship in 1916, and a disappointing second-place finish nine games behind the Chicago White Sox the following year, Hooper's Red Sox entered the 1918 season in a tenuous position. Although Boston's roster suffered fewer losses to the military and war-related industries than other teams, the lineup managed a woeful team average of .249, the second-worst in

Hooper, 1912. Courtesy of Chicago History Museum.

the American League; Hooper posted a .289 average and a .405 slugging percentage (second on the team to Babe Ruth in both categories). He also helped the team to another pennant in a war-shortened season (126 games) that ended with a dramatic labor challenge during the World Series.

During the Fall Classic against the Chicago Cubs, Hooper demonstrated his clear thinking and effective leadership, representing his fellow players' concerns in a manner that preserved the integrity of baseball, while also exposing some of the inherent weaknesses of baseball's ruling system. Due to wartime travel restrictions, the teams played the Series in a 3–4 format, with the first games in Chicago (ironically at Comiskey Park). The rest of the games took place at Fenway. The Red Sox returned home enjoying a 2–1 lead, but all was not well. For several war-related reasons, attendance and gate receipts during the regular season and World Series in 1918 fell well below pre-war levels. However, at this time the players' postseason bonuses came from gate receipts and the owners would not guarantee a minimum payment. The two teams, traveling on the same train, appointed four representatives, including Hooper, to speak to the governing National Commission and press their case. Specifically, the teams sought a guarantee of $2,600 each for the winners and $1,400 for the losers, with 10% going as a donation to the Red Cross. The National Commission begrudgingly listened, and agreed to consider the matter, but made no promises.

With Boston leading three games to one, the players delayed the start of the fifth game by more than one hour in an attempt to secure concessions from the Commission.

Although Hooper negotiated an end to the strike, and secured a verbal promise from Ban Johnson of no reprisals, he forever regretted not securing the guarantee in writing. After Boston won the Series 4–2, its last for 86 years, the players received the smallest financial awards in World Series history ($1,108.45 for each Red Sox player and $574.62 for each Cub). In December the Boston players all received letters from John A. Heydler, acting president of the National League and a Commission member. It informed them that, "Owing to the disgraceful conduct of the players in the strike during the Series . . . (the players) would be fined the World Series emblems that were traditionally awarded to the winners." Although a modest symbol, the emblems — really lapel pins — became a symbol of the lack of respect accorded the players in the years before a strong players union and free agency.

After a .312 season in 1920, Harry Hooper's career with the Boston Red Sox ended on March 4, 1921, when Boston owner Harry Frazee thwarted a holdout by trading him to the Chicago White Sox for Shano Collins and Nemo Liebold. Hooper posted some of the best offensive seasons of his career during his five years with the White Sox. In 1921 he batted .327; the following year he notched career highs in runs scored (111), home runs (11) and RBIs (80). In 1924, he posted a career-best .328 batting average and .413 on-base percentage. In 1925, his last major league season, Hooper batted .265. Playing in his final major league game on October 4, 1925, Hooper went 1-for-4 with a double.

Upon his retirement, Hooper returned to California and worked in real estate for one year before accepting a job as player-manager with Mission (San Francisco) in the Pacific Coast League. Hooper lasted one year with the club, batting .282 in 81 games and guiding the Missions to a disappointing 86–110 record. Let go after the season, Hooper returned to the real estate business for a few years while also playing minor league baseball in nearby Marysville and Santa Cruz, then became coach of the Princeton baseball team in September, 1930. Hooper stayed at the post for two years, posting a 21–30–1 record before Depression-era finances forced the college to cut back on Hooper's salary, leading to his resignation. He once again returned to the real estate business in California, survived the Depression, and became wealthy in his old age. He also served as postmaster of Capitola for over 20 years. His greatest honor came in 1971, when the Veteran's Committee elected him to the Baseball Hall of Fame. Hooper was also one of the inaugural inductees when the St. Mary's College Athletic Hall of Fame was established in 1973; his son John, a center fielder during the 1940s, was inducted four years later. Harry Hooper died at the age of 87 on December 18, 1974, following a stroke. He was laid to rest in an above-ground crypt in the center of Aptos Cemetery, in Aptos, California. He was survived by two sons and a daughter.

SAD SAM JONES *by Alex Edelman*

G	ERA	W	L	SV	GS	GF	CG	SHO	IP	H	R	ER	BB	SO	HR	HBP	WP	BFP
24	2.25	16	5	0	21	2	16	5	184	151	66	46	70	44	1	8	6	750

G	AB	R	H	2B	3B	HR	RBI	BB	SO	BA	OBP	SLG	SB	HBP
24	57	6	10	1	0	0	1	13	14	.175	.329	.193	0	0

For a player so significant in Red Sox history, surprisingly little is known about Samuel Pond "Sad Sam" Jones. Despite his incredible contributions to the Red Sox World Series victory in 1918, the most often discussed thing about Jones is his curious nickname.

Born July 26, 1892, to Delbert and Margaret Clingan Jones, in Woodsfield, Ohio, about 20 miles west of the West Virginia Panhandle, Sam developed his arm on his grandfather's farm by throwing potatoes across a field to his brother Robert. He pitched well in high school, but quit ball after his junior year to take a full-time job at Schumacher's grocery store. Though he intimated to family that he preferred basketball, and would have played it professionally had there been a league at the time, he kept pitching in pickup games, and in 1913, he was asked to try out for Zanesville of the Inter-State League. That was where he first broke into professional baseball, winning two games and losing seven but also getting good experience — including pitching in a June exhibition game against the New York Giants. However, Jones was only 20 years old and very homesick, so when he was forced to take a pay cut[1], he refused, and when he saw his manager, Marty Hogan, on the street the following day, the young hurler demanded to be released immediately. In what Sam's son, Paul, would later call "probably the craziest release in baseball history," Hogan obliged, writing Jones' release in pencil on the inside of a chewing tobacco packet.

Sam was not home for long. Just three days after he returned to Woodsfield, he was offered a contract by Lee Fohl, the manager of the Columbus team in the same league as Zanesville. Ironically, Sam ended up taking a pay cut from his $175 a month Zanesville wage anyway, and when the league folded on July 15, Sam went home to work as a clerk in the grocery store. During the offseason, Jones played semipro basketball, a sport he claimed to be better at than baseball, but in the spring of 1914, he returned to baseball, spending some time at the Bill Doyle baseball school in Portsmouth, Ohio. Later that summer, Jones left the school to sign with the Portsmouth team in the Ohio State League, where he posted another losing record (5–6) but showed some potential when it mattered. One day, with Cleveland Indians scout Bill Reedy watching the game, Jones pitched well enough to earn a victory and hit a triple and home run to help his own cause. Reedy was impressed and signed Jones for the Indians later that year. He spent most of the year pitching

for Cleveland's American Association team (10–4 in 23 games, with a 2.44 ERA), earning a promotion to the big-league club for one game in the middle of the year.

Jones debuted with the Indians on June 13, 1914. After starter Casey Hageman gave up nine runs to Philadelphia, Jones threw the final three and one-third innings, allowing two hits and one run, while going 1-for-2 at the plate. Though that was his only appearance of 1914, in 1915 he became a regular — his first of 21 seasons pitching for six of the eight American

Sam Jones.
Detail from 1919
*Spalding's Official
Base Ball Guide.*

League clubs. In his only full year with the Indians, Jones was 4–9 (3.65 ERA) and walked more (63) than he struck out (42). Jones batted .156 for the Indians — his career batting average was .197 in 1,243 at-bats. In the book *The Glory of Their Times*, Jones told Lawrence Ritter that he "loved" playing with the Indians — probably because it was so close to where his sister lived.

On April 12, 1916, the Indians traded Jones to the Red Sox with Fred Thomas and $55,000 for future Hall of Famer Tris Speaker. The Joseph Lannin-owned Red Sox were dumping Speaker and his high salary, to the distress of Red Sox fans. Thomas was the man Lannin wanted; Jones himself seemed an afterthought at best, though later it was learned that manager Bill Carrigan had insisted the Sox secure Sam as part of the deal. The 1916 pitching staff was essentially the same one that had won the 1915 World Series; Vean Gregg who got most of the work the sore-armed Smoky Joe Wood had previously handled, while Jones threw only 27 innings, all in relief, losing his only decision. During the summer of 1916, on his 24th birthday, Sam married his childhood sweetheart, the former Edith Kerr; they would remain happily married for almost 50 years until Sam's death in 1966.

Jones was used even less in 1917, reprising his 0–1 record. The loss came in his only start of the year, in Cleveland on August 19. He was hammered for two runs in the first and two in the fourth; the *Boston Globe* said that when it was over, "he looked like a crazyquilt."

At the start of his tenure with the Red Sox, Jones hardly seemed a big part of the ballclub. The *Boston*

Sad Sam, 1918. Courtesy of Chicago History Museum.

Herald and Journal reported that Jones "wasn't even sent a contract [in 1918] by the Hub Hose. The team was at Hot Springs when owner Harry Frazee got a letter from Sam along these lines: 'Forgotten me altogether? I'm not worth a contract of any sort? If I am through, let me in on it.'" Red Sox executives told the *Globe* that they thought he was at Camp Sherman in the Army and had placed him on the voluntarily retired list in error. They wired Jones to come quickly, and told the newspaper they expected him to get a fair amount of work.

Fortunately for Jones, the Red Sox were right. The new manager for 1918, Ed Barrow, saw that Jones had a "most baffling delivery" and nurtured him into a pitcher who delivered 16 victories against only five losses (2.25 ERA). Though Barrow would later say that he was equally as proud of turning Babe Ruth into an outfielder as he was of turning Jones into a great pitcher, Jones and his manager had a contentious relationship at best. In his interview with Laurence Ritter for *The Glory of Their Times*, Jones admitted that he was a bit hard to handle as a ballplayer in his younger years, something that would become a semi-serious problem in his years with the Washington Senators. On May 23, 1918, Jones had his first start of the season (the second of his career) and pitched extremely well against Cleveland—though he was on the short end of a 1–0 decision.

Jones's next two starts were brilliant. He outpitched Walter Johnson—his childhood hero—on May 29, winning a 3–0, five-hit shutout, and followed that with a 1–0 shutout of Cleveland on June 6, again allowing just five

hits, but this time in 10 innings. (The June 6 game was interesting in that pitcher Babe Ruth played left field for Boston and pitcher Joe Wood played left field for Cleveland.) After allowing just one run in three starts, Sam Jones had cemented himself in as part of the starting rotation.

In the first 29 innings he threw against his former ballclub, Jones allowed Cleveland just one run. After he beat the Indians on August 20, the very player he had been traded for, Tris Speaker, told the *Boston Herald and Journal*:

> *"Sam Jones is the best pitcher Boston has. . . . Those two years Sam sat on the bench made him. He simply absorbed everything that went on in the games. He's smart and learns rapidly. That slow ball of his simply floats up there and you swing your head off, and then he has a fast one that is on top of you before you realize it. In addiction, he has as good a curve ball as anyone in the league. Yes, I believe he's the best pitcher on the team."*

A baffling delivery might be one thing, and it seemed to take him a while to harness his pitches (he walked more than he struck out in each of his first five full seasons in the majors), but Jones maintained that during a five-year stretch he only once threw over to first base to hold back a runner, believing that "there are only so many throws in an arm," something future Hall of Famer Eddie Plank had told him.

When Ernie Shore left for the Navy, Dutch Leonard took a shipyard job, and Babe Ruth cut back a bit on pitching, both Joe Bush and Sam Jones got the opportunity to pitch in 1918. Bush won 15, Jones won 16, and Carl Mays won 21. It was a terrific year, and Jones led the league in winning percentage as the Red Sox advanced to the World Series. Though Jones lost his start in Game Five, 3–0, the Sox won the Series—it would be their last world championship for 86 years.

The next year, 1919, wasn't as kind to Jones as 1918, and Sad Sam finished the season 12–20 with an inflated 3.75 ERA. The team itself had a losing record, and several headlines mentioned Jones' wildness and wobbling. Jones got more work than anyone else on the staff, but others pitched better. He did dominate Washington, throwing three shutouts in a row before losing in the last matchup.

In 1920, Jones's workload increased to 274 innings but he again had a losing record (13–16, with an ERA that grew to 3.94). He often pitched very well indeed, but was inconsistent and also often suffered from poor run support—though he perhaps single-handedly denied the pennant to the White Sox. Chicago finished two games behind the Indians, and Jones beat them six times. Only once in the first five of those wins did Jones give up as many as two runs. There were, though, the losses: On

June 12, he gave up six runs to the St. Louis Browns in the first inning, left the game, and lost. Trying again the very next day, he was left in to pitch the full game and lost again, 11–5.

It took until 1921 for Jones to turn it around again. Even though the team again had a losing record (as it did throughout the 1920s), Jones became a 20-game winner (23–16, 3.22 ERA), making himself an attractive target for the acquisitive New York Yankees.

Five days before Christmas 1921, Harry Frazee traded Jones, and Bullet Joe Bush (between them, the two pitchers had accounted for 39 of Boston's 75 wins in 1921) and threw in eight-year veteran Everett Scott, for four New York players: Roger Peckinpaugh, Rip Collins, Bill Piercy, and Jack Quinn. The three pitchers Frazee picked up each improved their win totals in 1922, and initially, the trade seemed like a very smart move.

Sam was 13–13 with the Yankees his first year, but went to the World Series again. Jones threw two late innings against the New York Giants without giving up a run, but the Giants swept the Series in four games (not counting a Game Two tie). It was back to the Series again in 1923, Sam's 21–8 and Herb Pennock's 19–6 pacing the Yankees during the season. In what he later called one of his proudest moments in baseball, Jones pitched a no-hitter on September 4, beating the Philadelphia Athletics, 2–0, without striking out a single batter. In the Series, he started and lost Game Three, but it was a 1–0 loss, a four-hitter spoiled only by Casey Stengel's home run for the Giants. Jones took his World Series record pretty seriously; he would later grumble to the press that he got "no run support," a fair assertion.

Jones entered 1924 with a sore right elbow that lasted two months and contributed to a disappointing 9–6 record. In 1925, he pitched a full year again but the Yankees collapsed all the way to seventh place. Jones was 15–21, and his ERA increased one full run from 3.63 to 4.63. The earned run average bumped up again to 4.98 in 1926, and his 9–8 record was mediocre on a team that featured 58 wins from Pennock, Urban Shocker, and Waite Hoyt, and took the World Series to Game Seven before losing to the Cardinals. Jones pitched just the ninth inning in Game Two, giving up the final run in a 6–2 loss.

Jones spent five years pitching in New York, but it didn't change him as a man. Jones was, according to those who knew him, a homebody. He hated leaving his Woodsfield hometown for spring training, and minutes after the season ended, he would hustle his belongings, his wife, Edith, and their sons, George and Paul, into their LaSalle automobile and drive straight to Woodsfield where he ran Sam's Corner Grocery store.

In early February 1927, Sam was swapped to the St. Louis Browns for Cedric Durst and Joe Giard. In his one season with St. Louis, Jones was 8–14 with a 4.32 ERA. Right after baseball wrapped up postseason play, St.

Sam's May 29 shutout of the Senators depicted in the following day's *Boston Post* cartoon.

Louis sent Sam and Milt Gaston to Washington for Dick Coffman and Earl McNeely.

Sad Sam pitched four years for Washington, rebounding nicely with a 17–7 campaign (2.84) in 1928, despite the Senators finishing 26 games out of first place. After a 9–9 year in 1928, his hopes for another strong season in 1929 were dashed when he sprained his back on May 22. He returned to Woodsfield for a month and next started in early July. He finished the season with a 9–9 mark and a 3.92 ERA. Owner Clark Griffith signed him again for 1930, but to a "bonus contract" based on incentives. Right as the season began, Jones ran afoul of manager Walter Johnson, something of an irony considering that "the Big Train" was Jones' childhood hero. Accused of "speaking out of turn" (*New York Times*) and displaying what Johnson termed "not the proper attitude" (*Washington Post*), Johnson sent Jones back to Washington while the Senators traveled from Boston to Philadelphia. The rift didn't last long, though, and Jones was back in a few days. Jones was what we could call a "difficult sign" during his years in D.C., but in this case it was perhaps Johnson who "possibly may have been a little harsh" in the words of *Post* correspondent Frank H Young. Perhaps the bonus clause worked; he won 15 and lost seven (with a 4.07 ERA).

In 1931, Jones was 9–10, and in December the Senators traded him and Irving "Bump" Hadley to the White Sox for Carl Reynolds and Johnny Kerr. The *Washington Post* said that Jones "undoubtedly is nearing the end of his career." He would turn 40 during the summer of 1932.

Sam Jones won 10 games for the White Sox in 1932 and again in 1933, but was under .500 each year. Chicago was competing with the Red Sox for last place in those years and in his four seasons with the White Sox, Jones's won-loss percentage was higher than his team's. In 1934, he celebrated his 42nd birthday with a five-hit, 9–0 shutout of Washington. In November 1935, after he had posted a winning 8–7 record, the White Sox gave Sam Jones his unconditional release at age 43. His 22-year career was finally over.

Sam had pitched in the odd local exhibition game during the offseasons. After retiring from baseball, he kept busy, teaching kids in Woodsfield how to play ball (and securing donations of major-league equipment from some of his old teammates.), according to his friend, Ronald Turner; one of those children, from nearby Stewartsville, Ohio, was another Sam Jones, nicknamed "Toothpick Sam," who would go on to play 12 years in the major leagues. Sad Sam spent four summers coaching the Woodsfield Junior Merchants. In 1939, a brief INS wire story reported on a "married men vs. single men" ballgame from the prior summer, in which a batter drove a liner back to the mound and broke Sam's finger. In December, he signed on as a coach-player with the International League Toronto Maple Leafs, where he worked under manager Tony Lazzeri, a former teammate with the Yankees.

Jones' last season as a professional came in 1940, after four years out of the game. He appeared in eight games for the Maple Leafs, for a total of 12 innings, with a winning 1–0 record and a somewhat meaningless 2.25 ERA. Soon after his 48th birthday he was released by the Maple Leafs. In his final appearance, he'd thrown one inning without giving up a hit or a run. Two years later, he briefly dipped back into baseball when he was hired by the manufacturers association in Springfield, Vermont, to coach a team in the city league. His son Paul played for the team, and lived in Springfield after Sam had moved back to Woodsfield.

In the years after baseball, Jones prospered in his hometown as president of the board of directors of the Woodsfield Savings and Loan Co., and was active in Presbyterian Church and Masonic circles. As far back as 1922, the president of the local board of trade said that one of the pleasing features of Jones's success was that "he always wears the same size hat." Sam suffered an illness that lingered and then took his life on July 20, 1966, just 20 days before his 50th wedding anniversary.

The Associated Press obituary explained the origin of his nickname, "Sad Sam, the Cemetery Man," as emanating from "a new sportswriter whose only acquaintance with the pitcher was watching him from the press box. The dour features of the pitcher at that distance completely hid the twinkle in his eye." The story deemed him a "whimsical and quietly humorous man, brimful of quips and backwoods humor."

Old friend Ronald Turner recalled Sam as a hunter and horseman who never flaunted his career as a baseball star. One player Turner recalled Sam mentioning with a sense of disapproval was Babe Ruth, whose flashy lifestyle didn't sit well with the modest "Squire of Woodsfield." But Jones was well liked by many of his old teammates and he counted Hall of Famers like Joe Cronin and Cy Young as his friends.

Jones loved his town above everything else — with the exception of his family. When Paul, who inherited Jones' love for baseball (and, apparently, ice skating), moved to Erie, Pennsylvania, Jones, who always hated traveling away from Woodsfield, would often drive the seven hours to visit his son and granddaughters. Sam's other son, George, emphasized the great pride that his father took in his small-town hometown. He loved coon hunting and rabbit hunting, George said. He was a brilliant pianist, who played by ear, something he passed on to son George, who would work in the music industry and play in bands for a time. George says Sam was loved unanimously by everyone in town, and his "coon feed" barbecues were hits. He relished and seized every possible opportunity to immerse himself in Woodsfield. During the time after his career he worked as a delivery man for a grocery store, sold furniture, drove a hearse, labored as a church custodian, was president of his county's World War II draft board and spent part of almost every day sitting in his brother Bob's clothing shop, surrounded by friends and baseball pictures.

Sam Jones, throughout a lengthy baseball career that took him from Cleveland to Washington, Boston to Chicago, and many places in between, was a small-town man at heart; he was a local institution in Woodsfield when he lived, just as much a part of the village as the County Library or the abandoned railroad. A marker detailing his career in baseball stands on Creamery Street in Woodsfield, ensuring that the village remembers the man who cherished it more than any other place until the day he died. While Jones admitted he may have been a bit tough to handle during his younger years, he clearly developed and matured from a brash rookie into a true gentleman, and the values of modesty, devotion, and stoicism that he grew to embody are summed up neatly in this poem he composed later in his life.

BASE BALL IS BUT A GAME OF LIFE

*First base of Egotism, Second base of
    overconfidence,*
*Third base of indifference, Home Plate of honest
    achievement.*
A good many men lose by reason of pop-flies;
*the short-stop of public opinion frequently nips
    short the*
*career of a man who fails to connect with the ball
    of life*
with a good sound wallop.

The winner is the man who knocks the horse-hide
of opportunity
loose with the bat of honest effort.
When you have batted for the last, made the
rounds of the bases
and successfully negotiated home-plate,
may we hope to hear the Umpire of LIFE, which
after all,

is the esteem of friends and acquaintances,
call to you that you're safe.

Note

1. The reason for the pay cut is outlined in an article by Jim B. Bullard in the *Martins Ferry* (Ohio) *Times Leader*. 1913 was a bad flood year, and Zanesville's ballpark was damaged by the flood — forcing the team to move its games to a fairground. Attendance suffered, and the players were asked to take a pay cut.

WALT KINNEY *by Allan Wood*

G	ERA	W	L	SV	GS	GF	CG	SHO	IP	H	R	ER	BB	SO	HR	HBP	WP	BFP
5	1.80	0	0	0	0	5	0	0	15	5	3	3	8	4	0	2	0	57

G	AB	R	H	2B	3B	HR	RBI	BB	SO	BA	OBP	SLG	SB	HBP
6	5	0	0	0	0	0	0	0	1	.000	.000	.000	0	0

July 1918 was perhaps the most momentous month in Walt Kinney's life. The Texas League — like all minor leagues during the summer of 1918 — had been facing dwindling attendance and a steady stream of young players leaving for the Great War in Europe, or accepting war-related employment. Finally, on July 7, the league canceled the remainder of its season. Kinney, a left-handed pitcher for the Dallas Giants, returned to his home in Denison, Texas.

On July 12, Kinney's wife, the former Jessie Elizabeth Ringo, gave birth to their first child, Walter Jr. A couple of days later, Kinney's contract was purchased by the Boston Red Sox and the 23-year-old pitcher headed north to Chicago to join his new teammates. On July 26, he made his major league debut at Comiskey Park.

Kinney appeared in only six games for the 1918 Red Sox, pitching a total of 15 innings (all in relief) and playing right field in the late innings of the last game of the season. He was not on the team's World Series roster, but he did serve as a batting practice pitcher. He later pitched parts of three seasons for the Philadelphia Athletics.

Walter William Kinney was born in Denison, Texas, on September 9, 1893, to John William Kinney and Cora Estelle Sabin. Kinney's maternal grandmother was the daughter of Ezra Chandler and Louisa Ann Kendall. One of Ezra's brother's descendants was Albert Benjamin "Happy" Chandler, commissioner of baseball from 1945 until 1950.

Kinney first pitched professionally at the age of 20 for the Denison Railroaders in the Texas-Oklahoma League in 1914. In 27 games, he pitched 187 innings, allowing 123 hits and 57 walks, while striking out 112 batters. It is not known how many of the 58 runs Kinney allowed were earned, but his runs against average was 2.79.

On February 20, 1915, Kinney, then 21, married Jessie Ringo, a 27-year-old native of Texas.

Kinney had two more good seasons with Denison (a 1.94 ERA in 210 innings in 1915 and a 2.48 ERA in 269 innings in 1916). In 1916, he first exhibited the control problems that would plague him for most of his professional career. In 269 innings, he walked 154 — an average of 5.2 per nine innings. He did win 22 games against 11 defeats, however, and that may have earned him the opportunity to finish that season out west, appearing in 16 games for Oakland in the Pacific Coast League. In 54 innings, Kinney allowed a whopping 62 hits and 38 walks. He had an 0–6 record to go along with a 4.17 ERA.

The following year, Kinney was in the Western Association, pitching for Muskogee. He led the league in several categories: innings pitched (an astonishing 370), walks (191), and strikeouts (260). He posted a 23–16 record, with 30 complete games. Again, the number of earned runs allowed is not known, but Kinney's RA was 3.72.

Kinney was pitching for Dallas in the Texas League in 1918 — 17 games, 11 complete games, a 2.97 ERA in 112

Walt Kinney. Courtesy of Marjorie Sherrill.

innings, with more walks (51) than strikeouts (40) — when the league suspended its season.

The United States entered the Great War in April 1917 and Kinney registered for the draft two months later. His paperwork states that he was blind in one eye. Kinney's niece, Marjorie Sherrill, is unsure if Kinney was actually blind in one eye or was trying to get out of military service. Sherrill says that Kinney did have eye trouble much later in his life. The Boston newspapers made no mention of any possible issue with Kinney's vision.

When Kinney hooked up with the Red Sox, his first days with the team were spent serving as a batting practice pitcher, along with right-hander Dick McCabe. He struck up a friendship with another lefty on the team, Babe Ruth. At 6-foot-2, Kinney and Ruth were the tallest men on the team, but that wasn't all they had in common. Both men shared a love of pranks, crude jokes, and generally adolescent behavior. They would often box, wrestle, and carry on like two hyperactive kids.

On July 26, at Comiskey Park, the White Sox battered Red Sox starter Sam Jones for five runs in the third inning and two more in the fourth. As Boston was coming up to bat in the top of the fifth inning, an announcement was made that the War Department had granted all major league players an extension: They now had until September 1 to comply with the government's "work-or-fight" order (a May 1918 decree that all draft-age men had to enlist or find war-related employment).

A bit later in the game, Boston manager Ed Barrow went to his bench. Kinney relieved Jones and pitched the final four innings. He allowed only one hit, while striking out one batter and hitting another. He went 0-for-2 at the plate. Cuban-born Eusebio Gonzalez also made his big-league debut, taking over at shortstop for Everett Scott.

On August 2, exactly one week after his debut, Kinney pitched three perfect innings in Cleveland against the Indians, the Red Sox' main rival in the pennant race. Only one ball was hit out of the infield.

As the Red Sox continued their western road trip, Kinney saw action in Detroit on August 7, giving up three hits and three runs in three innings. During his stint on the mound, Kinney and Ty Cobb got into a shouting match when the Tigers star accused Kinney of trying to bean him. After walking Cobb to load the bases, Kinney surrendered a triple to Bobby Veach. The Tigers won the game, 11–8.

Two weeks later, the Red Sox were back home, getting set for another big series with Cleveland. Kinney made his first appearance at Fenway Park on August 20, coming out of the bullpen after Babe Ruth had been shelled.

Walt Kinney with the 1918 Sox. Detail from 1919 Spalding's Official Base Ball Guide.

Kinney pitched two innings, allowing one hit and one walk, while striking out two. The Red Sox lost the game, 8–4.

(Two days earlier, a bunch of Red Sox bench warmers and a few regulars played a Sunday exhibition game in New Haven, Connecticut. Kinney and Bill Pertica pitched for Boston, which lost to the locals, 4–3.)

During the last weekend of the regular season, Kinney appeared in two games. On August 31, he hurled three innings against Philadelphia in the second game of a double-header. He allowed only one hit, but walked three. Boston lost the game, 1–0, as A's pitcher John Watson pitched two complete games. Carl Mays had done the same thing for the Red Sox in a twin bill the previous day.

In New York, on September 2, in the late innings of the season's final game, Barrow made numerous substitutions. Kinney ended up playing right field.

In his 15 innings, Kinney allowed six hits, walked eight and struck out six. His ERA was 1.80 and opposing hitters batted only .106 against him. Although he did not receive a decision in any of his five games, the Red Sox lost all five. As a batter, he was 0-for-5.

Kinney and the rest of the Red Sox left New York by train and headed straight to Chicago for the World Series. Because the Cubs would be relying heavily on their two left-handed pitchers, Jim Vaughn and Lefty Tyler, Barrow wanted Kinney to pitch batting practice, to get the Boston hitters more accustomed to southpaw deliveries.

Kinney's star turn on the 1918 Red Sox was not on the playing field. Rather, it occurred on the train ride back to Boston after the first three games of the World Series. Boston had defeated the Cubs in the first and third games and Babe Ruth — who had thrown a complete game, 1–0 shutout in the opener — was set to take the Fenway mound for Game Four.

The team's train hadn't even pulled out of Chicago on Saturday evening, September 7, a few hours after Game Three, when Ruth, Kinney and a few other players began racing through the cars, grabbing every straw hat they could find and ramming their fists through them. Game Four was set for Monday the 9th — Kinney's 25th birthday — and he and the Babe apparently started celebrating a little early.

As the train traveled through western Massachusetts, Ruth somehow injured his pitching hand. The first accounts of what happened were not exactly consistent.

Boston Herald and Journal:

Babe Ruth . . . narrowly escaped serious injury on the baseball special outside of Springfield last night. He was standing in the aisle of the Sox car, talking to Carl Mays, when the train lurched, sending the Colossus aspinning and crashing against a window. The heavy glass was shattered and fell clattering, inside and outside. Babe did not know how seriously he had been injured, but he had the presence of mind not to put out his hands, and was fortunate enough to escape with only a small cut in his trousers.

Boston Traveler:

A slight accident made its appearance in the Sox camp on the way home from the middle West. Saturday night Babe Ruth was walking out of the smoker when the train gave a lurch and he was thrown against the side of the car. He put out his left to save himself from a fall and bent the third finger of his left hand so far that the middle joint was slightly strained. It swelled a little, but [team trainer] Doc Lawler was on the job with iodine and it isn't in any serious condition this morning.

One of the Boston papers — the *American* — and the *Chicago Herald and Examiner* came a little closer to the truth.

American:

Battering Babe Ruth did bump one of his pitching fingers "fooling" on the train, but the digit was not affected badly enough to harm his hurling ability.

Herald and Examiner:

[L]ast night Ruth put his pitching hand on the bum. Babe made a playful swing at a brother athlete in the smoking room of the Pullman. The brother athlete dodged and Babe bent the third finger on his left hand.

When Barrow learned what had happened, he was livid, but Ruth assured him that he could still pitch the fourth game. Babe did well in the game, though he needed some relief help from Joe Bush in the eighth inning. Boston won the game 2–1; the two Red Sox runs scored on Ruth's fourth-inning triple.

Afterwards, the Big Fellow confessed he had been in pain for the entire game. "I still don't know how I did as well as I did," Ruth said. "I was lucky to get that far." Once the victory was secure, giving the Red Sox a 3–1 lead in the series, Edward Martin could inform the *Globe*'s readers that Ruth's hand "was bruised during some sugarhouse fun with W.W. Kinney."

The Red Sox beat the Cubs in six games to win an unprecedented fifth World Series championship. It was the third title in four years for the Red Sox, and the fourth in seven years. Kinney was awarded a winner's share of $300.

On Sunday, October 13, 1918, just over one month

Kinney, 1918. Courtesy of Chicago History Museum.

after the World Series, Kinney pitched an exhibition game for the Tulsa Federals in Cleveland, Ohio. Washington Senators ace Walter Johnson pitched for the Cleveland team and Jim Thorpe (an outfielder with the New York Giants in 1918) was scheduled to appear. The White Way Café offered to give "$10 in cash to the first player to knock a home run" in the game. An ad for the game states:

In the game at Oilton last Sunday Johnson
Beat Kinney 1 to 0 in a ten-inning game,
Kinney desires another opportunity to defeat
The peerless pitcher Johnson.

Major league baseball was considering canceling the entire 1919 season, but the Great War ended on November 11. Released after the season, Kinney signed with the Philadelphia Athletics.

In 1919, Kinney split his time between the starting rotation and the bullpen, appearing in a team-high 43 games (two fewer than the league leader). He led the AL with 21 games finished; a former 1918 Red Sox teammate, Jean Dubuc, led the NL with 22.

In $202\frac{2}{3}$ innings, Kinney posted a 3.64 ERA (the league average was 3.32); his nine victories were exactly one-quarter of the team's season total. Kinney had the fourth-best rate of strikeouts per nine innings in the American League, although his lack of control was still an issue (91 walks and 97 strikeouts).

In 1920, Kinney made eight starts and two relief appearances for the Athletics before jumping the team in late May. An independent team in Franklin, Pennsylvania, had offered him $500 more than his annual salary with the Athletics.

Philadelphia manager Connie Mack tried to persuade

Kinney to return to the club and the pitcher apparently told Mack he'd meet the team in Detroit. When he didn't show up, Kinney was charged with violating his contract. According to news reports, Athletics management also had loaned Kinney $1,000 at the start of the 1920 season, in addition to giving him a 60 percent increase in salary from the previous year. When Kinney left the A's, he still owed the club about $800.

It's unclear how long Kinney stayed with the Franklin club, but his second child — a daughter named Mary Jean — was born in Wisconsin in September 1920. This means that after leaving the Athletics, Kinney and his family must have moved away from Texas.

The following spring, Kinney showed up at the Athletics' spring training camp in Lake Charles, Louisiana, and asked Mack if he could rejoin the team. Mack referred him to Commissioner Kenesaw Mountain Landis, who denied Kinney's application for reinstatement on March 29, 1921, and banished him from the major leagues for five years.

Kinney was out of organized baseball for only two years. He returned to the Athletics for five games in 1923. On May 9, Kinney came out of the bullpen with the Athletics trailing the St. Louis Browns, 3–0. He helped Philadelphia tie the game in the sixth inning by hitting a home run off Urban Shocker, but then he allowed four runs in the bottom half of the inning. The Browns went on to win the game, 10–5.

Nine days later, on May 18, Kinney demanded a trade. Connie Mack refused. Kinney said he would jump the team — and he was not in uniform for the A's game that day against Cleveland. It turned out to be the end of Kinney's major league career. His home run off Shocker was in his final major league at-bat.

Kinney did not play professional baseball for three years (1924–26), though he did pitch for a semipro team in Massillon, Ohio. During that time, he also did an ad for the Lonas-Nash Garage:

"While not Playing Base Ball with the Agathons he is driving his Nash. Is he satisfied with his Nash? We'll say he is!

He traveled over 15000 miles with his NASH during December and January 1923–24 through Missouri, Oklahoma, and Texas. He changed one tire during that time, the motor is in A-1 condition without repairs or tearing down. He drove for six days through the Ozark mountain region through roads so bad that for six days he could average only nine miles per hour. He broke the road ahead of 14 other cars, making the road for all of them.

Walter Kinney's Statement: I have driven eight different makes of cars since 1911, and will say that the NASH has given me greater pleasure and service than any other car. This leads me to believe

Kinney with the San Francisco Missions, 1930. Courtesy of Michael Mumby.

that the NASH really DOES lead the world in Motor Car Value. Signed WW Kinney"

In 1926, Kinney, his wife, and their two children were in Orange County, California. The city directory lists his job as "ballplayer." The following year, they had moved to a different address and Kinney was listed as a "pumper."

Kinney resumed his baseball career in 1927, when, at age 30, he signed with the Portland Beavers of the Pacific Coast League. He had a rough year, pitching in 172 innings over 35 games, allowing 189 hits, walking 72, and striking out only 36. His ERA was 4.50.

In 1928, Kinney was again working as a laborer, although he also pitched in 38 games for the Hollywood Stars (PCL) and compiled a record of 17–8. City records again list him as a ball player in 1929 and 1930. The US Census of 1930 lists Kinney and his family as renting a house at 1040 West 4th Street in Santa Ana, California. His occupation is professional ballplayer.

Kinney pitched 13 games for Dallas (Texas League, 1930), two for Mission (PCL, 1931), and eight for Tucson (Arizona-Texas League, 1931) before finishing his baseball career in Hollywood (PCL, 1932) with just 11 innings in two games.

Kinney and his wife remained in California, though it's not clear what Kinney did after his baseball career was over. According to Marjorie Sherrill, Kinney's niece, at one point Kinney tried his hand at prospecting. When the Kinneys lived in Redondo Beach, California, Sherrill says, "their major entertainment was to go to the thrift store down the street on Tuesdays when a new shipment would be delivered. They were excited by some of their little finds."

In a family history, Kinney's grandson notes, somewhat cryptically, that Kinney "did not know how to handle so much fame and money, etc. and he ran into some difficulties." Sherrill recalls Kinney telling her "how he was taken advantage of by flim flam men and lost money in the stock market due to his lack of education." Neither Kinney nor his two siblings finished high school.

In his later years, Kinney had diabetes and a drinking problem. After his wife died in January 1970, he took a turn for the worse. His eldest son, Jack, put him in an assisted living home in Escondido, California, where he died on July 1, 1971.

"DUTCH" LEONARD *by David Jones*

G	ERA	W	L	SV	GS	GF	CG	SHO	IP	H	R	ER	BB	SO	HR	HBP	WP	BFP
16	2.72	8	6	0	16	0	16	3	125²/₃	119	51	38	53	47	0	2	7	542

G	AB	R	H	2B	3B	HR	RBI	BB	SO	BA	OBP	SLG	SB	HBP
16	43	2	8	0	0	0	3	6	6	.186	.286	.186	0	0

Dutch Leonard.

A hard-throwing, spectacularly talented left-hander who in 1914 posted the best single-season earned run average in American League history, Dutch Leonard was also one of the Deadball Era's most controversial figures. At nearly every stop along his journey in professional baseball, Leonard feuded with management over salary, and at one point was even suspended from organized baseball for nearly three years for refusing to report for work. Regarded as a selfish, cowardly player by many of his contemporaries, Leonard frittered away much of his major league career, alternating periods of brilliance with long bouts of inertia. "As a pitcher, he was gutless," Hall of Fame umpire Billy Evans once declared. "We umpires had no respect for Leonard, for he whined on every pitch called against him." After exiting the game in 1925, Leonard touched off one of the biggest scandals in baseball history when he accused Ty Cobb and Tris Speaker of conspiring to throw a baseball game in 1919. Commissioner Kenesaw Mountain Landis dismissed the charges, and Leonard retired to his California ranch, where he earned millions of dollars growing grapes.

Hubert Benjamin Leonard was born on April 16, 1892, in Birmingham, Ohio, the youngest of six surviving children of David and Ella Hershey Leonard. For a time David worked as a real estate agent in Toledo, before moving the family to California in the early 1900s and finding work as a carpenter. While Hubert's older siblings became accomplished musicians (a brother, Cuyler,

eventually made a name for himself as a composer and trumpet soloist), Hubert gravitated toward the pitching mound. In 1911, "Dutch" (a moniker hung on him during his childhood because he "looked like a Dutchman") pitched for the highly regarded St. Mary's College team while attending classes there.

He was spotted by a scout for the Philadelphia Athletics, who signed him during the 1911 campaign. With the Athletics rotation already loaded with the likes of Jack Coombs, Eddie Plank, Chief Bender, and Cy Morgan, Leonard never appeared in any games. The following year, Leonard joined the Boston Red Sox for spring training, but developed a lame arm and failed to make the team. Sent to Worcester of the New England League, Leonard was bombed in one of his first outings and shortly thereafter abandoned the club. He showed up at Boston team headquarters and complained to club president Jimmy McAleer that "I didn't get any support. It's a rotten league. I won't play there any more." Still sensing promise in the young left-hander's arm, Boston sent Leonard to Denver of the Western League, where he overcame a midseason suspension for insubordination to win 22 games and strike out 326 batters in 241 innings of work. The following spring Leonard made the Red Sox squad out of spring training and joined the rotation.

Darkly-complexioned and built "more like a football player than a baseball player" according to writer F.C. Lane, the stocky 5'10½" Leonard relied on the classic combination of an overpowering fastball and sharp-breaking curve. Later in his career he mixed in the spitball, and in 1920 became one of the "grandfathered" pitchers allowed to continue throwing the pitch after it was made illegal. In his rookie season with the 1913 Red Sox, Leonard posted a 14–16 record and 2.39 ERA in 259⅓ innings of work. His biggest problem was his control: for the season he struck out 144 batters but also walked 94. All in all, it was a solid performance by the 21-year-old southpaw, but it gave little indication of the dominance he would achieve the following year.

Leonard's historic 1914 campaign was cut short by a wrist injury in early September, but in the 36 games in which he pitched, including 11 in relief, the left-hander posted an astounding 0.96 ERA, the lowest mark in the 20th century and the second best all-time, behind Tim Keefe's 0.86 recorded for the 1880 Troy Haymakers of the National League. (Keefe's record was established in just 105 innings, good enough to qualify for the record only because his team played just 83 games that season.) Leonard pitched $224^2/_3$ innings in his record-setting summer, striking out 176 (giving him a league-best strikeout rate of 7.05 per nine innings) and lowering his walk total to 60 while hitting eight batters. For the season, he allowed just 24 earned runs (10 unearned) and won 19 games against five defeats.

He didn't win his first game of the season until his fourth start, a 9–1 victory on May 4 against Philadelphia. After dropping a game to Washington on May 30 to run his record to 4–3, Leonard did not lose another game until August 13, running off a 12-game winning streak during which he struck out 91 batters in 116 innings. Despite his microscopic ERA, Leonard did not enjoy any long scoreless inning streaks or periods of noteworthy invincibility. Rather, he remained thoroughly consistent throughout the season, shutting out his opponents in seven of his starts and allowing just one run in 10 other outings. He surrendered more than two runs in a game just four times all season, and never allowed more than four runs in any start.

Because Leonard's season was curtailed by injury, the pitcher failed to reach many of the milestones that were most noted at the time. He failed to win 20 games, and except for ERA (which had only been an official American League statistic since the previous season) did not lead the league in any major pitching category. For this reason, Leonard's 1914 performance went largely unheralded in the press. Even Leonard regarded his work that year as incomplete. As he later told F.C. Lane, "If I hadn't broken my wrist I think I would have done very well that year."

Nonetheless, Leonard's 1914 season did raise expectations for the 1915 campaign, which would prove to be a resounding success for the Boston franchise but a

Dutch Leonard with Boston. Courtesy of the SABR-Ottoson Photo Archive.

turbulent year for its ace southpaw. After receiving a raise in salary to $5,000 per year, Leonard reported to the team out of shape, and started only three games in the first six weeks of the season. In late May, Leonard was suspended by the club for insubordination. According to newspaper reports, Leonard accused club owner Joseph Lannin of undermining manager Bill Carrigan's authority and generally mistreating his players. Leonard did not return to the starting rotation until early July, though he finished the season strong, posting a 15–7 record and 2.36 ERA. For the second consecutive year, Leonard led the American League in strikeouts per nine innings pitched, with 116 strikeouts in $183^1/_3$ innings. He rounded out his season in impressive fashion, beating Philadelphia's Pete Alexander in Game Three of the World Series, 2–1.

Leonard proved more durable over the next two seasons for the Red Sox, throwing a combined $568^2/_3$ innings in 1916 and 1917, and winning 34 games against 29 defeats. Although his strikeout rate continued to fall and he was no longer considered one of the game's overpowering pitchers, Leonard did pitch his first no-hitter in 1916, a 4–0 shutout over the St. Louis Browns on August 30. That autumn, Leonard also won his second and final World Series start, pitching Boston to a 6–2 victory over Brooklyn in Game Four. In 1918, Leonard pitched a second no-hitter, a 5–0 shutout victory, this time over the Detroit Tigers on June 3. His season came to an end a few weeks later when he circumvented the World War I military draft by joining the Fore River (MA) Shipyard team, for whom he won three games.

Prior to the 1919 season Leonard was included in the trade which also sent Ernie Shore and Duffy Lewis to the New York Yankees. Unlike Shore and Lewis, however, Leonard never appeared in a Yankee uniform and became a salary holdout. According to one report, Leonard demanded that his entire 1919 salary be deposited into a savings account, a request which infuriated New York owner Jacob Ruppert. "No man who doesn't trust my word can pitch for my team," Ruppert declared. In late May, the rights to the still-unsigned Leonard were sold to the Detroit Tigers for $10,000.

Now relying more on the spitball, Leonard spent the next three seasons with the Tigers, posting a modest

35–43 record. Prior to the 1922 season, Leonard again became tangled in a salary dispute, this time with Detroit owner Frank Navin, who refused to meet the pitcher's demands. Leonard in turn violated the reserve clause in his contract by jumping to Fresno of the independent San Joaquin League, an act which led to his suspension from organized baseball. After two years with Fresno, in which he compiled a 23–11 record, Leonard won his reinstatement and returned to the Tigers late in the 1924 season. Appearing in nine games for Detroit, Leonard went 3–2 with a 4.56 ERA.

In 1925 Leonard started 18 games for the Tigers, posting a solid 11–4 record despite a pedestrian 4.51 ERA. However, the pitcher feuded constantly with manager Ty Cobb, who had long disliked Leonard and would later claim that the southpaw was one of only two players he ever intentionally spiked during his career. As Cobb later explained, "Leonard played dirty — he deserved getting hurt." According to Cobb biographer Charles Alexander, Cobb punished Leonard by deliberately overusing him, even after the team physician warned that the work could do permanent damage to the pitcher's arm. When Leonard protested that his arm hurt, Cobb castigated him in front of the entire team, exclaiming, "Don't you dare turn Bolshevik on me. I'm the boss here."

Matters finally came to a head on July 14, when Leonard suffered the most brutal loss of his career, surrendering 12 runs and 20 hits to the Philadelphia Athletics. Despite the pounding, Cobb kept Leonard in the game for the full nine innings. Even Connie Mack, the opposing manager, pleaded Cobb to take Leonard out of the game, reportedly saying, "You're killing that boy." Cobb laughed at the suggestion. Later that month, he placed Leonard on waivers and pulled strings to make sure that no other team claimed him. Leonard was particularly hurt that Tris Speaker, manager of the Cleveland Indians and a former teammate, passed on him. Once Leonard had cleared waivers, Cobb traded him to Vernon of the Pacific Coast League, but Leonard characteristically refused to report. With that, his professional baseball career came to an end.

Dutch Leonard, glove in pocket.

Throughout his career Leonard had invested his money wisely, and by the time of his retirement operated a lucrative grape ranch just east of Fresno. But embittered by the manner in which he had been treated, Leonard quickly focused on exacting his revenge. Early in the 1926 season, Leonard told American League president Ban Johnson that on September 24, 1919, he had conspired with Cobb, Speaker and Indians outfielder Joe Wood to place bets on the following day's game against the Cleveland Indians, which Speaker had promised to lose in order to help the Tigers finish in third place. (It was Cleveland's first game after being eliminated from the pennant race.) The Tigers did win the game, 9–5, and Leonard, who did not play in the game, bet $1,500 on the outcome, receiving a modest $130 for his winning bet. To back up his story, Leonard produced two letters, one from Cobb and one from Wood, written shortly after the 1919 season, in which both made reference to the bets, though neither letter specifically stated what the bets had been for or whether the Indians had deliberately lost the game, as Leonard claimed.

Nonetheless, when presented with the letters, Johnson informed both Cobb and Speaker that their days in the American League were over, and after the 1926 season convinced both to resign their respective managerial positions and retire from the game. However, commissioner Kenesaw Mountain Landis, a long-time foe of Johnson's, saw the matter differently and decided to launch his own investigation. He asked Leonard to come to his office in Chicago to answer questions, but the ex-pitcher declined the invitation. Cobb, Speaker, and Wood, in turn, declared their innocence of the game-fixing charges and demanded an opportunity to face their accuser. With Leonard stubbornly refusing to leave his California ranch, the public sided with the accused stars. "Only a miserable thirst for vengeance actuated Leonard's attack on Cobb and Speaker," Billy Evans declared. "It is a crime that men of the stature of Ty and Tris should be blackened by a man of this caliber with charges that every baseballer knows to be utterly false."

Faced with a lack of evidence corroborating the game-fixing charge (indeed, Cobb, who supposedly had played the game to win, went only 1-for-5 at the plate with two steals that day, while Speaker, who was supposedly throwing the game, went 3-for-5 with two triples), as well as Leonard's unwillingness to come to Chicago, Landis publicly cleared Cobb and Speaker of any wrongdoing prior to the 1927 season, and Cobb signed with the Philadelphia Athletics, where he concluded his Hall of Fame career, while Speaker was sold to the Washington Senators.

Leonard, meanwhile, spent the rest of his days turning his grape ranch into a multimillion dollar enterprise. For a time he lived with his wife, Sybil Hitt, a vaudeville dancer known professionally as Muriel Worth. The marriage, which produced no children, ended in divorce in 1931. With the money from his grape-growing business, Leonard enjoyed a comfortable retirement in his lavishly-furnished home, which sat on a 2,500-acre plot of land.

Among his most prized collections was a record collection totaling 150,000 discs.

Leonard remained in good health until 1942, when he suffered a heart attack. To the end of his life he remained reluctant to discuss the details of his controversial career. As a nephew later told sportswriter Joseph E. Simenic, "Many times we pleaded with him to sit down and put it on a recording—the highlights of his career—but he never felt in the mood and when he was not in the mood he was not about to do anything regardless of what it might be."

Dutch Leonard died in Fresno of a cerebral hemorrhage on July 11, 1952. To his heirs (a sister, four nephews, and a niece) he left an estate totaling more than $2.1 million. He was buried in Mountain View Cemetery, in Fresno.

WALLY MAYER *by Doug Skipper*

G	AB	R	H	2B	3B	HR	RBI	BB	SO	BA	OBP	SLG	SB	HBP
26	49	7	11	4	0	0	5	7	7	.224	.321	.306	0	0

A journeyman who spent parts of seven seasons in the American League, Wally Mayer joined the Red Sox in 1917 and spent two campaigns as a reserve catcher. Although he did not appear in the 1918 World Series, "Kid" Mayer did help Boston get there by smacking a pair of 12th-inning game-winning hits against AL runner-up Cleveland.

A light hitting, fine fielding backup backstop, the 5-foot-11, 168-pound right-hander batted .193 in 132 games for the White Sox, Red Sox and Browns, with 14 doubles, three triples and no home runs, drew 42 walks, drove in 20 runs, and scored 22. Although he saw scant action in the major leagues, Mayer was a durable and capable catcher, and a solid hitter with an ability to draw walks in the minor leagues. As a minor leaguer, he appeared in more than 1,300 games between 1911 and 1928, collected more than 1,000 hits, drew more than 600 walks, and scored nearly 600 runs.

Walter A. "Wally" Mayer was born July 8, 1890 (although one source lists his birth date as August 3, 1889), in Cincinnati. The Queen City boasted 296,908 residents that year, a rich heritage of German immigration, and a powerful baseball tradition. Mayer's parents, Julius, a lithographer, and Mathilda, had moved to Cincinnati from Wartenburg, Germany, separately in the early 1880s, married shortly after their arrival, and became U.S. citizens in 1888. They had three children, sons Julius Jr. and Walter, who both apprenticed in the printing business as teenagers, and Vera, who became a piano teacher and later

a railroad stenographer. While Julius Jr. followed his father into the printing profession that the elder Mayer had learned in Germany, young Walter was more engaged in Cincinnati's American tradition, baseball.

In 1911, Mayer burst into professional baseball 90 miles south of Cincinnati with Paris, Kentucky, of the Blue Grass League. Just 20 years old at the start of the season, Mayer led the league with a .352 batting average in 114 games, and fielded at a .969 clip. At the end of the season, he was released to Minneapolis of the American Association, which turned around and sold the young catcher to the Chicago White Sox, managed by future Hall of Famer Hugh Duffy.

Mayer made his major league debut at the age of 21 on Thursday, September 28, 1911, at Boston's Huntington Avenue Grounds. He went 0-for-3 in his only appearance of the season, but drew two walks in Chicago's 6–3 loss to the Red Sox. He made seven putouts, recorded two assists, and committed an error. Under the headline "Mayer Plays Good Game," the next day's *Chicago Tribune* reported, "Walter Mayer, a young catcher secured by the Duffites from the Paris club of the Blue Grass league, made his first appearance in big league clothes. His clothes, at that, were slightly out of fashion, being of a vintage used by the White Sox years and years ago. Despite the deep purple of his uniform, the Kentuckian played a nice game behind the plate. He pegged swiftly to second twice in time to nail would be stealers and gobbled up a couple of hard fouls." Kentucky, of course, is across the Ohio River from

Cincinnati, and Mayer was an Ohioan, not a Kentuckian.

Young Mayer made the White Sox roster again for new player-manager Nixey Callahan in 1912, but rode the pine for nearly the entire year, behind veterans Walt Kuhn and Billy Sullivan. Callahan did use Mayer in nine games, but the youngster collected nothing more than a walk in 10 plate appearances, and scored a run. He donned a catcher's mask in six games, handling 13 putouts and an assist, with a pair of passed balls. Any thought Mayer may have had about being the White Sox catcher of the future was dispelled during the final two months of the season, when Ray Schalk arrived on the scene as a 19-year-old and played the first 23 games of a Hall of Fame career.

With Schalk entrenched at catcher and Kuhn as his backup, Mayer wasn't needed by the White Sox in 1913,

Wally Mayer with the White Sox.
Courtesy of Chicago History Museum.

though he did appear on "the First Published List of the Members of the Baseball Players' Fraternity, Embracing 296 Names." The player union's member list was published in *Baseball Magazine* and also included Grover Cleveland Alexander, Ty Cobb, Eddie Collins, Christy Mathewson, Tris Speaker, and Hans (Honus) Wagner. "A large number of the members of the Fraternity are now wearing a pin as an insignia of the organization," the article said. "It is of gold with enamel face representing two bats crossed and at their juncture, a ball of unique workmanship. The whole makes a very neat and attractive piece of jewelry."

Neither the jewelry nor the Fraternity could keep Mayer in the majors, and he was optioned to Birmingham in the Southern League before the 1913 season started. There he batted .270 and fielded a nifty .984 in 112 games, and was recalled in August, along with pitcher Bill Prough, a 20-game winner for the Barons.

"The star Birmingham battery, Prough and Mayer, has been secured by the Chicago American League Club," the *Atlanta Constitution* reported on August 14. "Exercising an optional agreement, Walter Mayer, the young Barons catcher, was regained for $1,500. When Chicago placed Mayer with the Barons club, a blanket option was exacted for the choice of (another) player for $3,500. Prough's wonderful pitching attracted the attention of the

White Sox, and he was chosen. Mayer has starred with Birmingham since his entrance into the Southern, batting .271 and fielding at a merry clip. He seems to be about the best in the league. It is not known whether the players will report at the close of the season or next spring."

Neither player made an appearance for Chicago in 1913, though Mayer saw action of a different kind during the off season in his hometown. "Walter Mayer was a hero at a Salvation Army home fire in Cincinnati," Ring Lardner wrote in the December 17, 1913, *Chicago Daily Tribune*.

Mayer returned to Chicago in 1914, where he jumped ahead of Kuhn to serve as Schalk's understudy. And though he batted just .165, he did collect his first major league hit, when he went 2-for-5 on May 9, two years and 221 days after breaking into the American League. The 23-year-old Mayer achieved what would be major league career highs with 40 games played, 85 at-bats, and 14 walks. He also established career bests with 14 hits, seven runs scored, three doubles, a triple, and five runs batted in, marks that he would later match, but never eclipse, and he stole a base for the only time in his major league career. Mayer appeared behind the plate 33 times, recorded 137 putouts and 47 assists, committed six errors for a .968 fielding percentage, and took part in three double plays. Mayer also made his only major league defensive appearance in fair territory, turning in a putout and an error in one game at third base.

New White Sox manager Pants Rowland relied heavily on Schalk (who played in 134 of 154 games) in 1915, and Mayer split time with newcomer Tom Daly as the backup as Chicago moved up to third place behind World Champion Boston and Detroit. In July, after playing in two straight games, Mayer was featured in a photo in the *Chicago Daily Tribune*. The caption read, "Because of the difficulty of keeping the mask and shin guards off Ray Schalk, the other catchers on the White Sox staff have had little chance in the last two seasons." When he did see action, Mayer collected 12 hits, including a triple, in 54 at-bats for a .222 average, and drove in five. In 20 games as a catcher, Mayer fielded .990, well above the league's .965 mark for catchers.

That wasn't enough for Rowland to keep Mayer around in 1916. At the age of 25 and no longer a prospect, Chicago released Mayer to Milwaukee on April 22, and Milwaukee later shipped him to St. Paul, both in the American Association. He appeared in 104 games for the two clubs, batted .210 in 328 at-bats, smacked two homers, drove in 84 runs, and stole 12 bases. In 93 games as a catcher, he registered a .951 fielding percentage.

Mayer moved east to Providence of the International League in 1917, where he appeared in 79 games, 78 of them behind the plate, batted .291 with a pair of home runs, and stole eight bases. Behind the plate, he was superb, making 345 putouts, collecting 105 assists, and making nine errors, a fielding percentage of .980. Mayer hit an inside-the-park home run, the result of a collision between two Baltimore Orioles outfielders, on September 6, shortly before he reported to Boston to consummate an August 11 deal in which Red Sox sent pitcher King Bader to Providence in exchange for Mayer.

The transaction would come under question a year later, when the Providence Grays president, B.P. Moulton, who had purchased the team from Detroit Tigers owners Frank Navin and William Yawkey, sued National Commission members Ban Johnson and August "Garry" Herrmann. Moulton contended that the Boston club had actually issued a note to purchase Mayer, and that Moulton had obtained the note when he purchased the club. Moulton argued that when he attempted to collect from the Red Sox, the team used World Series proceeds to pay Navin and Yawkey, who still owned the Providence ballpark, and that the National Commission had allowed the payment to Navin and Yawkey to occur.

Meanwhile, Red Sox manager Jack Barry used Mayer in four 1917 late season games, and the 27-year old catcher collected two singles and five walks in 17 plate appearances, and made 19 putouts, eight assists, and an error.

Before the 1918 season started, the Red Sox acquired Wally Schang from the Philadelphia Athletics to share backup backstop duties with Mayer behind starter Sam Agnew. During the war-shortened season, manager Ed Barrow used Mayer in 26 games, and he collected 11 hits in 49 at-bats. In 23 games as a catcher, he fielded .964.

He also played a valuable role out of the lineup. "Mayer has been camping out in the bullpen all season," the *Boston Globe* commented, "his job being to get relief pitchers ready when Ed Barrow is going to rig the derrick on some wavering boxmen."

Wally Mayer, c. 1918. Charles Conlon photo. Courtesy of Michael Mumby.

And while he played sparingly, Mayer did make an impact on Boston's pennant race with Cleveland. On July 9, he slammed a 12th-inning double that beat the Indians at Fenway Park, and on August 4, Mayer singled in the 12th inning to plate the winning run and secure Babe Ruth's 2–1 complete-game victory at League Park in Cleveland.

In between the two big hits, Mayer made a side trip. The United States had entered World War I earlier in the year. Eligible men were ordered to join the military or perform jobs that contributed to the war effort. Baseball was not designated as an essential industry.

On July 18, the *Chicago Tribune* observed that "Catcher Walter Mayer rejoined the Red Sox after a visit to his draft board at Cincinnati, where he was called for investigation. The board will let him know in a couple of days just how long he has to obtain another job."

It turned out that he had the rest of the shortened season. Baseball owners agreed to end the 1918 season on Labor Day, and the World Series started three days later, but not without turmoil. The Chicago Cubs and Boston Red Sox players, unhappy with how they would share the proceeds from the first four World Series games, engaged in an impromptu strike before Game Five on September 10. The two teams skipped pre-game batting and fielding practice, and kept the 25,000 fans at Fenway Park waiting for an hour after the scheduled start time. While player representatives from the Red Sox and Cubs fruitlessly negotiated with the two National Commission members in attendance, the third member, American League President Ban Johnson, was summoned from a celebration at bar of the Copley Plaza Hotel. Johnson, reportedly inebriated, arrived at the park, threw his arm around Red Sox player rep Harry Hooper, and pleaded, "Harry, do you realize you are a member of one of the greatest organizations in the world — the American League. And do you realize what you will do to its good name if you don't play? Harry, go out there and play. The crowd is waiting for you." Hooper and the Red Sox took the field, and won the Series for the American League in six games. Johnson and the National Commission rewarded them by withholding their commemorative World Champions pins. Despite years of efforts from Hooper, members of the 1918 Red Sox never received their pins. Meanwhile, the media portrayed Johnson and the National Commission as heroes.

"Both the Red Sox and Cubs wilted when the national commissioners stood pat and finished the world's series," the *Chicago Daily Tribune* reported in early October, "but the Red Sox wound up with a demand that the 10 per cent of their share of the receipts be devoted to 'local war charities' instead of being handed over to some national war chest, as was proposed. One of the former Red Sox already has absolved himself from that class. On his return from the world's series to Cincinnati Walter Mayer, the former White Sox catcher, who finished the season with Barrow's men, donated 10 per cent of his check to war funds in Redland."

While he may have done the required thing in that instance, Mayer joined teammates Joe Bush, Wally Schang, and Amos Strunk on a barnstorming tour after winning the World Series, billing themselves as "the Red Sox," which further irritated the National Commission. The commissioners canceled the tour and disciplined the quartet for attempting to achieve financial gain while the national pastime was shut down.

Later in October, Mayer conformed to the draft board's earlier orders. "Twenty Red Sox are in some branch of the active service, and that does not include any who entered shipyards at the conclusion of the world's series," I.E. Sanborn of the *Chicago Daily Tribune* reported. "Dutch Leonard, Paul Smith, Carl Mays, Fred Wilder, Walter Mayer, John McInnis, and William Pertica went into uniform by the draft route, several of them being allowed by their exemption boards to finish the world's series before reporting for duty."

With the end of the war in November came the end of military service for many of the men recently inducted. And while Mayer's patriotism was praised, his baseball skills at age 28 were not. "Mayer, a clever catcher who has been 'third string man' for years in the big show, has been displaying much less class recently," W.A. Phelon of the *Washington Post* wrote. The Red Sox apparently agreed, and peddled Mayer to the St. Louis Browns for $5,000 on February 28, 1919. That season, Mayer matched his career high for hits with 14, including four doubles and a triple, walked eight times, and drove in five runs. In 25 games as a catcher, Mayer made 84 putouts, 33 assists, and five errors.

Mayer played his final game in the majors at the age of 29 on September 2, 1919, a 4–3 Browns loss to Cleveland at Sportsman's Park. He was one of four catchers to attend spring training with the Washington Senators the following year, but did not make the team.

He caught on with Minneapolis of the American Association and spent the next five seasons as the regular catcher for the Millers. Manager Joe Cantillon used Mayer 152 times during the 1920 season, and the backstop batted .271 with six home runs and 59 runs batted in, and led the league in chances accepted. Although he played in just 112 games in 1921, Mayer again led the loop in

chances accepted with 691. He batted .277, with 6 home runs and 54 runs batted in for the Millers, who became the first American Association team to hit more than 100 home runs, and were not shut out the entire season.

Mayer's 1922 season was a tremendous display of durability and ability. A 31-year old at the start of the season, he appeared in 164 games, 163 of them behind the plate, catching in 98 percent of the team's games. He batted .317, socked 19 home runs, drove in 114 runs, led the league with 111 bases on balls, and struck out just 26 times. For the third straight season, he led the league with 889 chances accepted, and he fielded .983 for the season to lead the Millers to a second-place finish in the AA.

He played in 111 games for Minneapolis in 1923, batting .280 with four home runs and 59 RBIs, and the following year, at the age of 34, played in 96 contests, batting .265 with four homers and 26 RBIs for new Millers manager Mike Kelly.

In 1925, Mayer moved from Minneapolis to Little Rock in the Southern Association, where he hit just .206 with five home runs and 43 RBIs in 107 games. He batted .232 in 25 early season games in 1926 before the Travelers released him. Mayer finished out the season with Greenville, South Carolina, of the South Atlantic League, where he batted .296 with 10 homers and 38 RBIs in 83 games. He caught on with the Spinners again in 1927, and batted .200 with eight home runs and 34 RBIs in 88 games. Mayer closed out his career in organized baseball at the age of 38, starting the 1928 season at Greenville and finishing with Sally League rival Spartanburg, South Carolina, hitting .233 with seven home runs and 31 RBIs in 89 games with the two teams. A finger injury caused him to call it quits.

By the time of the 1930 United States Census, Mayer was living at the Hennepin Hotel, a boarding house in downtown Minneapolis. Although out of organized baseball for two years, he still listed his occupation as "ballplayer." Later, Mayer made his home at 408 Nicollet Avenue, 27 blocks north of the Millers' Nicollet Park at West 31st Street and Nicollet Avenue, and became a cigar store clerk.

In June 1950, Mayer was diagnosed with chronic pulmonary tuberculosis, and he entered the Glen Lake Sanitarium in Minnetonka, Minnesota, southwest of Minneapolis. He died there 18 months later, at the age of 61, on November 11, 1951. Separated from his wife, the former Myrtle Nelson (they married in 1923), at the time of his death, Mayer left as his only surviving relative Vera Bauer, a sister in Cincinnati. He was cremated at the Lakewood Crematory in Minneapolis, and his ashes were returned to Cincinnati, where a private funeral service was held.

CARL MAYS *by Allan Wood*

G	ERA	W	L	SV	GS	GF	CG	SHO	IP	H	R	ER	BB	SO	HR	HBP	WP	BFP
35	2.21	21	13	0	33	1	30	8	293²/₃	230	94	72	81	114	2	11	6	1162

G	AB	R	H	2B	3B	HR	RBI	BB	SO	BA	OBP	SLG	SB	HBP
38	104	10	30	3	3	0	5	9	15	.288	.357	.375	1	2

Carl Mays is best remembered for throwing the pitch that led to the death of Cleveland shortstop Ray Chapman in August of 1920. But he also had a career record of 207–126 and a 2.92 ERA over 15 seasons, and remains one of the best pitchers not honored in the Hall of Fame. Throwing with a submarine motion so pronounced that he sometimes scraped his knuckles on the ground while delivering the ball, Mays looked "like a cross between an octopus and a bowler," *Baseball Magazine* observed in 1918. "He shoots the ball in at the batter at such unexpected angles that his delivery is hard to find, generally, until along about 5 o'clock, when the hitters get accustomed to it — and when the game is about over."

Perhaps the most disliked player of his era, Mays was once described by writer F.C. Lane as "a strange, cynical figure" who "aroused more ill will, more positive resentment than any other ballplayer on record." A noted headhunter even before the Chapman beaning, Mays refused to apologize for how he pitched. "Any pitcher who permits a hitter to dig in on him is asking for trouble," he once said. "I never deliberately tried to hit anyone in my life. I throw close just to keep the hitters loose up there." One teammate said Mays had the disposition of a man with a permanent toothache. Throughout his professional career, Mays had trouble making friends — even on his own teams. "When I first broke into baseball, I discovered that there seemed to be a feeling against me, even from the players on own team," Mays said after a few years in the big leagues. "I always have wondered why I have encountered this antipathy from so many people wherever I have been. And I have never been able to explain it, even to myself."

Carl William Mays was born on November 12, 1891, in

Carl Mays in 1918. Courtesy of Chicago History Museum.

Liberty, Kentucky, one of eight children. The family soon moved to Mansfield, Missouri, where Carl's father William was a traveling Methodist minister. After his death when Carl was 12 years old, Mays's mother moved the family to Kingfisher, Oklahoma. It was there that Carl met his cousin, John Long, a catcher who introduced him to the game of baseball.

In 1912, Mays signed with Boise, Idaho, in the Class D Western Tri-State League, for $90 a month; he finished the season 22–9 with a 2.08 ERA. He played the next season in Portland, Oregon, and in 1914 was drafted by the Providence Grays, a team the Detroit Tigers owned in the International League. During his stay with Providence, the Grays were sold to Red Sox owner Joe Lannin.

Mays's 24 victories led Providence to the 1914 IL pennant; in the final month of the season, he was ably assisted by Babe Ruth, who had made his debut in Boston that summer. The two young men were called up for the final week of the Red Sox's season, but Mays did not appear in any games.

Mays joined the Red Sox staff in 1915 and made his debut on April 15. During the Red Sox's pennant-winning season, he was used mostly in relief, appearing in 38 games. He went 6–5, with a 2.60 ERA, and (though the statistic hadn't been invented yet) led the league with seven saves. He did not appear in the World Series.

Mays's abrasive personality grated on opponents. In his rookie season, Mays often sparred with Detroit's cantankerous outfielder Ty Cobb. In one game, after Mays threw high and inside on Cobb, the Tiger laid down a bunt along the first base line for the sole purpose of spiking Mays and cutting his leg. Though bitter rivals — the Red Sox and Tigers battled for the American League pennant that season — the men held a grudging respect for each other's single-minded pursuit of victory.

In 1916, Mays split his time between the rotation (24 starts) and bullpen (20 other appearances), winning 18 games and posting a 2.39 ERA. In that fall's World Series against Brooklyn, Mays recorded a save in Game One — bailing out Ernie Shore by recording the final out with the bases loaded and the tying run on third — but was the losing pitcher in Game Three, the Red Sox's only loss in the series.

In 1917, Mays became a star. With a 22–9 mark, his 1.74 ERA was the third-lowest in the major leagues, and he ranked among the top five in the American League in fewest walks and hits allowed per nine innings, and lowest opponents' batting average and on-base percentage. But Mays also hit a league-high 14 batters and earned a reputation as a headhunter that dogged him for the rest of his life. "Mays is a low-ball pitcher," one opponent noted. "How does it happen that when he puts a ball on the inside it generally comes near the batter's head?"

Mays would often berate his fielders for making errors behind him. "I have been told I lack tact, which is probably true," he said. "But that is no crime." Late in his career, Mays praised another pitcher: "This fellow has no friends and doesn't want any friends. That's why he's a great pitcher." He could have easily been talking about himself.

Yankees infielder Roger Peckinpaugh said Mays threw "a very 'heavy' ball. It sinks and when you catch it, it feels heavy enough to almost go through your glove." Horace Ford, who batted against Mays in the National League, said that hitting Mays's fastball "was like hitting a chuck of lead. It would go clunk and you'd beat it into the ground."

Mays got an incredible amount of outs via ground balls, especially with the Red Sox. From 1916–18, he recorded 117, 118, and 122 assists, which remain the top three season totals in Red Sox history. In 1918, Mays, then 26 years old, was the ace of the Boston staff, winning 21 games with a 2.21 ERA. He tied Walter Johnson for the league lead with eight shutouts and tied Scott Perry for the lead with 30 complete games. He finished fifth in strikeouts and fifth in fewest hits allowed per nine innings. He also hit 11 batters, the second-highest total in the league.

Mays started and completed Games Three and Six of the 1918 World Series against the Cubs; Boston won both games by identical 2–1 scores. Seven days after he helped pitch the Red Sox to the World Series championship, Mays married Marjorie Fredricka Madden, a graduate of the New England Conservatory of Music whom he had met at Fenway Park during his rookie season.

But things went downhill for Mays in 1919. While he was at spring training, his farm house in Missouri burned to the ground; he suspected arson. During a Decoration

Carl Mays, 1917, at Comiskey Park, Chicago.
Courtesy of Chicago History Museum.

Day series in Philadelphia, when Athletics fans were pounding on the roof of the visitors' dugout, Mays threw a baseball into the stands, hitting a fan in the head. He also ran into a lengthy streak of bad luck on the mound, as the slumping Red Sox gave him almost no run support. Over a 15-day period in June, Mays lost three games by a combined score of 8–0. The last straw came on July 13, during a game against the White Sox. When Eddie Collins tried to steal second base, catcher Wally Schang's throw hit Mays in the head. At the end of the inning, the pitcher stormed off the mound, left the team, and headed back to Boston.

Mays told sportswriter Burt Whitman that he needed to make a fresh start with another team. "I'm convinced that it will be impossible for me to preserve my confidence in myself as a ballplayer and stay with the Red Sox as the team is now handled," he said. "The entire team is up in the air and things have gone from bad to worse. The team cannot win with me pitching so I am getting out.... Maybe there will be a trade or a sale of my services. I do not care where I go." On July 30, the Red Sox traded Mays to the New York Yankees for Allen Russell, Bob McGraw, and $40,000 in cash.

A fierce legal battle ensued, as enraged American League president Ban Johnson attempted to block the trade. Several days before Mays was dealt, Johnson had privately suspended Mays and issued a secret order to all eight American League clubs prohibiting them from acquiring the pitcher until his suspension had been served. Johnson feared that Mays's actions could set a bad precedent for the league, by giving players the power to subvert the reserve clause and force trades simply by refusing to play for their clubs. "Baseball cannot tolerate such a breach of discipline," Johnson said of Mays's abandonment of the Red Sox. "It was up to the owners of the Boston club to suspend Carl Mays for breaking his contract and when they failed to do so, it is my duty as head of the American League to act."

The league's owners fractured over the matter, with five franchises (Cleveland, Detroit, Washington, St. Louis, and Philadelphia) siding with Johnson, while three (New York, Chicago, and Boston) defied him. Because the three "Insurrectionist" clubs held control over the league's five-man board of directors, Johnson was forced to back down from his stance on the issue, particularly after the three clubs began holding meetings with the National League to discuss the formation of a new 12-team circuit. Mays reported to New York, and the incident marked the first time in his long tenure as AL president that Ban Johnson had been outmaneuvered on a major issue. Mays pitched in 13 games for the Yankees in the second half of 1919, posting a sterling 1.65 ERA. Mays won 26 games for New York in 1920, and in 1921 he led the American League in both wins (27) and saves (7). He also hit .343 that year. Mays batted .268 over his career and, despite his reputation, was hit by a pitch just four times in 15 years — and only once after 1918.

On August 16, 1920 — a dark, overcast day at the Polo Grounds — Mays hit Indians shortstop Ray Chapman in the temple with an inside fastball leading off the fifth inning. A loud crack resounded through the stadium, and Mays, thinking the pitch had hit Chapman's bat, fielded the ball and threw it to first base. Chapman was helped off the field, but collapsed in the clubhouse; after a late-night operation on his fractured skull, he died early the following morning. As Chapman staggered off the field, Mays pointed out to the umpires a scuff mark on the baseball which he claimed had caused the pitch to sail inside. Later that day, Mays would also claim the ball was wet from the rain that had fallen earlier. A few hours after Mays was informed of Chapman's death, he told a Manhattan District Attorney: "It was a little too close, and I saw Chapman duck his head in an effort to get out of the path of the ball. He was too late, however, and a second later he fell to the grounds. It was the most regrettable incident of my career, and I would give anything if I could undo what has happened." Almost all other witnesses to the incident, however, reported that Chapman never moved an inch and probably never saw the ball.

Sorrow over Chapman quickly turned to anger against Mays. Several teams, including the Red Sox, Tigers, and Browns, sent petitions to league president Ban Johnson, demanding Mays be thrown out of baseball. Mays spent a week in seclusion, then returned to the mound on August 23. Yankee fans were supportive — a clearly nervous Mays defeated Detroit 10-0 at the Polo Grounds — but there was an increase in calls for a boycott of any game pitched by Mays.

He made three starts in New York before his first appearance on the road, on September 3, in a relief stint at Fenway Park. He was greeted with a mixture of boos and cheers, but by the time he had pitched the second game of a doubleheader the following day, most of the crowd was on his side. He decided, however, to not accompany the Yankees on a road trip to Cleveland later that week.

In the 1921 World Series against the Giants, Mays pitched three complete games without allowing a walk, but he was charged with two losses and the Yankees lost the Series. According to sportswriter Fred Lieb, there were suspicions Mays may have lost those two games on purpose. In *The Pitch That Killed*, Mike Sowell details the concern among several writers and Commissioner Kenesaw Mountain Landis after Mays's meltdown in Game Four. Sowell also quotes Yankees co-owner Cap Huston as saying many years later that Mays and others (possibly Joe Bush) had deliberately lost World Series games in both 1921 and 1922. Lieb believed the unanswered questions about those Series were what really kept Mays out of the Hall of Fame.

The rumors also were a likely reason that, despite Mays's 65 wins in three years, the Yankees tried to dump him before the 1923 season. That didn't work, so manager Miller Huggins simply refused to use him. Mays appeared in only 23 games for the Yankees in 1923, and at the end of the season was sold to Cincinnati. He pitched for the Reds for five years — rebounding to a 20–9 record in 1924 — and ended his career in 1929 with the New York Giants.

After his retirement from the major leagues, Mays pitched in the Pacific Coast League and American Association for two seasons, then worked as a scout for 20 years for the Cleveland Indians and the Milwaukee and Atlanta Braves. For a number of years, he also ran the Carl Mays Baseball School at Jantzen Beach in Portland, Oregon. Among his students was Johnny Pesky, allowed to attend free of charge since he was a clubhouse kid for the Portland Beavers. Mays died on April 4, 1971, in El Cajon, California at age 79, and was buried in Riverview Cemetery in Portland. He was survived by a second wife, Esther, and two children.

DICK MCCABE *by Nicole DiCicco*

G	ERA	W	L	SV	GS	GF	CG	SHO	IP	H	R	ER	BB	SO	HR	HBP	WP	BFP
3	2.79	0	1	0	1	2	0	0	$9\frac{2}{3}$	0	4	3	2	3	0	0	0	40

G	AB	R	H	2B	3B	HR	RBI	BB	SO	BA	OBP	SLG	SB	HBP
3	2	0	0	0	0	0	0	0	0	.000	.000	.000	0	0

Dick McCabe was the only child of Margaret and Richard James McCabe, Sr. He was born on February 21, 1896, in Mamaroneck, in Westchester County on the outskirts of New York City. In 1914, at the age of 18, the 5-foot-10½, 159-pound right-handed pitcher played with New Rochelle's semipro baseball team before signing a professional contract to pitch for the Eastern Association team in Bridgeport, Connecticut. For Bridgeport, McCabe pitched eight games with a 5–1 record, chalking up 30 strikeouts in 41 innings of work.

In 1915, McCabe played in the Class B New England League, splitting his time between Lewiston and Lynn. League records are less than complete, but he posted a 13–9 mark in 27 games. This earned him a tryout with the Boston Red Sox, so in 1916 he was invited to his first big league spring training camp in Hot Springs, Arkansas. He lacked both experience and sufficient control and was unable to break onto the roster of the reigning World Champions. Instead, he took up again with Lynn before joining Hartford of the Class B Eastern League. He was injured for most of 1916, appearing in only nine games. One report from July while he pitched for Hartford said he couldn't get the ball "within a yard of the plate." He was 2–3 for the season.

McCabe had a second stint with the Sox during 1917 spring training, but his contract was placed with the Buffalo Bisons of the International League. The World War was on and the entire Buffalo team, McCabe included, registered for the military draft, waiving any rights to claim exemption. As it happened, though, he gained some real pitching experience in 1917 as he logged 259 innings, appearing in 38 games, and posting a 15–13 record and a 3.06 ERA.

McCabe made his third appearance in Red Sox spring training camp in 1918, and this time he made the club. He appeared in seven springtime games, including an April 2 appearance in which he relieved Babe Ruth, hurled 10 innings, and recorded the win. Six of his seven spring games were played against the Brooklyn Dodgers, the only team the Red Sox played that spring. The other was a split squad game in which McCabe pitched for the Yannigans against the regular Red Sox. He pitched a shortened seven-inning game and proved to be an exceptionally fast worker pitching the entire seven innings in just 35 minutes. McCabe ended the spring of 1918 having pitched 37 innings, giving up 38 hits and nine runs, with four walks and eight strikeouts.

McCabe made the trip to Boston with the major league team and became the 1918 batting practice pitcher, a decision that pleased the hitters. He'd developed good control and they liked how perfectly he grooved the ball for their tune-ups. On May 30, as uncharacteristically arctic air filled Fenway, the 22-year-old McCabe made his major league debut. He went from putting the ball right over the plate day after day to facing the Washington Senators in the afternoon game of the day's doubleheader. Boston had won the first game, 9–1. McCabe gave up three singles in a row in the second inning, with one run scoring. In all, he pitched eight innings, allowing 11 safeties. There were two errors behind him; the final result was a 4–0 defeat. Today, that could be considered a quality start, but in 1918, the 11 hits raised a few eyebrows. The *Boston Globe* commented, "Dick pitches every day in batting practice and has to stick it over so the boys can tune up their batting eyes. He stuck it over pretty well for the Griffmen yesterday and they indulged in a little batting harmony, too, but no complaint can be made about Dick. Put him into a few more ball games and he will show something." Manager Ed Barrow underscored the point: "A few more games and he would be okay." That proved to be his only start for the Red Sox. He had two at-bats, but did not get a hit. McCabe apparently had a deceptive motion. He picked off two runners from first base during the game; Clark Griffith charged it was a balk move.

McCabe made just two other pitching appearances for the Sox, for a total of two additional innings. On June 7, he was the last of six Red Sox pitchers, yielding one hit in two-thirds of an inning of work as the Cleveland Indians clobbered the Red Sox, 14–7. By the middle of July, still subject to the "work or fight" order imposed by Secretary of War Newton D. Baker, he was released and picked up by the Jersey City Skeeters of the International League. With Jersey City, he got in 85 innings of work; his dismal 2–8 record was not a reflection of the 2.86 earned run average he recorded.

The following year, 1919, McCabe played again in the International League, splitting his time between Binghamton and Newark, winning 15 games (while losing 16), but with an even better ERA (2.63) and a strikeouts to walks ratio of more than two to one.

In 1920, he settled in with the Buffalo Bisons again, where he would pitch for 2½ seasons. Toward the end of the 1920 season, he won 13 straight games ending 1920 with a 22–6 record, with 232 innings of work and a 2.56 ERA. He struck out 103 and walked just 40. In 1921, McCabe was 17–17 with a 2.42 ERA. He'd begun to make a name in the minor leagues, primarily as a starter, and in June 1922, he was acquired by the Chicago White Sox. It was his second shot at major league baseball. The day he reported to the team, manager Kid Gleason thrust McCabe into the ninth inning of a game. His stint with the White Sox was even shorter than with Boston, however. He appeared in three games, but won a game on June 21, the beneficiary of two runs scored in the bottom of the ninth as the White Sox salvaged the game with a 5–4 win over the Washington Senators. McCabe had thrown a scoreless top of the ninth. In all, he pitched only 3⅓ innings for Chicago, giving up four hits and three runs. He had evened his major league totals at 1–1, but never did get another at-bat. McCabe was purchased for $5,000 in August 1922 by the Salt Lake City Bees president, William Lane.

McCabe pitched for Salt Lake for a little more than four seasons before Lane moved the Pacific Coast League franchise to Hollywood, renaming the team the Hollywood Stars. In five of his seven seasons in the Pacific Coast League, McCabe pitched over 200 innings. A serious bout with the flu limited him to 196 innings in 1927, just four innings short of six seasons in a row. His record in the PCL was 98–99. McCabe was inconsistent in his outings. There was never a mention of a fastball, just a good twister. One speculates that his batting practice fastball just wasn't good enough to make it in the majors, though the Coast League always played a high level of baseball and he fared well there. He was with Hollywood from 1927 into the 1929 season, and the *Los Angeles Times* once described his pitching as "classy" and said he had a "method to every pitch."

McCabe was a very smart pitcher and was used from time to time to scout the opposition, for instance an April 1928 game against Sacramento in which he sat in the stands behind home plate. He was also physically tough; in one inning on August 28, he took a ball off his left shin

Dick McCabe. Zeenut card, 1923.
Courtesy of the Mark Macrae Collection.

and then was struck in the head with a ball thrown to home plate, but he finished the inning.

After eight seasons of Pacific Coast League play, McCabe was sold to the Texas League's Fort Worth Panthers in June 1929. Despite a 1–4 record for Hollywood at the time of the sale, McCabe bounced back for the Panthers to post eight wins against three losses. 1930 was a bounce-back year for McCabe all the way around. He remained with the preseason favorite Fort Worth team and for the second time became a 20-game winner with a league-leading 20–7 mark. He made three appearances in the baseball classic of the South, the Dixie Series, in which the champions of the Texas League and Southern Association squared off in a series patterned after the World Series. McCabe was ineffective in the series, though, complaining of a dead arm.

1931 proved to be his best year and he was touted as the smartest hurler with an easy style. On May 8, he pitched a full 16 innings but four days later made his next scheduled start. He was called Dick "Control" McCabe in July after picking up his 16th win. In September he notched his 22nd win in his league-leading 27th complete game. He ended the year at 23–7 with 310 innings pitched. He yielded only 86 runs while striking out 111 and compiling a spectacular 1.97 ERA. McCabe even hit his second minor league career home run. Dizzy Dean of the Houston Buffaloes was named the 1931 Texas League MVP with his 26 wins. McCabe came in fourth place in the voting.

While pitching in a September game, McCabe earned the respect of Dean's Houston teammates with his crafty ability, which led the Houston Buffaloes to borrow McCabe to pitch for them in the 1931 Dixie Series when they needed to replace an injured Tex Carleton. In the first game, Dizzy Dean pitched in a 1–0 losing effort against the Birmingham Barons. McCabe pitched the second game and was brilliant, shutting out the Barons with a 3–0 gem. McCabe's final appearance came in the fifth game, which he lost, 3–1, giving up four hits in four innings. Dizzy Dean finished the series 1–2 with four appearances, including relief in the sixth game, but Birmingham won the series in seven games.

The Fort Worth Panthers rewarded McCabe for

superb seasons in 1930 and 1931 by naming him player-manager of the 1932 team. He boasted that the team would be in the fight for the pennant. His main focus was to develop the youngsters to sell to higher leagues by making sure their confidence was never broken. His toughness came out again when cold climate prevented a workout and McCabe vowed that from then on, the team would hold workouts no matter what the weather conditions. He was one of the league's fastest pitchers, completing a 1–0 win over Houston in 63 minutes. In August, age began to win out over gritty determination and toughness when McCabe pitched only one inning of a game before being knocked out; he came back to start the next night but gave up three runs in the second inning.

McCabe resigned from Fort Worth at the end of August, signed with Dallas on the 29th and pitched a 3–0

shutout. It proved to be his last hurrah as he retired from baseball in 1933 after appearing in seven games combined for Montreal of the International League and Birmingham of the Southern Association. McCabe's minor league career spanned 20 years and 3,814 innings. He ended with a 259–212 record, 4,175 runs, 766 walks, 1,355 strikeouts, and a 3.64 ERA.

McCabe spent the offseasons in Buffalo, New York, where he took up permanent residence after baseball. He secured employment as a salesman for the William Simon Brewery in Buffalo. McCabe rose in the ranks, and was promoted to sales manager before ultimately being named vice president three years before his death. He died at the age of 53 on April 11, 1950, in Sisters Hospital in Buffalo from complications following a stroke. He was survived by his wife, Theresa Ball McCabe.

STUFFY MCINNIS *by Aaron M. Davis and C. Paul Rogers III*

G	AB	R	H	2B	3B	HR	RBI	BB	SO	BA	OBP	SLG	SB	HBP
117	423	40	115	11	5	0	56	19	10	.272	.306	.322	10	2

"It was the best of times, it was the worst of times...." During his 18-year career in the Major Leagues, John Phalen "Stuffy" McInnis' teams finished in first place six times, winning five World Series, and in last place four times. He started his career by becoming the youngest member of Connie Mack's famed "$100,000 infield," replacing veteran Harry Davis at first base for the Philadelphia Athletics in 1911, and joining Eddie Collins, Frank (soon to be "Home Run") Baker, and Jack Barry in that fabled infield. Following the dismantling of the Athletics after the 1914 season, Stuffy stayed on, suffering through three straight last-place A's finishes. But whether it was feast or famine for his teams, McInnis remained a consistent singles hitter, an outstanding defensive first baseman, and a savvy clubhouse leader. A spry 5'9½" right-handed line-drive pull hitter, McInnis has a career batting average over .300, having amassed more than 2,400 hits. However, he is best known as one of baseball's best defensive first basemen, due to his amazing consistency covering first base.

The fourth of five sons of Stephen and Udavilla (Grady) McInnis, Stuffy was born September 19, 1890 in the fishing town of Gloucester, Massachusetts. His father provided a good living for the family variously as a caretaker of a stable of driving horses, a chauffeur, and a "call" fireman for the Colonel Allen Hook and Ladder, No. 1.

Stuffy McInnis. Detail from 1919 *Spalding's Official Base Ball Guide.*

All McInnis' brothers played baseball, but Stuffy stood out from an early age. He gained his unique nickname during his boyhood playing days, when teammates and spectators would shout, "That's the stuff, kid, that's the stuff!" after he had made a good play.

Playing shortstop, McInnis led Gloucester High School to championships in 1906 and 1907. In the summers of 1907 and 1908, he played for the Beverly, Massachusetts amateur baseball club. In July 1908, he joined the Haverhill Hustlers professional baseball club, and "soon became the sensation of the New England League," according to the Philadelphia Athletics' 1910 Championship Season Souvenir Program. He was paid $100 per month by the Hustlers, batting .301 in 186 at-bats under the tutelage of the legendary Billy Hamilton. On the advice of Dick Madden of the Beverly amateur club — who acted as a scout for the Athletics — McInnis was signed by A's owner-manager Connie Mack at the end of 1908.

Stuffy's slight stature and boyish looks were the cause of some confusion in his earlier years. Once, before a New England League game, umpire Steve Mahoney asked Hamilton when he was going to get his mascot off the field, pointing at McInnis. "Mascot nothing!" snapped Hamilton, "That's my shortstop and he's one of the best you've ever seen."

In 1909, just 18 years old, McInnis was considered a potential rival for the starting shortstop position over Jack Barry, who had joined the major leagues just a year earlier. He stuck with the Athletics out of spring training, but ended up playing only 14 games — all at shortstop — in this first season. His major league debut on April 12 was an auspicious occasion for another reason, the grand opening of Shibe Park, the first steel and girder ballpark in the country. Jack Barry was injured, so Stuffy started in front of over 30,000 fans, a huge crowd for that era. Stuffy acquitted himself well, making an error but getting a hit as the Athletics defeated the Red Sox, 8–1, behind Eddie Plank. Stuffy finished the season with only a .239 batting average, but made himself useful off the bench, as he became particularly astute at stealing signs from opponents.

In 1910, McInnis played at shortstop, second base, third base, and even in the outfield, batting .301 in 38 games. It was during this season that Connie Mack told Stuffy to start working out at first base, despite his short stature and lack of experience at the position. Ben Houser, who was trying to become the A's regular first baseman, tried to run McInnis off first every time he tried to take groundballs or throws. But in 1911 Mack kept Stuffy and released Houser who had hit only .188.

Before the 1911 season, Mack determined that McInnis would supplant regular first baseman Harry Davis, whose production had declined considerably in the previous year. However, when, early in the season, Jack Barry became sick, McInnis took over at shortstop instead. He played 24 games at shortstop, keeping Barry on the bench even some time after he recovered, due to his hot hitting. Eventually, Barry reclaimed shortstop, and McInnis took over first base from Davis.

On September 23, 1911, Connie Mack included McInnis' name on the list of the 21 players eligible to represent the A's in the World Series. However, two days later, Stuffy sustained an injury to his right wrist when he was struck by a pitch from the Tigers' George Mullin. Though no bones were broken, McInnis' right forearm became

Stuffy McInnis. Charles Conlon photograph. Courtesy of the Boston Red Sox.

badly swollen, and he was unable to throw even from first base to the pitcher's mound with any speed or accuracy. McInnis did not play the rest of the season. In 126 games in 1911, Stuffy hit for a .321 batting average.

The Athletics won the 1911 American League pennant, limping into the World Series with the aged Davis replacing Stuffy at first base. It was the second year in a row that McInnis' team played in the World Series without Stuffy taking a meaningful part in the outcome. However, with the Athletics up 13–2 with two outs in the ninth inning, and a 3–2 series lead, Mack put Stuffy into the game defensively at first base, so that Stuffy could say he'd played in a World Series. A's pitcher Chief Bender promptly induced Giants catcher Artie Wilson to ground weakly to Frank Baker at third base. The Series ended as Stuffy touched the ball for the first time, nabbing Baker's throw for the final putout. For Stuffy, it was the first of five World Series with three different teams.

McInnis entered the 1912 season surrounded by great expectations and with huge shoes to fill. Harry Davis, despite his declining performance over the previous two seasons, had been one of the American League's premier power hitters, and the A's regular first baseman since Mack formed the team in 1901. McInnis responded to the expectations with an excellent season, batting in 101 runs, the fourth most in the league, and scoring another 83 in the effort, while batting for a .327 average. However, for the first time in three years, the Athletics failed to win the American League pennant.

In 1913, the A's got back on track, winning the American League pennant for the third time since McInnis joined the team. During the season, McInnis batted for a .324 average, with 90 runs batted in, which tied for second in the league. His defense also improved dramatically, providing a glimpse of his future defensive greatness. In the World Series, the Athletics beat the New York Giants in five games for the World Championship. McInnis slumped badly at the plate in the Series, garnering only two hits in 17 at-bats for a paltry .118 batting average.

McInnis had another strong offensive year in 1914,

finishing with a .314 batting average, including 95 runs batted in, second most in the league. The Athletics again won the American League pennant. They entered the 1914 World Series as heavy favorites over the Boston Braves. The Athletics managed only a lackluster offensive performance, scoring six runs in the improbable four-game sweep by the "Miracle Braves." Stuffy again struggled at the plate in the Series, going 2-for-14 for a .143 average. The entire A's team hit only a lackluster .172 for the four games.

Nineteen fourteen had begun with the defection of outfielder Danny Murphy, a team member since 1902, to the newly-formed rival Federal League. While the loss of Murphy, no longer a regular player, did not greatly weaken the Athletics in 1914, it was the harbinger for what was to be the end of the Philadelphia Athletics' first dynasty. Philadelphia entered the 1915 season after losing starting pitchers Chief Bender and Eddie Plank to the Federal League, third baseman Baker to a rebellious one-year retirement, and second baseman Eddie Collins, in a sale by Mack, to the Chicago White Sox. The result was that they had no hope of winning even half their games, let alone competing for the pennant. To make matters worse, in July, Mack sold Barry's contract to the Boston Red Sox, thus leaving McInnis as the sole remaining member of the Athletics' once-feared infield. Although McInnis, too, was wooed by the Feds, he reportedly opted to stay with the Athletics out of loyalty to Connie Mack, even for considerably less money.

Not surprisingly, however, McInnis' next three years with the Athletics were unhappy ones as the A's finished in the cellar in 1915, 1916, and 1917. Stuffy, however, continued to be productive, batting .314, .295, and .303 in those years to remain one of baseball's premier first basemen.

Stuffy had an interesting encounter with future teammate Babe Ruth early in the 1916 season. McInnis was walking across the lobby of the Bellevue-Stratford Hotel in Philadelphia on an April evening when he saw Babe Ruth relaxing in an easy chair. That afternoon Ruth had defeated the Athletics in Shibe Park and allowed only five hits, including one by McInnis. McInnis walked over to the Babe and said, "You pitched a fine game out there today, Babe. That fastball of yours was really hopping all afternoon."

Stuffy McInnis, 1918. Courtesy of Chicago History Museum.

McInnis later reported that although he had batted against Ruth many times in the past, the Babe looked him squarely in the eye and said, "Yeah, kid, it was a pretty good game. Glad you could get out to the ballpark and see it."

After the end of the 1917 season, Mack demanded that McInnis take a salary cut. When McInnis refused, Mack traded him to the Boston Red Sox in January 1918 for third baseman Larry Gardner, outfielder Tillie Walker, and backup catcher Hick Cady.

After nine years with the Athletics, McInnis helped lead his new team to the war-shortened 1918 American League pennant. The Red Sox won the World Series four games to two primarily on the pitching of Babe Ruth and Carl Mays, but also with the timely hitting of McInnis and a few teammates. In the first game, McInnis singled home the only run of the game in the fourth inning as Babe Ruth shut out the Cubs, 1–0. In Game Three, Stuffy singled in the fourth and scored the deciding run on a squeeze bunt by Everett Scott in a 2–1 Red Sox victory. For the Series McInnis batted .250, well above the team's lowly .186 average. He also fielded his position flawlessly. For example, in Game Four he took part in three double plays and made the pivotal defensive play of the game in the ninth inning, forcing Fred Merkle at third base on Chuck Wortman's little tapper in front of the plate.

Boston's fortunes fell in 1919, 1920, and 1921, as first Mays and then Ruth were traded or sold. The team finished in the bottom half of the American League each season, as McInnis again found himself on a team that had been dismantled for cash by its owner. McInnis hit for averages of .305, .297, and .307 in the three years, respectively.

It was during this period that McInnis honed his first base defense to a point of near-infallibility. In 1919, he made seven errors in 118 games for a .995 fielding average. In 1920, he again made seven errors, this time in 148 games, for a league-leading .996 fielding average. In 1921, McInnis made only one error in 152 games for a record .9993 fielding average.

Even that lone error was debatable. It occurred on May 31st in Fenway Park against the Athletics. Jimmy Dykes was leading off first and the Red Sox catcher fired to McInnis on an attempted pick-off play. Stuffy dropped the ball on the tag and the official scorer charged him with an error. The next season, Dykes, knowing that was the only error McInnis committed all year, would bring the play up whenever he got to first base against the Red Sox. He would say, "You know, Stuffy, that really wasn't an error. I was safe either way, whether you dropped it or not."

According to Dykes, Stuffy would purse his lips and make believe he wasn't listening. Finally, during one game when Dykes brought up the play once again, McInnis said out of the corner of his mouth without looking at Dykes, "Shut up Dykes. You just shut up about it. If you mention that error one more time, so help me Dykes, so help me...."

Even with that single bobble in late May, Stuffy's 1,300 chances accepted without an error in 1921 set the record for errorless chances in a season. Further, from May 31, 1921 to June 2, 1922, McInnis went 163 games and 1,625 chances without making an error at first base. In 2007, Kevin Youkilis wrapped up an error-free season at first base, handling 1,080 chances without a single miscue. He has handled a club record 1,586 straight errorless chances at first base since his last miscue on July 4, 2006 at Tampa Bay. He has played in 214 consecutive games without an error.

According to one report, Stuffy disputed the error that brought an end to his errorless streak, a wide throw that he believed should have been charged to the thrower. McInnis reportedly encountered the sportswriter who had served as the official scorer on the train afterward and, after a brief discussion, socked him in the nose. The story may be apocryphal as Stuffy was generally considered one of the true gentlemen in the game.

Stuffy did not drink or smoke and was "careful" in his speech. But he was proud of his fielding prowess. On June 23, 1919 McInnis was charged with his first error of that season after 526 chances when he could not handle a low throw from his old Athletics' teammate, Jack Barry, who was playing as a part-time second baseman. Some 30 years later McInnis was coaching baseball at Harvard and Barry was the coach at Holy Cross. According to one of Stuffy's former players, whenever Harvard played Holy Cross, the two old teammates would meet at home plate before the game to present their lineups and their greeting never varied: "How are you, Stuffy?" Barry would say. "Good. How are you, Jack?" Stuffy would reply, "You know that was a low throw, don't you, Jack."

There is evidence that McInnis was well aware of his batting average as well. In an interview late in his life, Smoky Joe Wood related that McInnis would approach him at the tail end of a season if the game didn't mean anything in the standings and say, "Look, it doesn't matter to you, let me get a hit or two and I'll get picked off or caught stealing." According to Wood, if McInnis got a hit, he would keep his end of the bargain and make an out

on the bases. Wood made it clear that Stuffy never bet or took advantage but was just trying to pump his batting average up a little at the end of the year.

Before the 1922 season, McInnis was traded to the Cleveland Indians. He hit for a .305 batting average, making only five errors in 140 games. Cleveland finished fourth in the American League. After the season, McInnis was released on waivers. He signed with the Boston Braves, with whom he spent two seasons, batting .315 and .291 in 1923 and 1924, respectively. The Braves finished at or near the bottom of the National League in both seasons, and released McInnis in April 1925. After the 1924 season, however, Stuffy had toured Europe as part of John McGraw's White Sox — Giants exhibition series. While there he met with British royalty, partook of an audience with the Pope, and visited Monte Carlo.

McInnis ultimately signed with the Pittsburgh Pirates for 1925. Playing in only 59 games, he hit for a .368 average, with a .437 on-base percentage and a .484 slugging average. Stuffy's veteran leadership was instrumental in helping the young Pirates win the National League pennant. In the World Series against the Washington Senators, the Pirates lost three of the first four games. John McGraw, whose Giants had lost to the Senators the previous year, suggested to Pirates manager Bill McKechnie that he play McInnis at first base instead of the struggling George Grantham, to take advantage of Stuffy's World Series experience. McKechnie took McGraw's advice and the Pirates won three straight to come back for an improbable World Series win. McInnis' steadying hand and timely hitting were major contributors to the Pirates comeback. McInnis played part-time for the Pirates again in 1926. He hit for a .299 average, but recorded only 127 at-bats in 47 games. The Pirates finished third in the National League.

In 1927, McInnis returned to Philadelphia as manager of the Phillies. Despite some early-season heroics by the perpetually woeful "Flying Phils," the team lost 103 games and ended up in its usual spot at the bottom of the National League. In 1928, Stuffy served as player-manager of the Salem Witches in the New England League. The 38-year old batted .339 in part-time duty. He went on to coach baseball at Norwich University, Cornell, and Harvard. After six seasons of coaching Harvard, McInnis resigned in 1954 because of failing health.

In his private life, McInnis was as steady as he was on the ball field. He married Elsie Dow in 1918. They had one daughter, Eileen, and three grandchildren. For the last 40 years of his life, McGinnis lived at 11 Tappan Street in Manchester-by-the-Sea, Massachusetts, a few miles down Cape Ann from his native Gloucester. On February 16, 1960, after a lengthy illness, McInnis passed away in Ipswich, Massachusetts. He was 69 years old and had been preceded in death the previous year by his wife Elsie.

Stuffy McInnis, Harry Frazee, and Jack Barry as McInnis signs his contract for 1918.
Courtesy of the Boston Public Library.

Tris Speaker, Stuffy hit a warm-up pitch by Ed Karger into short center field, which the Boston outfielders were not in a position to field. McInnis circled the bases for an inside-the-park home run against the unprepared Red Sox. The umpire upheld the homer and on appeal, American League president Ban Johnson refused to overturn the umpire's ruling or the Athletics victory, based on a new, soon-to-be-withdrawn, rule prohibiting warm-up pitches between innings. Johnson had implemented the rule after complaints that games were taking too long to play, sometimes lasting as long as two hours!

Although known for his fielding wizardry, McInnis was an outstanding hitter as well. For his 19-year big league career, he batted .307 and hit over .300 14 times. He was known as a consummate contact hitter, striking out only 189 times in about 7,822 career at-bats. For three years of his career, he struck out fewer than 10 times in over 500 plate appearances. Only Joe Sewell has ever topped that feat. In 1922, Stuffy struck out only five times in 537 at-bats. In 1924, he whiffed only six times in 581 at-bats. On April 29, 1911, Stuffy went five-for-five, all singles, against the New York Highlanders' Hippo Vaughn and Jack Quinn while seeing only seven pitches. He hit the first pitch he saw for a single three times and the second pitch twice.

Typical of Deadball Era players, McInnis did not hit many home runs — only 20 for his career — and many were inside-the-park jobs, including two in one game on August 12, 1912 versus Vean Gregg of the Cleveland Naps. His most memorable home run, however, came on June 27, 1911 in a game at Huntington Avenue Grounds in Boston. McInnis stepped to the plate to lead off the seventh inning while the Red Sox were still warming up between innings. With Eddie Collins of the A's still on the field talking to Red Sox center-fielder

McInnis with the Pirates in 1925.

While McInnis was an excellent hitter, it was as a fielder that he truly left a legacy. He was one of the earliest first basemen to excel at catching throws one-handed and he did so in a way that appeared natural and not flashy, as was often the case with his contemporary Hal Chase. His one-handed style enabled him to reach for high and wide throws, and helped him overcome the disadvantage of his rather short stature. He is also credited as the inventor of the "knee reach," during which maneuver he performed a full, ground-level split in stretching for a throw. According to one report, he was also the first to wear the claw-type first baseman's glove to improve his efficiency in scooping balls out of the dirt.

With his fielding prowess, his lifetime batting average of .307 in 18 major league seasons, his participation in five World Series, and his membership in the best infield of the Deadball Era, Stuffy McInnis is certainly worthy of consideration for Baseball's Hall of Fame. One thing is certain: in his long career he lived up to his childhood nickname.

HACK MILLER *by Mike Sowell*

G	AB	R	H	2B	3B	HR	RBI	BB	SO	BA	OBP	SLG	SB	HBP
12	29	2	8	2	0	0	4	0	4	.276	.276	.345	0	0

In many ways, Lawrence "Hack" Miller was baseball's version of the circus performer his father "Sebastian the Strong Man" had once been. Hack Miller entertained teammates by using his bare hand to pound tenpenny nails through two-inch planks of wood and taking the same-size nails and bending them with his fingers. It has been written that he pulled up "fair-sized trees by the roots" during spring training. He once was photographed holding a baseball bat above his head like a barbell, with a teammate hanging from each end. He bragged that one winter he lifted a car to free a woman who had been trapped beneath its wheels. And though he normally swung a 47-ounce bat, on occasion in the minor leagues he wielded a 65-ounce club that was more than twice as heavy than those used by modern major leaguers of the 21st century.

Miller was short and squat at 5-foot-9, with a massive chest, broad shoulders, powerful arms and a listed playing weight between 195 and 208 pounds, although for much of his career he was overweight and slow.

But Hack Miller was more than a circus freak or a stuntman. He could hit, as evidenced by batting averages of .352 and .301 with 32 home runs in his two seasons as a regular with the Chicago Cubs in 1922–23. Sadly, Miller never became the star that he might have been had he been able to control his weight and utilize his amazing strength on the field and not just as a sideshow.

His career with the Red Sox was similarly tantalizing but brief. Called up in the final weeks of the 1918 pennant race, Miller made just one appearance in the Fall Classic, which, ironically, was against the Cubs, the team with

Hack Miller pounding a nail into the Weeghman Park (later Wrigley Field) ballpark fence, 1922. Courtesy of Chicago History Museum.

which he later would spend three and one-half seasons. That one at-bat came at Fenway Park in the ninth inning of Game Five of the Series, with the Red Sox trailing the Cubs, 3–0. Facing righthander Hippo Vaughn, Miller hammered the ball into deep left field toward the farthest reaches of Duffy's Cliff, so named for the great Red Sox outfielder Duffy Lewis, who was a master at fielding flies hit onto the steep incline in front of the left-field fence. The ball seemed headed for an extra-base hit that might spark a last-gasp Red Sox rally.

But as the crowd roared in anticipation, Cubs outfielder Les Mann raced up the incline, turned to gauge the arc of the ball, and then, even as he lost his footing and fell to a sitting position, somehow managed to reach up and make the catch in the webbing of his glove. As Burt Whitman wrote in the next day's *Boston Herald and Journal*, "It was the most unusual [catch] made in that hilly stretch of territory which surely has seen some queer catches."

That one moment was symbolic of Miller's major league career: brief, dramatic, colorful, memorable, but just short of the stardom that many thought was his destiny.

Miller joined the Red Sox from Oakland of the Pacific Coast League on August 7, 1918, and Boston manager Ed Barrow said in the August 10 *Herald and Journal* that the young outfielder reminded him of the great Hans Wagner. But after the Series ended, Miller never again appeared in a Boston uniform. He terrorized PCL pitchers for the next three seasons, then turned in those two tantalizing seasons for the Cubs that put him on the verge of becoming one of the game's premier power hitters. But following part-time duty in 1924 and the first month of 1925, a losing battle

Hack Miller. Charles Conlon photograph. Courtesy of Michael Mumby.

Miller, batting.

with weight problems drove Miller back to the minor leagues, where he continued to thrill fans in the Pacific Coast League, Texas League, and Three-I League with his hitting prowess and feats of strengths.

Despite his relatively short stay in the big leagues, Miller did leave his mark. He was widely considered the strongest man in baseball during his playing days.

Both F.C. Lane, the widely respected writer for *Baseball Magazine*, and Cubs first baseman Charley Grimm wrote of witnessing Miller hammering nails through boards with his hand covered only with his baseball cap. Historian Art Ahrens wrote in *The National Pastime* that as an 18-year-old apprentice steamfitter, Miller would hoist 250-pound radiators onto his shoulders and carry them up several flights of tenement stairs.

But there were many baseball men around the National League who looked at Miller's powerful frame and dismissed him as "muscle-bound," with his strength actually handicapping him as a player.

Grover Cleveland Alexander, the great pitcher for the Phillies, Cubs, and Cardinals, seemed to endorse this view of Miller when he was quoted in Lane's 1925 book *Batting*:

Even slugging at its worst is something of a science. It is surely not a matter of strength and weight. If it were, Hack Miller would be the greatest slugger in either league for he is by all odds the strongest man on the major circuits. But Rogers Hornsby can hit the ball harder than Hack. Miller is short, thickset, ponderous. Hornsby is tall, loose-jointed, of slender build. Hack could take him in his two hands and double him over his knees. In strength, there is simply no comparison. Besides, Hack probably outweighs Hornsby by 40 pounds. Still, Hornsby is the harder hitter of the two.

Miller also rivaled Babe Ruth in using the heaviest bat in baseball history. Ruth's 48-ounce bat is regarded by many as the heftiest in the major leagues, and Lane wrote in *Baseball Magazine* in 1925 that Ruth once used a 54-ounce club. While Miller's 47-ounce bat was not quite as weighty as Ruth's normal club, the 65-ounce

one Hack claimed to use in the minors (he said he liked it because it didn't sting his fingers when he hit with it) was off the scales compared with that of other baseball strongmen.

Despite his many feats of strength, Miller was a good-natured man who also entertained his teammates with his musical ability, playing a guitar that Grimm remembered as "held together with bicycle tape" in the Cubs' string band. Sportswriters described Hack as having "a killing smile" and an easy-going disposition that allowed him to laugh off hecklers in the bleachers or pranks played on him by his teammates. On one occasion, while playing for Danville, Illinois, of the Three-I League late in his career, Miller found a snake in the outfield grass at Bloomington, Indiana. He took great delight in using the serpent to joke with the fans in the left-field bleachers, acting as if he were about to toss what Robert Poisall of the *Danville Commercial News* described as a "rattler" into their midst.

Miller came about his strength and muscular build naturally. He was born New Year's Day in 1894 in New York City, but the next year, his father, Sebastian (a German immigrant whose real name was Mueller, according to the February 7, 1923, *Los Angeles Times*), moved the family to Chicago, where he operated a saloon. Miller later told *Baseball Magazine* that the establishment was a hangout for wrestlers and other toughs who liked to show off their strength with feats such as lifting 400 pounds using only one finger. The elder Miller, known as "Sebastian the Strong Man," was himself a wrestler who could break cobblestones with his bare hands, according to *Baseball Magazine*. The *Los Angeles Times* reported that among Sebastian the Strong Man's other stunts was taking a horse's tail in each hand and holding the animals back while trainers tried to lead them in opposite directions.

Hack Miller inherited his father's strength and stocky

build, but the younger Miller said he was neither as large nor as strong as his father. However, as young Hack matured, he began to resemble a famous wrestler of his day, the Russian strong man George Hackenschmidt. This generally is considered the source of Miller's nickname "Hack," although Edwin F. O'Malley of the *Los Angeles Times* wrote in 1918 that Miller earned his nickname in 1917 because his fat did a ballet dance as he "scudded after a fly ball."

As a boy, Hack played in neighborhood football games, but he told *Baseball Magazine* that "there was a rough crowd, nothing like rules and I got badly hurt." His parents forbade him to play again, so he turned his attention to other athletic endeavors.

Despite his size and strength, Miller was surprisingly agile and athletic. He worked three years at the Chicago department store Marshall Field, which entered teams in local athletic competitions. Miller told *Baseball Magazine* that he collected a boxful of medals in these meets, displaying his versatility by pole-vaulting more than nine feet, broad-jumping more than 17 feet and running the 60-yard dash in less than 11 seconds.

But it was in baseball that Miller would gain national acclaim. After playing semipro ball in the Chicago area, he began his professional baseball career at the age of 20 with Wausau of the Wisconsin-Illinois League, where he batted an impressive .333 with nine homers and nine stolen bases in 72 games in 1914.

Miller moved up to the Class C Northern League the following season, and he showed the speed he later boasted of by hitting 12 triples and stealing 14 bases to go with a .306 batting average for St. Boniface, prompting Brooklyn of the National League to draft him in August.

In 1916, Brooklyn assigned Miller to Winnipeg of the Northern League, and he not only won the batting title with a .335 average but also set what was reported as a world record for the longest drive with a fungo bat. Competing in a contest on June 19, Miller hit a fungo 438½ feet, beating the old record held by major league pitcher Big Ed Walsh by a full 19 feet, according to *Minor League Encyclopedia*. Hack also experienced night baseball more than 20 years before it was introduced in the major leagues, as the long summer days in Winnipeg allowed the team to play games until 10 or 11 P.M.

Miller's strong season earned him his first shot at the major leagues, as Brooklyn called him up in August 1916. He appeared in three games, hitting a triple with an RBI in three at-bats, but he was sold to Oakland of the Pacific

Hack with the Cubs.
George Brace photo.

Coast League on September 26, before the Robins played in the World Series against the Red Sox. It wouldn't be long before Miller got another shot at the Fall Classic.

Playing in Class AA, the minor leagues' highest designation at the time, Miller batted .296 with 12 triples for the Oaks in 1917. Despite his stats, Miller carried too much excess weight to suit Oakland manager Del Howard, who ordered him to shed some pounds over the winter.

Miller did just that, reporting to camp in the spring of 1918 more than 20 pounds lighter. The benefits were immediate, as Hack batted .316 through 102 games and was leading the PCL in hits with 131, prompting O'Malley of the Los Angeles *Times* to marvel that Hack could run the 100-yard dash in under 11 seconds and "base it like a Ty Cobb."

The glowing reports on Miller caught the attention of Red Sox manager Ed Barrow, who signed the young outfielder on August 3 to provide Boston with a much-needed right-handed bat to play the outfield on days when Babe Ruth was called upon to pitch. Although Miller batted only 29 times in 12 games as a pinch hitter and occasional starter in left field against left-handed pitchers in the stretch drive of the pennant race, he hit a respectable .274 with two doubles and four RBIs. Still, by the end of the regular season, Miller had lost out to another late-season addition, 35-year-old George Whiteman, as the backup left fielder, and Hack made only the one pinch-hit appearance in the World Series.

That would mark the end of Miller's career with the Red Sox, as the following spring he was sold back to Oakland, where over the next three seasons he posted batting averages of .346, .347, and .347. A broken leg in 1919 limited him to 54 games, but in 1920 Miller led the PCL with 280 hits and in 1921 his .347 average was second only to former Red Sox Duffy Lewis' .403 in 300 fewer plate appearances (league records show Miller as the batting champion, but official records confirm Lewis as the winner, according to SABR's Bob Hoie).

Still struggling to keep his weight under control, Miller played winter ball that offseason, and in January 1922 he was signed by the Cubs to fill a void in left field. Hack's reputation as a batter and a strong man preceded him to the Cubs training camp on Catalina Island, off the Southern California coast, so he was under a lot of scrutiny from the time he stepped off the boat following the two-hour ride from Los Angeles. A writer for the *Chicago Daily Tribune* took one look at Miller and reported that he was "carrying enough beef to make a couple of ball-players. He looked much like Ping Bodie when the latter was not in trim. Hack has a pair of shoulders that appear to measure something like a city block across."

Although Miller got off to a slow start that season, he began hitting when the weather warmed up, and he finished the season third in the league in batting with a .352 average as well as 12 homers and 78 runs batted in. Hack's most memorable moment came on August 25 when he hit a pair of three-run homers to help the Cubs beat the Phillies 26–23 in the highest-scoring game in major league history.

When Miller followed up with a .301 average, 20 homers, and 88 RBIs in 1923, he appeared to some to be on his way to stardom. More savvy baseball experts had their doubts. Hugh Fullerton, the great baseball writer for the *Chicago Daily Tribune*, wrote of him on October 1, 1923:

Miller is a sturdy and always trying type of ball player, a fence buster, and one of those fellows who will kill the weak pitching. He can take toe holds and crack 'em high up and far away, and then prove a sucker to an ordinary pitcher with control. He is slow on the bases, but covers an amazing amount of ground in the outfield for one so slow. He is working all the time and fairly good in aiding his center fielder. In retrieving balls hit between left and center he is all right until it comes to throwing.

Decades later, in the October 4, 1982, issue of the *New York Times*, Bill Veeck Jr. wrote that his father, Bill Veeck Sr., the general manager of the Cubs in the 1920s, was so enamored with Miller that in 1924 he added new bleachers to shorten the left-field fence at Cubs Park by 50 feet, hoping to boost Hack's home run total. According to Veeck Jr., opposing pitchers responded by pitching Miller low and away, causing him to hit harmless popups, and after Giants first baseman Bill Terry hit two homers into the shortened bleachers his first two at-bats, the Cubs tore down the bleachers before the next game.

However, Veeck's memory was faulty. It was Hack's weight and manager Bill Killefer's preference for speed, not the Chicago ballpark, which led to Miller's demise with the Cubs. The only changes to Cubs Park that the *Chicago Daily Tribune* reported in 1924 were the removal of advertisements from the outfield fences and a rebuilt scoreboard that could display the American League scores in addition to those of the National League. It was in 1926 that Cubs Park was renamed Wrigley Field and the bleachers in left field removed as part of a renovation that almost doubled the stadium's seating capacity.

Hack was gone by then, but he did play with the Cubs throughout 1924. Although losing his starting job in left field to Dallas Grigsby that season, Miller was a valuable

part-time player and pinch hitter, batting .336 in 53 games. According to Arthur Daley of the *New York Times*, Miller also passed on his nickname to a future Cubs great who, when joining the team as a rookie in spring training 1924, reminded his teammates of "a sawed-off Hack Miller," leading him to become known as "Hack" Wilson.

Miller played only sparingly early in the 1925 season, and on May 21, he made his last big-league appearance, hitting a pinch-hit triple in a 5–4 loss at Brooklyn. Three days later, he was given his release and returned to Oakland, where he had made his winter home.

He clearly was struggling to keep down his weight, and although Hack batted .321 after joining Oakland in 1925, the following spring he reported to camp "so fat he hasn't been able to perform," according to the *Chicago Daily Tribune*. Midway through the season, the Oaks sold Miller to Houston, where he rounded into shape well enough to bat .367 for the Buffs.

In 1927, Hack split his time between Houston and Beaumont of the Texas League, batting .340, and Danville of the Three-I League, where he batted .311 and led his team to the pennant.

Danville marked the end of Miller's playing career, although some record books incorrectly credit him with playing for Houston in 1929. The mistaken identity was understandable considering that in the same circuit there was another Hack Miller, who in 1926 had led the league in home runs to power Dallas to the pennant and the Dixie Series championship over the Southern Association champions. To add to the confusion, both Hack Millers were stocky, muscular power hitters.

In 1928, Dallas sold its Hack Miller to Minneapolis of the American Association, where he enjoyed a solid season before weight problems led to his being shipped back to the Texas League in 1929. Both the *Houston Post* and *Houston Chronicle* heralded the signing of the former Dallas slugger who, as the *Chronicle* warned, "is not to be confused with the Hack Miller who played with Houston three years ago."

By that time, Lawrence "Hack" Miller, once hailed as the strongest man in baseball, had returned to his home in Oakland, where his strength gained him employment as a dock worker. Miller eventually became a crew boss on the waterfront before retiring in 1959. He remained in Oakland until his death at 77 on September 17, 1971. He was buried in Oakland's St. Mary Cemetery.

Miller's legacy is that of a baseball strong man who performed amazing feats of strength in an era before weight training and steroid use. But one can only wonder how good Miller might have been had he had the discipline and the training to better utilize that strength and control his weight. He never was able to do that, and as a result Hack Miller's feats on the field never matched those off it.

VINCE MOLYNEAUX *by Bill Nowlin*

G	ERA	W	L	SV	GS	GF	CG	SHO	IP	H	R	ER	BB	SO	HR	HBP	WP	BFP
7	4.91	0	0	0	0	0	0	0	22	3	4	4	8	1	0	0	3	43

G	AB	R	H	2B	3B	HR	RBI	BB	SO	BA	OBP	SLG	SB	HBP
6	2	0	0	0	0	0	0	0	2	.000	.000	.000	0	0

He never had a hit, never made an error, and only pitched 32²/₃ innings in 13 major league games, but he was a member of the World Champion 1918 Red Sox. Standard reference books show Vincent Leo Molyneaux as born near Niagara Falls, in Lewiston, New York, on August 17, 1888 although August 17, 1890 was the date he provided when he registered for the military draft during the First World War. A six-foot, 180-pound right hander, Molyneaux was signed out of college and brought to the major leagues at the somewhat advanced age of 28 (or, perhaps, 26). The 1890 birth date seems more reliable. It confirms information his parents provided during the United States Census of 1900, which indicated Vincent was nine years old at the time, born in August 1890.

Vincent was the older child of parents who each traveled some distance to settle near Niagara — Joseph Molyneaux, a laborer from Louisiana born in February 1863, and Kathryn "Kate" Dempsey, who was born in Ireland in August 1869. The couple also had a daughter, Christina, born in January 1897. Joseph Molyneaux was listed as a Louisiana native in the 1900 census, but as born in New York in the 1880 census at which time he was working as a book binder. The 1890 census records were lost to fire, but the 1910 census shows Vincent and Christina still living at home in Niagara Falls, and Maggie Dempsey, Kate's sister, working as a stitcher in a book factory at age 25 and also living in a house on Garden Avenue. Vincent was working at the time as a laborer in the food industry. Joseph Molyneaux was a cooper working for the railroad. (Oddly, none of them appear in the 1920 census, yet in 1930 Kathryn Molyneaux and Margaret Dempsey were both still living at Garden Avenue. Vincent shows

Vince Molyneaux. Collection of Allan Wood.

up nowhere in the country in either 1920 or 1930.) There were other Molyneaux in the area, and even today there is a section of Lewiston known as Molyneaux Corners.

As a student at Niagara Falls High School, Vincent played with the Carter Crume company ball team. Carter Crume Co. Ltd. was a manufacturer of sales books, perhaps where his father and Aunt Maggie worked. As an ace pitcher for the Crumes, Vince caught the eye of major league scouts, several of whom attended a seven-game series in early 1914. "Squinch" Molyneaux was the starting pitcher in the first game of the series, and pitched a no-hitter.

In late May that year, Molyneaux was acquired by the Jamestown (New York) Giants of the Interstate League. He debuted with a 7–1 complete game win over the Wellsville (New York) Rainmakers. The *Jamestown Evening Journal* wrote that he "showed up in great style. He has everything required by a successful pitcher in the flinging line with a beautiful change of pace thrown in, and in addition fields his position in fine style." He had a tendency to walk a lot of batters, but did very well, running up his record to 9–2 by July 11. He suffered three consecutive losses from July 15 to 19, the latter two by scores of 4–3 and 3–2, and then disappeared from the box scores for three weeks having been injured in a "street car smashup." Coming back, "Molly" generally pitched quite well but saw his record deteriorate. Jamestown was no-hit by Wellsville in one of his starts; the Warren (Pennsylvania) Bingoes beat them 2–1 in another, and the Bradford (Pennsylvania) Drillers shut them out, 2–0. Then he lost a 1–0 game to the Hornell (New York) Green Sox despite throwing an excellent five-hitter with eight strikeouts and no walks. By year's end, he had a record of 11–12 earning the final win on September 12 throwing six innings of relief while going 2-for-3 at the plate, and driving in the final three runs in the 6–5 win over Wellsville.

Jamestown played Bradford in a postseason series for the Interstate League pennant, and Molyneaux came on in relief in Game Four after Jamestown was down 5–1. He pitched five innings of scoreless ball but in the top of the ninth "Molyneaux somehow or other forgot that Zurfluh was perched on third base and during one of his mighty windups, Zurfluh stole home, reaching the plate before the ball had been delivered." Mention of Molyneaux's elaborate windup would turn up again.

Molyneaux started Game Five and threw three scoreless innings, but then allowed two runs in the fourth and another in the fifth. Molyneaux, never much of a hitter despite the one standout game, was 0-for-5 at the plate. Jamestown lost the game, 4–2, but won the series in seven games.

After the season, Jamestown included him on their reserve list — as they did with a man named William Molyneaux. This presents a bit of a mystery. There was no William in Vincent's immediate family, and there never was any other Molyneaux mentioned in any of the *Evening Journal* game accounts throughout the season. The newspaper added to the mystery, though, in its August 25 edition when it reported "Secretary Molyneaux of the Jamestown club announced this morning that he had booked the Newark club" for an exhibition game on August 30. Secretary Molyneaux? Some relative was a team executive? There is nothing in any of the other sports page coverage that year that referred to a Secretary Molyneaux. Further, the team that Jamestown played on August 30 was Jersey City, not Newark. Perhaps it was a mistake of some sort.

Molyneaux had won a baseball scholarship to Villanova College in Pennsylvania and was a standout pitcher for Villanova in both 1915 and 1916, first raising eyebrows with a 14-inning 1–1 tie with Fordham on May 25, 1915. A "Philadelphia expert" cited by the *Washington Post* in June 1915 listed his "all-star" choices for an All-Eastern baseball team. He selected Harvard's Eddie Mahan as pitcher, but said that some of the other contenders lacked a good team behind them, adding, "Molyneaux, of Villanova, with a star nine, would have shown almost as well as any pitcher who can be mentioned."

Mysteries continue to confound. It's not clear why Jamestown let him go but Molyneaux was released to Wellsville, also in the Interstate League, for 1915. Inexplicably, the National Board canceled the deal (a handwritten note in Molyneaux's Hall of Fame files indicates he was suspended) and he never played for Wellsville. He is shown as having signed with a team in Buffalo instead, in June 1915, but never played for Buffalo, either.

He was released to the London (Ontario) Tecumsehs (in the six-team Canadian League.) Molyneaux joined a team in a bit of turmoil. Players were coming and going, and the London club in particular was under financial constraints worse than those of the other teams. Frustrated manager F. C. "Doc" Reisling, who often pitched for the team, too, at one point grumbled that London was "used to $1,800 a month baseball" but owner A. E. Somerville had placed a stricter salary cap on his ball club. The Tecumsehs (they played in London's Tecumseh Park) began the season with 16 players on the roster, but by June 28 were down to just 11 players and Reisling!

On July 7, Reisling telegraphed the *London Evening Free Press* that he had obtained "a pitcher by the name of Mulina, with a fine college reputation." Due to pitch his first game on July 8 against the St. Thomas (Ontario) Saints, he "received the sad news of his sister's sudden death in New York State" and so left the club before he had a chance to throw a pitch. Instead, the Tecs signed Tom "Julius" Caesar. Our man returned, though, and got his first start on July 17. Described in the *Free Press* as "Mike Mulina" he was removed in the fifth inning after giving up three runs on five hits, but he had been working with a big enough lead that London beat the Brantford (Ontario) Red Sox, 6–5. Throughout the season, which ended on September 1, the London newspaper consistently spelled his name as Mulina, though one or two box scores showed him as "Molina." Apparently, Molyneaux never read the newspaper or never bothered to correct it.

He started again on July 23 and last-place London lost a close 3–1 game to first-place Ottawa. Three errors hurt the London team. Winning against Hamilton, 3–2, in his next outing three days later, he displayed "fine form." Eight errors (!) cost him the July 31 game against St. Thomas, despite combining with pitcher Hammond on a five-hitter, only one of which was charged to "Mulina." He allowed six hits and lost a fine 1–0 effort to Brantford on August 2; three bunched hits in the sixth sealed his fate.

On August 4, London named second baseman Wally Hartwell as manager, replacing Reisling; the newspaper said Reisling was "not a driver . . . he might have got better results had he refrained from treating some players like human beings."

The next day was a spectacular one for "Mike Mulina." He pitched both halves of a doubleheader against the Guelph (Ontario) Maple Leafs and nearly won them both. Only a bad first inning in the first game (six runs scored while he was "wild as a hawk" before settling down) prevented him from winning both. After the one bad frame, he allowed just three runs for the rest of the day. London lost the first game, 8–5, and won the second, 3–1. He was 2-for-7 at the plate.

On August 9, he won an efficient 6–0 shutout and then beat St. Thomas 9–1 just five days later. An August 18 pitch buzzed by the head of Ottawa pitcher Urban

Shocker ("Herb" Shocker in the London paper) and he had words with Molyneaux, who charged the Ottawa batter and hit Shocker in the face. Shocker came back with a couple of haymakers before the two were separated. The Senators won the game, 2–1. Late in the year, there was one game when "Mulina" played right field, batting ninth, going 0-for-3 at the plate, and never making a play on a ball. On the final day of the year, he won a three-hitter against St. Thomas, 3–0, on a day when both games of the doubleheader were completed in a combined one hour and 55 minutes.

Molyneaux finished the year with a 6–4 record on the mound and a .162 average (6-for-37) at the plate. All six hits were singles. As far as *Free Press* readers ever knew, however, this was the record of a man named Mike Mulina.

Vince pitched for Villanova again in 1916, and had a record of 8–4. The *Boston Globe* first took notice on June 6, 1916 with a story headed "Red Sox in the Bidding." The story, filed from Philadelphia the day before, reported "Vincent Molyneaux, star pitcher of the Villa Nova [sic] College baseball team, who has bested the University of Pennsylvania, Penn State, and other strong college aggregations this year, has received five offers from major league clubs." The report ended, "Molyneaux, who is a big right-hander with speed, good curves, change of pace, and an easy pitching motion that should make him last for years if he proves good enough to stay in fast company, has just completed his sophomore year at Villa Nova, but is willing to play professional ball if he gets what he considers a fair offer." Both Philadelphia teams, the White Sox, the Red Sox, and the Cincinnati Reds had expressed interest.

"He was one of those students who favored summer ball," reported the *Chicago Tribune*'s James Crusinberry in his special report from Philadelphia on July 14, and found Molyneaux more than ready to play. According to Crusinberry, Molyneaux had just graduated Villanova and was looking for a job with the White Sox. The writer's story said, "When the Sox arrived, they found a new pitcher waiting to become one of them.... Immediately after lunch the recruit went to the ball park and was fitted up with a big league suit. He was to be allowed to pitch to the batters during their practice session, but the rain spoiled his chance. He will work out tomorrow before the eyes of the manager and will do the same for several days. If he shows class he may be retained or farmed to some minor league team to get experience."

Apparently, he hadn't graduated, since he was pitching once more for Villanova on May 3, 1917, throwing a three-hitter against the University of Pennsylvania — but losing 3–0. It wasn't too long after school ended he was brought into the St. Louis Browns offices and, after a conference with manager Fielder Jones, signed a contract at the behest of his escort, Browns scout Charlie Kelchner.

Pitchers Eddie Plank and Tom Rogers were both ailing and the team needed some help.

The signing was announced on June 7 and Molyneaux debuted at home against the visiting Cleveland Indians on July 5, just a few weeks before he turned 29. He pitched very well in relief, allowing just two hits and one run in five full innings, but granting four bases on balls in the process. He struck out two. Thrown into the game the next day, too, Molyneaux walked two more and gave up three hits, tagged for two earned runs in $2\frac{2}{3}$ innings of middle relief. On July 11, Molyneaux walked five more batters and gave up four hits in another five innings, charged with three earned runs. On the 15th, facing the Boston Red Sox, once more he pitched in middle relief (the Browns lost every one of these games). He pitched the eighth, allowing just one hit, but when he walked the first two Red Sox in the top of the ninth, he was pulled from the game. The next pitcher induced a double play and got out of the inning; neither runner scored, and the game ended in a 6–3 defeat for the Browns.

Molyneaux, though, was hardly "lights out" as a reliever, and it appears he worked throwing batting practice awaiting another appearance for nearly six weeks. Vincent next pitched the ninth inning in an 8–0 August 27 loss to Philadelphia, with one walk, one hit, three runs (one earned) in one inning of work. During the August 30 game in Chicago, he took over as the third Browns pitcher after the first two yielded six runs in the first two innings. St. Louis manager Fielder Jones "sent a kid named Molineaux [sic] to the slab." Vince completed the game, allowing two runs in six innings, walking four and striking out two, giving up six hits, but batting 0-for-2 at the plate.

In Cleveland on September 3, he came on in middle relief during the morning game and was ineffective, with two walks and two hits in $1\frac{1}{3}$ innings — allowing a few more runs. He threw a wild pitch and struck out one. He compiled a 4.91 ERA in 22 innings of work, giving up 18 hits and 15 runs (12 earned). His strikeouts-to-walks ratio was the inverse of the desired one: he struck out four but walked 20.

At the end of spring training 1918, as he was leaving St. Louis with his team to open the season in Chicago, Browns business manager Bob Quinn gave Molyneaux his unconditional release, announced on Opening Day, April 16. The *St. Louis Star* wrote, "An over-abundance of right-handers on the Browns resulted in his release." The Cardinals pounced and signed him the same day. Branch Rickey had his eye on "the collegiate hurler" (as he was described by the *St. Louis Post-Dispatch*) the year before but had lost out when Vincent had been signed by the Browns. The Cardinals were in financial straits; at one point in the first half of May they were down to 17 players on the team, and Rickey was wheeling and dealing. Still, Molyneaux failed to sufficiently impress; he was given his release on May 7 and the *Star* politely wrote, "As manager Hendricks' pitchers have been hurling good ball, he was unable to find a place for the former collegian." Apparently the team "tried to place him with in a minor league" but Vincent may have declined, hoping instead for another shot at The Show.

If such was his plan, it may have paid off. Two weeks after his release, on May 21, Boston's Ed Barrow announced the signing of "Molyneaux, the former crack Villanova right-hander." The brief report in the *Boston Globe* said, "Molyneaux recommended himself to the Sox and as some of the Boston players had seen him in action, Barrow decided to take him on. He will report today or tomorrow." He reported in Boston on the 23rd, and was immediately put to work pitching batting practice. That may have been the reason Barrow signed him. A July 24 comment in the *Boston Herald* indicated he was a pitcher "Barrow picked up because he had absolutely no practice-flingers."

He got a chance to play, though, and his Red Sox debut came in Boston during the second game of a Memorial Day morning/afternoon doubleheader against Washington. The Red Sox won the first game with ease, 9–1, but Dick McCabe allowed four runs in eight innings and the Red Sox failed to score in the second game. Molyneaux pitched the ninth inning, without allowing a man to reach first base.

On June 7, the Indians worked 11 walks off six Red Sox pitchers and slammed out 13 hits and took the game, 14–7. Neither Dutch Leonard nor Joe Bush, nor Babe Ruth, nor "Victor" [sic] Molyneaux, nor Sam Jones, nor "McCabe, a batting practice hurler" could stop them. Molyneaux walked two and threw two wild pitches in his $2/3$ of an inning, but didn't give up a hit.

He appeared in the second game of a June 20 Fenway Park doubleheader and walked a couple of batters but helped preserve Leonard's 3–0 shutout of the Athletics after Tillie Walker's line drive injured Leonard's hand in the sixth and forced him to leave the game. Molyneaux came on in relief and threw $3 2/3$ innings of hitless relief, picking up his only major league decision — a win — when the Red Sox scored all three of their runs in the bottom of the sixth.

On July 3, Lore Bader started the game and threw the first seven innings, allowing five runs. Red Bluhm batted for Bader in the top of the eighth (Bluhm's only appearance in a major league game), and Vince pitched the bottom of the eighth — the two hits and a walk, and one run made little difference in the 6–0 Philly win. The next day — Independence Day — Vince took over for Sad Sam Jones in the sixth inning of the first game in Philadelphia and got the Sox out of the inning before Joe Bush took over for him in the seventh. He'd recorded three outs over the two innings but he'd walked two in the seventh, and the *Boston Herald* wrote, "Molyneux (sic) didn't allow a

hit, but Barrow was afraid he might, and preferred to take a chance with Bush." Molyneaux was "hit hard" in a July 14 exhibition game against Queen Quality of Jamaica Plain, though the Sox won the Woonsocket RI game, 5–2.

The Browns beat the Red Sox on the 18th, and "Molly" (as the *Boston Record* called him) threw the final three innings, allowing just one hit and one run on a walk, a sacrifice, and a single. His outing earned him a subhead in the *Boston Daily Advertiser*: "Molyneaux Does Well When Given Chance to Finish Game." Like in London, this paper also called him Mike Molyneaux; Vince and Squinch and Molly were not his only nicknames. At the plate for the Red Sox, he'd batted only twice and struck out both times. When it was his turn to bat in this game, there was one out in the Boston ninth. Barrow had Carl Mays, another pitcher, hit for him, and Mays ended the game grounding into a double play.

The next day, July 19, Molyneaux was given his outright release to the Jersey City Skeeters (International League). Molyneaux balked, though, and said he would not go. The *Boston Herald* wrote, "Vincent had a chance to go to the Jersey City team but passed it up and got the blue envelope instead." The July 20 *Globe* reported: "Molyneaux says that the Red Sox did not have to pay a cent for him, that he wrote asking for work and they signed him. He says that they have no right to sell him now and he intends to make an issue of the matter. He insists that he has the goods as a big league pitcher and knows of several clubs that will give him employment if he becomes a free agent. What work Molyneaux has done for the Sox he did well." It's true he was 1–0 with a 3.38 ERA in $10 2/3$ innings of work, and had only given up three hits to the 43 batters he faced, but (as with the Browns) he had an "upside-down" walks to strikeouts ratio (one strikeout, eight walks), and threw two wild pitches. There was at least one untoward moment after his release. "Molyneaux says that an effort was made to bar him from the clubhouse yesterday," noted the *Globe*.

Even if there were several other clubs interested, Molyneaux suffered from poor timing. The next day Ban Johnson ordered all American League ballclubs to cease operations within 48 hours. Though his order never went into effect, it was just a week after Molyneaux's release that Secretary of War Baker announced the baseball season should end on September 1. Teams were not looking for new players, and one could hazard a guess that announcing plans to "make an issue" regarding his employment would not have endeared him to the magnates of the game under any circumstances.

Vincent returned to Niagara Falls in 1918 and went to work for "the Aluminum company" — likely a job he undertook as an alternative to military service during the World War. Molyneaux pitched one inning for the Salt Lake City Bees (Pacific Coast League) in 1919. He'd been acquired in March and the *Salt Lake Herald* reported manager Eddie Herr was "sweet on pitcher Molyneaux." Herr had worked as a scout for the Browns and knew Molyneaux, who joined the Bees during spring training on March 23. He was apparently not in the best of shape as a *Herald* note on April 5 reported him having the only sore arm in camp; a week and a half later, the *Salt Lake Telegram* reported his arm giving him "considerable trouble." An earlier report in the April 15 *Herald* described Molyneaux (and his windup) as "the man with the 'special delivery' — a style that is all his own." He had a spitter as well "that it is declared has some stuff on it."

His one inning late in the April 24 game against Los Angeles was far from successful: he retired no one, allowed two earned runs, and lost the game. The winning pitcher was former Red Sox teammate Bill Pertica. It was a bad outing, and Bees manager Herr wasn't in a patient mood. Writing in the *Los Angeles Times*, Harry A. Williams told the story: "Monsieur Molyneaux started. That remark about covers his career. M. Molyneaux began slipping as soon as he started, and didn't stop until he had slipped clear out of the park." The first batter he faced was Red Killefer, who walked. Then he threw a wild pitch that was so wild that Herr apparently shouted, "Come out of that!" Williams wrote that the Salt Lake manager's "anguished bellow could be heard all over the park." There was no one warming up. Herr just wanted him out of there. The final score was 7–1, Los Angeles, so Molyneaux took the loss. It was his windup that caused concern, one that Williams called an "eight-day windup." The game story said Molyneaux "has a most complicated delivery, indicating that he is an athlete of complex mechanism…when he would finish winding up, he appeared to have lost his sense of direction, not being sure whether [first baseman] Earl Sheely or [catcher] Tub Spencer was behind the plate. So he played safe by throwing the ball into neutral territory." Even though relief pitcher Schorr finished walking the second Angels batter, the walk was assigned to Molyneaux. Both runners subsequently scored.

Herr already had his eye on a replacement, and wasted little time making a move. The *Salt Lake Herald* headlined its story: Molyneaux Jerked Off Rubber After Skyscraper Throws: Is Released. Researcher Craig Fuller offered some detail from the paper's account: "Weird pitching cost Salt Lake the game today. It also cost pitcher Molyneaux his job after he had tossed up six consecutive balls, the last of which was ten feet about Spencer's head. Manager Herr wigwagged him from the mound and thereupon decided to release him." Al Gould joined the pitching staff the next day, and Molyneaux was reported heading back east.

It was Molyneaux's last appearance in professional baseball. A May 15 *Reading Times* article reported — it was deemed headline material — "Vin" Molyneaux had arrived in Reading and had agreed to terms offered him by the Reading ballclub's assistant manager, Charlie Kelchner. Molyneaux had wisely sought out Kelchner, the scout who'd signed him to the Browns two years earlier. The team was on the road at the time and Kelchner wired manager Red Dooin asking whether Molyneaux should join the team or await their return. Just two weeks later, without ever appearing in a game for Reading, he was released. The May 29 *Times* explained, "His arm is not in shape and the team could not afford to carry him along."

It was apparently not long after his abortive attempt to continue in baseball that Molyneaux began work as an auditor with the United States Government. He developed a heart condition in 1949 and died on May 4, 1950 in Stamford, Connecticut. The death certificate describes him as a "retired traveling accountant U.S. Gov. R.F.C." and indicates he had been living in Stamford for two years. (R.F.C. almost certainly refer to the Reconstruction Finance Corporation.)

The city directory in Stamford shows him as living at 369 Atlantic Street in 1950 — the address was, at the time, the address of the YMCA. Molyneaux had been married earlier in life, but his obituary indicates he was survived only by two cousins, Mrs. Samuel Johnson and Mrs. Harold Flynn. Funeral services were held at Sacred Heart Church in Niagara Falls, and he was buried at St. Mary's Cemetery. The *Niagara Falls Gazette* obituary described Molyneaux as "probably one of the finest hurlers in baseball history in Niagara Falls."

BILL PERTICA *by Bill Nowlin*

G	ERA	W	L	SV	GS	GF	CG	SHO	IP	H	R	ER	BB	SO	HR	HBP	WP	BFP
1	3.00	0	0	0	0	0	0	0	3	3	1	1	0	1	0	0	0	11

G	AB	R	H	2B	3B	HR	RBI	BB	SO	BA	OBP	SLG	SB	HBP
1	1	0	0	0	0	0	0	0	0	.000	.000	.000	0	0

Bill Pertica was a right-handed pitching prospect who showed promise early in his career, had one prime season with the Cardinals, and ultimately faded into obscurity. He was born in Santa Barbara, California, on

August 17, 1898, and made the big leagues (albeit about as briefly as possible) in his first year of pro ball.

Pertica was short in stature at 5-foot-9 (some sources list him as 5'7"), but he had a major league arm. His listed weight was 165 pounds. Almost nothing is known about his early life. His father, Frank J. Pertica, was a saloonkeeper in Santa Barbara at the time of the 1900 United States Census, and he lived with his wife, Martina, and their three sons, Frank A. (born in 1894), Roberto (born in 1897), and Angelo (born in August 1898 and apparently later known as William Andrew Pertica). Frank's father was born in Italy; his mother in California.

Bill Pertica first crops up in the *Los Angeles Times* during spring training of 1918. The March 19 edition labeled the 19-year-old Los Angeles Angels (Pacific Coast League) pitcher as "one of the most promising recruits on the squad." Just a couple of weeks later the paper reaffirmed the assessment while commenting on his final spring training outing: "Pertica, who pitched the second real game of his career, showed that he is one of the most promising youngsters that ever ambled to a mound. The newcomer is already a find...has already shown an assortment of heaves that are baffling in the extreme." He lost that game, 4–2, but pitched well enough that it was said he'd have won eight of 10 such games; he was "calm and steady as a veteran, and always had control."

His professional debut came on April 5 and earned him a *Times* subhead reading "Dazzling Debut is Made by Mister Pertica." He threw a spitball—legal at the time—but it was just one pitch in his repertoire. His poise was noted: Pertica "appears to have the hall mark of sterling quality," the *Times* wrote. "At no time during proceedings did he wobble in the least."

Pertica started for the Angels in 1918 and appeared in 23 games, completing 14 and totting up a 12–7 record (2.25 ERA) in 180 innings of work. With the U.S. now in World War I and a "work or fight" order in effect, player after player in the majors enrolled in industries deemed essential to the war effort, or enlisted, and the ranks of a number of teams were drastically depleted. The PCL was forced to end its season early, and the July 27 *Times* reported the departure of four Angels who had been able to secure slots with major league teams. Jack Quinn, Ray Mitchell, and Al DeVormer all were to leave L.A. that day for the White Sox, while "Bill Pertica, the child wonder," had landed a job with the Red Sox. Perhaps not coincidentally, Pertica was under the age 21–31 draft age.

His first and last official game with the Red Sox came on August 7 in Detroit. Joe Bush started for the Red Sox but was hit mercilessly and was tagged with six runs in

Bill Pertica, 1920. Courtesy of the Mark Macrae Collection.

the first inning and one more in the second. Pertica came in to pitch the third and threw three innings, allowing just one run in the fourth when the Tigers secured two of their three hits off him. Manager Barrow had pitcher Jean Dubuc pinch-hit for Pertica in the sixth; he drew a base on balls. Pertica had hit once for himself, but for an out—a career 0-for-1 in American League action.

Pertica traveled with the team to Boston, one of several new arrivals on the Red Sox, who pulled into town on August 10—the others being Dubuc, George Cochran, Eusebio Gonzalez, and Hack Miller. The only other action that Pertica saw with the Red Sox, though, was in an exhibition game at New Haven on August 18. The Sox lost to the New Haven Colonials in a 4–3 game in front of about 3,000 fans at Lighthouse Point. Pertica started the game and threw six innings, giving up six hits (one a first-inning triple by Wally Pipp, who scored on third baseman George Cochran's error) and all four Colonials runs. The game account suggests that all four runs were unearned. He struck out five, but walked four and committed two errors. Walt Kinney closed it out with two hitless innings. There was just one home run hit in the game, by Babe Ruth.

When it came time for the World Series, Pertica joined both Dubuc and Kinney as backup pitchers on the roster, but the only action any of them saw was at the plate: one strikeout by Dubuc in a Game Two pinch-hitting role. When the Red Sox party traveled to Chicago, Barrow took the whole club with him "even little Pertica, who he at one time thought he would leave in Boston." (*Boston Globe*) Pertica's contribution to Series play involved a little expectorant. He threw batting practice to help Red Sox hitters. Since Cubs relievers Phil Douglas and Claude Hendrix were known to be "exponents of the damp delivery" (*Boston Globe*), Pertica—himself a "moist ball chucker"—pitched in. He earned a $300 Series share, the same as late arrivals Cochran, Coffey, Dubuc, Kinney, and Miller. A full share was $1,108.45. Pertica awaited an expected call to the Navy, leaving Boston for his home out west on a September 13 train.

Pertica got in a bit of post-Series play, traveling from Los Angeles to Santa Barbara to play for the United States Railway team in early October. He kept active at least occasionally over the winter, being reported as playing in a mid-January game in Hollywood. The Red Sox still had their eye on him. The March 5, 1919, *Los Angeles Times* wrote that Ed Barrow was "discovering a glad eye on 'Solemn Bill' Pertica. For some time local fans had been led to believe that Bill would don Angelic array this spring." However, the paper said, Barrow had sent an offer to the Angels to purchase his contract. The offer, the *Times* explained in a gratuitously anti-Semitic comment, was one "with an eye centered on the Yiddish percentage" — he dropped the purchase price from $2,500 down to $1,000, "giving as his reason that Pertica is not as yet matured enough to be more than a volunteer of the Red Sox roster." Angels owner Johnny Powers was "not averse to letting Bill go, but would rather make use of him in a trade with the Red Sox than sell him outright. Pertica's fingers have already felt the ecstatic thrill of a world's series split, and the chances are that he will sign for eastern climes."

Barrow reportedly offered the Angels outfielder George Whiteman and another player for him, but Powers and Angels manager Red Killefer declined. Angels business manager Jim Morley explained, "We don't want to stand in Pertica's way, but if we let him go we must get something good in return.... I regard Pertica as the most promising young pitcher that ever broke into the Coast League." High praise indeed.

"Silent Bill" pitched a full two seasons for the Angels, in 1919 and 1920. He won 17 games (though he lost 20) in 1919, with a 3.24 ERA, and was 15–13 with a 2.83 ERA in 1920, throwing 602 innings in the two seasons. He started the first year well, even throwing a no-hitter through $8^2/_3$ innings on May 10 against the San Francisco Seals. The *Times* wrote with verve, "His spitter and fast drop were simply unfathomable at all times and as for speed, he shot 'em over the plate as fast as a cyclone whizzes past milestones in a graveyard." His season was one of ups and downs. He won 1–0 games against Portland on August 2 and over Sacramento on August 23, but threw away a game on July 25, a costly error earning him the subhead "Pertica Gives Lurid Exhibition of Throwing Pill." Summarizing the season in early October, the paper declared, "'Solemn Bill' has been an in-and-outer, but when right is practically unbeatable." November rumors had Pertica being packed off to the Phillies, but come February, the Angels had once again concluded that they weren't being offered good enough value.

The 1920 campaign was another up-and down one for Peretica. As of the end of June, he was the PCL's leading pitcher — but on July 9 the "slugging Mormons" from Salt Lake City drubbed him for 12 hits and six runs and he had to leave after just $1^2/_3$ innings. Six days later, "Bill had

Pertica with the 1918 Red Sox. Detail from the 1919 *Reach Official Base Ball Guide.*

little or nothing on the pill." He regained his form, losing a tough 1–0 game to Vernon on July 23 and another even tougher 1–0 loss to Portland in early August during which he threw all 15 innings. In mid-December, it was reported that he'd been dealt to the Cubs, but the deal fell through when the Cubs failed to exercise an option. In early January of 1921, the St. Louis Cardinals announced that they had acquired Pertica for three players: Ed Bogart, Dorsey Carroll, and George Lyons.

Pertica subsequently traveled to Japan with a group of ballplayers for a tour that proved a financial bust and resulted in mutiny by several of the players. He'd played exhibition games before the Japanese trip, playing with Ty Cobb as his center fielder for a game he threw in a San Francisco uniform on November 15. He pitched and lost the third of three games to the Colored All-Stars while working for Pirrone's Major Leaguers team in a weekend tournament; Pertica's wild pitch in the bottom of the ninth brought home the winning run. In mid-February, back from Japan, a confusing report surfaced in the *L.A. Times*, saying that Pertica and catcher Johnny Bassler were involved in a trade for Tigers veteran Oscar Stanage, a deal that somehow resulted in Bassler playing with Detroit while Pertica wound up with the St. Louis Cardinals. A profile of legendary scout Charley Barrett in the January 24, 1935, issue of *The Sporting News* credits Barrett with recommending Pertica to the Cardinals.

Pertica was particular about signing with St. Louis, however. He planned to object if the Cardinals farmed him out to Seattle, and he returned their contract when they offered $3,000 instead of the $4,500 he felt he deserved. The *Los Angeles Times* noted, "Most unbiased baseball men ... will regard his demands as unreasonable." Branch Rickey invited him to come to spring training to talk it over, but Pertica requested a roundtrip ticket in case the two failed to come to agreement. They reached agreement, though, and Bill pitched well for St. Louis in 1921. In 31 starts and seven relief stints, he won 14 games and lost 10, with a 3.37 ERA. *The Sporting News* noted Pertica's "Sunday school disposition" — maybe another allusion to the "Solemn Bill" nickname.

Bill struggled with the Cardinals in 1922, but still appeared in 34 games — though starting just 15 of them. His record was 8–8, but with a very discouraging 5.91 ERA. After the season, Pertica again played ball in the wintertime, in the California Winter League. He did so with Branch Rickey's encouragement. "One reason for a willingness to let Pertica continue work is that he has been trying to develop something besides the spitball he started out with," wrote *The Sporting News* on January 25, 1923. Pertica had not been one of the 17 pitchers who were grandfathered in when the spitball was banned in 1920 and his decline in 1922 was attributed to doing without his spitter. Ty Cobb was quoted as saying, "I don't see how the Detroit scouts ever overlooked him." The Tigers tried to trade Red Oldham for him, but once more something went wrong—Oldham was suspended for playing winter ball without permission—and Oldham wound up in the Coast League instead.

Despite his drop in 1922, the Cardinals kept him on for 1923, but he appeared in only one game before he was traded to Houston of the Texas League. The *Los Angeles Times* noted the trade, which proved to put an end to his major league career: Pertica "was with the Cardinals two years but was unable to win in major company so Branch Rickey shipped him to his Texas League club." The June 7 *Sporting News* said Pertica had failed to get along with Houston and was transferred from Houston to Memphis on the orders of St. Louis, that the Cardinals sent Lester Bell to Houston to replace Pertica, and that Pertica "attributes his poor work to a sore soup bone." Whether Pertica was sent to Houston in a true trade or an arrangement of another kind is unclear. He never appeared in a game for Memphis. Even against lesser competition, Pertica had found it difficult in Houston. He threw 50 innings, but was 1–4 with a 5.58 ERA. He walked 30 and struck out but 14. He apparently had broken one of the small bones in his arm, according to a report from Houston in January 31, 1924 *Sporting News*, and when properly diagnosed, he wore a cast until it healed.

Come 1924, the comeback failed as he again appeared in only seven games for Houston, for 32 innings, and posted a sorry 0–5 record with a 9.56 ERA. He missed much of the season due to an injured arm. It's not surprising that he retired from baseball, though he was still pitching semipro ball for the Pasadena Merchants in a January 1, 1925, game against Gilmore Oil. Pasadena lost, 4–3. Ultimately, Bill decided he didn't have what it took and he is listed as "voluntarily retired" from 1925 through 1930. He made his way to New York at some point and was living in Brooklyn at the time of the 1930 U.S. Census.

As a hitter, Pertica was no great shakes. Whether in the PCL or the major leagues, in the years he had 20 or more at-bats, the highest he ever hit was .206 in 1919 with the Angels. All told, he hit .174 in pro ball, .152 in the major leagues.

Surprisingly, after six years out of organized baseball, Pertica shows up as pitching for the Scranton Miners in 1931. In midsummer, he was in touch with manager Ernie Vick (with whom he'd played in St. Louis), agreed to terms, and kicked off his Scranton career as the starting pitcher in an exhibition game against the World Champion Philadelphia Athletics on August 5. The A's were leading the American League by a full 12 games at the time. The game ended in a 1–1 tie after nine innings, when the overflow crowd swarmed onto the field and it was impossible to continue. Despite the low score, Pertica's performance—in the words of the *Scranton Republican*—"should be sent into 'Believe It or Not' Ripley." In four of the five innings he pitched, he loaded the bases but was touched for only the one run.

He pitched the second game of an August 13 doubleheader against the Hazleton Mountaineers and found the Scranton fans cheering for opposing Hazleton hitter Pat Wright. Wright was 3-for-3 in the first game, with a single, a double, and a home run. He walked once. He was 2-for-2 against Pertica in the second game with a triple and the two-run second-inning home run that proved the game winner. The fans wanted another homer, but Pertica didn't give him anything good to hit and he walked again. Pertica took the loss. His only other appearance was two-thirds of an inning in relief against Harrisburg on August 16. He was charged with one run, on two hits. The *Republican* wrote that being swept by last-place Hazleton essentially spoiled Scranton's chances for the pennant; the next day, Pertica was given his release. He was back home in Brooklyn the day after that. His line read 0–1 with 12 hits surrendered in eight innings.

Bill Pertica then disappears from the baseball record books. In fact, he pretty much disappears altogether. Despite being 43 at the time, he enlisted in the U.S. Army in 1942 but was discharged six months later, according to baseball researcher Dick Beverage. He was inducted on August 28, 1942, and stationed at Camp McQuaide in California. Researcher Walter Kephart says that was the West Coast Processing Center for AWOL servicemen and other "troublemakers"—sort of a stockade—and that Pertica was serving in the Military Police Section, Headquarters Detachment at the time of his discharge on February 20, 1943. Army records do not indicate the type of discharge, so we are left to speculate that he may have become involved in a fracas of some sort and become injured; it may simply be that he became ill. What we do know is that he was sent to San Francisco's Letterman General Hospital on February 8, on to Hammond General Hospital in Modesto, and was discharged from there on February 20.

What he did after discharge is not known, but he perhaps returned to the L.A. area to work as a bartender. In September 1950, he was invited to the silver anniversary of Los Angeles' Wrigley Field to play in an old-timers game there. On the last day of March, 1953, *Los Angeles Times* writer Braven Dyer wrote, "The last I heard of Bill, he was tending bar in Boyle Heights, which seems appropriate as it was in the Stag Saloon right across the street from Jim Jeffries' bar that Red Killefer signed him to an Angel contract. Walter McCredie walked through the swinging doors two minutes later with a contract that would have landed Pertica with Portland and later Cleveland." Dyer characterized Pertica as "an unknown Mexican lad from a Santa Barbara hacienda" but in this we suspect Dyer erred. Pertica was more likely of Italian ancestry, though

attempts to trace his lineage have so far proven fruitless.

Bill Pertica died on December 28, 1967, at his home in Los Angeles and is buried in the Willamette National Cemetery, just outside Portland, Oregon — a final resting place run by the Veterans Administration.

GEORGE HERMAN "BABE" RUTH *by Allan Wood*

G	AB	R	H	2B	3B	HR	RBI	BB	SO	BA	OBP	SLG	SB	HBP
95	317	50	95	26	11	11	66	58	58	.300	.411	.555	6	2

G	ERA	W	L	SV	GS	GF	CG	SHO	IP	H	R	ER	BB	SO	HR	HBP	WP	BFP
20	2.22	13	7	0	19	0	18	1	166⅓	125	51	41	49	40	1	2	3	660

During his five full seasons with the Boston Red Sox, Babe Ruth established himself as one of the premier left-handed pitchers in the game, began his historic transformation from moundsman to slugging outfielder, and was part of three World Series championship teams. After he was sold to the New York Yankees in December 1919, his eye-popping batting performances over the next few seasons helped usher in a new era of long-distance hitting and high scoring, effectively bringing down the curtain on the Deadball Era.

George Herman Ruth was born to George Ruth and Catherine Schamberger on February 6, 1895, in his mother's parents' house at 216 Emory Street, in Baltimore, Maryland. With his father working long hours in his saloon and his mother often in poor health, Little George (as he was known) spent his days unsupervised on the waterfront streets and docks, committing petty theft and vandalism. Hanging out in his father's bar, he stole money from the till, drained the last drops from old beer glasses, and developed a taste for chewing tobacco. He was only six years old.

Shortly after his seventh birthday, the Ruths petitioned the Baltimore courts to declare Little George "incorrigible" and sent him to live at St. Mary's Industrial School, on the outskirts of the city. The boy's initial stay at St. Mary's lasted only four weeks before his parents brought him home for the first of several attempted reconciliations; his long-term residence at St. Mary's actually began in 1904. But it was during that first stay that George met Brother Matthias.

"He taught me to read and write and he taught me the difference between right and wrong," Ruth said of the Canadian-born priest. "He was the father I needed and the greatest man I've ever known." Brother Matthias also spent many afternoons tossing a worn-out baseball in the air and swatting it out to the boys. Little George watched, bug-eyed. "I had never seen anything like that in my life," he recalled. "I think I was born as a hitter the first day I ever saw him hit a baseball." The impressionable

Babe Ruth, bat in hand.

youngster imitated Matthias's hitting style — gripping the bat tightly down at the knobbed end, taking a big swing at the ball — as well as his way of running with quick, tiny steps.

When asked in 1918 about playing baseball at St. Mary's, Ruth said he had little difficulty anywhere on the field. "Sometimes I pitched. Sometimes I caught, and frequently I played the outfield and infield. It was all the same to me. All I wanted was to play. I didn't care much where." In one St. Mary's game in 1913, Ruth, then 18 years old, caught, played third base (even though he threw left-handed), and pitched, striking out six men, and collecting a double, a triple, and a home run. That summer, he was allowed to pitch with local amateur and semipro teams on weekends. Impressed with his performances, Jack Dunn signed Ruth to his minor league Baltimore Orioles club the following February.

Although he was a bumpkin with minimal social skills, at camp in South Carolina Ruth quickly distinguished

Ruth warming up on the sidelines, 1917. Courtesy of Chicago History Museum.

In 1916, Ruth won 23 games and posted a league-leading 1.75 ERA. He also threw nine shutouts — an American League record for left-handed pitchers that still stands (it was tied in 1978 by the Yankees' Ron Guidry). In Game Two of the World Series, Ruth pitched all 14 innings, beating the Brooklyn Dodgers, 2–1. Boston topped Brooklyn in the series four games to one.

Ruth's success went straight to his head in 1917, and he began arguing with umpires about their strike zone judgment. Facing Washington on June 23, Ruth walked the Senators' first batter on four pitches. Feeling squeezed by home plate umpire Brick Owens, Ruth stormed off the mound and punched Owens in the head. After Ruth was ejected, Ernie Shore came in to relieve. The baserunner was thrown out trying to steal and Shore retired the next 26 batters for an unofficial perfect game. Ruth got off lightly with a 10-day suspension and a $100 fine. He ended the year with a 24–13 record, completing 35 of his 38 starts, with six shutouts and an ERA of 2.01.

Although Ruth didn't play every day until May 1918, the idea of putting him in the regular lineup was first mentioned in the press during his rookie season. Calling Babe "one of the best natural sluggers ever in the game," Washington sportswriter Paul Eaton thought Ruth "might even be more valuable in some regular position than he is on the slab — a free suggestion for Manager [Bill] Carrigan." The *Boston Post* reported that summer that Babe "cherishes the hope that he may someday be the leading slugger of the country."

In 1915, Ruth batted .315 and topped the Red Sox with four home runs. Braggo Roth led the AL with seven homers, but he had 384 at-bats compared with Babe's 92. Ruth didn't have enough at-bats to qualify, but his .576 slugging percentage was higher than those of the official leaders in the American League (Jack Fournier .491), the National League (Gavvy Cravath .510), and the Federal League (Benny Kauff .509).

With the Red Sox offense sputtering after the sale of Tris Speaker in 1916, the suggestion to play Ruth every day was renewed when he tied a record by hitting a home run in three consecutive games. Ruth hated the helpless

himself on the diamond. That spring, the Orioles played several major league teams. In two outings against the Phillies, Ruth faced 29 batters and allowed only six hits and two unearned runs. The next week, he threw a complete game victory over the Philadelphia Athletics, winners of three of the last four World Series. Short of cash that summer, Dunn sold Ruth to the Boston Red Sox.

On July 11, 1914, less than five months after leaving St. Mary's, Babe made his debut at Fenway Park: He pitched seven innings against Cleveland and received credit for a 4–3 win. After being hit hard by Detroit in his second outing, Ruth rode the bench until he was demoted to the minor leagues in mid-August, where he helped the Providence Grays capture the International League pennant. Ruth returned to Boston for the final week of the 1914 season. On October 2, he pitched a complete game victory over the Yankees and doubled for his first major league hit.

Babe spent the winter in Baltimore with his new wife, Boston waitress Helen Woodford, and in 1915, he stuck with the big club. Ruth slumped early in the season, in part because of excessive carousing with fellow pitcher Dutch Leonard, and a broken toe — sustained by kicking the bench in frustration after being intentionally walked — that kept him out of the rotation for two weeks. But when he returned, he shined, winning three complete games in a span of nine days in June. Between June 1 and September 2, Ruth was 13–1 and ended the season 18–8.

feeling of sitting on the bench between pitching assignments, and believed he could be a better hitter if given more opportunity. In mid-season, with all three Boston outfielders in slumps, Carrigan was reportedly ready to give Babe a shot, but it never happened. Ruth finished the 1917 season at .325, easily the highest average on the team. Left fielder Duffy Lewis topped the regulars at .302; no one else hit above .265. Giving Ruth an everyday job remained nothing more than an entertaining game of "what if" — until 1918.

In April of 1917, the United States had entered the Great War; many players had enlisted or accepted war-related jobs before the season began. Trying to strengthen the Red Sox offense, about two weeks into the season, manager Ed Barrow, after discussions with right fielder and team captain Harry Hooper, penciled Ruth into the lineup. The move came only a few days after a Boston paper reported that team owner Harry Frazee had refused an offer of $100,000 for Ruth. "It is ridiculous to talk about it," Frazee said. "Ruth is our Big Ace. He's the most talked of, most sought for, most colorful ball player in the game." Later reports revealed that the offer had come from the Yankees.

On May 6, 1918, in the Polo Grounds against the Yankees, Ruth played first base and batted sixth. It was the first time he had appeared in a game other than as a pitcher or pinch-hitter and the first time he batted in any spot other than ninth. Ruth went 2-for-4, including a two-run home run. At that point, five of Ruth's 11 career home runs had come in New York. The *Boston Post*'s Paul Shannon began his game story, "Babe Ruth still remains the hitting idol of the Polo Grounds."

The next day, against the Senators, Ruth was bumped up to fourth in the lineup — he hit another home run — where he stayed for most of the season. Barrow also wanted Ruth to continue pitching, but Babe, enjoying the notoriety his hitting was generating, often feigned exhaustion or a sore arm to avoid the mound. The two men argued about Ruth's playing time for several weeks. Finally, after one heated exchange in early July, Ruth quit the team. He returned after a few days and, after renegotiating his contract with Frazee to include some hitting-related bonuses, patched up his disagreements with Barrow.

"I don't think a man can pitch in his regular turn, and play every other game at some other position, and keep that pace year after year," Ruth said. "I can do it this season all right, and not feel it, for I am young and strong and don't mind the work. But I wouldn't guarantee to do it for many seasons." [*Baseball Magazine*, October 1918]

Ruth then began what is likely the greatest nine- or ten-week stretch of play in baseball history. From mid-July to early September 1918, Ruth pitched every fourth day, and played either left field, center field, or first base on the other days. Ruth's double duty was not unique

during the Deadball Era — a handful of players had done both — but his level of success was (and remains) unprecedented. In one 10-game stretch at Fenway, Ruth hit .469 (15-for-32) and slugged .969 with four singles, six doubles, and five triples. He was remarkably adept at first base, his favorite position. On the mound, he allowed more than two runs only once in his last 10 starts. The Colossus, as Babe was known in Boston, maintained his status as a top pitcher while simultaneously becoming the game's greatest hitter.

Ruth's performance led the Red Sox to the American League pennant, in a season cut short by the owners, partially because of dwindling attendance. All draft-age men were under government order to either enlist or take war-related employment — in shipyards or munitions factories, for example — which led to paltry turnouts of less than 1,000 for many afternoon games that summer.

Ruth opened the World Series on September 5 against the Chicago Cubs with a 1–0 shutout. He pitched well in Game Four, despite having bruised his left hand during some horseplay on the train back to Boston, and his double drove in what turned out to be the winning runs. Those performances, together with his extra-inning outing in 1916, gave Ruth a record of $29^2/_3$ consecutive scoreless World Series innings, one of the records Ruth always said he was most proud of. His scoreless streak was finally broken by Whitey Ford of the Yankees in the 1960s.

While with the Red Sox, Ruth often arranged for busloads of orphans to visit his farm in Sudbury for a day-long picnic and ballgame, making sure each kid left with a glove and an autographed baseball. When the Red Sox were at home, Ruth would arrive at Fenway Park early on Saturday mornings to help the vendors — mostly boys in their early teens — bag peanuts for the upcoming week's games.

"He'd race with us to see who could bag the most," recalled Tom Foley, who was 14 years old in 1918. (Ruth was barely out of his teens himself.) "He'd talk a blue streak the whole time, telling us to be good boys and play baseball, because there was good money in it. He thought that if we worked hard enough, we could be as good as he was. But we knew better than that. He'd stay about an hour. When we finished, he'd pull out a $20 bill and throw it on the table and say 'Have a good time, kids.' We'd split it up, and each go home with an extra half-dollar or dollar depending on how many of us were there. Babe Ruth was an angel to us."[1]

To management, however, Ruth was a headache. His continued inability — or outright refusal — to adhere to the team's curfew earned him several suspensions and his nonstop salary demands infuriated Frazee. The Red Sox owner had spoken publicly about possibly trading Ruth before the 1919 season, when Babe was holding out for double his existing salary and threatening to become a boxer. However, Ruth and Frazee came to terms and the Babe's hitting made headlines across the country all season long. He played 111 games in left field, belted a record 29 home runs, and led the major leagues in slugging percentage (.657), on-base percentage (.456), runs scored (103), RBIs (114), and total bases (284). He drove in or scored one-third of Boston's runs. But while Ruth also won nine games on the mound, the rest of the staff fell victim to injuries and the defending champs finished in the second division with a 66–71 record.

The sale of Ruth to the Yankees was announced after New Year's Day 1920 and although it was big news, public opinion in Boston was divided. Many fans were aghast that such a talent would be cast off, while others, including many former players, insisted that a cohesive team (as opposed to one egomaniac plus everyone else) was the key to success.

Ruth with the Red Sox, 1914.
Courtesy of Chicago History Museum.

and a greater emphasis on the pursuit of pleasure. (Prohibition, instituted in 1920, had no effect whatsoever.) Sportswriter Westbrook Pegler called it "the Era of Wonderful Nonsense."

It was also a time when "trick pitches"—the emeryball, the spitter, and various ways of scuffing the ball—were outlawed. Both leagues began using a better quality (i.e., livelier) baseball. Ruth thrived—and over time, so did the players in both leagues.

The Babe got off to a slow start in 1920. He was in spring training for nearly three weeks before he crushed his first home run. Ruth also jumped into the stands to fight a fan who had called him "a big piece of cheese" (probably not a direct quote). While tracking a fly ball during an exhibition game in Miami, Ruth ran into a palm tree in center field and was knocked unconscious.

"[T]here is no getting away from the fact that despite his 29 home runs, the Red Sox finished sixth last year," Frazee said. "What the Boston fans want, I take it, and what I want because they want it, is a winning team, rather than a one-man team that finishes in sixth place." Frazee also called Ruth's home runs "more spectacular than useful."

He also intimated that the Yankees were taking a gamble on Ruth. It was a statement he would be later ridiculed for, but at the time the Yankees felt the same way. The amount paid ($125,000) was astronomical, Ruth ate and drank excessively, frequented prostitutes, and had been involved in several car accidents. It would have surprised no one if, for whatever reason, Ruth was out of baseball in a year or two.

Amid this speculation over his future, on February 28, 1920, Babe Ruth left Boston and boarded a train for New York. He was still just 25 years old.

• • •

Babe Ruth arrived in New York City at the best possible time for his outsized hitting and hedonistic lifestyle. It was the Roaring Twenties, the Jazz Age, a time of individualism, more progressive social and sexual attitudes,

After a disappointing April, in which he missed time due to a strained right knee, Ruth began May with home runs in consecutive games against the Red Sox. He went on to set a major league record for the month with 11 homers. That record lasted less than 30 days, when he smacked 13 long balls in June. He tied his own single-season record of 29 home runs—set the previous year with Boston—on July 16. Two weeks later, he had 37.

He finished the year with the unfathomable total of 54 home runs. He outhomered 14 of the other 15 major league teams. The AL runner-up was George Sisler, with 19; Cy Williams needed only 15 to top the National League. Ruth hit 14.6% of the American League's 369 home runs. For Barry Bonds to outdistance his peers in 2001 (when he set a new single season mark of 73 home runs) as Ruth did in 1920, Bonds would have needed to hit 431 homers that year.

In addition to this stunning display of power, Ruth was fourth in batting average at .364. His slugging percentage of .847 stood for more than 80 years—until Bonds reached .863 in 2001.

Ruth's arrival in New York began a stretch of offensive dominance the game will likely never see again. In the 12 seasons between 1920 and 1931, Ruth led the AL in slugging 11 times, home runs 10 times, walks 9 times, on-base percentage 8 times, and runs scored 7 times. His batting average topped .350 eight times. In half of those 12 seasons, he batted over .370. (Ruth once said that if he shortened his swing and tried to hit singles, he'd hit .600.)

Ruth also starred in a short movie entitled *Headin' Home*, which was filmed in Fort Lee, New Jersey. The plot, such as it was, starred Babe as a country bumpkin who makes good in big league ball — not exactly playing against type. According to *Variety*, "It couldn't hold the interest of anyone for five seconds if it were not for the presence of (Ruth)." Babe often returned to the Polo Grounds after a morning of filming still wearing his movie makeup and mascara, much to the annoyance of manager Miller Huggins.

Ruth quickly became one of the most famous people in the country. On Yankees road trips, people with no interest in baseball traveled hundreds of miles to get a glimpse of the Babe. He was cheered wildly in every park — for rival fans, if Ruth smacked one out of the park, it hardly seemed to matter what the final score was.

Sunday baseball became legal in New York in 1919 and the fan base changed forever. Women and children came out regularly to the park. One of Ruth's most enduring nicknames — the Bambino — came from the Italian fans in the upper Manhattan neighborhood around the Polo Grounds.

Everyone wanted to know as much about Ruth as possible. The New York papers (more than 15 dailies) began devoting more and more space to the Babe's exploits. Nothing was too trivial. According to sportswriter Tom Meany, if Ruth was seen "taking an aspirin, it was practically a scoop for the writer who saw him reach for the sedative." Marshall Hunt was hired by the *Daily News* to write about the Babe — and only the Babe — 365 days a year.

In the 1920s, giddy sportswriters were coming up with nicknames for Ruth nearly every day. His Boston nickname — the Colossus — morphed into the Colossus of Clout. From there, a seemingly endless — and often silly — list emerged: the Wizard of Wham, the Sultan of Swat, the Maharajah of Mash, the Rajah of Rap, the Caliph of Clout, the Behemoth of Bash, the Potentate of Pow, the Wali of Wallop, the Prince of Pounders, and on and on.

His own name became a nickname, bestowed on someone who was the best in his or her field: the Babe Ruth of Surfing, the Babe Ruth of Bowling, the Babe Ruth of Poker. His teammates usually called him "Jidge" (for George).

The Yankees finished the 1920 season in third place with a 95–59 record, only three games behind Cleveland. It was their best showing in 10 years. They followed that up in 1921 by winning 98 games and their first-ever pennant. And somehow Ruth may have actually had a better year at the plate than he did in 1920. His batting average improved slightly (.376 to .378), and while his OBP (.532 to .512) and slugging (.847 to .846) dipped slightly, he drove in 171 runs and hit a career-high 16 triples. (According to manager Huggins, Ruth was the second fastest player on the team.) He also broke his own single-season home run record — for the third consecutive year — with 59. On July 18, Ruth became the game's career home run leader, hitting his 139th homer, passing Roger Connor. Ruth also set new season records for runs scored (161), extra-base hits (107), and total bases (412).

Ruth also pitched in one game. He started on June 13 and allowed four runs in five innings. He also hit two home runs that day and finished the game in center field as the Yankees won, 11–8.

In September 1921, Ruth underwent three hours of tests at Columbia University to determine his athletic and psychological capabilities. Sportswriter Hugh Fullerton wrote up the findings for *Popular Science Monthly*:

> The tests revealed the fact that Ruth is 90 per cent efficient compared with a human average of 60 per cent. That his eyes are about 12 per cent faster than those of the average human being. That his ears function at least 10 per cent faster than those of the ordinary man. That his nerves are steadier than those of 499 out of 500 persons. That in attention and quickness of perception he rated one and a half times above the human average. That in intelligence, as demonstrated by the quickness and accuracy of understanding, he is approximately 10 per cent above normal.

The psychologists also discovered that Ruth did not breathe during his entire swing. They stated that if he kept breathing while swinging, he could generate even more power.

The Yankees faced their landlords in the Polo Grounds, the New York Giants, in the 1921 World Series. Ruth cut his left arm (which then became infected) during a slide in the second game and wrenched his knee in the fifth game. Babe made only one pinch-hitting appearance in the final three contests. The Yankees won the first two games, but the Giants took the best-of-nine series, five games to three.

After the World Series, Ruth and some other Yankees went on a barnstorming tour to earn extra money. This was in violation of the National Commission's 1911 edict that players on the two pennant-winning teams could not barnstorm after the World Series — enacted, perhaps, to preserve the integrity of the World Series or to limit the players' total income. Kenesaw Mountain Landis, newly installed as the game's first commissioner, suspended Ruth and fellow outfielder Bob Meusel for the first six weeks of the season, and fined them each $3,362 — the amount of their 1921 World Series share).

When Ruth returned to the lineup on May 20, he was named the team's captain, succeeding Hal Chase (1912) and Roger Peckinpaugh (1914–21). The honor lasted less than one week. Ruth was again slow to get his bat started and after five games, he was hitting .093 and being booed.

On May 25, he was thrown out trying to stretch a single into a double and, furious at the call, threw dirt in umpire George Hildebrand's face. On his way towards the dugout, he spied a heckler and jumped into the stands, ready to fight. The fan ran away and Ruth ended up standing on the dugout roof, screaming, "Come on down and fight! Anyone who wants to fight, come down on the field!" Ruth was fined $200 and was replaced as captain by shortstop Everett Scott.

Babe was suspended for three days in mid-June for his part in an obscenity-laced tirade against umpire Bill Dinneen. When Ruth got the news the following day, he challenged Dinneen to a fist fight — and the suspension was increased to five days. In the wake of the suspensions, Ruth made an effort to check his temper. On June 26, as some of his teammates argued with Dinneen, Babe merely sat down in the outfield grass and watched.

Ruth played in only 110 games in 1922. His batting average dropped to .315, but he led the league with a .672 slugging percentage and his OBP of .434 was fourth best.

The Yankees and the Giants met in the World Series for the second straight year. After a three-year experiment as a best-of-nine, the series was back to being a best-of-seven, where it has remained to the present day. The Giants swept the Yankees in five games (Game Two ended in a tie due to darkness). Ruth went 2-for-17.

The Yankees left the Polo Grounds and began 1923 in their own ballpark, directly across the Harlem River in the borough of the Bronx. Yankee Stadium was dubbed the House that Ruth Built, but with its short right-field porch, a more appropriate title might be the House Built for Ruth. Babe returned to his battering ways with a vengeance. He hit .393 — if only four of his 317 outs had fallen for hits, he would have batted .400 — and hit 41 home runs. Harry Heilmann of the Tigers led the AL with a .403 average.

The Yankees won their third straight pennant, finishing 16 games ahead of the Tigers. And for the third straight year, the World Series was an all-New York affair. This time, it was the Yankees, after losing two of the first three games, who prevailed. Ruth went 7-for-19 in the series, with three home runs. However, all three came at the Polo Grounds. Giants' outfielder Casey Stengel hit the first World Series home run at Yankee Stadium.

Ruth won his only batting title in 1924, easily topping the AL at .378 — almost 20 points higher than Charlie

Jamieson's .359. Babe hit 46 home runs and finished second with 121 RBIs. His .739 slugging percentage was more than 200 points higher than runners-up Harry Heilmann and Ken Williams (both at .533). However, the Yankees finished in second place, two games behind the Washington Senators.

In 1925, the Yankees fell all the way to seventh, 69–85, 28½ games out of first place. It was a bad year from the start. Ruth showed up for spring training at 256 pounds and went on to have the worst year of his career. He hit .290/.393/.543 (batting/on-base/slugging), with 25 home runs and a paltry 66 RBIs. This was also when Ruth suffered the famed "Bellyache Heard 'Round the World." Ruth fell ill during the team's spring training exhibition tour. The initial story was that Ruth had eaten too many hot dogs, and the *New York Evening Journal* ran a photo of Ruth with 12 numbered franks superimposed on his stomach.

It was clearly more serious than indigestion. On April 17, Ruth had minor surgery for what doctors termed an "intestinal abscess." Several teammates hinted it might have been a sexually-transmitted disease; one teammate said it wasn't a bellyache, "it was something a bit lower."

Whatever it was, it didn't cramp Ruth's style. Babe was staying out all night more often than not and by the end of the season, he was a physical wreck. In mid-December, Ruth realized that if he wanted to continue playing ball into his thirties, he needed to do something different. He showed up at Artie McGovern's gymnasium on East 42nd Street in Manhattan, a well-known gym used by New York's rich and famous.

Ruth committed himself to McGovern's strict regimen of exercise, diet, and rest. Six weeks later, by the time he was ready to head south for spring training, Ruth had lost 44 pounds and shed almost nine inches from his waistline.

The Babe still had plenty of fun, obviously, but he never let himself get seriously out of shape again. As Robert Creamer wrote in *Babe: The Legend Comes to Life*, "From 1926 through 1931, as he aged from thirty-two to thirty-seven, Ruth put on the finest sustained display of hitting that baseball has ever seen. During those six seasons, he averaged 50 home runs a year, 155 runs batted in and 147 runs scored; he batted .354.... From the ashes of 1925, Babe Ruth rose like a rocket."

As Ruth rose, so did the Yankees. The Bombers went from seventh place to first, winning 91 games and the 1926 pennant. Ruth batted .372/.516/.737, with 47 home runs (runner-up Al Simmons had 19), and drove in 155 (41 more than his nearest challenger). The Yankees were also boosted by the great play of two rookie infielders: second baseman Tony Lazzeri and shortstop Mark Koenig. First baseman Lou Gehrig, in his second full season at age 22, led the league with 20 triples and 83 extra-base hits — one more than Ruth.

In Game Four of the World Series against the St. Louis Cardinals, Ruth belted three home runs. It was the first time he had ever hit three in one game — and it was the first time that had been done in a World Series game. This was also the game before which Ruth allegedly promised to hit a home run for 11-year-old hospital patient Johnny Sylvester.

The 1926 Series came down to a deciding seventh game at Yankee Stadium. New York trailed 3–2 in the bottom of the ninth inning, when Ruth walked with two outs. Bob Meusel was facing Grover Cleveland Alexander when Ruth took off for second. He was thrown out trying to steal — ending the game and the World Series.

The 1927 Yankees are often talked about as the greatest team in baseball history. New York finished with a 110–44 record, winning the league by a whopping 19 games and sweeping the Pittsburgh Pirates in the World Series. They scored 975 runs, 130 more than second-best Detroit.

Ruth's fabled 60 home runs — which he had become obsessed with since hitting 59 six years earlier — captured the headlines, but Gehrig, at age 24, had a better season. He outhit Ruth (.373 to .356) and nearly matched him in on-base percentage (.474 to .486), and slugging (.765 to .772). Gehrig had more extra base hits (117 to 97), total bases (447 to 417), and RBIs (175 to 164). He also led the league in doubles, was second in triples, second in home runs, second in hits, and was third in batting average.

The Yankees won 13 fewer games in 1928, but their 101–53 record was still good enough for a third straight pennant. Ruth batted only .323, but his 54 home runs helped him lead the major leagues in slugging at .709. He and Lou Gehrig each drove in 142 runs. The Yankees used only three pitchers as they swept the Cardinals in the World Series. Ruth batted .625 (10-for-16), with three doubles, three home runs, and a 1.375 slugging percentage. Gehrig hit .545 (6-for-11) and slugged 1.727.

In January 1929, Babe's first wife, Helen, died in a house fire in Watertown Massachusetts. At the time, Helen was living with Edward Kinder, a dentist, and while the deed on the house listed Helen and Kinder as husband and wife, they were not, in fact, married. (Babe and Helen had never officially divorced.) Ruth was devastated by the news. At the funeral, he wept uncontrollably.

Babe married Claire Hodgson on April 17. The following day, the Yankees — with numbers on the back of their uniforms for the first time — opened the season against the Red Sox. Babe, wearing his new #3, whacked a first-inning home run to left field and doffed his cap to Claire as he rounded the bases.

On August 11 in Cleveland, Ruth hit the 500th home run of his career. The *New York World* called it "a symbol of American greatness." The man who retrieved the homer got two signed baseballs and, after posing for a photo with Ruth, the Babe slipped him a $20 bill.

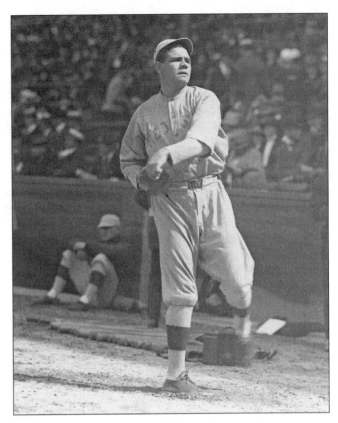

Ruth, 1918. Courtesy of *Chicago History Museum*.

Miller Huggins died suddenly near the end of the 1929 season — and Babe lobbied for the manager's job for 1930. (Ruth would drop hints about wanting to manage for the next four years, but the Yankees never seriously considered it.) Ruth also asked for his salary to be increased to $100,000 — this coming a few months after Black Tuesday and the start of what became the Great Depression. He ended up signing a two-year deal for $80,000 per season. With exhibition game receipts, movie shorts, personal appearances, and endorsements, Ruth probably earned close to $200,000 in 1930.

By the end of June 1930, Ruth was ahead of his 60-homer pace of 1927, but injuries slowed him down and he finished with 49.

The Yankees were an offensive juggernaut. In both 1930 and 1931, they scored more than 1,000 runs — an average of nearly seven runs per game. But it was the Philadelphia Athletics who won the pennant in 1929, 1930, and 1931 behind the big bats of Jimmie Foxx and Al Simmons and the pitching of Lefty Grove.

In 1931, at age 36, Ruth had one of his finest seasons. He hit .373/.495/.700, with 46 home runs, 163 RBIs, 128 walks and 149 runs scored.

Ruth made his final trip to the World Series in 1932. Amazingly, in the seven-year reign of Ruth and Gehrig from 1929 to 1935, the Yankees won only one pennant. Gehrig (.349/.451/.621, 34 HR, 151 RBI) and Ruth

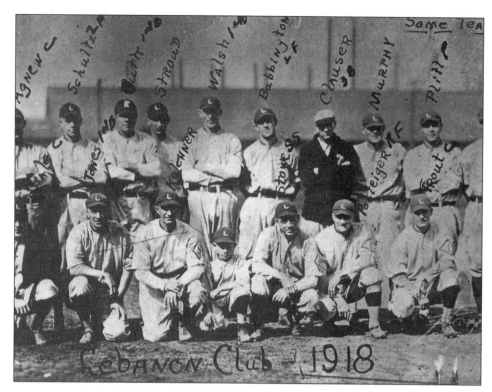

Ruth, Agnew, and others with the Bethlehem Steel Mill ballclub.
Courtesy of the Lebanon County Historical Society.

(.341/.489/.661, 41 HR, 137 RBI) were ably assisted by Lazzeri, Bill Dickey, Ben Chapman, and Earl Combs. However, it was Jimmie Foxx of the A's who led the league in home runs (58).

The Yankees swept the Chicago Cubs in the 1932 World Series, giving them wins in 12 straight World Series games. It was during the third game — October 1 at Wrigley Field — that Ruth added to his legend. The game was tied 4–4 when Ruth stepped in against Cubs starter Charlie Root with one out in the fifth inning. Ruth had already homered in his first at-bat and the Cubs' bench-jockeying was at a fever pitch.

Everyone agrees that as Root threw two called strikes to Ruth, the Babe held up one and two fingers. What exactly happened before Root threw his 2-2 pitch will never be definitively known. The legend says Ruth pointed, perhaps with his bat, towards the center field bleachers, indicating that was where he was going to hit the next pitch. Or he may have been saying "I've still got one strike left."

Either way, Ruth swung and belted the ball to deep center field — one of the longest home runs seen at Wrigley — for his second home run of the afternoon. He laughed as he jogged around the bases, pointing and jeering at the Cubs dugout.

Of the many game stories written that afternoon, only one mentioned Ruth "calling his shot." Within two or three days, however, writers who had initially made no reference to Ruth's theatrics were offering their own

recollections. And thus a legend was born. A 16mm home movie of the at-bat surfaced in 1999. The grainy film does show Ruth pointing his arm, but it's impossible to determine exactly what he is doing.

Root maintained that Ruth "did not point at the fence before he swung. If he had made a gesture like that, he would have ended up on his ass." As for the Babe, when asked whether he had really pointed to the bleachers, he smiled and said, "It's in the papers, isn't it?"

It was Ruth's last trip to the World Series. He had played on seven World Series champions: four with the Yankees (1923, 1927, 1928, 1932), and three with the Red Sox (1915, 1916, 1918). He was also on the losing side of three World Series teams with New York (1921, 1922, 1926).

The year 1933 was Ruth's 20th season in major league baseball. He batted only .301 with 34 home runs, though he still led the league in walks. One of the season's highlights was the inaugural All-Star Game, played at Comiskey Field in Chicago. Ruth hit the game's first home run. He also robbed Chick Hafey of a home run in the eighth inning, to preserve the AL's 4–2 win.

The Yankees finished seven games behind the Senators and, in an effort to boost attendance for the last home game of the year, announced that Ruth would pitch against the Red Sox. The 39-year-old outfielder held the Red Sox without a run for five innings. With a 6–0 lead, he stumbled in the sixth, allowing a walk, five singles, and four runs. He gave up another run in the eighth, but hung on and won the complete game, 6–5.

Although Ruth had prepared for the start, it took a toll on his arm. He couldn't so much as comb his hair with his left arm for about a week.

Ruth took a $17,000 pay cut in 1934. His $35,000 contract was still the highest in the game, but it was his lowest salary since 1921. On July 13, in Detroit, Babe hit his 700th career home run. Three days later, he drew his 2,000th walk.

In August, during the Yankees' last trip at Fenway, a record crowd of 48,000 turned out, assuming it would be Ruth's last appearance in Boston. The fans cheered everything Ruth did. When he grounded out in his final at-bat, he was given a long standing ovation. "Do you know that some of them cried when I left the field?" Ruth said afterwards. "And if you wanna know the truth, I cried too."

On the other hand, for what was rumored to be his final home game in a Yankees uniform, only 2,000 fans showed up. Babe played only one inning, being replaced by a pinch-runner after drawing a walk. He ended the year with a .288 batting average.

During the off-season, Ruth agreed to travel with an all-star team to Japan. In arranging for a passport, he discovered that his date of birth was February 6, 1895. He had always believed he was born on February 7, 1894. He was actually a year younger than he had thought.

Yankees owner Jacob Ruppert, not wanting Ruth to return in any capacity in 1935, worked out a secret deal with Boston Braves owner Emil Fuchs. Fuchs would offer Ruth a contract that included the titles of "assistant manager" and "vice president." Ruth loved the idea and when he informed Ruppert, the Yankee owner said he wouldn't stand in Ruth's way. At spring training in 1935, Ruth learned that the Yankees had already assigned his uniform number 3 to George Selkirk. They were also using his locker to store firewood.

Ruth ended up playing in 28 games for the Braves, batting .181. The one bright spot came on May 25 in Pittsburgh. Ruth belted the final three home runs of his career, and drove in six runs. Career home run 714 disappeared over the right-field roof—the longest home run ever hit at Forbes Field.

Many of the hitting records Ruth once held have been broken, but what cements Babe's status as the best to ever play the game is the combination of hitting for average, hitting with power, and his work on the mound. In addition to his batting exploits, Ruth also pitched in 163 games, with a record of 94–46 and a career ERA of 2.28. For 71 years, he was also the unlikely answer to a great trivia question: Who is the only major leaguer to pitch in at least 10 seasons and have a winning record in all of them? Ruth had winning records in 10 seasons: 1914–1921, 1930 and 1933. Andy Pettitte now holds the record at 13 seasons (1995–2007).

Ruth retired to a life of golf, fishing, bowling, and public appearances. In November 1946, he checked into French Hospital on 29th Street in Manhattan, complaining of headaches and pain above his left eye. It was cancer, though the newspapers never printed the word.

Babe Ruth Day was held at Yankee Stadium (and every other major league park) the following April. A crowd of 58,339 was there and many of them, players as well as fans, were shocked at how frail and shrunken the mighty Babe had become.

Ruth returned to the Bronx one more time, on June 13, 1948. Yankee Stadium was celebrating its 25th anniversary and Babe's number 3 was being retired. Ruth was back in the hospital 11 days later. The cancer had spread to his liver, lungs, and kidneys. He knew he was dying.

Babe Ruth died at 8:01 P.M. on August 16, 1948. He was 53 years old. He is buried at Gate of Heaven Cemetery in Valhalla, New York, next to his second wife Claire, who died in 1976.

Leigh Montville, author of *The Big Bam*, called Ruth "the patron saint of American possibility." Ruth's obituary in the *New York Times* concluded: "Probably nowhere in all the imaginative field of fiction could one find a career more dramatic and bizarre than that portrayed in real life by George Herman Ruth."

Note

1. Allan Wood, telephone interviews with Tom Foley, 1995 and 1997.

WALLY SCHANG *by Don Geiszler*

G	AB	R	H	2B	3B	HR	RBI	BB	SO	BA	OBP	SLG	SB	HBP
88	285	36	55	7	1	0	20	46	35	.244	.377	.284	4	2

A switch-hitter who was adept at getting on base, Wally Schang was considered by many of his contemporaries to be the best catcher of his time. Behind the plate, the 5'10", 180-pounder was one of the most athletic catchers of his day, so agile and alert that he occasionally played third base or in the outfield. An excellent hitter who posted a career .393 on-base percentage, second only to Mickey Cochrane among catchers, Schang could hit for power, too: in 1916 he became the first player to homer from both sides of the plate in the same game. The energetic and likeable Schang batted better than .300 six times and caught for seven different American League pennant winners. In his six World Series appearances, Schang batted .287, including a .444 mark for the Boston Red Sox in the 1918 World Series. Yet despite his impressive resume, Schang never received recognition for his accomplishments, earning only 22 votes in five appearances on the Hall of Fame ballot. In the words of one baseball writer, "the only thing Wally's career lacked is the recognition he deserved."

Walter Henry Schang was born on August 22, 1889 in South Wales, New York, a small farm community some 25 miles southeast of Buffalo, one of nine surviving children of Frank and Mary Schang. The Schangs owned and worked over 170 acres of farm land, principally raising dairy cows. Despite the daily grind of schoolwork and chores around the farm, young Wally was preoccupied with baseball. As he later remembered, "From the moment I crawled out of bed my thoughts had to do with baseball, with the result that I raced the poor nag to the creamery every morning. I wanted to get my job over as early as possible so I could drive back home, walk the two miles to the school and get in forty five minutes to an hour of baseball before the bell called us to our studies." Baseball injuries did not excuse Wally from his farm chores. Said Schang: "For a while I had to milk one-handed."

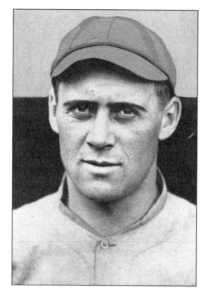

Wally Schang, 1914.

Wally was not the only member of his family obsessed with baseball. Indeed, the national game became something of a family passion. Frank Schang, a catcher for the local town team, inspired at least three of his sons to pursue the game professionally. Wally's older brother Bob enjoyed a short major league career as a catcher for Pittsburgh, New York, and St. Louis in the National League. Another brother, Quirin, spent 20 years as a catcher in the semipro circuit.

While still in high school Wally started playing semipro ball for a team in nearby Holland, New York. He played many positions including shortstop, third base, and the outfield before finally settling in behind the plate. Over the next three seasons, Wally garnered a reputation as one of the area's best semipros, culminating in 1911, when he starred for the Buffalo Pullmans. George Stallings, then skipper of the Buffalo Bisons of

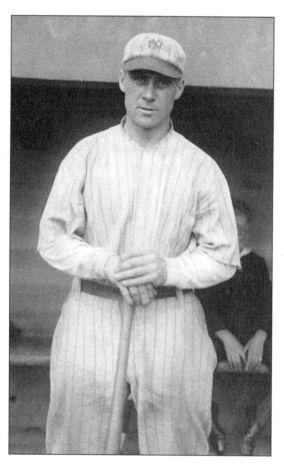

Wally with the Yankees.

the International League, was impressed and picked up Schang's contract near the end of the season. Appearing in 48 games for the Bisons in 1912, Schang batted .333 and cemented his excellent defensive reputation with 41 assists. Word spread quickly of the young backstop's talent, and prior to the 1913 season 13 of the 16 major league

clubs attempted to draft the 23-year-old switch hitter. The Athletics were the fortunate team to land Schang and he traveled to Philadelphia to learn the ropes.

As the 1913 season opened, Connie Mack knew he had a talented roster. With Jack Lapp and the aging Ira Thomas already on board, Mack allowed the young rookie to observe his major league colleagues and slowly eased him into action. When the season was concluded, Schang had managed 207 at-bats, hitting a healthy .266, and ranked first among all major league backstops with three home runs and a .392 on base percentage. Defensively, Schang quickly developed into one of the league's best backstops, with 92 assists in 72 games behind the plate. "Schang has proved one of the wonders of the year," veteran sportswriter Hugh Fullerton observed. "Schang is steadier and works with more judgment than he did during the early part of the year, studies batters better, and works better with the pitchers."

In that year's World Series against the New York Giants, Schang performed like a seasoned veteran, batting .357 in four games and leading the team with seven RBIs, including a Game Three solo home run off Doc Crandall.

With some success and money in his pocket at the conclusion of the 1913 season, the young man focused on his personal life. To cap off a fantastic year in 1913, Schang married a Philadelphian named Marie Aubrey. Wally was ready to settle down financially thanks to his $3,243.94 World Series paycheck, which was a very generous bonus compared to his regular $1,000 annual salary. The couple would have one child, Joan Marie, born in 1926.

The 1914 season was another good one for the Philadelphia A's, who captured another American League pennant with a 99–53 record. Once again they were aided by the continuing development of Schang, who established himself as the best offensive catcher in the game. Wally led all American League catchers in batting average (.287), extra base hits (22), home runs (3), slugging percentage (.404), and RBIs (45). Defensively, Wally struggled as he played through a broken thumb on his throwing hand, and as a result committed 30 errors, tied for the most among AL backstops.

Like most of his teammates, Schang fared poorly in the A's shocking loss to the Boston Braves who swept that year's World Series. Starting all four games, Wally batted just .167 and struck out four times in 12 at-bats. When later asked about the A's poor performance in the Fall Classic, Schang was quoted as saying, "We went into [the World Series] too cocky, and we lived it up too much." Following the A's stunning defeat, star pitchers Eddie Plank and Chief Bender departed for the Federal League, slugging third baseman Frank Baker held out the entire season, and second baseman Eddie Collins was sold to the White Sox. Virtually overnight, the A's dynasty evaporated and the team tumbled into last place in 1915, where it would remain for the next seven years.

Schang continued to perform well for the next few years on some miserable teams. Despite Schang's growing reputation as an excellent catcher, Mack needed to utilize Wally in a utility role, playing him more in the outfield and at third base than behind the plate. Nonetheless, the 1915 *Reach Guide* described Schang as "one of the most sensational catchers in recent years. He is a remarkably fast runner, a good hitter, and a strong thrower." He finished the season with a .248 batting average, a career-high 18 stolen bases, and a team-high .385 on base percentage. In 1916, Schang led the 36–117 Athletics in home runs, with seven, a figure he reached with the help of his historic performance on September 8 at Shibe Park, when he became the first switch hitter in baseball history to homer from both sides of the plate in the same game.

After the 1917 season, in which he batted .285 in 118 games, Schang, Joe Bush, and Amos Strunk were traded to the Boston Red Sox. Schang appeared in 88 games for Boston in 1918, batting .244 with only eight extra-base hits, but still posted a stellar .377 OBP. With the entry of the United States into World War I, the baseball season was cut short, and the Red Sox captured their third pennant in four years with a 75–51 mark, 2½ games ahead of second place Cleveland.

Schang with the Red Sox. Courtesy of the SABR-Ottoson Photo Archive.

Though that year's Fall Classic, played in early September, was overshadowed by events overseas, Schang enjoyed a fabulous series, batting .444 over six games and making some key defensive contributions. In Game Three, with Boston leading 2–1 with two outs in the bottom of the ninth, Chicago's Charlie Pick singled, putting the tying run on first. Pick stole second and on the next pitch broke for third on a ball that got away from Schang. Wally reacted quickly and fired to third beating the sliding Cub to the bag. But Pick's hard slide knocked the ball out of third baseman Fred Thomas's glove. As Thomas argued with the umpire, Pick raced for home. Thomas retrieved the ball and threw a strike to Schang who was waiting for Pick to arrive. The Cub may have had more success running into a brick wall. When the dust settled, Schang was standing over the fallen Cub, ball in hand, having tagged Pick with the final out of the game. In Game Four, Schang scored the winning run and in Game Six his stellar defense, including a pickoff of Les Mann in a key situation, helped lead to the final Red Sox victory.

Following the 1919 season, in which the Red Sox finished a disappointing sixth, Boston owner Harry Frazee dismantled his team, selling Babe Ruth to the Yankees in January 1920. A year later Schang and three teammates were also sent to New York for catcher Muddy Ruel and three other players. Once again, Schang had the good fortune to be traded to a winner. Now in his 30s, Schang put together three excellent seasons in his five years with the Yankees, batting better than .300 twice and appearing in three more World Series. After hitting a disappointing .188 in the Yankees' 1922 World Series defeat, Schang batted .318 and scored three runs in the Yankees' first World Series triumph in 1923.

Though Schang remained a productive player, by 1925 his offensive numbers began to decline, leading to rumors that his eyesight might be failing. At the end of the season, Schang was traded to the St. Louis Browns for cash and pitcher George Mogridge. Determined to prove he wasn't finished as a player, Wally enjoyed one of his best seasons in 1926, batting .330 with a .405 OBP and a .516 slugging percentage in 103 games. Appearing in 97 games for the Browns in 1927, Schang posted a .318 batting average. The following year his average dipped to .286, but he still managed to post a career-high .448

OBP. In 1929, his average dipped still further, to .237, but Schang adjusted by drawing 74 walks on his way to a .424 OBP. Nonetheless, at the end of the season the Browns traded the 40-year-old catcher to Philadelphia for Sammy Hale. Back with Connie Mack and the pennant-bound Athletics, Schang appeared in only 45 games, posting a .174 average. He did not appear in the World Series, and was released by Mack at season's end. The following year he finished out his major league career with the Detroit Tigers, batting .184 in 30 games. Even at the end, however, Schang's defensive abilities left an impression on his teammates. As one Tiger observed, "Just to watch him was an education in the art of catching.... I've never seen anyone so graceful behind the plate."

Released by Detroit on June 29, 1931, Schang signed two weeks later with the Chattanooga Lookouts of the Southern Association, batting .247 over the remainder of the season. Struggling financially in the early years of the Great Depression, he almost signed on with the House of David in 1932 for $230 per month. At the last minute he was saved by George Sisler, manager of the Texas League's Shreveport Sports, who offered him a roster spot. Schang batted .214 as the team's third-string catcher.

Having stretched his playing career as far as it would go, Wally returned to the farm he'd purchased in Dixon, Missouri, but the Great Depression continued to bring economic struggles. Since farming and baseball were all Wally knew, he headed back to the latter in 1934, as player-manager for the Joplin (Missouri) Miners of the Western Association, batting .257 in 71 games. In 1935, after trying and failing to land a job as a Pacific Coast League umpire, Schang returned to the Western Association, batting .256 for Muskogee, Oklahoma. In 1936, the Cleveland Indians hired him as a coach, where he helped develop pitchers Denny Galehouse and Bob Feller. In fact he roomed with Feller that year, instructing the young phenom on the nuances of the game. Schang served as player-manager for various minor league clubs from 1938 to 1940. He finished out his career in 1942 with Owensboro (Kentucky) of the Kitty League, reaching base in five of his seven plate appearances at age 52.

In retirement, Schang was often seen at the ice cream shop in Dixon, where he would regale listeners with his stories of Ruth, Collins and other teammates, or on the golf course, where he often played 36 holes even after he was 70 years old. He died at St. Luke's Hospital in St. Louis on March 6, 1965 at 75 years of age, and was buried in Dixon Cemetery.

EVERETT SCOTT *by Ray Birch*

G	AB	R	H	2B	3B	HR	RBI	BB	SO	BA	OBP	SLG	SB	HBP
126	443	40	98	11	5	0	43	12	16	.221	.242	.269	11	0

Shortstop Lewis Everett "Deacon" Scott was the steady infield leader of several championship Red Sox and Yankee teams of the 1910s and 1920s. Beginning June 20, 1916, and ending May 6, 1925, he played in 1,307 consecutive games, which was the major league record until Lou Gehrig and then Cal Ripken broke it. Not only was Scott an accomplished ballplayer, but he also wrote a children's book and became a skilled bowler. Although he was never seriously considered for baseball's Hall of Fame, Scott was considered to be the finest fielding shortstop of his time.

Lewis Everett Scott was born on November 19, 1892, in Bluffton, Indiana. He graduated from Bluffton High School, where he was a pitcher, in 1909. His family moved to Auburn, Indiana, while Everett started his pro baseball career in 1909 in Kokomo of the Northern State of Indiana League. That same year, he went to Fairmont, West Virginia, of the Pennsylvania-West Virginia League; he played for both teams in 1910 but in reverse order. In 1911, he moved on to Youngstown (Ohio-Pennsylvania League).

While Scott was playing for the Youngstown Steelmen (now in the Central League) for a second year in 1912, the Boston Red Sox minority owner, Jimmy McAleer, a native of Youngstown, observed him on June 6, and, two days later, tendered an offer for Scott to the Youngstown owner; the Boston Braves also made an offer, of $5,400. The Washington Senators were scouting Scott, too. The Senators determined that Scott's body weight of around 120 pounds would not allow him "to keep up the strenuous pace demanded in the big show," certainly ironic in light of Scott's later consecutive games streak.[1] After marrying Gladys Watt, his childhood sweetheart, on August 20, 1912, Scott signed with the Red Sox on August 22. In the offseason he worked as an inspector in a piano factory.

In 1913, Scott was assigned to the American Association's St. Paul Saints. Called "Scottie" by the St. Paul fans, he received rave reviews for his speed in the field, his throwing arm, and, most importantly, "baseball brains."[2] His .269 average that year was virtually identical to that of his two previous seasons. On January 31, 1914, Scott signed a contract with the Red Sox for $2,500, despite having been offered $4,000 by the Federal League's Indianapolis team.[3]

Scott, who batted and threw right-handed, arrived with a great advance buildup in Boston in 1914; even the great Connie Mack of the Philadelphia Athletics was impressed by his fielding prowess after an early season game against the Red Sox. On Opening Day, April 14, he played his first big league game, succeeding the incumbent, Heinie Wagner. His rookie year .239 batting average was good for a shortstop during this era, and his fielding was good enough, too. He cut his errors almost in half in his second season with the Red Sox.

In 1915, Scott's brother, Charles, a pitcher, was invited to spring training with the Red Sox, but did not make the club. During the season, the diminutive shortstop, at 5-feet 8 inches and 135 pounds, saw his batting average dip to .201, but his steady defense was one of the main reasons why the Red Sox advanced to the World Series, defeating the Philadelphia Phillies in five games. Scott had just one hit, a single, in 18 Series at-bats.

The 1916 Sox returned to the World Series once more and they defeated the Brooklyn Robins in five games. For the season, Scott had improved his batting average to .232, as well as being the American League leader in fielding average for shortstops. Wilbert Robinson of the Robins nicknamed him "Trolley Wire," a tribute to his accurate throws from shortstop to first during the Series. Scott was 2-for-16 with one RBI in the 1916 Series.

After two world championships in his first three years, Scott felt he deserved more money and sent back the contract the Red Sox offered to him for the 1917 season, which (after the collapse of Federal League competition) had offered a slight decrease in salary. However, within a few days, Scott came to terms with the Red Sox and earned a substantial raise, from $3,000 to $4,500.[4] During the offseason, though, Scott's wife, Gladys, spent time in a sanitarium and it was reported that when Scott reported to spring training, he appeared drawn.[5] He later left camp to be with his wife when she needed surgery. He nonetheless played a full 157 games in the regular season, hitting .241 in 528 at-bats as the Red Sox finished nine games behind the Chicago White Sox, the eventual World Series champion.

Beginning with spring training, the 1918 season was directly affected by World War I. Players were not able to get into game condition, resulting in many lame arms among pitchers. In addition, the office of Secretary of

Everett Scott. Courtesy of Chicago History Museum.

War Newton Baker issued a "work or fight" order that required eligible men of draft age to enlist in the armed services or find work in war-related industries. Some 237 players left their teams during the season. However, neither Scott nor teammate Harry Hooper missed a league game all season and, by the time the World Series against the Chicago Cubs was played, the two players (and Sam Agnew) were the only position players left from Boston's 1916 championship team.

During the shortened season, which ended on September 2, Scott continued his consistent play, making only 17 errors and, despite hitting only .221, contributed 26 sacrifice hits and struck out only 11 times. The World Series ended in a Red Sox victory in six games, with Scott contributing 26 assists in the field and turning three double plays. Before Game Five, the players on both teams briefly refused to take the field because of problems with the way the World Series money was to be allocated.[6] The dispute was resolved and the Red Sox had their fifth championship. After the season, Scott was honored in Spalding's 1919 baseball record book as a baseball "Hall of Fame" member (this was before the official Baseball Hall of Fame was established), recognizing his achievements during the 1918 season. He had also surpassed previous longevity marks, established by Eddie Collins (470 games) and George Burns (459 games). On April 23, 1919, it was announced that Scott had signed a three-year contract with the Red Sox.

After five full seasons in the major leagues, Scott had established himself as a consistent and dependable, if not flashy, player. Although his batting average was usually low, he was considered to be a player whom a manager would like to have up at the plate in a difficult situation.[7] In the 1915 World Series, for instance, he bunted on a third strike, catching the Philadelphia infield flat-footed and advancing a runner who later scored a decisive run.[8] He showed an uncanny knack for playing batters correctly in the field and his throws from any part of the infield were accurate.[9] Entering the 1919 season, he had played 524 consecutive games, despite being afflicted by a recurring condition of boils, and assorted injuries. Covering his wounds with bandages, he was able to continue playing, although in considerable pain.[10]

Although the 1919 season was a disappointment

for the Red Sox, Scott hit a career-high .278 and led all American League shortstops in fielding. But his wife was unhappy being away from him and alone with their child in Indiana, and it was reported that Scott requested a trade to a team closer to home, such as Chicago, Detroit, or St. Louis, after the season concluded.[11] Scott disputed the rumored trade possibility, attributing it to unreliable sources.[12]

The Red Sox began spring training in 1920 with a team in transition, held together by Scott, Hooper, and John "Stuffy" McInnis. Despite their efforts, the Boston club eventually finished 25½ games behind the American League champion Cleveland Indians. Scott played in 154 games, amassing a career-high 210 total bases, with four home runs and 61 RBIs. During the season, he passed the 533 consecutive games mark of the Phillies' Fred Luderus, hitting a rare home run in the process. On April 26 he broke the record of 577 consecutive games played set by George Pinckney of Brooklyn from 1885 to 1890, and played his 600th straight game on July 14. Throughout the season, his streak withstood a wrist injury caused by a pitched ball, and an ejection from a game in which he played 3½ innings.

In the offseason, Scott continued his conditioning program, preparing himself for the rigors of playing shortstop in an era when players regularly sharpened their spikes and were not afraid to use them to cut middle infielders when they slid into a base. To reduce injury, Scott wore padded shoes to protect his ankles from spike wounds.

Early in 1921 spring training, Scott suffered a charley horse injury that lingered throughout the spring training schedule. However, the injury did not stop his streak, which reached 700 on May 17, in a game during which he made a phenomenal force out by diving face first into second base. Stating a goal of attaining the 1,000 mark, he played in number 800 on September 2. Still esteemed by fans and press alike, Scott continued to be praised for his consistency in the field and at bat. It was strongly felt that his record for consecutive games was unbeatable. His 62 RBIs in 1921 were the most he'd driven in for the Red Sox.

Despite his fine play, trade rumors persisted during the offseason: first, a two-way deal between the Yankees and the Red Sox and then a three-way deal between the Yankees, Red Sox, and Tigers. Finally, a trade with Boston was announced in which the Yankees received Scott and pitchers Joe Bush and Sam Jones in exchange for shortstop Roger Peckinpaugh and pitchers Bill Piercy, Rip Collins, and Joe Quinn. In addition, in a separate deal, the Red Sox traded Stuffy McInnis to Cleveland, further raising suspicion that owner Harry Frazee was in the process of selling the club, and that perhaps there was money involved coming from the Yankees to the Red Sox in the Scott deal.[13] The local press in Boston

Scott with the Yankees.

denounced the deal as being strongly in favor of the Yankees, while the national press was mixed. In retrospect, it seems apparent that Frazee was systematically dismantling the Red Sox, sending them into a free fall that would put them out of serious pennant contention for a generation.

Scott's reaction to the trade was that he would have preferred to stay in Boston, but, if he had to go anywhere, he was glad to go to New York, since he would be reunited with many of his old Red Sox teammates, such as Babe Ruth, Waite Hoyt, and Wally Schang. He felt that he had been treated well in Boston.[14]

During spring training in 1922, the Yankees announced that Babe Ruth would become the captain of the Yankees, replacing the traded Peckinpaugh. However, because of an incident the previous season, Ruth was suspended until May. It was suggested that perhaps Scott, having been the captain of his Red Sox team, might be appointed captain until Ruth's return. It is easy to see why Scott would be considered for this honor, for beyond his stellar play on the field, he also was adept at many hobbies, including auction bridge, whist, poker, fishing, and bowling. Scott became the captain of the Yankees, serving in that role until he left the club in 1925.

Although Scott's first game as a Yankee was a loss, his consecutive games streak continued. The great sportswriter Grantland Rice remarked: "After Everett Scott is dead we expect to see his ghost out there playing short through force of habit. No such shallow barrier as the grave will ever check the Deacon's tireless pace."[15]

After Scott played in his 900th consecutive game, the *Washington Post* referred to him as the "iron man" and also mentioned his ability as a "great money player," citing his penchant for performing strong when much is at stake.[16] However, the streak almost came to an end on September 14 when, after visiting his home in Indiana, he caught a train to Chicago to meet up with his teammates there. The train blew out a cylinder head along the way, and Scott was forced to take a car, another train, and then a taxi to arrive at the ballpark late. He entered the game in the seventh inning, enough to count for a game to continue his string of 972 games. That year, Scott was again the American League's leader in fielding at shortstop.

A highlight of the 1922 World Series between the Yankees and the New York Giants was the anticipated battle of the shortstops, with Scott being the better fielder, and the Giants' Dave Bancroft being the better hitter during the regular season. At Series end, won in five games (one tie) by the Giants, the two shortstops had played to a virtual tie. But it was evident, especially to Scott, that he was unable to cover as much ground in the Series as he normally would. To Scott's credit, he mentioned that he was getting older, but also said the Fenway Park infield which he manned for so many years was a slower track, allowing him to get to balls more easily than both the Polo Grounds and Yankee Stadium.[17]

When Yankee contracts went out to players for the 1923 season, the general consensus was that several star players would be asked to take a cut in salary. Scott's salary remained the same and he promptly returned it signed. After a period of conditioning in Hot Springs, Arkansas, and spring training in New Orleans, Scott entered the season knowing that he needed only to play 14 games to reach his goal of 1,000 consecutive games. On April 13 in an exhibition against Brooklyn, though, he sprained his left ankle while falling over second base and it was feared that he had also torn his tendons. Because of his age and the nature of his injury, it was generally thought that he would miss at least the first game of the season. In fact, Yankee manager Miller Huggins said he anticipated that Scott would be sidelined for two or three weeks. However, after using crutches and wrapping his ankle in bandages, he was able to play on Opening Day, the first game ever played in Yankee Stadium. More than 74,000 fans were treated to a home run by Babe Ruth in a 4–1 win over the Red Sox. Scott was credited with the first assist at the new Stadium.

Scott persevered despite his injury and, on May 2, 1923, at Washington's Griffith Stadium, he participated in his 1,000th consecutive game. To mark the occasion, he was presented with a solid gold medal in a pregame ceremony in which he was praised by Secretary of the Navy Edwin C. Denby as "the greatest ballplayer in point of service and achievement that ever trod the diamonds of America, the home of baseball."[18] Despite his accomplishment, it was reported that, although Scott held the major league record, a minor leaguer named Perry Lipe had participated in 1,127 consecutive games.

As the season progressed, the whispers began that Scott was getting old and getting slower and that he was not doing the Yankees any favors by playing with nagging injuries. He began to make costly errors when he could not get to balls that he used to field with ease. On August 23, he ran his streak to 1,100 games and soon claimed the world's record by playing in his 1,128th game, surpassing Lipe. In a rematch of the previous two years' World Series, the Yankees finally won their first title, defeating the Giants, four games to two, with Scott getting a key hit and scoring a run in a five-run rally to win Game Six.

After the season, Scott considered retiring from baseball to enter business, hinting that he wanted to leave baseball with pride in his accomplishments. It was thought that manager Huggins might bench Scott for a couple of games at the start of the season in order help him improve his play over the course of the season; another consideration was to involve Scott in a trade. This possibility gained credence when the Yankees acquired Earle Combs in a trade to serve as an understudy. Despite all the talk, Scott signed a contract for the 1924 season, after spending the winter resting his legs by staying away from playing basketball. Clearly, though, Scott's star in New York was fading.

By the beginning of the season, Huggins had backed away from benching Scott, saying that he might need a rest in July or August when the weather became hot. Scott played on, reaching 1,200 straight games on June 28.

At season's end, the Yankees had finished two games behind the Washington Senators and Huggins strongly hinted that he needed a new shortstop for the following season. It was suggested that Scott had an "obsession" with his streak and by playing every day was not exercising common sense. For years, he had taken to wrapping his legs in bandages in order to compensate for various injuries. Scott performed well, however; his .250 average in 1924 was a notch above his .246 of the previous year, and his 64 RBIs a career high. His number of putouts and assists was significantly larger, and his fielding percentage improved.

Scott showed his bowling prowess during the offseason, participating in several tournaments. He also hoped to purchase a bowling establishment when he retired. Despite reports that he would not play on Opening Day because of a pulled muscle, Scott continued his streak. But criticism of his "obsession" continued, and, finally, on May 5, 1925, the streak ended when Paul "Pee Wee" Wanninger started in Scott's place. At first, it was reported that Scott was "not feeling well," but later it was reported that he had been sat down because of a shakeup in the Yankee lineup.

Scott was angered by the move, and returned to Indiana for a few days to consider his options. He insisted that he was not upset by the end of the streak, but rather that he had been playing better and expected to play. In an attempt to add humor to the end of the streak, writer James R. Harrison of the *New York Times* noted that it had been reported that Scott was benched by the same type of stomach ailment that had sidelined him the day before his streak began in 1916. Harrison joked, "If such is the case, the thing is getting chronic and Everett should see a doctor." Critics also noted that Scott's streak was aided by the fact that he had not played every inning of every game, sometimes playing only a small portion of a game. Regardless, Scott made only a few more appearances in a Yankee uniform, his last start coming in the second game of the May 30 doubleheader. Scott's final 18 games with the Yankees saw him bat just .218. Two days later, on June 1, teammate Lou Gehrig began his own consecutive game streak that would eventually reach 2,130 games.

Scott's streak broken, the impasse with the Yankees ended when Scott was finally claimed on waivers by the Washington Senators on June 17, 1925. Coincidentally, he initially played behind Roger Peckinpaugh, who had been involved in the trade with the Red Sox that sent Scott to the Yankees. After an injury to Peckinpaugh, he played well (hitting .272) in 33 games for the Senators, who went to the World Series but lost to the Pittsburgh Pirates, four games to three.

Scott's desire to leave baseball increased, and his successful bowling and billiard establishment in Fort Wayne, Indiana, led him to consider retirement again. Nevertheless, Scott's passion for baseball still burned and he was claimed on waivers by the Chicago White Sox from the Senators in March 1926, and appeared in 40 games for them. He then was claimed on waivers by the Cincinnati Reds from the White Sox on July 6 and appeared in four games.

The following season, 1927, Scott was signed by the Baltimore Orioles of the International League, for whom he played 109 games, hitting 11 home runs and driving in 69 runs before being unconditionally released on August 4. He signed with the Toledo Mud Hens of the American Association eight days later, playing 33 games before being released on December 7.

In 1928, Scott signed with Reading (International League), playing in 131 games and batting .315, and returned to the team for the 1929 season, appearing in 62 games, before being released in July.

After baseball, Scott continued to manage bowling alleys and billiard parlors in Fort Wayne, as well as continuing to participate professionally in bowling tournaments, rolling 51 perfect games in his career. In 1928, a children's book he wrote called *Third Base Thatcher* was published by Grosset and Dunlap as part of the Christy Mathewson series of books.

As a result of his streak, Scott was also uniquely qualified to comment on the consecutive games mark that was being established by Lou Gehrig of the New York Yankees. In a July 7, 1939 column written by Bob Considine, Scott, reflecting upon Gehrig's streak, felt that Gehrig should have first broken the streak established by Scott by about a hundred games and then should have played about 125 games a year from that point on, thus prolonging his career.[19] In an ironic twist, it was Pee Wee Wanninger whom Gehrig pinch-hit for to begin his own streak, which eventually reached 2,130 games. Cal Ripken Jr. currently holds the all-time record of 2,632.

Everett Scott died on November 3, 1960, at Parkview Hospital in Fort Wayne, Indiana. He had been in poor health in the years prior to his death. He was survived by his wife, Gladys; a son known as Everett Jr.; a grandchild; two brothers; and a sister. Scott was buried in Bluffton's Elm Grove Cemetery.

Notes

1. *Youngstown* (Ohio) *Vindicator.* June 6 and July 31, 1912.
2. *Boston Daily Globe.* August 8, 1913, p. 6.
3. *New York Times.* January 31, 1914, p. 9.
4. *Boston Daily Globe.* February 22, 1917, p. 4.
5. *Boston Daily Globe.* March 11. 1917, p. 14.
6. *Boston Daily Globe.* September 11, 1918, p. 1.
7. *Chicago Daily Tribune.* January 12, 1919.
8. *New York Times.* September 23, 1919, p. 25.
9. Trachtenberg, Leo, "The Durable Deacon." *Yankees Magazine,* December 17, 1992, pp. 38–41.
10. Sebring, Blake, "Our Own Iron Man." *Fort Wayne News Sentinel* (online), April 20, 2006.
11. "Red Sox Will Lose Clever Shortstop." *Washington Post,* October 20, 1919, p. 10.
12. "Boston Club Suits Everett Scott." *Boston Daily Globe,* October 29, 1919, p.9.
13. *New York Times.* December 26,1921, p. 21.
14. *Atlanta Constitution.* January 8, 1922.
15. *Boston Daily Globe.* May 12, 1922, p. 18.
16. *Washington Post.* June 25, 1922, p. 44.
17. *Boston Daily Globe.* January 1, 1923, p. 6.
18. *Boston Daily Globe.* May 3, 1923, p. 12.
19. *Washington Post,* July 7, 1939.

DAVE SHEAN *by Les Masterson*

G	AB	R	H	2B	3B	HR	RBI	BB	SO	BA	OBP	SLG	SB	HBP
115	425	58	112	16	3	0	34	40	25	.264	.331	.315	11	3

Dave Shean was the epitome of the Deadball baseball player on the field — he sacrificed runners to the next base, played a steady second base, and collected his share of singles. Off the field, Shean was the opposite of a hard-charging deadballer — he didn't smoke, drink, chew tobacco, or swear, and regularly attended Sunday Mass.

Shean was born to Irish immigrants, Patrick Shean (a police officer) and Mary Scannell, on July 9, 1883, in Arlington, Massachusetts, a suburb five miles northwest of Boston. He grew up with three sisters in a deeply Catholic household at 58 Medford Street, next to Mt. Pleasant Cemetery, and across the street from St. Malachy's (later St. Agnes) Church, which played a central role in the Sheans' religious lives.

While attending Arlington High School, Shean's athletic abilities became evident. The school's *Clarion* reported in June 1899 that the left fielder was "playing in good style, capturing nearly everything which comes [his] way." Shean became a star of the team both at the plate and on the mound before transferring to Boston College High School. After graduating from BC High, he attended Fordham University where he played the infield and outfield and occasionally pitched against other college, semipro, and major-league teams.

During time off from school, he played for a team in Rutland, Vermont, in the Twin Mountain League, where he was spotted in 1906 by Philadelphia Athletics scout Jim Byrnes. Rather than finish his schooling, Shean jumped at the chance of signing with the Athletics, who were coming off an American League pennant. Second base was already occupied by Danny Murphy, who batted just over .300 the year Shean signed. But it wasn't only Murphy who stood in Shean's way. A week after Shean's debut with the Philadelphia American League team, another second-sacker and college boy, Eddie Collins, started his 25-year career. Collins went on to become one of the best second basemen in baseball history and was inducted into the Baseball Hall of Fame in 1939.

With the Athletics finishing a disappointing fourth in 1906, Connie Mack gave Shean some playing time at the end of the season. He played in his first major league game on September 10, 1906, collecting a hit and a sacrifice in a 2–1 win over Washington.

Within two weeks of his first game, Shean initiated of the rarest feats in baseball — a triple play. In a game against the St. Louis Browns, Bobby Wallace stepped to the plate with runners on first and second. The two runners took off with the pitch and Wallace hit a line drive to

Dave Shean, with the Philadelphia Athletics, 1906, at Chicago's South Side Park. Courtesy of Chicago History Museum.

Shean, who snared the ball and threw to shortstop Simon Nicholls, who touched second to double off Pete O'Brien and relayed the ball to first baseman Harry Davis, who retired Ike Rockenfield before he could get back to the bag at first.

After a trial in which Shean played in 22 games, collecting 75 at-bats and batting .213, the A's sent him to Montreal in the Eastern League in 1907. The following year, Shean played for Williamsport in the Tri-State League, where he led the league with 97 runs scored and hit .282 for the league winners.

With Murphy still the starting second baseman for the A's and young Eddie Collins waiting in the wings, Mack sent Shean to the crosstown Phillies, where he played shortstop for 14 games (with a .146 average) in 1908.

Shean's stay with the Phillies did not last long. After he had played 36 games in 1909, the National League team sent Shean to the Boston Doves, later renamed the Braves.

Back in his hometown, Shean got the chance to play

regularly for the second-division team. He led the National League in putouts, assists, double plays, and chances per game for the position in 1910, while batting .247. One of his highlights that year came when the Doves played Brooklyn. Shean was on second after a walk and a sacrifice bunt. He took off for third with the pitch to Bill Sweeney. Sweeney grounded the ball in the hole between Jake Daubert and John Hummel. Hummel gobbled up the ball and threw to Daubert at first to get Sweeney for the out. At the same time, Shean rounded third and continued to home, beating Daubert's throw to the plate. The scamper from second to home was becoming Shean's "specialty," according to the next day's *Boston Globe*.

Following the Doves' 100-loss season, Boston management tried to trade Shean to the New York Giants, but the team's board of directors ultimately killed the deal. A month later, though, Shean escaped baseball purgatory and was sent to the Chicago Cubs, who had won the National League pennant in 1910.

With Heinie Zimmerman and Johnny Evers already splitting time at second base, Shean spent 1911 playing both middle infield positions as a backup. The *Chicago Tribune* called Shean "an infielder of sufficient experience to jump in a regular job with the Cubs should he be needed."

When Shean hit camp before the 1911 season, manager Frank Chance had spoken positively of him, as someone who could play all four infield positions. The *Tribune*, however, was more impressed with the second baseman's wardrobe. "Shean really is in the class by himself when it comes to the glad rags. When he struck Cub headquarters, he looked as if he had been on a strap hanger all the way from the east, for there wasn't a crease in his garments except those put there by his valet," according to the *Tribune*. The crowded infield reduced his playing time, as Shean hit .288 in just 54 games for the Cubs.

The following year, 1912, the Cubs sent Shean to Louisville of the American Association, but he refused to go to Kentucky. The Louisville team suspended him. He was traded to the Braves in May 1912. After a week, Shean was on the move again, signing with the Providence Grays of the Eastern League.

Shean played the next few seasons with the Grays and resurrected his career by showing his leadership and new-found batting prowess in addition to his hard-nosed

Dave Shean, 1911 Chicago Cubs. Courtesy of Chicago History Museum.

base-running and defensive ability. In Providence, Shean "had a chance to show some stuff. He was associated with players who had ability and pep," Fred Hoey wrote in the *Boston Herald and Journal*.

That first year with Providence also proved a turning point in his life off the field. He married Eleanor Toomey, who the *Boston Globe* called a "popular East Boston girl," a handball player and entertainer in shows like the unusually-named East Boston Catholic Literary Association. They settled in his hometown of Arlington.

Back on the ball field, Shean replaced Roy Rock, a Providence favorite, at shortstop for the 1912 season. Out of his natural position, Shean struggled. He moved to second the following year and his play improved.

The year 1914 proved a successful one for both Shean and the Grays. The Grays won the International League pennant (the Eastern League had changed its name) as Shean, the Grays' captain, batted .334 in 150 games, while knocking out 173 hits, 22 doubles, 14 triples, and seven home runs; he also collected 35 sacrifice hits and 25 stolen bases.

During a one-week period that season, Shean also became acquainted with two people who would impact his life. On August 18, 1914, the Boston Red Sox sent a 19-year-old pitcher named George Herman Ruth to Providence for some seasoning. "Babe" later played with Shean on the 1918 Red Sox and the two remained friends after their playing days.

The other person to make his presence felt that week

was David W. Shean Jr., born on August 22, 1914, to David and Eleanor. David Jr. was the Sheans' only child.

Following the pennant-winning 1914 season, manager Bill Donovan left Providence and took the top job for the New York Highlanders. Rather than search outside the organization, the Grays turned to their popular second sacker to take over the Providence reins.

The Sporting News reported Shean was "the popular choice for the job. . . . Shean will be the manager that the fans are sure to cotton to. He is a clever second baseman — the best in the International League — and will be a worthy successor to Bill Donovan."

The Providence fans also rejoiced with the naming of the new manager. At a preseason dinner for Shean, "Fighting Dave," as the *Providence Journal* called him, was celebrated.

"No leader of a Providence club ever received heartier assurance of support and cooperation than those extended to popular Bill Donovan's successor on the occasion of his official introduction as guardian of the destinies of the champions," the paper reported.

Shean was confident of a first-division finish, though he warned fans that the pitching was not as strong as in its championship year.

Shean picked up his first win as a manager over the Buffalo Bisons in the second game of the 1915 season. The Grays fought with the Bisons throughout the year and headed into September with a slight lead.

The Grays' season soured, though, when the team lost doubleheaders to Buffalo and Toronto, then dropped two more games to Toronto. Buffalo edged the Grays by two games for the title. Though the Grays came up short, fans didn't cancel an already scheduled victory party after the season. Shean received a sterling silver tea set. The *Providence Journal* wrote that the Grays' fans believed "no manager ever fought harder to give the city a pennant" than had Shean.

Shean managed one more year in Providence, but before the 1917 season, with the Grays under new ownership, he lost his job in Rhode Island. Hoey wrote that Shean "was a good manager, whose maxim was 'Never drive the men. They are human. The easiest way is the best.' This put Dave 'in right' with the players and the result was teamwork in its truest sense."

In 1917, Shean was back in the majors, playing for Christy Mathewson's Cincinnati Reds. Shean played in 131 games for the .500 team that included Hal Chase, one of the finest first baseman and crookedest players in baseball history. Though the Reds suffered through mediocrity that year, and Shean hit just .210, there were memorable moments. One game of note was when Fred Toney and James "Hippo" Vaughn hooked up for nine innings of double no-hit ball. Shean played second base that day as Cincinnati knocked out its first hit in the 10th inning and won 1–0.

Shean witnessed not only near perfection while playing second base that year. He also played a part in some lunacy. One play in particular was one of the strangest scoring plays possible. The Braves' Wally Rehg didn't run out a ground ball hit to Chase at first base. Rather than step on the bag for the out, Chase instead flipped the ball to Shean at second, who tossed the ball to Larry Kopf at shortshop. Kopf rifled the ball to right fielder Tommy Griffith, who completed the putout to pitcher Peter Schneider, who was covering first. The scoring line was 3-4-6-9-1.

Shean continued playing steady ball, leading the league's second basemen in putouts, assists, double plays, and chances per game. "Any player who can survive a year with Cincinnati without impairing his baseball health is indeed a wonder," Hoey wrote.

That was the last year Shean would have to play with major league mediocrity. During spring training in 1918, the Boston Red Sox traded pitcher George "Rube" Foster — who had refused to attend spring training because of a pay cut — to the Reds for the gritty second baseman from Arlington. Shean was back home once more, but a starting job was not guaranteed. Second-base legend Johnny Evers, who played with Shean on the Cubs, was once again his competition.

The Sox made the move for Shean because they were concerned with Evers' age coupled with the fact that a number of Boston's players were eligible for the draft and the nation was at war. Shean, on the other hand, was not subject to the draft because he was 34 years old (draft age at that time was 21 to 31) and married with a son. The Sox were also concerned with Evers's temperament. His win at all costs attitude caused serious problems during the spring training tour and having him and Barrow around was not going to end well.

After reuniting with his old Providence teammate Ruth, Shean got the start at second base for the 1918 Red Sox on Opening Day, and the Sox beat the Athletics, 7–1, with Ruth getting the win.

The early season was not all good times, though. In the second game of the season, Shean was on the wrong side of pitcher Carl Mays' surly nature. On that day, Mays was hurling a no-hitter going into the eighth inning. Joe Dugan led off for the Athletics with a hard groundball into the hole. Shean tried to trap the ball with both hands, but slipped on the outfield grass. Dugan crossed first base safely and was awarded a single. Still fuming about the play after the game, Mays told the newspapermen that Shean should have been given an error.

Following that brief bump in the road, Shean's 1918 campaign was one of his finest. "His skill in blocking off the stick, his value as a sacrifice hitter, and his effective batting in the pinches was one of the biggest factors in the Red Sox' drive to victory," reported the *Boston Post*. "And every ballplayer in both the big leagues will freely

Shean with the 1910 Boston Doves.

admit that Dave is one of the wisest infielders in the game and that neither Cobb nor anyone else can put anything across while Shean is on the watch."

He batted .264 and played in 115 games in the 126-game season, shortened because of the war. Shean missed time that year because of neuralgia, foot problems, a stomach virus, and an infected foot.

The injury bug bit Shean again while the Red Sox practiced for the 1918 World Series. He dove for a line drive and the ball struck his throwing hand, ripping the nail and skin off the tip of his middle finger. Trainer Martin Lawler wrapped the finger in a splint and Shean was ready to play in his first World Series.

In the first game, Shean scored the only run of the contest. Stuffy McInnis singled him home from second base. *The Sporting News* wrote of Shean's journey home that he "runs like a turtle on an iceberg."

After the Sox won two of three games in Chicago, the teams rode the rails back to Boston. While on the trip, players discussed their possible winnings. Dissatisfied with the new rule that the World Series pot would be split between more teams (the two league champions would take 55½ percent of the money — not the full 100% — and split it 60/40), coupled with cheaper ticket prices that hurt the size of player bonuses, the players discussed taking action.

Shean, Harry Hooper, and the Cubs' Les Mann tried to meet with the National Commission, which ran baseball at the time, but were rebuffed. The dispute resurfaced

later in the Series and the players threatened to strike before Game Five.

Back on the field, Shean made one of the best plays of the Series in Game Four. In the sixth inning, Ruth walked Lefty Tyler. Max Flack grounded back to the pitcher, who threw wildly to second past shortshop Everett Scott. But Shean, backing up the play, caught the ball while on his knees and dove toward the base, crawling on his stomach to tag the base before Tyler's foot made contact. Ruth retired the next two batters and continued his scoreless innings streak that stood as a World Series record until 1962.

The Red Sox wrapped up their fifth world championship in Game Six. Shean scored the winning run and fielded the ground ball that secured the 2–1 win. Though Shean hit only .211 in the Series, he scored the first and final runs. Those were the only runs he scored in the six games but, then again, the Red Sox scored only nine runs in all.

World Series champion teams usually have a joy-filled offseason, but not the 1918 Red Sox. Baseball's hierarchy was upset with the players' "greedy" demand for more money during the Series. While previous winners received $3,000 to $4,000 for winning the Series, which was more than the annual salaries of most of the players, the Red Sox players collected only slightly more than $1,100.

National Commission member John Heydler told the players they would not receive their World Champion emblems "owing to the disgraceful conduct of the players in the strike during the series." In response, Sox owner Harry Frazee bought several of the players pocket watches engraved with their names and "Red Sox 1918 champions," but the National Commission snub haunted the players long after their playing days.

Shean's grandson, Henry, said his grandfather didn't talk much about his baseball career, which he said could have been because of the 1918 slight. "Growing up, we always talked about the Red Sox. But he didn't talk about his career. I think he may have been unhappy about the way things went down," said Henry Shean.

For the following decades after the snub, Hooper sent letters to the baseball commissioners asking for the team's emblems. In one printed letter, the Hall of Famer even mentioned Shean, noting that 1918 was his only World Series appearance. Seventy-five years after the snub and nearly 10 years after Hooper's death, the relatives of the

1918 Red Sox finally received their honors. During a ceremony at Fenway Park, the Red Sox (and not Major League Baseball) gave the families commemorative pins in honor of the 1918 season.

After the World Series year of 1918, Shean played in only 29 games, and was batting just .140 when the Red Sox released him in August 1919.

Many baseball players struggle with lives after baseball, but not Shean. He returned to his position at Nathan Robbins Company, a poultry firm that employed him during the offseason.

In a December 1918 story in the *Boston Post*, Hoey wrote, "When the baseball season is over, Dave does not sit around clubrooms or pool halls and tell the natives what's best in baseball. Instead he exchanges his baseball uniform for a butcher's frock and (goes) to the big market where he handles more fowls." Shean spent decades after baseball working for the poultry company in the dank basement of Boston's Quincy Market.

"You get a tough one now and then just the same as you do in baseball," Shean said of his poultry work. "Once in a while, I run across one that has spurs like those that Ty Cobb wears. I sidestep those babies. There are all kinds of birds in the poultry game as there are in the big leagues. I get plenty of chances to size up all the varieties."

Shean worked his way up the company ladder and became president of the business. "His personality is one of the firm's biggest assets and the Dave Shean smile brings hundreds of new customers every year," reported the *Boston Post*.

Shean stayed in touch with the game. According to reports at the time, the Arlington man made trips to Fenway Park when his old friend Babe Ruth came to town with the Yankees. During those visits, Shean presented the Babe with poultry, which the Sultan of Swat devoured.

"He didn't make it a point to talk about his famous friends," recalled his granddaughter Leslie Flanagan. "He didn't make a big deal out of it though he really had quite an exciting life as a younger man. He was very modest about the whole thing."

Shean remained with the poultry business until the end of his life. His only child, David Jr., who graduated from Harvard University and served in World War II, followed in his father's footsteps by taking over the leadership role at Nathan Robbins Company. Though Shean did not return to pro ball after his retirement, he played and coached baseball on Arlington's Spy Pond Field. He also participated in old-timers games in the Boston area.

Shean's life came to an end in 1963 after the 77-year-old widower suffered numerous injuries in a car accident. He died at Massachusetts General Hospital on May 22. His death was mourned by his hometown. The local newspaper, the *Arlington Advocate*, called Shean "one of Arlington's best known and loved citizens."

Advocate columnist Leonard Collins wrote that Shean was "a very quiet and unassuming man. Dave hardly talked about his playing days, but on such occasions he was wonderful to listen to as he spoke of the men who were known all over the country." Shean's funeral was held at St. Agnes Church, where he had spent many hours attending services. He was buried at St. Paul's Cemetery in his hometown.

Thinking back on her father-in-law's life, Helen Shean remembered the former ballplayer as the "most generous, thoughtful, quiet man I ever knew."

After his death, *Advocate* columnist Collins summed up Shean's life by writing, "On or off the field, Dave did just great. His quiet charities over the years were many and no one would know about these if the recipients had not divulged his name. Arlington was his home always and he never lost interest in its people or activities."

JACK STANSBURY *by Tony Bunting*

G	AB	R	H	2B	3B	HR	RBI	BB	SO	BA	OBP	SLG	SB	HBP
20	47	3	6	1	0	0	2	6	3	.128	.241	.149	0	1

Like the Selective Service System and liberty bonds, Jack Stansbury's brief major league career was a product of America's involvement in World War I. Early in the summer of 1918, while the United States war effort siphoned teams' rosters, Stansbury, until then a fixture in the minors, suddenly became a 32-year old rookie pursuing a pennant with the Boston Red Sox. The former New Orleans Pelicans utilityman failed to distinguish himself during 21 games in the American League, but his month-long stint turned out to be surprisingly eventful. Just days after he joined the Red Sox, he became an accidental participant in a sensational episode involving young slugger Babe Ruth. He also had diamond encounters with four other baseball immortals.

After his brush with fame, Stansbury quietly retreated to the minors, where he completed a serviceable 19-year professional baseball career, moving effortlessly from outfield to infield to catcher. His versatility prompted *The Sporting News* to call him "a champion all-around man in the field" and "the star of utility men."

John James "Jack" Stansbury began his life on December 6, 1885, in Phillipsburg, New Jersey, a thriving industrial town on the banks of the Delaware River. The youngest of four children born to David and Rose-ann (Mooney) Stansbury, Jack played amateur ball in the Easton-Nazareth area of Pennsylvania, across the river from Phillipsburg. At 5'9" and 165 pounds, Jack possessed a valuable combination of speed, strength, and the ability to play a variety of positions.

Scouts recognized Stansbury's array of skills, and Williamsport of the Tri-State League acquired the 22-year-old for the 1908 season. Following a pair of unspectacular years in which he played outfield, infield, and catcher, the man frequently known as "Stans-berry" in the box scores (and even "Shrewsbury" on at least one occasion) turned heads in 1910 when he batted a sparkling .294 in 92 games. Yet it was the afternoon of September 5 that likely proved to be the turning point in his career. On that day, the right-hander blasted three home runs over the left-field wall in a doubleheader sweep at Altoona — a gargantuan feat near the midway point of baseball's Deadball Era. The stunning accomplishment against the eventual Tri-State champs received national press coverage.

Propelled by his late-season power burst, Stansbury landed with the Louisville Colonels of the American Association in 1911. There, he logged the best years of his professional career and flirted with making major league clubs. Playing second base and left field early on, he became a regular and quickly proved he could hit the offerings of a pair of former major league stars. On May 5, he went 1-for-3 off Nick Altrock of Minneapolis, then followed it up the next day with a 3-for-4 performance against the Millers' Rube Waddell.

George Biggers, Louisville correspondent for *The Sporting News*, raved about the newcomer's multi-dimensionality and spirited attitude: "The showing of this little player has been most amusing and still gratifying to everyone concerned . . . So far, he has played left field, second, short and is now going to center. He can also go behind the bat in a pinch. But the beauty part of it is that he is hitting at a .314 clip and rapidly improving. This swatting ability of his will sure keep him on the team. Stansbury is not a center fielder but he is a hard worker, always willing to ask for advice from the older heads and is giving

Jack Stansbury, 1918. Courtesy of Chicago History Museum.

(manager) Del Howard all that he has every minute."

Later, the Colonels moved Stansbury to third base and placed him the leadoff spot, where he thrived. Jack turned out to be a bright spot for the last-place squad. He hit .283 in 569 at-bats, cracking 23 doubles and 10 triples. Late in 1911, he attracted the notice of major league clubs. In August, Charles Murphy, owner of the defending National League champion Chicago Cubs, headed to Louisville to scout the prospect, but decided not to work a deal for him. Murphy instead secured Stansbury's teammate Larry Cheney, a pitcher who went on to dominate the National League the next season, winning 26 games and losing 10.

Though the Cubs passed on Jack, the Cleveland Naps did not. They obtained the services of Stansbury in the fall and took him to spring training in 1912. Jack competed for Cleveland's third base position, but became the first casualty of camp when he was cut and shipped back to Louisville. Again holding down third and leading off, Stansbury got off to a blistering 29-for-64 start before being injured in a freak accident at Minneapolis on May 1. As he sat on the bench, Colonels second baseman Lynn Bell sliced a line drive into the Louisville dugout. "Stansbury threw up his arm to guard his head and the ball struck him on the bone, fracturing it," reported *Sporting Life*. "He will be out of the game for a month or six weeks."

Stansbury suffered a broken left wrist, but recovered swiftly and returned to the lineup on June 4. He showed no ill effects from the injury. Splitting his time between the outfield and infield, Stansbury batted .301 for the seventh-place Colonels. This time, the St. Louis Cardinals snapped up the utilityman extraordinaire for their 1913 spring training session. *The Sporting News* gushed about Stansbury's potential: "If all dope on this Louisville recruit is correct, Manager Miller Huggins will make a mistake in not giving him a full trial. He was a .300 hitter in the American Association last year, with 25 two-baggers to his credit, and is a champion all-around man in the field. . . . Judging from his ability to cover any position he might even fill Ed Koney's [Ed Konetchy] job at first, though a little light on weight and short on height."

Alas, Stansbury was discarded once again. The try-out with the Cardinals seemed to be his final shot at the big time. Jack's performance dropped off significantly in 1913, and though he rallied in the ensuing year (.278, 96 runs, 182 hits, 26 doubles, 11 triples in 160 games), Louisville dealt him to New Orleans of the Southern Association at the end of the 1915 campaign.

Now 30 years old, Stansbury appeared to have his best seasons behind him. Nonetheless, he remained a valuable player. His versatility was perhaps no more evident than in 1917, when he played 17 games at second base, 19 at shortstop, 22 in left field, 14 in center field, 16 in right field, and 16 at catcher and pinch hit in 11 contests as the Pelicans finished second in the Southern Association. Stansbury's ubiquitous ways continued into the next season for New Orleans, when World War I intruded on Organized Baseball and turned Jack's life, and those of many other players, upside down.

A set of circumstances resulting from America's involvement in the war conspired to elevate Stansbury to the major leagues in 1918. The first was the announcement in May of the U.S. government's "work-or-fight" order. This rule, requiring men between 21 and 31 to find "essential" or "useful" employment by July 1, or risk induction into the armed forces, sent some young major leaguers scurrying off to factories and shipyards. Others enlisted. While owners awaited a sweeping government ruling on whether the order would be applied to baseball, the situation forced big-league clubs to seek additional sources of players to offset losses. Several minor circuits, including Stansbury's Southern Association, decided to halt operations near the end of June and in early July due to the war, creating a supply of professional players. At 32 years old — just beyond the age limit for the draft — Stansbury suddenly became an attractive commodity. The Red Sox, already smarting from losses of personnel to the armed forces and essential industry, and girding for more, purchased Jack, along with fellow infielders Walter Barbare and Red Bluhm, from New Orleans on June 25.

Sporting a big league uniform at last, Stansbury made his debut at third base in place of the ailing Fred Thomas (who would soon enlist) on June 30 in a road contest against Washington. On the mound for the Senators that afternoon: Walter Johnson. The rookie refused to be intimidated by the future Hall of Famer, who would finish 23–13 in the war-shortened season, with a 1.27 ERA. Although hitless, Stansbury put the ball in play on every at-bat and "laid down a neat sacrifice" his first time up, according to the *Boston Post*'s Paul H. Shannon. The bunt helped produce a run. In the field, Stansbury's fine play on a "hard chance" on a slick surface prevented a game-winning score by Washington in the ninth and allowed the Red Sox to win it in the 10th, 3–1. He had survived his first major league test.

Unbeknownst to Jack, the excitement was only beginning. Two days later, he stood at the epicenter of an explosion by his new teammate Babe Ruth. In the sixth inning of a game against the Senators, Ruth, who was making his transition to everyday player in 1918 and had started in center field, struck out for the second time. When Babe reached the bench, Red Sox manager Ed Barrow lashed into him for jumping too hastily at pitches. The rebuke set off what the *Boston Herald and Journal* described as a "verbal pyrotechnic debate" between the two men. "I thought he (Barrow) called me a bum and I threatened to punch him," Ruth said. "He told me that would cost me $500, and then I made a few more remarks and left the club."

After Babe's angry departure, Stansbury took over in center field and finished the game. Ruth failed to show up for the following day's contest in Philadelphia, causing news to spread that he had quit the team. Jack once again replaced the slugger in center and batted cleanup (he went 0-for-4). A choice bit of irony then occurred. At the same time Stansbury was filling in for the Red Sox star, Ruth busily made arrangements to play for the Chester (Pennsylvania) Shipbuilding Company team. (The shipyard was on the Delaware River not far from where Jack grew up.) But it never came to pass. With Boston owner Harry Frazee threatening legal action against the shipbuilding company, and Ruth finally calming down, the home run hitter returned to his squad and played the second game of a Fourth of July doubleheader versus the Athletics. Stansbury substituted one last time for Babe in the opener, going 2-for-5 in an 11–9 Boston victory.

The Ruth incident laid to rest, Stansbury's big league life began to settle down. He started at third base on a semiregular basis (Barbare alternated with him) and batted seventh or eighth in the order as the Red Sox waged a fierce battle with the Cleveland Indians and Washington Senators for first place. Yet Jack never seemed far from an adventure with one of baseball's greats. In a key skirmish with the Indians at Fenway Park on July 9, the rookie third baseman made a sensational sprinting catch in front of the stands of Tris Speaker's "high, wavering, wind-tossed" foul ball. The crowd roared its approval. The *Post*'s cartoonist depicted the play in its next edition, showing an outstretched Stansbury saying to himself, "This is tough on Tris." He got even tougher on the star center fielder the following afternoon. By smothering Speaker's blazing shot to third, Stansbury was able to catch a Cleveland baserunner in a rundown and squelch a rally. He also started a pair of double plays from the hot corner. Jack's defensive gems contributed to a pair of Boston shutouts (1–0, 2–0), helped push the team's lead to 2½ games, and elicited the praise of the Boston press. "Stansbury works like an artist," said the *Boston Globe*'s Edward F. Martin. "He gets them everywhere, shoots the ball away quick and throws true to the mark." His inability to solve major league pitching, however, bothered

Barrow, and his 4-for-32 start earned him a spot on the bench for several games.

Stansbury returned to the lineup on July 19 for the opening of a four-game set with the Detroit Tigers at Fenway. The next day, while patrolling third, he had a base-path rendezvous with Ty Cobb. On a double steal attempt in the sixth, the Georgia Peach charged toward Stansbury, who held the ball — perhaps nervously — well in advance of Cobb. At the last moment, the Tigers' superstar slid and deftly maneuvered his body to avoid the infielder's tag, reaching the bag safely. The crowd, the largest of the season at Fenway to that point, howled at the seemingly supernatural Cobb.

Despite his meager offensive output — and the little lesson by Cobb — Stansbury's prospects for remaining with Boston for the rest of 1918 appeared bright. While Jack and the Red Sox were scrapping it out with Detroit, Secretary of War Newton Baker, ruling on the draft appeal of Senators catcher Eddie Ainsmith, definitively proclaimed baseball to be a nonessential industry. The judgment guaranteed that draft-age players would face induction into the armed forces under the work-or-fight order unless they found employment deemed vital to the war effort. As a result, more major leaguers left their teams for jobs in factories, shipyards, and the like. Stansbury seemed more valuable than ever.

His hitting even picked up briefly, and on July 26, Jack enjoyed his finest day as a big-leaguer. In a contest against the White Sox at Comiskey Park, he smacked two hits and drove in a run, off one of the game's best hurlers, Eddie Cicotte. He was outstanding in the field, too, collecting six assists and two putouts. Stansbury's moment of glory was short-lived, though. He failed to hit safely in the remaining two Chicago games, and Barrow finally benched him in favor of new recruit George Cochran.

Perhaps more damaging to Stansbury's hopes for big league survival was Secretary Baker's announcement of an extension until September 1 of the deadline of the work-or-fight order to baseball players. Jack's most precious asset — his age — immediately became worthless in the wake of the major-league owners' decision to end the season on Labor Day. Less than a week after Baker's statement on July 26, the Red Sox, on the road for a series with St. Louis, sent Stansbury, Frank Truesdale (34 years old), and Lore Bader home to Boston. They were soon dealt to teams in the International League, Stansbury heading to Newark. The *Herald and Journal* writer with the nom-de-plume Bob Dunbar described the players as "very disconsolate" over their departure from the Red Sox. "It is easy to sympathize these days with a big leaguer who has been sent down to the minors. . . ." Dunbar continued, "Then, too, this trio is deprived of any split (of money) in the world series, if w.s. there be."

Indeed, Boston went on to win the American League pennant in the truncated campaign and defeated the Chicago Cubs in the World Series, four games to two. Fred Thomas returned from naval training long enough to play third base for the Red Sox. Stansbury had performed admirably in his month-long stay with Boston. In 21 major league games (one more than record books credit him for), he batted a paltry .154, but committed just one error in 56 chances, making several difficult plays. When he debuted with Boston on June 30, the Red Sox were percentage points behind the Yankees in the A.L. standings. When he left on July 31, Boston owned a 4½-game first-place lead over the Indians.

His dalliance with the game's elite over, Stansbury eased back into minor league life, spending another eight years in the bushes. In 1919, he made his way back to New Orleans, where he lived with his wife, Edith, and concluded the season with Beaumont of the Texas League. Jack found the oil-rich city near the Gulf of Mexico to his liking and settled there for the next 40 years. Once again playing multiple positions for the Beaumont Exporters in 1922, the 36-year-old Stansbury hit .287 in 592 at-bats, scored 86 runs, and drove in 61. He served another three years in the Texas League, before receiving an offer to be the player-manager of Palestine of the Texas Association in 1926. His endeavor with the franchise was as brief and unsuccessful as his Boston foray. Palestine's president, Thomas M. Campbell Jr., fired the new skipper without explanation after a loss to Austin late in May. "I can not understand why I was released," a crestfallen Stansbury said. "The club was running fine and we are in third place in the league." He wrapped up his 19-year pro career the same season with Tyler-Texarkana of the East Texas circuit.

Jack finally decided to reap some of the opportunities furnished by Beaumont's Spindletop gusher of 1901. He worked as a machinist for the Magnolia Refinery Co. (now part of Exxon Mobil) and plunged himself into the social scene of Beaumont. Despite having no children of his own, Jack maintained strong ties to his family in New Jersey, and developed a close relationship with his nephew, also named Jack.

"My dad said when Uncle Jack was playing ball he would send him balls home and he was the only kid in the early '20s with real baseballs," said Jane (Stansbury) Miller, the daughter of the younger Jack Stansbury. "They were all very proud of Uncle Jack, and though he only played in the majors a short time, it was very exciting to his family. My dad is named after him and he really had great affection for Uncle Jack. He once sent him a glove and my dad thought that was the greatest thing. Uncle Jack received a gold pocket watch for Most Valuable Player. My brother said he remembers my father telling him it was from an industrial league."

After his wife died in 1960, Jack moved back to Phillipsburg in New Jersey to be closer to his family, bringing his life full circle. Stansbury eventually developed

Parkinson's disease and died of bronchopneumonia on December 26, 1970, at the age of 85. The man who challenged Walter Johnson at the plate, replaced Babe Ruth in the outfield, met Ty Cobb on the basepaths, and had a small role in helping the Boston Red Sox win a world championship — all in one amazing month in the war-plagued summer of 1918 — rests in Fairmount Cemetery in Phillipsburg.

AMOS STRUNK *by John McMurray*

G	AB	R	H	2B	3B	HR	RBI	BB	SO	BA	OBP	SLG	SB	HBP
114	413	50	106	18	9	0	35	36	13	.257	.316	.344	20	0

Lanky and lightning fast, Amos Strunk was one of the best defensive center fielders of the Deadball Era and a major offensive contributor to Connie Mack's powerhouse Philadelphia Athletics teams which appeared in four World Series from 1910 to 1914. A patient hitter, the left-handed Strunk placed in the top 10 in the American League in slugging three times from 1913 to 1916, but his power was a derivative of his speed: though "The Flying Foot" never became a great base-stealer, he was one of the fastest in the league on the basepaths, placing among the league leaders in doubles twice and triples four times. Strunk's exceptional speed allowed him to go from first to third on bunt plays, and his quickness led J.C. Kofoed of *Baseball Magazine* to remark: "Some call him the Mercury of the American League, but all know Amos Strunk whatever the handle they plaster on him. He is of a type one instinctively calls rangy, because he moves with the speed you would exert should you accidentally touch a red-hot range."

Amos Strunk.

Amos Aaron Strunk was born on January 22, 1889 in Philadelphia, Pennsylvania, the fifth child of Amos, a carpenter, and Amanda Strunk. Young Amos learned baseball playing at Fairmount and Huntington Parks in Philadelphia, where the players were called "Park Sparrows" since they spent so much time on the baseball field. There, it was noted that "the lanky kid was too fast for his protagonists. He ran rings around them, and they confessed it." After playing with an amateur team in Merchantville, N.J. in 1907, Strunk began playing professionally with Shamokin of the outlaw Atlantic League in 1908. From there, he was recommended by teammate Lave Cross to Athletics manager Connie Mack, who brought Strunk to the major league team and played him for the first time on September 24, 1908; Strunk collected a pinch hit single in his debut. Mack was intent on assembling a group of speedy players, and "he wanted men who could travel

fast enough to burn their galoshes. Collins, Barry, Oldring, and the rest were in that class, and Amos fitted in like a drink on an August day." Strunk was sent out to Milwaukee of the American Association for some additional seasoning early in the 1909 season, but he was soon back with Philadelphia to resume a major league career that would last for 17 seasons.

At age 21 in 1910, the 175-pound Strunk was described as being "built like a panther, standing six feet in height, and without an ounce of superfluous flesh upon him." Strunk, however, played in only 16 regular season games in 1910 due to a knee injury. Strunk was plagued by injuries throughout his career, which is a major reason why he played in fewer than 100 games in eight of his major league seasons. Strunk came back late in the season and played in four of the five games in that year's World Series, collecting five hits in 18 at-bats and driving in two runs.

Strunk quickly established himself as one of the premier defensive outfielders in baseball. In 1913, one writer claimed that "Amos has justly earned the verdict of being the greatest defensive outfielder that the game has ever produced. In the matter of fielding his position on the defense, the Ty Cobbs of today and the Curt Welches of other days never even approximated the same class displayed by Amos. It is impossible to even conceive of anything in human form performing more sensational and unerring feats than Amos shows consistently day in and day out. An accurate judge of a batted ball, off at the crack of the bat, his great speed takes him to wallops that other great outfielders would never reach, and he has no weaknesses to either side, in front or back there, by the palings." *Baseball Magazine* three years later noted that "for five years now Amos has demonstrated to his fellow townsmen that, barring a few immortals like Cobb and Speaker, he need doff his chapeau to none." High praise to be sure,

Sox centerfielder Strunk featured in April 5, 1918 *Boston Post* sports page cartoon.

but Strunk elicited it through his superlative play, leading the league in fielding percentage four times from 1912 to 1918, and regularly ranking among the league leaders in putouts per game. Despite such accolades from the press, Mack felt his center fielder was undervalued, calling Strunk "the most underrated outfielder in baseball." Mack went on to say that "Amos made his job of playing center field look a lot easier than it really was."

Strunk was also a key man in Mack's famed double squeeze play. With Strunk on second and a runner on third, Mack would have the batter bunt. The speedy Strunk would break from second base with the pitch and would follow the runner from third home, allowing the Athletics to score two runs on a single squeeze bunt. In addition to the 1910 championship team, Strunk was a major contributor to Connie Mack's

Strunk with the A's.

World Series teams in 1911, 1913, and 1914, though injuries kept him from appearing in more than 122 games in any of the three seasons.

During his career, Strunk was considered one of baseball's great storytellers. It was said that he had a "De Wolfe [*sic*] Hopper way of telling stories," in reference to the legendary Broadway actor and orator. *Baseball Magazine* commented: "Some time when you're not busy get Amos to tell you stories on old John McCluskey. He'll make you laugh so hard you'll lose your wrist watch."

Strunk did not enjoy his best season in a Philadelphia uniform until Mack had dismantled the A's dynasty, selling off most of the team's best players and sending the club plummeting in the standings. In 1916, when the A's lost an astounding 117 games — still the worst record in modern baseball history — Strunk was by far the team's best player, setting career highs in doubles (30), hits (172), and on-base percentage (.393), while ranking fourth in the league with a .316 batting average. He followed that performance with another strong campaign in 1917, scoring a career-high 83 runs while batting .281 with a .363 OBP. Following the season, the cash-strapped Mack completed his fire sale, sending Strunk, Joe Bush, and Wally Schang to the Boston Red Sox in return for $60,000 cash and three players.

Strunk's average slipped to .257 in 1918, as the Red Sox captured the pennant and won the World Series. In June 1919, Strunk was traded back to the Athletics from the Red Sox along with Jack Barry in return for Bobby Roth and Red Shannon. Claimed off waivers by the White Sox in July 1920, Strunk had another outstanding season in 1921 with Chicago, and he went on to play primarily a part-time role with the White Sox through 1923. Though Strunk continued to be effective when he played, persistent leg injuries often kept him on the bench and chipped away at his defensive range. In 1922, Strunk batted .289 in 92 games, and in 1923 he posted a .315 batting average in 54 at-bats. During spring training 1924 Strunk suffered serious head injuries in an outfield collision with teammate Roy Elsh, and was released by the White Sox a month later after appearing in only one game as a pinch hitter. On May 2, 1924, the Athletics acquired him for a third time, signing the 35-year-old outfielder as a free agent. In 30 games for the Athletics, Strunk posted a .143 batting average and was released at season's end. Appointed as the player-manager of the Shamokin Shammies of the New York-Pennsylvania League in 1925, Strunk resigned in August, citing recurrent leg injuries, although he was batting .396 at the time. It was his last job in organized baseball.

In retirement, Strunk became an insurance broker, and he remained in that business for 50 years. He was also an expert photographer. A 1958 article described how "Strunk might be taken for a retired admiral. His hair is white, and he is youthful in movement and dress." His wife Ethel, whom he married in 1915, was a successful portrait painter, and the two were married for more than 50 years until her death in 1966.

Strunk occasionally bemoaned the lack of aggressiveness in contemporary baseball after he retired. He felt that baseball needed more of the competitive fire that teams like the Dodgers and Giants showed during Strunk's era. "Baseball needs more of that bitterness today," he said, "but it's still a wonderful game."

Amos Strunk died on July 22, 1979 at age 90 in Llanerich, Pennsylvania after a brief illness. He was survived by two nephews. Strunk was buried in Greenmount Cemetery in Philadelphia.

FRED THOMAS *by Craig Lammers*

G	AB	R	H	2B	3B	HR	RBI	BB	SO	BA	OBP	SLG	SB	HBP
44	144	19	37	2	1	1	11	15	20	.257	.331	.306	4	1

After eight years as a Boston regular, longtime third baseman Larry Gardner was sent by the Red Sox to Philadelphia in early 1918 as part of the Stuffy McInnis trade. Including McInnis, nine men were used at third base by Boston during 1918. Playing the most games at third (41) was 25-year old Fred Thomas. Thomas had arguably the most interesting season of any member of the Red Sox. He was a member of two championship teams (the Red Sox won the World Series and his Great Lakes team took the Navy Championship), had five future Hall of Famers as teammates, and played in seven games against the Chicago Cubs (six in the Series and one exhibition game while with the Great Lakes Naval team).

Fred Thomas was the grandson of immigrants. His grandfather, also named Frederick, was from the Hesse region of Germany. In 1880 Frederick was a saloonkeeper in Menominee Falls, Wisconsin. The second of his eight children, George, was born in Wisconsin about 1868. George Thomas became a carpenter and married in 1891. George and Martha Thomas had four children, only one living to adulthood. That child, Frederick Harvey Thomas, was born in Milwaukee on December 19, 1892.

George and Martha soon moved to the village of Mukwonago in Waukesha County, southeast of Milwaukee. This area would be Fred's home through most of his baseball career. The Mukwonago area is still largely rural and a sizable lake is located near town. Fred enjoyed the outdoors. In addition to baseball, he fished in the lake and hunted on the nearby farmland. He also made money trapping muskrats in the lake. Trapping was lucrative, and Fred continued trapping even after entering professional baseball. He later remembered making almost as much trapping as he made during a season of professional baseball. Money saved from his offseason vocation later allowed Thomas to buy land in Northern Wisconsin

on which he built a resort that is still operated by family members.

Fred played high school baseball and with the local Mukwonago team. During his high school career, he was seen by a scout from the Milwaukee City League. To preserve his amateur status, he played in the City League under the name of Wallace.

He graduated from Mukwonago High School in June, 1911, and almost immediately began his professional career. The day after graduation, George and Fred Thomas traveled together to Fond Du Lac, Wisconsin. Fred later remembered "being scared to death." Fond Du Lac was a member of the Class C Wisconsin Illinois League.

When Fred and his father arrived in town, they went to the ballpark since the team was playing that day. It often took a little luck to break into professional baseball in 1911, and Fred Thomas remembered in a 1973 interview how that luck came about: "They had their team all set but — would you believe it — their third baseman got hurt that day. The manager of the club took a look at me and I know what he thought. He said, 'Kid, do you think you can play third base?' I said, 'Sure I can play third base.' So he says, 'Tomorrow morning, I'll hit you a few grounders to see what you can do.' That infield was as smooth as glass and I thought they'd never get it by me there. So the next morning he hit me a few grounders and said, 'I guess you'll do.'"

Fred Thomas was in the lineup that very afternoon. "It was the first professional ballgame I ever played and I'll never forget it. We played Rockford and they were the best team in the league. They had a pitcher by the name of [Cy] Slapnicka going for them — the best pitcher in the league, too. You know it was the best game I ever played as far as fielding is concerned. They hit more groundballs down towards third base and, boy, I got them every which way. I just had confidence on that good infield."

Rockford broke a scoreless tie in the top of the ninth, but Thomas was presented a chance to become a hero. "We got a man on first base in our half of the inning and I was the next man to bat, to sacrifice. I'd never sacrificed in my life and so everyone was telling the manager what to do:: 'You should put somebody up there to sacrifice for the kid.' The manager said, 'Nope, after the way he's played today, I'm not putting anyone in there for him. I don't care what he does. So I went up there to sacrifice and I made a half sacrifice down towards third base. The pitcher tried to get the man at second and he threw the ball a mile into right-centerfield. That man scored and I scored, too, and we won the ballgame."

Thomas went with the team on a road trip to Aurora and Rockford. He said of those games: "I went along great, but I couldn't seem to hit. I don't know why." After the last game at Rockford, manager Bobby Lynch received a phone call from the team president. "The third baseman was ready to play and we can't afford to carry an extra man." Lynch told Thomas, "I'll just have to let you go home. I hate to do it. I'd rather let another man go and keep you, but they won't stand for it."

Thomas spent the rest of the summer playing semipro ball in Mukwonago, and late in the season got another chance at professional baseball. "Around Labor Day, the Green Bay club sold their third baseman to Los Angeles and called to ask if I'd finish the season. It was a funny thing. Where I couldn't hit at Fond Du Lac, they couldn't get me out at Green Bay. Playing in the sandlots around my home town, I got a bad charley horse and could hardly run up there [at Fond Du Lac]." Statistics for Thomas' first professional season are unavailable.

That fall, Fred enrolled at Carroll College in Waukesha. He wasn't sure if he wanted to continue in professional ball, but when Green Bay sent a contract that winter, Thomas decided to give professional baseball another try. Fred's son Warren Thomas believes there was some parental influence involved, and that decades later Fred wasn't entirely certain he had made the right choice. Thomas remembered having a good year in 1912, and he did. He batted .235 with decent power for the era.

Moved to shortstop in 1913, he was one of the league's best infielders. He led the league with 127 games played, 81 runs, and 13 triples. He batted .290, stole 29 bases, and hit 10 home runs. Triples and home runs would prove

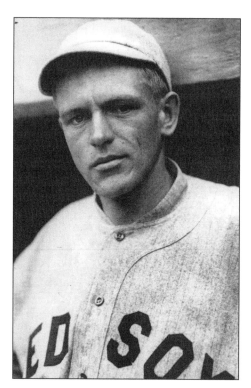

Fred Thomas. George Brace photo.

lucrative for Thomas that season. "The Continental Clothing Company in Green Bay used to give $3.50 of merchandise for every home player that hit a three-base hit or a home run. I roomed with a fellow by the name of Earl Smith who also went up to the big leagues afterwards. I was just a skinny kid and everybody was kidding him because roommates used to split whatever they got. They didn't think he'd get any help from me. Would you believe it? By the end of the summer we had a couple of trunks filled and didn't know what to buy afterwards."

Clothing wasn't the only extra Thomas and Smith received for their hitting that summer. "With a home run you got a carton of Bull Durham tobacco and if you didn't want that they'd give you $2.85 in cash. On one road trip at Wausau, I don't know how many home runs Earl Smith and I hit, but we had enough to carry us on the whole road trip. The Bull Durham Company [also] put a big frame of a bull in the outfield and every time you hit the bull you got $50. I hit the bull the first year I played with Green Bay, and the second year I played with Green Bay, I hit it three times."

Fred's play in 1913 also impressed veteran manager "Pa" Rourke of the Omaha team of the Class A Western League. After his second season with Green Bay, Omaha drafted him in the fall of 1913.

Pa Rourke was legendary for his run-ins with Western League umpires. The *Topeka Daily Capital* said: "The stream of expletives which flows from Pa's lips during the progress of a ball game is a never diminishing current five feet wide and eleven feet deep." The manager was popular enough in Omaha that the 1914 team was nicknamed the Rourkes. Rourke was an astute judge of young talent. During the offseason he sold a pair of veteran infielders including former major leaguer Jim Kane to make room for Thomas and another young player. The *Daily Capital* was initially skeptical, but later wrote: "Thomas, the svelte blonde third bagster of the Omaha team, looks to be a pretty sweet ballplayer due to go higher some time." Playing shortstop much of the season, Thomas maintained an average over .300 before finishing at .285 with excellent extra-base power.

Thomas was one of three future 1918 Red Sox third basemen to play in the Western League in 1914. George Cochran played third for Topeka and Jack Coffey was the manager-shortstop at Denver. Cochran and Coffey would remain in the Western League, but for Fred Thomas another promotion was in order. Drafted by Cleveland after 1914, he was assigned to New Orleans of the Southern Association After spending spring training with the major league team, Fred Thomas had another outstanding season at New Orleans in 1915. He hit .265, and led the league with 11 home runs and 53 steals. He later remembered, "I just about ruined that league." New Orleans newspapers referred to him as "The Rabbit." That season and a decision by the Boston Red Sox would soon change the course of Fred Thomas's career.

In April, 1916, Boston dealt Tris Speaker to Cleveland for two players and an estimated $50,000. One of those players was Sam Jones, the other Thomas. A *Boston Globe* columnist wrote of Thomas: "It has been a long time since Boston has had a baserunner with a record of 53 stolen bases for a season. May Fred Thomas, the new infielder for the Red Sox, via the Speaker deal, be another Billy Hamilton. There is many a time when a fast man on the bases in place of a slow one means the winning of a game." The Red Sox left Thomas at New Orleans for the 1916 season. Despite a disappointing season, Thomas was invited to Boston's 1917 spring training camp in Hot Springs, Arkansas.

An early intra-squad game demonstrated Thomas's strengths and weaknesses as a player. At the plate, he "twice tripled and drove in a run with a sacrifice fly. He kicked one in the field and pegged poorly to [Mike] McNally in the final frame." Thomas remained with the Red Sox until they returned to Boston. He even got his first look at Ty Cobb that spring. When Boston played a pair of exhibition games at Toledo, Cobb was in the Mud Hens' lineup, while Thomas watched from the bench. A few years later, Thomas would have a closer meeting with Cobb. "He slid into third base once and thought I got a little bit careless in touching him out. He called me everything he could think of—but he put himself out that time [and] he didn't like that I told him that."

The *Boston Globe* said that when Harry Frazee informed Thomas he would be sent back to New Orleans for the 1917 season, "Thomas said he would go home first." Instead he was sent to Boston's Providence farm club in the International League. The *Globe* reported: "The recruit is satisfied with the Providence berth and said that he did not expect to stick with the Sox, saying that a club that was good enough to win the world's championship should be good enough to stick together for awhile." Playing in a top-classification league for the first time, Fred hit .252, tripled 16 times and stole 20 bases.

As 1918 began, the *Globe* reported that the Red Sox "had a string" on Thomas and several other players, noting that "there has never been a great demand for them." The article said Boston was seriously pursuing a trade with the Philadelphia Athletics for first baseman Stuffy McInnis. When the deal was made, incumbent third

baseman Larry Gardner was among three players sent to Philadelphia. Like the Speaker trade, this would have a profound effect on Thomas's baseball future. The trade reduced the Boston roster to just 21 players with Thomas one of just two with previous experience at third. The appointment of Ed Barrow as the new Red Sox manager also improved Thomas's chances of making the 1918 roster. Barrow, International League president the previous season, was aware of the young infielder's abilities. Though it was a break for Thomas, he didn't like Barrow's noted temper, feeling that Barrow "blew his stack at times and not for good reason." Warren Thomas says his father didn't like hot-tempered managers.

Making the roster and being expected to start are two different things. As the time to report to the Hot Springs training camp neared, deals for infielders were a frequent topic in the *Boston Globe*. Fritz Maisel, Oscar Vitt, Eddie Foster, and Ray Chapman were some names mentioned. None of those deals was made, but Barrow expected McInnis to be "another Jimmy Collins" and announced plans to play him at third. Thomas arrived in Hot Springs on March 16, and a day later was the starting third baseman and cleanup hitter in the exhibition opener against Brooklyn. He went 1-for-3 with two runs scored, both on home runs by Babe Ruth. Thomas was still considered a utility player, and worked out at shortstop, second, and the outfield during the spring.

Throughout spring training, Boston was still seeking infielders. The *Globe* said: "The infield utility man is a hard working conscientious little fellow named Fred Thomas. He will probably hold his job; but he does not compare with either [Harold] Janvrin or [Mike] McNally." He played in seven spring games for the Red Sox, batting .167 with a double and six runs scored. Defensively he made three errors in 21 chances.

Thomas spent the first week of the 1918 season on the bench, and made his major-league debut on April 22 against New York. He was unsuccessful in a pinch-hitting appearance against George Mogridge of the Yankees. Still the last man off the bench, Thomas next saw action late in another one-sided loss to Washington on May 8. Those brief appearances gave no indication he would soon receive an opportunity as a major league third baseman.

May 13, 1918, was a big day for Fred Thomas. Dick Hoblitzell was injured and Ruth was scheduled to pitch, so Barrow put Thomas in the starting lineup in what was supposed to be a temporary move. Fred didn't think he'd play that afternoon, and even neglected to wear his sliding pad, not expecting to be in the lineup. As it turned out, this "temporary" lineup change lasted much longer than expected. Thomas got his first major league hit, off Allan Sothoron of the Browns, in the first inning of a 7–5 win. Hoblitzell was expected to leave for military service soon, but he was also batting .123 at the time of the change. Before his departure, he played only a handful of games, and Thomas remained in the starting lineup.

A mid-May series in Fenway against the Tigers convinced Barrow of Thomas' abilities. In the first game of the series, he tripled in a run, the next day he scored three runs, and the following game he went 2-for-4 with an RBI. His defense was even more important. The *Globe* said he was "handling himself superbly at the hot corner. Freddy is doing everything to . . . Ed Barrow's taste these days." The first negative comment concerning Thomas had nothing to do with his playing ability. It was the likelihood he'd "be called any day in the draft." Happily for Thomas and the Red Sox, any day was still over a month off.

During that month, Thomas played solid defensively with steady batting. He hit safely in 17 of 22 games and made just two errors during one stretch of June. Offensively he had back-to-back two-hit games during a series at Cleveland. Defensively he made an outstanding catch of a foul fly to help preserve Dutch Leonard's no-hitter. Alert baserunning by Thomas gave the Red Sox a run in a game at Chicago. The *Globe* said: "Scott deposited a Texas leaguer in short right, good for one base. Thomas kept right on running and rounded third with the ball in [Eddie] Murphy's hands. He pegged it to second and the run counted."

On June 25, Thomas hit his only home run of the 1918 season. In a game at the Polo Grounds, "in the eighth he hammered a four-baser into the right-field stands" off Yankees pitcher Joseph "Happy" Finneran.

The next day, Thomas was injured making an outstanding play. The *Globe* said: "[Carl] Mays was well supported by the Sox, too, Thomas making a fine stop of [Peckinpaugh's] savage grounder in the eighth. Thomas's hand was injured in the play and he retired in favor of Heinie Wagner."

Thomas made just one more regular season start in a Red Sox uniform. In early July, the *Globe* reported that he had left the team and was at his Wisconsin home for his pre-induction physical. The article stated: "Thomas was proving a sterling performer for the Barrowmen and will deliver the goods for Uncle Sam if the latter wants him. . . ." Initially, Uncle Sam didn't want Fred Thomas. He was rejected by the Army because of diabetes. Thomas said diabetes had been diagnosed after his second professional season. He remembered that the Army didn't want diabetics and placed him in Class 4. He later amplified, "I didn't know what to do. They said if you go back to playing baseball, we'll have to pull you back because there was so much publicity about professional athletes being exempt from the draft. In this case we have to exempt you, but it would be a bad thing to go back playing ball. I asked them to give me a release so I could enlist in the Navy. They said they won't accept you there. They'll ask why you're in Class 4. But I tried it. I went into Milwaukee

and they hardly asked me to take off my clothes. They accepted me without an examination. So I went to Great Lakes as a sailor."

The Great Lakes Naval Station was located in Chicago, and its commander, Captain William Moffett, was a baseball fan. "We are asking [baseball players] to join the navy because we want the best men we can get" he said. The *Chicago Tribune*, quoting Moffett, said there would be no permanent "shore duty" for the players. Thomas later said "[I] had it made at Great Lakes. All [I] had to do was play baseball." The offer was attractive to a large number of talented players. More than a dozen men who previously or later played in the major leagues spent at least part of 1918 playing for Great Lakes. The team was managed by former major leaguer Felix Chouinard. Three of those players were future Hall of Famers: Red Faber in the Baseball Hall of Fame, and infielder Paddy Driscoll and outfielder George Halas in the Pro Football Hall of Fame.

Fred Thomas first appeared in the Great Lakes lineup in a 7–0 win over the Naval Auxiliary Reserve Officers Training School team. Thomas went 0-for-2 against Brooklyn pitcher Jeff Pfeffer. A few days later, plans were made for three games in the Chicago area with a team representing the Atlantic Fleet. Rabbit Maranville, Whitey Witt, and Del Gainer were the best known members of the Atlantic Fleet team. Before Thomas joined Great Lakes, they'd beaten the Atlantic Fleet team during an eastern trip. The two games at the Great Lakes park and one at Chicago's Weeghman Park would determine the naval championship (though a couple of teams based on the West Coast were reportedly strong as well).

The first game was played on August 3, and featured pregame entertainment from a 300-piece battalion band. Captain Moffatt threw out the first pitch, and according to the *Tribune*, "Never had the air been rent with such bedlam. . . . .fifteen thousand jackies yelled and cheered themselves hoarse." Faber pitched Great Lakes to a 6–2 win, Thomas going 0-for-4. The Atlantic Fleet team won the next day, setting the stage for the deciding game. That game was the highlight of Fred Thomas's time at Great Lakes. He had four hits, including a home run, against former Brooklyn pitcher Dick Durning. Faber got the win for Great Lakes in relief of aptly named starter John Paul Jones. Later in August, Great Lakes lost a pair of games to the Camp Grant Army team of Rockford, Illinois. Thomas had one hit in that series. He went hitless when Great Lakes hosted the Chicago Cubs (the Red Sox' World Series opponent just a week later) on August 27. The Cubs won, 5–0.

As the World Series between the Cubs and Red Sox neared, it appeared Boston would use either Coffey or Cochran at third. Thomas remembered that Barrow had hopes of getting his third baseman back. "[He] sent me a telegram asking if I could get a furlough to play in the

World Series because they were having a lot of trouble at third base, and my commanding officer got me a furlough." He was the first major leaguer to receive a service furlough to play in the Series. When the Red Sox reached Chicago, they received a surprise. Edward Martin of the *Globe* informed readers: "Freddy Thomas was conspicuous. He looks as fit as an armful of fiddles and is in good shape. Thomas met the team at the hotel wearing his seaman's uniform and the boys were so glad to see him they nearly shook his hand off." It was also an opportunity for a family reunion: Thomas's parents were at the games in Chicago. Fred's father was described as "such a young looking gent that if he jumped into a uniform and stood down around the hot corner one would be almost willing to bet it was Freddy."

Stability more than spectacular play characterized Thomas' contribution in the World Series. Batting seventh, he singled once each in Games Three and Five. More important was his defense. Thomas played errorless ball and made a couple of outstanding plays in the deciding sixth game. The *Globe*'s Edward Martin considered the plays key to the Boston win: "Freddy Thomas knocked down a hard hit ball from Merkle behind third base in the seventh, the pill coming at him with such force that it drove him onto foul territory, but he held up, pegging while off his balance and getting Merkle with the assistance of 'Stuffy the Stretcher.' In the ninth, Thomas went out to the Cubs bullpen for Flack's foul fly." Thomas kept the ball Flack hit and had it autographed by his Red Sox teammates. In 2007, the baseball — the final ball put in play during the 1918 World Series — was put up for auction and ultimately repurchased for something over $12,000 by a member of the Thomas family. When the World Series shares were voted on by Boston players, Thomas received $750, about two-thirds of a full share.

With World War I ending in November, Thomas was soon discharged from the Navy. That winter, the Red Sox acquired Ossie Vitt to play third, and Thomas was sold to the Philadelphia Athletics. Boston had been trying to get Vitt for a year, but Thomas remembered uncertainty over his discharge also being a factor in the decision to trade for Vitt.

Playing in 124 of Philadelphia's 140 games, he hit just .212, but tripled 10 times and his two home runs were against two of the league's best pitchers, Dutch Leonard and Red Faber. Thomas enjoyed playing for Connie Mack, calling him "a gentleman to play for." Thomas said of the 1919 Athletics: "We should have been better than we were but we just couldn't make it. We had some fellows who didn't play up to the standards they should have and we didn't finish very well."

In 1920, Thomas wrapped up his major-league career, playing in 76 games with the Athletics and three more with Washington. Fred later remembered: "Connie come up to me and said, 'Griffith of the Washington club has been after me all year. He wants me to let you go to them because he needs a shortstop.' I didn't like the proposition but there wasn't anything I could do about it."

In late July, though needing a shortstop, the Senators needed a power hitting OF-1B more, and sought Frank Brower from the Reading ballclub of the International League. Reading demanded Thomas in trade. Thomas later said his seemingly inexplicable inactivity with Washington might have been an attempt to hide him from Reading. "I never could understand that. I did afterwards, though. When we got to the end of our road trip in Chicago, the traveling secretary said we're going to let you go to Reading. Right then and there I had a notion to go home but I thought it's the latter part of August and I might as well stick it out for the money. I found out the Reading club was supposed to have a choice of any of the infielders except one. When the Reading manager [John Hummel] found out I was in the Washington lineup, he changed his mind and decided to take me."

Initially discouraged by the demotion, Thomas thought about retirement to finish his education. When the contract for 1921 arrived, his father suggested that Fred should at least write back to the team. "I wrote to them and told them I was going to quit if I couldn't play in the big leagues. So they wrote and told me we'll give you a big league salary. They gave me more money by $1,000 than I ever got in the big leagues." He made $3,500 a season in the International League. Connie Mack, whom Thomas remembered as being stingy in terms of salary, had paid Thomas about $2,500 a season.

Fred Thomas was one of the best players in the International League in 1921. He batted a career-best .335. His 220 hits, 38 doubles, and 21 triples were also career highs, Thomas said diabetes may have cost him another shot in the major leagues after that season. "They were always afraid something was going to happen to me. The first year I was with Reading I did the same thing in the International League I did in the Southern League. I just about did everything in that league, and a scout for the New York Giants had it all fixed that I was going to go to the Giants but when they found out I was diabetic they just wouldn't have anything to do with it." Thomas remained in Reading for two more seasons. In neither season did he approach his 1921 totals, though he did lead the league with 17 triples in 1923.

Fred married Susan Sawyer at East Troy, Wisconsin, also in Waukesha County, on December 24, 1921. They'd known each other for several years. Her brothers had played baseball against Fred in the area. Eventually, they went on a double date to a ballgame in Chicago. They hit it off and soon began seeing each other. Fred and Susan had two sons, Robert and Warren. Thomas finished his professional baseball career at Buffalo in 1924. Son Warren was born in Buffalo during Thomas's season there.

After his retirement from professional baseball, Thomas began a career that allowed him to follow his passion for the outdoors. He owned and operated the Fred Thomas resort at Birchwood, in northwest Wisconsin, until 1960. Thomas's uncle was a homesteader in the area, and Fred regularly visited to hunt and fish. His uncle urged Fred to buy land across the lake. Though he had a nice home in Mukwonago, he moved to the Birchwood area late in 1925. Warren Thomas remembers that the material for the family's first cottage on the lake had to be brought in by barge. Despite the remote location, the fishing brought guests in from the beginning. The Thomases met guests at the railroad station, several miles away, and brought them to the resort. Son Warren Thomas believes today that an eye for quality and continual improvements made the resort successful. Teammate Everett Scott from the 1918 Sox would spend six weeks every year fishing at the resort. Warren Thomas remembers that Scott enjoyed his privacy, and would tell business associates in Fort Wayne, Indiana, that he was in Canada. Other former players, including outfielder Bob "Braggo" Roth, were also visitors.

Thomas played semipro ball in Rice Lake, Wisconsin, after opening the resort. Rice Lake had a strong team featuring Thomas and former major leaguer Clay Perry. The team traveled through the region, often playing in tournaments. Thomas received $25 a game, the same amount as a week's rent at one of the resort's cottages. The Rice Lake team also played teams of barnstorming professionals after the major league season ended.

Even after his playing career ended, Fred Thomas still had a strong accurate arm. Warren Thomas remembers family snowball fights. "He could make a snowball and throw that darned thing standing on his head, almost, and hit us every time. We gave that up because we were getting hit every time and he threw it pretty darn fast."

During the winters, Thomas often went to Florida. Warren Thomas isn't sure how they became acquainted, but in the 1950s, Fred often went fishing with Braves third baseman Eddie Mathews. During spring training, Mathews and other members of the Braves were frequent dinner guests at the Thomas home in Florida. The family understandably prizes a Milwaukee team ball that includes the signatures of Mathews, Hank Aaron, and Warren Spahn.

A back injury suffered when he was hit in the back by a pitched ball at some point eventually led to chronic degenerative back problems that required surgery. The surgery didn't go well, and Fred Thomas spent the last several years of his life in a wheelchair.

During the latter years of his life, Thomas continued to follow the game, but was a critic of modern baseball. He felt fielders "should never let a ball get by them. They're wearing a bushel basket on their hands." Thomas's glove was described as a piece of leather with a hole cut in the center to hold the ball. Warren Thomas remembers that his father was also dismayed by high salaries in the game. "He said they're getting fantastic salaries and they haven't even put their shoes on yet." Fred held particularly fond memories of Babe Ruth, feeling that he was the greatest player in baseball history.

Fred Thomas died at a nursing home in Rice Lake on January 15, 1986, the last survivor of the 1918 Boston Red Sox. In addition to his wife, Susan, and sons, Robert and Warren, he was survived by eight grandchildren and 12 great-grandchildren.

In 1993, Warren was among descendants of 1918 Red Sox players invited to Boston for the 75th anniversary of the championship season. The family received a plaque, and Warren Thomas recalls that it was "quite a thrill to walk around third base where my father played in 1918."

FRANK DAY TRUESDALE *by Jim Elfers*

G	AB	R	H	2B	3B	HR	RBI	BB	SO	BA	OBP	SLG	SB	HBP
15	36	6	10	1	0	0	2	4	5	.278	.350	.306	1	0

Frank Truesdale was the classic journeyman player. Generally a weak-hitting switch hitter, he was also something of a stone hand around second base, his usual position. Truesdale possessed enough talent to latch on to several major league teams, yet not enough to stick around long. Lacking in physical prowess, Truesdale stood 5'8" and weighed just 145 pounds. The minor leagues are where Frank made his name and established his reputation. His long minor league career took him everywhere from the Texas prairies to the Pacific Coast, to the shores of the Great Lakes, playing at every level of the game.

Frank Day Truesdale was born in St. Louis, Missouri, on March 31, 1884, and grew up playing ball on the city's sandlots. Like many in that city, Frank was a first generation resident. His father had been born in New Jersey and moved to St. Louis to better his position in the world. Getting his start in the professional game a bit late, Frank was assigned, at age 21, to Houston in the South Texas League in 1905. Like so many minor leaguers Frank worked his way steadily up the ladder.

He spent four years with Houston, usually as a second baseman. In both 1905 and 1906 Truesdale led all second sackers in the league in games played. In 1907, Houston tried him at shortstop and Frank responded by leading the league's shortstops in assists. But the move was only temporary; in 1908 Frank was back at second base and compiling his first minor league hitting season of note.

Placed in the role of leadoff hitter, Frank responded marvelously. He set tongues wagging and was voted the best player in the Texas League by the fans. The *Dallas Morning News* wrote: "Notwithstanding near every baseball fan has his individual preference among the various baseball players, most of them will agree that Frank Truesdale stands out head and shoulders above the other men of the Texas League when it comes to native ability, baseball prowess and execution."[1] After appearing in 113 games he was batting .278 with 44 stolen bases when his contract was purchased by the Oakland Oaks of the Pacific Coast League for $750.

After a respectable final 60 games of the 1908 season with the Oaks, Truesdale's skills took a noticeable nosedive the following season. In 26 games he was hitting .284 but lacking in most other offensive categories. He scored only seven runs and stole just seven bases. The Pacific Coast simply did not agree with Frank. Unused to the chilly San Francisco Bay weather he lost according to the *Oakland Tribune* "between twenty and thirty pounds"[2] off his already slim frame. Because of his weight loss and subsequent evaporation of his skills, Frank was reduced to a part time role with the Oaks in 1909. His prior performance in Texas was recalled fondly, though. When the Dallas franchise of the Texas League noticed that Truesdale's name was not appearing in the Oaks box scores, they sent telegraphic inquiries about his status. As a result the Oaks gave him his release and in May 1909, Frank reported for duty on his old stomping grounds.

The results were dramatic yet mixed. While his batting average dropped 30 points to .255, the move to Texas seemed to do him good. Certainly it was a boon to his professional career. Playing every day in Texas, he caught the eye of St. Louis Browns scout Charley Barrett who signed him for the upcoming season. The Browns, under manager Jack O'Conner, went with an almost entirely new lineup for 1910. The changes were largely for naught. As the *Washington Post* bluntly stated, the "Browns Are Not Strong."[3] Frank was invited to spring training with the Browns and he impressed O'Conner. Frank made the club as the Brownies made their way northward. This first season in the big leagues is the closest Frank Truesdale ever came to being a star.

Given the starting job at second, and making his major league debut on April 27, Frank played in 123 games in 1910. He showed some speed on the basepaths, stealing 29 bags. His noticeable lack of skill at the plate however, resulted in an anemic, by today's standards average of .219. That average was actually not too bad for the Deadball era; in fact, it was one point higher than the entire Browns team averaged in 1910. His lack of power also was not a concern that year. He did have occasions to put his good speed to use. On August 23, he hit a three-run inside-the-park home run off the Red Sox' Ed Karger at the Huntington Avenue Grounds. It would be his only major league home run. The Browns as a team netted only 12 homers that season. In the Deadball era, teams took their runs wherever they could get them. His propensity for errors, however, drew considerable fire and even put him in the record books.

Frank fielded an abysmal .914, poor even for the error-laden Deadball era. In the history of major league baseball, his .914 is the lowest fielding average ever compiled by a second baseman who appeared in more than 100 games. Frank amassed a dizzying 56 errors to lead the league. So notably poor was his fielding that four years later columnist John J. Ward singled out Truesdale in an article he wrote for *BaseBall Magazine*. The title of the article said it all, "The Kings of Error Makers."[4] Truesdale was selected as starting second baseman for the bad fielding team. Selected as a counterpoint for "A Great Fielding

Frank Truesdale with the 1910 St. Louis Browns. Charles Conlon photograph. Courtesy of Michael Mumby.

Truesdale with Boston, 1918. Detail from the 1919 *Reach Official Base Ball Guide.*

Team" was the Athletics' Dave Shean, who fielded a nifty .981.

Apart from his disastrous fielding Frank did make another mark in the record books, this one considerably better. When brand new Comiskey Park opened on July 1, 1910, the Browns faced the White Sox. Frank recorded the first single (though not the first hit) ever in that fabled park as the Browns spoiled the Pale Hose's home opener, 2–0. The high points aside from his lone home run were the 29 steals and his 35 RBIs.

In 1911, Frank appeared in just one game for the Browns as a pinch runner before he was shipped off to Buffalo of the International League. He spent the next three seasons with the Bisons, playing in the shadow of Lake Erie. As usual, he put up mixed numbers, although in 1912 he did lead the league in runs scored with 120. In 1914, after the first game of the season, the Bisons traded Truesdale to the New York Yankees.

The Yankees gave the Bisons outfielders Frank "Flash" Gilhooley and Lester Channell. The deal turned out to be a steal for the Bisons, as both players they obtained for Truesdale brought them huge benefits. Gilhooley led the club in hitting, runs scored, hits, triples, and walks. Channell placed second in most of these same categories. Together the duo led the Bisons to the International League title in 1915 and 1916, while the Yankees got a .212 hitter with an alarming fielding average of .947 for 77 games.

The Yankees cut their losses and sold Frank to the International League's Jersey City franchise for the 1915 season. Instead of becoming despondent, Frank responded with his best season to date. He hit .303, breaking .300 for the first time in his professional career. The next two seasons found him in Toronto playing for the fabled Maple Leafs, but he was only with the Maple Leafs for a grand total of 15 games in 1917 before he disappeared from their roster. Apparently the Leafs gave him his outright release. There are no notations in his minor league file describing his departure as being caused by injury, so the Leafs must have been unhappy with him.

Out of professional baseball for the first time since 1905, Frank Truesdale made his way to New Mexico. The 47th state had joined the Union just six years earlier, in 1912. Frank settled in St. Rita, New Mexico, a town that is notable because it no longer exists. The site of a copper mine which is still active, St. Rita was completely devoured by the company's mining operations in the 1920s. Since St. Rita was a company town, all of its inhabitants were employed by the mine in some capacity. Frank was no exception. According to the 1920 Federal census of the town, Truesdale was employed in the none-too-strenuous position of mechanic's helper. By this time he had a young family to support. His wife, Willie, was a native of Alabama but the two had met in Texas while Frank was playing in the minors. Texas is also where their only child, a daughter named Elaine, was born.

Apparently the pay and the work in the mines were not enough to kill his passion for baseball. On April 29, 1918, he got a call to join the Red Sox; his signing was announced the following day. Frank was given a week to report to the team. He arrived in time to witness the Yankees sweep a three game series from the Red Sox. The Sox manager at the time, Ed Barrow, had probably seen Frank play many times while he served as president of the International League. He may have recalled Frank and put in the request for him to join the team. The manpower drain occurring as a consequence of World War I and the fact that Frank's age would likely spare him from the military draft may well have been factors in Frank's recruitment.

Frank spent nearly all of his time on the Red Sox bench, getting into just 15 games. Only one of his appearances was of note: his debut. He was the last batter to face Red Faber before Faber departed for military service on June 11, in Chicago. Future Hall of Famer Faber had enlisted in the Navy and signed up for submarine duty as the United States involvement with the Great War escalated. Faber left for duty with Uncle Sam with a whale of a game, surrendering just a single run while scattering seven hits in a 4–1 win over the Red Sox. Truesdale was sent to the plate in the ninth as a pinch hitter for pitcher Dick McCabe and never came close to breaking up Red's party. He struck out, giving Red a great going-away present. Truesdale got a rare start on June 19, playing without distinction in a 5–0 loss to the A's in Boston.

Typical of his time in Boston was a doubleheader against the A's on July 4. He had perhaps his best game with the Sox in the first game, collecting four hits in five at-bats, including a double, as his team clawed out a 9–7 victory. However, Truesdale cost the Red Sox the nightcap when his error at second base allowed the A's to plate the decisive run in a 2–1 victory.

On July 9, he scored the winning run, however, in a 12-inning 1–0 win over Cleveland. He pinch-hit, bounding the ball back to Jim Bagby, reaching base on a fielder's choice and making second on the play. He scored on Wally Mayer's walkoff single.

On July 14 the Red Sox sent a team of scrubs to Woonsocket, Rhode Island, to play for the town against

Frank Truesdale, Bill Killefer, and Hub Northen, St. Louis Browns, 1910.
Courtesy of Chicago History Museum.

the Queen Quality team from Jamaica Plain, Massachu-setts, a section of Boston. At the time, in-season exhibi-tions against local industrial and town teams were quite common and lucrative events for major league teams. The Sox sent no one of note to defend the honor of Woon-socket. The Queen Quality men were no slouches. Several major leaguers played for Jamaica Plain under aliases. The Sox defeated Queen Quality, 5–2, in front of 2,000 fans, a quite respectable crowd. Truesdale batted leadoff and scored a run in the winning effort.

Frank Truesdale found himself mentioned in virtu-ally every newspaper in the country a few days later. On July 19, Secretary of War, Newton D. Baker issued his fa-mous "work or fight order." The edict declared that every major leaguer 30 years old or younger would either have to work in a military-related industry or face induction into the military. Newspapers all across the country listed the members of the various teams who were exempt from the order. Frank Truesdale, Dave Shean, Heinie Wagner, and George Whiteman were the only members of the Sox over the age limit and thus exempt.

Despite this, Truesdale's days with the Sox were num-bered. His last major league game came on July 30, 1918. His final numbers: 36 at-bats, 10 hits, six runs scored, and a fielding average of .913, a point below even his record-setting standard for abysmal fielding. With little fanfare he was shipped off to Jersey City of the Interna-tional League, but he played only a single game for his new club.

Frank did not depart the Sox on good terms. Appar-ently believing that he had a verbal contract with the team to be on salary for the last two months of the sea-son, Truesdale sued the Red Sox for the money he felt he was owed. The end result of the lawsuit was not especially satisfactory to Frank. On January 10, 1919, the National Commission declared him a free agent but said he was not entitled to the two months' additional salary.[5]

1919 found Frank back in familiar Texas where he would play out the rest of his professional life. He was with both Dallas and San Antonio, appearing in 98 games and hitting a nightmarish .196. Among the mys-teries about Truesdale is where he spent 1920. The 1920 federal census places him in St. Rita but at the same time a Truesdale was playing for a semipro team in the tiny hamlet of Elmo, Texas. Was it Frank? He popped up again for sure in 1921 with the San Angelo Broncos of the Class D West Texas League. He hit .249 in 101 games and this time led the league in fielding.

1922 could be best summed up with the phrase "down-ward spiral." He began the season with the Red Snappers of the Texas-Oklahoma League as their starting second baseman. At midseason the Red Snappers cut him and he latched onto Ardmore in the same league. In early Au-gust, Ardmore dropped him as well so it was on to Clovis of the West Texas League. At Clovis, Frank was able to gain some consolation in having fallen so far down base-ball's professional ladder by having the best two weeks of his life. He hit .358 in 19 games. Unfortunately, on August

30, Frank's season came to an end when he suffered a sliding injury. He never fully recovered from it and the injury would dog him for the rest of his life.

The end of Truesdale's baseball career neared. In 1923 he traveled to Paris, Texas, and spent spring training with the Paris Grays of the Class D East Texas League. It is unknown whether he appeared in any games with the Grays as stats for that league have not been compiled.

Frank Truesdale's last contact with professional baseball came in 1924. He turned up for spring training with the Terrell Terrors of the Class D Texas Association. He had reached rock bottom. Although he trained with the team, Frank was not on the Terrors' opening day roster. After parts of 19 years in the professional game, Frank Truesdale was out of baseball at the age of 40.

A real mystery is why he never joined the managerial ranks. He certainly knew the Texas leagues inside and out. But instead of managing, he returned to New Mexico for another go at the mining industry. Frank Truesdale is probably the only major leaguer in history who lived in not one, but two ghost towns. He settled in the small community of Gamerco, New Mexico, just north of Gallup. Gamerco began and ended life as a coal mining boom town. The Gallup American Coal Company began sinking shafts and setting up the town in 1920. Gamerco was a model company town complete with company store, meat market, a hotel, and a clubhouse. For the residents, use of the coal company also made available a shower house, a golf course, a swimming pool, tennis courts, and a feature that Frank especially liked, a baseball field. The company had its own doctor and nurse and, unlike some coal mining companies, the emphasis in Gamerco was on safety.

Gamerco was a happy company town until the mine went bust in the 1960s. With the shuttering of the mines, Gamerco was gradually absorbed by the New Mexico wilderness. Today only a few of the old buildings remain.

Although Truesdale spent most of his final years in Gamerco, it was not where he died. He spent his last year in ill health being tended to by his daughter, Elaine, in Albuquerque. He died on August 27, 1943, at the young age of 59. Survived by his wife and only daughter, Frank was buried at Sunset Memorial Park in Albuquerque.

Notes

1. "Frank Truesdale Rated as Greatest Player in Texas League by the Fans," from the. *Dallas Morning News* as quoted in the *Oakland Tribune* Friday July 23, 1909 p.14.

2. *Ibidem.*

3. "Browns are Not Strong," *Washington Post* April 10, 1910 p. MS8.

4. "The Kings of Error Makers," *Baseball Magazine* August 1914, p. 79.

5. "Players Lose Suit Against Two Clubs," *Washington Post* January 11, 1920 p. 14.

CHARLES FRANCIS "HEINIE" WAGNER

by Michael Foster with Joanne Hulbert

G	AB	R	H	2B	3B	HR	RBI	BB	SO	BA	OBP	SLG	SB	HBP
3	8	0	1	0	0	0	0	1	0	.125	.222	.125	0	0

"I don't care for Rockefeller's millions and I have no desire to share Wilson's honors," Heinie Wagner once quipped to a group of players during a long, hot train ride out west. "But I would like to be as good a pitcher as Walter Johnson and always be able to pitch for a team as strong as the Athletics."[1] Although never regarded as especially fast, the longtime Red Sox shortstop and coach made a name for himself for covering wide territory from deep short and occasionally slipping his oversized feet in front of opposing base runners to trip them up as they headed for third. On and off the field, his quiet leadership, dogged loyalty and wry humor earned him the respect of teammates, adversaries, and fans in Boston for over two decades.

His nickname, "Heinie," was a lifelong reminder of his German ancestry, but Charles Francis Wagner, son of German-born John Wagner and American-born Catherine Siedle, born in New York City on September 23, 1880, was as American as they came. As a boy, Wagner mastered the inside game in gritty fashion, playing barefoot on the rough-and-tumble side streets and vacant sandlots of Harlem. His first experience on the baseball diamond took place on the streets of Manhattan, and by the age of 17 he was among the most prominent amateurs on the island. Billy Rodenbach, a player and manager of a semi-pro team on the upper West Side, had a game scheduled with a crack team in New Jersey when his third baseman fell ill. Dismayed, Billy searched for a substitute, and he nearly gave up the search when a friend urged him to check out a kid playing on the streets in Hell's Kitchen. "Go take a slant at him," he was told.

Rodenbach would not regret the trip. On a cobblestone street near 39th Street and 11th Avenue, he found the "championship of the Kitchen" in progress. He was impressed by what he saw, and between innings he approached Wagner and complimented him on his ability to scoop hot grounders off the uneven surface.

"Say, Kid," he said, "come over to Jersey and play with my club."

"Aw, I can't play with you big fellows," Heinie retorted.

"I'll take a chance on you," said Rodenbach. "Now, I'll tell you what I'll do. You come over with us and if you make good I'll slip you half a dollar." Wagner agreed.[2]

Believing there was no better way to "gather in easier money than in baseball," after graduating from high school in 1898 Wagner landed his first regular paying work on the New York semipro circuit, earning a dollar a game for the Murray Hills nine.[3] In the spring of 1902, after a brief jump to Waverly in the New York State League, Wagner signed on to play short with the Columbus Senators, the smallest by population of the six charter cities in the newly re-formed American Association.

Wagner's break into the big leagues came in Columbus at midseason of 1902. Desperate to fill the spikes of ailing Joe Bean at shortstop, in late June John McGraw offered Wagner a shot with the Giants in New York. Heinie accepted without batting an eye, and in his July 2 debut he brought the New York fans to their feet with a spectacular grab of a Fred Tenney line drive.[4] Wagner made 17 appearances over the next two weeks, hitting .214 in 56 at-bats, but McGraw — perhaps mistaking Wagner's mellow demeanor as a lack of competitive fire — was unimpressed. He handed Heinie his unconditional release on July 17.

Wagner was not out of the game for long. The following spring, Heinie signed on with Walt Burnam's Newark Sailors in the Eastern League (today's International League). He never hit better than .241 in his four years with the club, but his deft fielding and deadly accurate arm solidified his reputation as a premier middle infielder. Wagner also made a name for himself as one of the league's most gifted brawlers, even winning an arrest during a contest with Jersey City in September of 1906 for punching an umpire in the face for a call Wagner deemed off the mark. Big league eyes may well have been watching that afternoon, for not two weeks later his contract was picked up by the New York Highlanders. Almost overnight, and amid little fanfare, the Highlanders turned him over to owner John I. Taylor and the Boston Americans.

On September 26 in Chicago, Heinie Wagner appeared in the first of the 805 games he would eventually play in a Boston uniform. He committed an error to open the contest but went on to nail out two clean hits to win accolades from the press. "Wagner played a great game," the *Boston Globe* wrote the next day. "He has all the earmarks of a real find."[5] A "real find" was exactly what the beleaguered 1906 Boston team needed that summer.

Heinie Wagner, 1910 Red Sox.
Courtesy of Chicago History Museum.

Only two years away from championship glory, Taylor's club had inexplicably sputtered and spiraled their way from first to dead last in the American League. Taylor, hoping to infuse his aging club with young guns, made Wagner and rugged Holy Cross catcher Bill Carrigan the first installments of a team Taylor vowed would be rebuilt on youth, power, and, above all else, speed.

Wagner's work in late 1906 was more than enough to earn him an invitation to train with Boston the following spring, and on March 1 he dutifully joined his teammates aboard the 9:50 A.M. train out of New York bound for Little Rock. It was a taxing summer from the outset. After enduring five weeks of camp as a rookie newcomer, on the eve of opening day Wagner and his teammates were rocked by the horrifying suicide of enormously popular manager, Chick Stahl. For Wagner, the season only went downhill from there. Playing under no fewer than four managers over the next five months, Wagner fought bitter battles with disgruntled Freddy Parent, who was none too pleased to be dumped from his regular position at short to make way for the upstart Wagner. "Naturally, the presence of Parent on the same team worried Wagner a great deal," the *Boston Post* later wrote. "[Wagner] did not do himself full justice and was at times moody and morose."[6] In October, John I. Taylor put an end to the conflict by sending Parent to Chicago as part of a three-team deal that brought infielder Frank LaPorte from New York to Boston.

With Parent now out of the picture, in the spring of 1908 Heinie Wagner found a home for himself in Boston;

that was no less the case away from baseball, where the pieces of Wagner's personal life similarly fell into place. Back in '04, Wagner had wed fellow New Yorker Martha Hahn, whose sister, Augusta, had married Heinie's older brother, George, a year prior. Within a year of their wedding, Martha gave birth to the couple's first child — a girl, Elizabeth — and in 1906 Heinie and George moved their growing broods 45 minutes north of Harlem to the tiny hamlet of New Rochelle, where the duo purchased a sprawling duplex on Webster Avenue. In addition to serving with his brother as a volunteer firefighter, Wagner — famously at the time — began raising chickens in the back yard of the property.

"He was something of a star in his hometown," daughter Eleanor Wagner recalled with great fondness in 2001. "Dad was always manager of the kids on the New Rochelle team. Even when my oldest brother was very little, he was the manager. And he always made it a point to make sure the black kids and the white kids all had the opportunity to play alongside one another — he was adamant about it, in fact."[7] Outside of coaching neighborhood youngsters during the offseason, however, rarely did baseball intervene in what was otherwise a quiet home life. During the regular season, Martha rarely traveled to New York or Boston to watch her husband play, and after spending weeks and months crisscrossing the American countryside by rail, Heinie had no interest in venturing anywhere outside New Rochelle when the season came to a close. "I regret to see Charley leaving home, as it seems so long each time before he returns," Martha lamented in a rare interview during the winter of 1910. "Some day, however, he will give up baseball and settle down to a quiet home life."[8]

That would be many years off. As Wagner etched steady work for himself with the newly christened Red Sox, club president Taylor followed up on his earlier promise and, one by one, assembled one of the youngest, swiftest squads in baseball: Eddie Cicotte, Harry Lord, and Tris Speaker; Joe Wood, Larry Gardner, and Ray Collins; Harry Hooper and Duffy Lewis. Off the field, they were cliquish and at times their own best enemies, divided — like most of America at the time — along the seemingly impenetrable lines of religion and ethnicity. But on the field it was a different matter. "I had heard there was a division on the team, but my dad never said much about it," recalled Eleanor Wagner. "They were divided at times, and possibly religion was a part of it. In spite of the differences, they got along, and when they were on the field they played baseball."[9]

Clubhouse tensions centered on ongoing ill-will between Catholics Lewis, Wagner, and Carrigan and High Mason Tris Speaker, and flared into open warfare more than once. In early August of 1910 things came to a head once again, this time over disgruntled team captain Harry Lord. The merits of Taylor's decision to deal Lord and

second baseman Amby McConnell to Chicago in August 11 would be debated for days, but no one at the time questioned manager Patsy Donovan's decision to appoint Heinie Wagner as Lord's replacement in the field. "Quiet and unassuming in his work, he has gradually worked his way to the front rank of ball players in this country," lauded one Hub scribe. "Although lacking grandstand playing and manners assumed by some players, he has rapidly made a place in the hearts of the fans all over the country by his wonderful stops and throws and knowledge of inside base ball."[10]

Just as Wagner found his permanent place on the Red Sox roster, a series of injuries began that would interfere with the rest of his professional career. The exhaustive schedule during the 1911 spring training trip to California left a number of men coming back from the coast in bandages. Wagner's injury happened right at the end of training, and caused him to be sidelined for much of the season.

On the heels of back-to-back disappointing seasons, in September 1911 the Taylor family sold their control of the American League franchise to Washington manager Jimmy McAleer and Robert McRoy, Ban Johnson's personal secretary. It was no secret to anyone that Johnson was behind the deal, but to Hub fans weary of nine years of John I. Taylor, it was welcome news regardless. Even better news came weeks later, when McAleer announced that he had enticed first baseman Jake Stahl out of retirement to manage the team for 1912. Under the firm hand of McAleer and with Stahl back in the fold, Boston looked to improve on its disappointing fourth-place finish in 1911. Still, few outside the Hub were ready to predict that Boston was in any position to challenge Connie Mack's powerful Athletics for supremacy in the American League.

After a series of maddening rain delays, on April 20, 1912, Heinie Wagner went 1-for-5 and stole a base in Boston's 7–6, 11-inning victory over New York to officially open Boston's new ball field, Fenway Park. The player-manager of any baseball team of the time also functioned as the captain of the team, but this was not the way the Red Sox were organized in 1912. Jake Stahl managed the team and also played first base, but Heinie Wagner was the Red Sox captain. What manager Stahl said before the game was law, but once the game started, and Jake covered the first base bag, Heinie Wagner took over control on the field, and the manager became just another player who took orders from Wagner over at shortstop. The system worked well, much to the astonishment of baseball purists of the time.[11]

Boston trailed Chicago for the first weeks of the summer, but a surge in early June put the Sox atop the American League to stay. Holding down shortstop "like a ballerina," as Joe Wood later put it, Wagner enjoyed the best season of his career, hitting a career-best .272 in 144 games to help lead Boston to its first pennant in eight years and a World Series date with John McGraw and the Giants.[12]

Through the ghost pen of the *Boston Post's* Paul Shannon, Wagner provided the day-to-day "inside dope" of each of the hotly contested games, which culminated in Fenway Park on October 16, the eighth game of the Series (Game Two had ended in a 6–6 tie, stopped by darkness after 11 innings).

Only 17,034 fans turned out for the Series finale — many rooters boycotting the game after a ticket blunder the day before caused a full-blown riot in center field — but Boston's 3–2 defeat of Christy Mathewson in the bottom of the 10th remains one of the storied finishes in World Series play.

During the 1912 World Series, John McGraw realized what he had missed by passing over young Charley Wagner. "If I had you with me the series would be all over now," he said at one point. "I always knew you would make a great ball player."[13] Smoky Joe Wood offered his own evaluation: "The work of one man stood out prominently all through the game. I never saw such playing at shortstop as that of Heinie Wagner."[14] The New York papers praised him as well, and lamented that Wagner, "one of the greatest shortstops that has represented Boston in the big leagues," had slipped through the otherwise astute grasp of John J. McGraw in 1902, only to extract a modicum of sweet revenge with a World Series win.[15]

Heinie returned to Hot Springs in March of 1913 carrying bold predictions of a second straight Red Sox championship. McAleer had the utmost confidence in his popular shortstop — he told James O'Leary, reporter for the *Boston Globe*, "I am not unreasonable enough to expect any improvement in 'Heinie' Wagner. No one could play a better game than he did last season, and if he does as well this year, that will be good enough. And he will be there, you may be sure."[16]

Wagner would not come close to his work at the plate the season before, hitting a disappointing .227, but in the field he turned out the finest defensive effort of his career. One of his specialties was covering second base on steals. He could take the catcher's throw on a run, often one-handed, and apply the tag just in the nick of time. Ty Cobb admitted that Wagner caught him far more often than did any other infielder in the American League.

Wagner was his reliable self at middle infield, but things were not nearly so memorable for the rest of his team. Dogged by injuries and persistent squabbles in the clubhouse and front office, the Sox never made it out of the starting gate. In the midst of a midsummer slump in July, Jake Stahl was shown the door; six months later, McAleer and McRoy were gone as well.

Injuries dogged the veteran players and ultimately doomed the team to fourth place. Wagner dealt with episodes of infection from spike injuries, blood poisoning,

and shoulder and arm pain that relegated him to the sidelines on several occasions, allowing greater opportunities for Harold Janvrin to preside over the shortstop position.

And when spring training rolled around in March 1914, it looked as though Heinie Wagner's days in Boston might well be at an end.

Over the winter, fans in Boston read that Wagner would likely be bumped to second base to make room for the enormously promising Everett Scott, who was already drawing a hefty salary from the franchise. When he arrived in Hot Springs with Carrigan in March, Heinie

Wagner. Charles Conlon photograph.
Courtesy of Michael Mumby.

appeared sickly and thin. He did not bother donning his uniform, limiting his workout to solo walks through the Hot Springs hills, and reporters looked on in disgust as he relied on teammates to cut his meat at the hotel dining room. Days later, accompanying sports scribes revealed that he had suffered an attack of rheumatism over the winter and was being shipped back north for treatment. Back in New Rochelle four weeks later, Heinie issued a statement saying he was suffering from "recurring weakness [and] rheumatism in the right arm," and had "given up all hope of ever playing big league ball again."[17]

Wagner's retirement was brief. Irked by his club's lax work and hungry for help from the coaching line, in late June Bill Carrigan called Wagner back to Boston to serve as his third base coach and "all around right eye." Wagner and Carrigan collaborated on strategy as well. They were inseparable friends and celebrated their accomplishments together. Wagner named one of his sons after Bill, and, as an ultimate tribute, Wagner, an amateur poultry raiser in the of-season, named his favorite rooster Rough.[18]

Heinie would not make a single plate appearance during the summer of '14, but his steady presence in the third base coaching box was a boost to the club and, in particular, to his friend Carrigan. The move clearly pleased new Sox owner Joe Lannin, too. In October he offered Heinie $4,000 to remain with the club for 1915.

Rumors about Wagner's future in Boston continued to percolate over the winter of 1914–15. One was that he was negotiating a jump to the Federal League; another had it that he was to take over as manager of the Eastern League Providence Grays. However, when the first day of training rolled around at Hot Springs in March, a surprisingly healthy Heinie Wagner was in uniform and ready to play. Now largely a utility infielder, he hit a modest .240 in 84 games in 1915 as the Red Sox won the pennant and spent his nonplaying time coaching at third. Wagner also found himself saddled with an additional, unforeseen duty on the road: overseeing the off-the-field shenanigans of a raw rookie from Baltimore, Babe Ruth. Heinie was included on the eligible players list, but he did not make an appearance during the Series, and instead collaborated with Bill Carrigan on strategy. Under the duo of Carrigan and Wagner and armed with a new generation of young guns on the mound, the Red Sox put their differences aside and again clawed their way to World Series victory, this time whipping Grover Cleveland Alexander and the Philadelphia Phillies, four games to one.

Fresh from victory, in January of 1916 the Red Sox released Wagner unconditionally, the franchise revealing only that he "might obtain a berth as a manager in one of the minor leagues."[19] For his part, Heinie had long been skeptical of the idea of managing anywhere outside of New Rochelle ("Managers, especially big league managers, have tough jobs," he said with a grimace six months earlier), but whatever his misgivings, in March he agreed to take the reins at Hartford in the Eastern League.[20] It was not a great fit. Wagner navigated the Senators to a 19–24 mark by midseason, but unable to "get big league players for nothing and develop a winning club," he was fired abruptly.[21] Wagner wasted no time in getting in touch with Carrigan, who on June 28 once again called him back to Boston.

The Red Sox were on their way to a second straight AL pennant by September, when Carrigan surprised Hub rooters by confirming his intention to retire when the season was out. Even the sweetness of a second straight World Series pin and promises of more money could not sway the resolute Carrigan, who over the winter affirmed that he was through. Wagner's name was mentioned prominently as a possible replacement for Carrigan, but in January Red Sox owner Harry Frazee announced captain and second baseman Jack Barry as the "logical choice" to manage the club in 1917. With Heinie again at third, Boston rolled up 90 wins to finish second in the AL, nine games back of pennant-winning Chicago.[22]

At the close of 1917, Harry Frazee assured Wagner that he would be back with Boston in 1918, and over the winter Wagner received a copy of his contract in the mail as usual. When Frazee hired Ed Barrow to replace Jack Barry at the helm of the team, however, the Red Sox owner did an about-face, announcing that he was dumping Wagner at third in favor of former Chicago Cub Johnny Evers. "Good, old Heinie...will not shout out 'stay up' from the third base lines this year," the *Globe* said with a hint of regret. "The Red Sox owner figures that...Evers will be more valuable to his club."[23]

As for Heinie Wagner, Frazee thought there might be a place for him somewhere. His loyalty and years of service to the Red Sox deserved something in return. The *Globe's* Ed Martin recalled that Wagner's loyalty also cost him financially. In 1914, Federal League agents offered him $25,000 to sign a three-year contract, Martin wrote, but Heinie remained loyal to the Red Sox and to his friend Bill Carrigan, although his salary with Boston was less than half of what the Federal League would have paid him.

When the players arrived at Hot Springs in March 1918 for spring training, they soon found out that this year's session would be different when manager Barrow and coach Evers announced some changes. Gone was the annual hike over the mountains, not a favorite of coach Wagner, either — he approved of the walk but deplored the snakes he often encountered. Manager Barrow complained, "You will understand we are not training to win a mountain climbing championship."[24]

The Evers experiment was doomed almost from the start. On the return trip from Hot Springs, weeks of tension between the sharp-tongued Evers and the explosive Barrow collapsed into all-out war.

Midway through spring training, a Hugh Fullerton dispatch carried in the *Boston American* weighed in on the 1918 Red Sox team. Frazee was throwing money around the league looking for players, but Fullerton asked, "Can money build a ball club?" He was skeptical of Barrow's ability to pull the team together, and considered Johnny Evers a smart man but incapable of coaching himself, let alone a team of notoriously fragile egos. He theorized that Frazee had hired Barrow and Evers as a "happy medium," but concluded that the result of the partnership would do practically nothing positive for team management. Fullerton said the Red Sox once had a great manager — Heinie Wagner — and called him one of the greatest of ball players who possessed every quality required of a manager, but he also conceded that Evers and Wagner never would have seen eye to eye. For their part, veteran players were incensed at losing Heinie, and the hiring of Evers provided no consolation.[25]

On opening day, April 15, Barrow issued a terse

HEINIE WAGNER, A SPECULATIVE HISTORY

by Joanne Hulbert

When Ed Barrow agreed to join the Red Sox organization in 1918, he intended to become the business manager and a prominent stockholder. Instead, Harry Frazee appointed him the team manager, thinking the former International League president could infuse new life in a team that ran out of steam during the 1917 season. Jack Barry would not be joining the team as manager nor playing at second base due to his military obligations as the war exceeded Frazee's pre-season predictions. A contract was sent to Heinie Wagner in February of 1918, but abruptly, and much to the dismay of the sports reporters and fans, the aging player, coach and "right eye" of Bill Carrigan was unceremoniously handed his unconditional release. Manager Barrow said he was looking for young blood to fire up the team, as he and Frazee announced that John Evers, of Chicago's Tinker to Evers to Chance fame, and also late of the 1914 World Champion Boston Braves would replace Heinie; the young blood was a mere 10 months younger than his predecessor.

When Opening Day arrived, Dave Shean presided over the second bag while Johnny Evers, feeling abandoned, stood bereft in the grandstand, and Heinie Wagner was called back to resume his place as coach. Red Sox management remained mum on the subject saying only that they'd heard a rumor that the Newark club, and a few other clubs not named, were interested in his services and they would not stand in his way as he considered alternate plans for his future, please and thank you. The sports reporters were less kind, and had predicted Evers

would have a hard time with teammates forced to endure his diatribes and sarcasm. One of the players declared Evers was so smart that he was incapable of understanding why they were all so stupid and had constantly harangued them when they made what he considered mistakes.

But now, Heinie was back, and a good thing, too, according to the fans. And a good thing, too, as it turned out in July, 1918 when Babe Ruth complained he was bored out there in the outfield and desired more time on the pitcher's mound, jumped the team, called it quits when Barrow accused him of not keeping in condition, and ran off to Baltimore where he intended to play ball and build ships in the Steel League. Ruth vowed he has done with the Red Sox and done with major league ball, and the money offered by the industrial league was pretty good.

Frazee and Barrow, realizing that losing the Babe would be a huge blow to the team, and what with his contract and the reserve clause and the threat to future gate receipts and the run for the American League pennant, they came to their senses and concluded that offering Ruth some time pitching as well as playing the outfield was a small price to pay—but how to get him back in the fold?

Babe Ruth "employee" card with Bethlehem Steel.

This was easy. Send Heinie Wagner, the Great Conciliator and Peacemaker to the rescue! And so it was done, and Heinie had his wayward charge returned to the team in three days' time.

Manager Barrow had been at the bottom of the argument that caused Ruth to quit the team, and was busy managing the rest of the team, so he could not possibly

continued on page 144

statement that Evers had been released and Wagner called back to Boston. With Evers awkwardly looking on from the Fenway Park grandstand, that afternoon Heinie was again in uniform and standing at his old post at third. Once again, it seems, the Red Sox needed Heinie Wagner far more than he needed them.

Under the dark cloud of war, the growing menace of the Spanish influenza, dwindling fan turnout, and staggering losses at the box office, the summer of 1918 was anything but ordinary. Still, as he had done for a dozen years now, Heinie Wagner served his team with loyalty

and dedication. He did his level best to keep an eye on an increasingly cantankerous Babe Ruth, and it was Wagner who was ordered to Baltimore to retrieve the slugging pitcher when he bolted the club in early July. "The veteran has seen the last of his playing days but is one of the cagiest coaches in the business," lauded one observer.[26] Indeed, Heinie rarely took the field, having appeared in only nine games in his final two years. In Washington on July 3, he made his third appearance of 1918. Heinie committed an error and was robbed of a hit by a brilliant stab by first baseman George Burns, but in the bottom of the

continued from page 143

serve as the posse. Harry Frazee had no patience for actors nor ball players who did not live up to their contracts. What if, instead, John Evers had still been around and had made that trip to Baltimore?

Baseball history might have been very different. During spring training Evers reserved some of his best verbal beatings for the Babe. Seeing his face at his door would not have smoothed the way for a return to Boston. The Babe might well have stayed in Baltimore despite threats by Evers delivered from Barrow and Frazee, threats that might not have intimidated him in the least, and could rather have strengthened his resolve to stay away from Boston. *The Sporting News*, in a scathing editorial published after Ruth's brief hiatus, called for a blacklist of players who jumped their major league contracts to play for the shipbuilding leagues during the war. What if all that had happened?

Thank you, Heinie Wagner. There are many who need to line up and offer you their undying gratitude. For one thing, the Red Sox would not have won the 1918 World Series, and Yankees fans would have had to chant "Nineteen Sixteen!" in 2004. The Babe would not have been available as trade bait for Harry Frazee in 1920. The New York Yankees must give credit to Heinie Wagner for their glut of World Series rings. Following the Black Sox scandal of 1919, Babe Ruth was instrumental in regenerating interest in the America's National Pastime by his larger than life public image, and his ability to hit home runs that, according to Frederick Lieb, "revolutionized baseball, creating what seemed to be an entirely new game." Major League Baseball's career home run record contenders would now be chasing the Double X, aka the "Beast" — Jimmie Foxx — instead of Babe Ruth. There would be no Babe Ruth League for young players, no Babe Ruth movies, far fewer baseball books, and much less roar in the Roaring Twenties. American lexicographers and Paul Dickson's *Baseball Dictionary* would be minus one adjective of colossal proportions: "Ruthian." So thank you, Heinie Wagner. You changed the course of baseball history and all of this might have happened if you had not been around to make that trip to Baltimore in July, 1918.

ninth he ripped a clean single to left off Vean Gregg for his 845th career hit. It would be his last at-bat.

His playing days were over, but at 37, Heinie Wagner had lost none of his competitive fire. "He was quiet but when something was important he'd speak right up and fight for what he wanted," Eleanor Wagner remembered. "My dad was a fighter."[27] That fact was never more in evidence than during Game Two of the 1918 World Series, when Wagner got into a fight with Chicago third base coach Otto Knabe on the floor of the Cubs dugout. Whoever was responsible for starting the fight was never fully sorted out (by all appearances, it was mutual), but in the end it was Wagner who got the short end of the fight. After being pulled from the melee with a broken finger and uniform that "looked like he had been working on a flivver," Heinie wrapped the injury and resumed work at third. However, Garry Hermann, president of baseball's governing body, the National Commission, was not about to let the event go unpunished. Two days later both men were called in front of the Commission and told in no uncertain terms that if either had any further desire to pick up where they left off, there was "lots of opportunity 'over there.'"[28]

In February 1919, Wagner was out again as part of the Red Sox club. There was a player limit imposed on teams, and non-essential personnel were cut. Wagner got his release once again. In April, he and Bill Carrigan teamed up again and looked into purchasing the rights to the Portland club of the New England League. They at first found Portland's Bayside Park management holding to an agreement they made with Hugh Duffy, and the two were required to wait Duffy out until he moved aside. Hugh

finally did, and the Carrigan-Wagner team was back in business on the baseball diamond. But by the middle of July the league crumbled as two of the six teams collapsed, and they sold out to John Donnelly of the Lowell franchise. Carrigan looked into movie house investments in Lewiston, and Heinie was once again footloose until Ed Barrow approached him to return to Boston in order to clear up the atmosphere of dissension that clouded the Red Sox as they dropped deeper in the American League standings. Despite his infusion of "pep" as the newspapers welcomed him back, it was too late for a comeback for the champions. In January 1920, just days before selling Babe Ruth to New York, owner Harry Frazee announced that he had released Heinie Wagner.

Wagner would return to the Red Sox in 1927, brought out of retirement by his old pal Carrigan to resume work at third base, but manager Carrigan had been handed little material to work with, and neither he nor Wagner was able to rekindle the magic of the previous decade. When Carrigan had seen enough at the close of the 1929 campaign, Heinie took up duties as manager of the Red Sox but with no more luck. After piloting the woeful 1930 Sox (52-102) to a last place finish in the American League (a whopping 50 games back of pennant-winning Philadelphia) to no one's surprise Heinie resigned the day after the season ended and returned to New Rochelle, this time for good. There Wagner spent his final years working as a supervisor at a local lumberyard, as a volunteer firefighter, and as manager of the New Rochelle police and fire department baseball teams.

Heinie Wagner suffered from numerous health problems in his later years, and on March 20, 1943, at the age of 62, he suffered a massive heart attack and died instantly at his home on Van Guilder Avenue. Although he had been employed at the lumberyard for twelve years, on his death certificate his family noted "baseball" as his "usual occupation" and "player and manager" his business.

Notes

1. *Atlanta Constitution*, January 21, 1914, p. 8.
2. "The Sporting Parade," Reviewed by a Veteran, October 1912. Wagner file in the Baseball Hall of Fame.
3. *Boston Daily Globe*, December 25, 1910, p. SM3.
4. *Boston Globe*, July 2, 1902, p. 5; *New York Times*, July 2, 1902, p. 7. Reports of Wagner's whereabouts when John McGraw brought him to the Giants vary. Three days after his debut, the *Washington Post* reported that Wagner had been playing for Providence; the *New York Times*, conversely, indicated that Wagner had been picked up from the Murray Hills club (a version of Wagner's story that was reiterated by the *Boston Post* eight years later when Wagner was made captain of the Red Sox). However, Wagner's obituary and Eleanor Wagner (as confirmed in Columbus papers) state clearly that he was in fact with Columbus when he was contacted by telephone by McGraw.
5. *Boston Globe*, September 27, 1906, p. 8.
6. *Boston Post*, August 7, 1910, p. 22.
7. Michael Foster telephone interview with Eleanor Wagner, October 10, 2001.
8. *Boston Daily Globe*, December 25, 1910. p. SM3.
9. Michael Foster telephone interview with Eleanor Wagner, October 10, 2001.
10. *Boston Post*, August 7, 1910, p. 22.
11. *Baseball Magazine*, "A Curious Situation" — November 1916.
12. Williams, Frank. "The 1912 Boston Red Sox." Unpublished article courtesy of Frank Williams.
13. Shannon, Paul H., "Journeys to the Homes of New England's Ball Players — Heinie Wagner," *Boston Post*, February 22, 1913, p.6.
14. Wood, Joe. "Wood Takes Off His Hat To Captain Wagner," *Boston Globe*, October 12, 1912, p. 7.
15. "Heinie Did It, Says McGraw," *Boston Globe*, November 5, 1912, p. 7.
16. "Credit to Wagner," August 3, 1912. Hall of Fame file.
17. *Washington Post*, April 28, 1914, p. 8.
18. Shannon, Paul H., "Journeys to the Homes of New England's Ball Players — Heinie Wagner," *Boston Globe*, February 23, 1913, p. 6.
19. *Washington Post*, January 11, 1916, p. 8.
20. *Washington Post*, July 18, 1915, p. SP2.
21. *Boston Daily Globe*, June 29, 1916, p. 9.
22. *Boston Daily Globe*, January 6, 1917, p. 1.
23. *Boston Daily Globe*, February 21, 1918, p. 11.
24. Martin, Edward F., "Schang Looked Good at the Hot Corner," *Boston Daily Globe*, March 14, 1918, p. 4.
25. Fullerton, Hugh S. "Fullerton Is Not Strong For Frazee," *Boston American*, March 19, 1918.
26. *Washington Post*, May 1, 1918, p. 8.
27. Michael Foster telephone interview with Eleanor Wagner, October 10, 2001.
28. *Washington Post*, September 8, 1918, p. 17.

GEORGE WHITEMAN *by Jon Daly*

G	AB	R	H	2B	3B	HR	RBI	BB	SO	BA	OBP	SLG	SB	HBP
71	214	24	57	14	0	1	28	20	9	.266	.335	.346	9	2

Who was George Whiteman? A simple answer might be a cross between Roy Hobbs and Crash Davis. Eleven years after having a cup of coffee with Boston and five years after having another one with the Yankees, he became an unlikely World Series hero for the 1918 Red Sox. Then he went back to the minors and played many more years, setting the minor league records for most hits and most games played.

Little is known of Whiteman's early life. He was born in Peoria, Illinois, on December 23, 1882. His father came to Illinois from New York State, while his mother was a German immigrant. He did not start playing professional baseball until he was 23 years old. Before that, he worked as a diving acrobat. He toured the country with a partner. His partner was killed one day while trying to dive into the shallow tank. George quit and turned to baseball.

In 1905, Whiteman played his first of 25 years of professional baseball with the Waco Tigers of the Class C Texas League. The next spring, he was traded to the Cleburne Railroaders, a new team in a town southwest of Fort Worth. The Railroaders won the 1906 Texas League pennant in their only year of existence. Whiteman would wind up on many pennant-winning teams which earned him the nickname "Lucky." It was here also that Whiteman first teamed up with Tris Speaker, who was converted from a pitcher to an outfielder that year. Whiteman himself typically played outfield throughout his later career, but with Waco he played second base and third base. Dode Criss was another teammate and Criss batted .396. This would have qualified him for the batting title, had he had enough at-bats. He did not and Whiteman won the title with a surprisingly low .281 average.

Whiteman and Speaker played together again in 1907, this time with the Houston Buffaloes. Scout George Huff sought to sign Whiteman for the Boston Americans. Huff was the University of Illinois coach who helped manage a few games for Boston earlier in the year after manager Chick Stahl committed suicide. Houston would not sell Whiteman unless Boston also took Speaker. Doak Roberts, the Houston owner, was trying to dispose of all of his baseball property. Whiteman played in four games in September 1907 for Boston and hit two singles in 12 at-bats. He would not play in the majors again until 1913.

On February 29, 1908, the *Hartford Courant* reported that Whiteman had been sold to Indianapolis, but he wound up playing in Houston again that year. After four years in the Texas League, Whiteman moved to the Montgomery Climbers of the Southern Association in 1909 and 1910. He mainly played outfield as he had in the Texas League. But he played some third base in August after the regular third baseman was released. On November 23, 1910, the *Atlanta Constitution* reported that George was sold to the Mobile Gulls for "the measly sum of $400." Apparently, he wasn't getting along with some of his teammates.

In any case, he didn't play in Mobile in 1911. He played 23 games for Missoula of the Union Association and returned to Houston to play 117 games. Whiteman played for Houston the next two seasons as well, leading the Texas League in triples both years.

He had a second shot at the majors toward the end of 1913. This time, it was with the Yankees and he hit safely 11 times in 32 at-bats (.344). He was released by New York in October and signed with the Montreal Royals of the International League. Whiteman played for Montreal for two years, leading the International League with 14 home runs and 106 runs scored in 1915.

Whiteman jumped to the Brooklyn Tip-Tops of the Federal League toward the end of the 1915 season, but he never appeared in a game with them. John McGraw expressed interest in him for the New York Giants, but the Louisville Colonels of the American Association purchased Whiteman. He stayed with Louisville for 1916 and for three games in 1917 before returning to Canada and the International League with the Toronto Maple Leafs. He helped Toronto win the pennant.

By 1918, the United States was deeply involved in

George Whiteman with the Red Sox.
Courtesy of National Baseball Hall of Fame.

World War I and many ballplayers were in the armed forces. The Chicago White Sox were relatively unscathed and favored to repeat, but the Red Sox entered the season without leftfielder Duffy Lewis, among others. Whiteman had turned 35 the previous winter and was old enough to not be subject to the military draft. Burt Whitman of the *Boston Herald and Journal* reported that Boston manager Ed Barrow had signed Whiteman for the coming season. Toronto had sold his contract for $750. It is possible that owner Harry Frazee knew George Whiteman when they were growing up. Both were natives of Peoria and Frazee was only two years older than the outfielder.

Whiteman had suffered from grippe ever since the Red Sox broke training camp in Hot Springs, Arkansas, and he stayed home while Boston went on the road to New York in early May. When he was playing, he wasn't hitting, according to the June 1 *Detroit News*.

Because of World War I, the 1918 baseball season ended about a month early. Whiteman didn't have that great a year at the plate. He had a batting average of .266 (and an OPS of .681.) But he did go 3-for-4 and hit a home run in the last regular-season game, against the Yankees. It was the only home run of his major league career. Boston won the American League pennant by 2½ games and moved on to face the Chicago Cubs in the World Series.

That last day of the regular season, Whiteman took a boat ride on the Hudson with reporter Burt Whitman. "I'm lucky against these left-handed pitchers," Whiteman said, referring to Chicago's star hurlers Jim "Hippo" Vaughn and George "Lefty" Tyler. "No one is figuring that I'll do much in the Series and you know it's the unexpected fellow who usually does the heavy work."

Whiteman's father came north from Texas to Comiskey Park for Game One to see his son in a big league game for the first time. Whiteman started Game One because Babe Ruth was pitching. Ruth had started to become more and more a position player in 1918, but manager Barrow wanted the Babe to pitch in the World Series and so the Sox needed a left fielder. Batting cleanup,

Whiteman went 2-for-4, including a fourth-inning single over the glove of Cubs shortstop Charlie Hollocher. His hit moved Dave Shean into scoring position and Shean scored the game's only run on a Stuffy McInnis single. In the sixth inning, with a runner on third and two outs, Charlie Deal hit a long fly to left that Whiteman caught, saving one run if not more. Ruth pitched a complete game shutout and the Sox won, 1–0.

Whiteman also started Game Two, again hitting fourth, while Ruth sat. Tyler was the starter for the Cubs and lefty junkballers had been giving the Red Sox trouble that year. Whiteman went 1-for-3 in the game with a triple, driving in Boston's only run of the game, but the Red Sox lost, 3–1, and the Series was even.

In Game Three, Whiteman drew first blood in the fourth inning when he was hit by a pitch and, two singles later, scored the first run. In the bottom of the fourth, with a man on second, he ranged back to the left-field fence and robbed Dode Paskert (the only participant in the World Series older than Whiteman) of an extra-base hit. The Red Sox won, 2–1, and took a two-games-to-one lead in the Series before it moved to Boston.

Both the Red Sox and the Cubs took the same train to Boston. Whiteman chatted with Chicago left fielder Les Mann about signing up players for YMCA work in Texas. But there were other discussions going on between players on the train. In a nutshell, they were dissatisfied with the World Series shares they would receive. Due to the war, and possibly the Spanish influenza pandemic that hit Massachusetts hard that September, attendance was low for the Series — and this was at a time when a World Series share could be as much as a player's annual salary, if not more.

Whiteman walked and scored on a Ruth triple in Game Four, won by the Red Sox, 3–2. Meanwhile, the talks between players on the two teams had resulted in a demand for increased compensation and came close to a refusal to play. The matter was resolved, but only at the last minute, and it caused a one-hour delay before Game Five.

Whiteman with the Yankees. George Brace photo.

In the fifth game, Boston's Sam Jones got into trouble in the top of the first, walking Max Flack and giving up a hit to Charlie Hollocher. Les Mann bunted them both into scoring position. Whiteman robbed Dode Paskert again, when he caught a sinking liner with a shoestring catch and threw on the run to second baseman Dave Shean, doubling off Hollocher. The Sox escaped that threat, but were shut out in the game, 3–0.

If Whiteman was already starring in the Series, Game Six was where he really shone. In the bottom of the third, with no score, the Cubs' George Tyler walked Carl Mays and Dave Shean. They moved into scoring position on an Amos Strunk grounder to second. The Cubs infielders conferred with Tyler and debated walking Whiteman to load the bases for Stuffy McInnis. Instead, they took their chances with the Texan and he hit a line drive to the opposite field. Cubs right fielder Max Flack was playing deep and got a bad read on the ball. He almost caught the ball, but he dropped it for an error. Both runners scored. Whiteman's liner gave the Sox a 2–0 lead. Later, in the eighth inning, Turner Barber pinch-hit for Chuck Deal and hit a sinking liner to short left. Whiteman made a shoestring catch and turned a somersault afterward. He hurt his neck on the play, and manager Ed Barrow put Ruth in as a defensive substitute. Whiteman received a thundering ovation. Mays allowed just one run and the Red Sox took the game and the World Series.

The press didn't vote for World Series MVPs back then, but it was widely felt that Whiteman was the hero, a word used over the years by writer Fred Lieb to describe his timely and crucial play. Even though he batted only .250 (5-for-20) and drove in just one run, he figured in eight of Boston's nine runs and made a number of key defensive plays. Hugh Fullerton called him "greater than Cobb and luckier than C. Webb Murphy (owner of the Cubs during their glory days)." George shared a black Cuban wood bat for most of the summer with another George, Babe Ruth. It was this bat that hit the Series winner. The Babe let Whiteman take it home to Houston.

WHITEMAN CLEANED THE BASES IN THE 1ST INNING WITH A DOUBLE TO CENTER SCORING HOOPER, SHEAN AND STRUNK.

Whiteman's three-RBI double helped the Sox beat St. Louis on May 13, 1918. Detail from *Boston Post* sports page cartoon.

White Sox. "I'll bet my money on the Sox..." he said, "They're what we ball players call a 'money team.' They have been through the mill and know what's expected of them. The experience will stand them in good stead when they meet Cincinnati."

Whiteman held out for a few weeks before signing a contract for the 1920 season. The 1920 Toronto Maple Leafs had an amazing season, finishing 108–46, but still finished 2½ games behind Jack Dunn's Baltimore Orioles for the International League title. Among his teammates was infielder Eusebio Gonzales, who also played for the 1918 Red Sox. But it was known even in July that Whiteman would go home to Houston and manage his hometown's Buffaloes. In 1919 Branch Rickey bought into the Buffaloes as a way to secure talent for his underfinanced St. Louis Cardinals.

Whiteman continued to play for another decade. His work took him to Houston, Oakland, Wichita Falls, Galveston, and other locales — more often than not as player-manager. He assumed the dual roles in the minors until 1929, when he was 46 years old.

(Whiteman's family was also in possession of Ruth's first Red Sox uniform. They later sold it to notable collector Barry Halper.)

Because of the standoff between the players and the National Commission prior to Game Five, Red Sox players were never awarded the traditional World Series emblem. Whiteman wrote several letters to league presidents Ban Johnson and Garry Herrmann in the early 1920s asking for his emblem, but he eventually gave up. These were finally awarded 75 years later in a ceremony at Fenway Park on September 4, 1993. Some relatives of the players were on hand for the ceremony, including Whiteman's sister-in-law, who was in her nineties.

After the 1918 season ended, World War I continued for two more months. Whiteman went into "ground aviation work." According to columnist J. V. Fitz Gerald, Harry Frazee declared that he would keep Whiteman in 1919. The Red Sox did keep him under contract until February, when Hooper and Ruth re-signed. On the 19th, Whiteman was one of five Red Sox waived. Toronto signed him for a second tour of duty in early March. Later that fall, George was asked to play prognosticator for that year's World Series and picked the Chicago

Even in his last season, working with Winston-Salem in the Piedmont League, he hit 10 homers and drove in 84 runs. When he finally hung up the spikes, he finished his minor league career with 3,388 hits (the record at the time.) Whiteman had 671 doubles and 196 triples; both good for third all-time in minor league history. He also holds the record for most minor league games played with 3,282.

Little is known about Whiteman's post-baseball life. He did work as a constable in his native Houston. George died of a heart attack at the age of 64 on February 10, 1947. He was buried in Hollywood Cemetery in Houston. His wife, Eva, lived to be 86 before passing away on April 15, 1973.

In the summer of 2005, George Whiteman was elected to the Texas League Hall of Fame.

While there is no evidence it ever happened, it would have been interesting if Whiteman dusted off his high diving act in 1918. The Red Sox had another outfielder by the name of Hack Miller who was the son of a circus strongman. Miller used a 47-ounce bat and could bend iron bars with his hands and pound spikes into wood with his fist. They would have made an entertaining duo.

JOHN WELDON WYCKOFF *by Christopher Williams*

G	ERA	W	L	SV	GS	GF	CG	SHO	IP	H	R	ER	BB	SO	HR	HBP	WP	BFP
1	0.00	0	0	0	1	1	0	0	2	4	1	0	1	2	0	0	0	1

G	AB	R	H	2B	3B	HR	RBI	BB	SO	BA	OBP	SLG	SB	HBP
1	1	0	0	0	0	0	0	0	1	.000	.000	.000	0	0

Without the benefit of hindsight, we can imagine that John Weldon Wyckoff thought himself lucky. Fresh from college at Bucknell and with a year of seasoning in the Tri-State League, he was called up to the big leagues in 1913, to the powerhouse Philadelphia Athletics no less, for which he pitched on two pennant winners. Then, in 1916, he was traded, in midseason, to the Boston Red Sox, the successor to the Athletics as the dominant powerhouse in the American League. He might have been full of hope, especially after escaping the debacle that was the 1915 Athletics, one of the worst clubs in major league history, and on which he served as the most successful workhorse pitcher.

But from there his career quickly fizzled. His role on the Red Sox world champion ballclubs of 1916 and 1918 was marginal at best, and he disappeared from the majors after making just one appearance early in the 1918 season. In hindsight, his career seems on one side doomed to frustration and on the other typical for a fringe ballplayer of his age, snatched up by a dominating team as a potential bit player. At the time Wyckoff was called up to the Athletics, manager Connie Mack was in the midst of sifting through young talent.

Then there is the matter of his talent. A curveballer, according to the 1915 Reach guide,[1] Wyckoff was difficult to hit during most of his major-league career. Only in the single-game 1918 campaign did he allow more hits than innings pitched in a single season. He led the Athletics in fewest hits per inning in both 1914 and 1915, and was among the top 10 in 1914 among pitchers with more than 500 batters faced. One newspaper account from 1915 spring training

Weldon Wyckoff.

Wyckoff with Boston, 1916. Courtesy of Chicago History Museum.

described him as faster than all but Walter Johnson and Dutch Leonard and with a better curveball than either. But he was wild. In those same two seasons, he also led the AL in wild pitches, with 14 each time. In his rookie season, his 6.7 walks per nine innings led all pitchers with more than 250 batters faced. In 1914, his 5.0 rate was the second worst (to Cleveland's Rip Hagerman) for any pitcher with more than 130 innings pitched, when the league average was 3.1. In 1915, when the league average was 3.3, Wyckoff's 5.4 was the worst for any pitcher with more than 200 innings, and was surpassed among pitchers with 500 batters faced only by his younger teammates Joe Bush and Rube Bressler. The disastrous 1916 campaign saw him allow almost a walk per inning in both Athletics and Red Sox uniforms, while striking out only four in more than 20 innings with the Athletics before he was sold. The increasing skepticism shown by the Red Sox management toward using the young pitcher was justified by his declining statistical performance.

It is easy to conjure an image of the 6-foot, 1-inch,175-pound right-hander nibbling at the corners, racking up pitch counts astounding for the times, especially in that grueling 1915 season, in which he was third in the league in strikeouts (with 157), was eighth in innings pitched, but led the American League in walks (with 165) by a margin of 46 over the next most walk-prone pitcher. The signs that his career may have been ended by what in the day was termed a "tired arm" were clear in the precipitous decline in workload and performance he experienced after having spent nearly two full seasons as the "iron man" of an overworked pitching staff. Indeed, in later years he would complain to his family that his arm had been "worked to death" during the 1915 season.

John Weldon Wyckoff was born in Williamsport, Pennsylvania, on February 19, 1892, the eldest of Sidney and Lily Wyckoff's three children. Sidney, a railroad conductor, had moved to Pennsylvania with his parents from New York. Lily's father had come from England and her mother from Maryland, and it is clear that at the time of the marriage both families were well established in the town that would later become famous as the home of the Little League World Series. There are some conflicting reports about Weldon's precise birthdate. Some baseball sources place it exactly one year earlier, and his obituary in the Wisconsin Historical Society Library places it as late as December 25, 1893. (One early baseball account places it on November 27 of that same year.) Though uncertain, his daughter MaryAnn Debbink favors the 1892 date and notes that the family tended to celebrate his birthday on Christmas Eve, but as a joke, never with the sense that it was the actual day, so that family tradition may have been the source of the obituary information. She also speculated that her father may have given different birth years in order to get around age barriers in the early stages of his career. The 1910 U.S. Census, however, sheds some clarity on matters: John W. is listed as an 18-year-old "laborer" who did "odd jobs" and who had been unemployed for 24 weeks in the prior year. His 15-year-old brother, William had a similar listing, and his sister, Alberta, is listed as being 7 at the time.

Shortly after the census, and during the 1910 season, John Weldon began to distinguish himself as a collegiate pitcher and outfielder at nearby Bucknell University, which had also been the alma mater of Christy Mathewson. The records here are scant; he never became sufficiently famous that it is easy to find more than a dim outline of his activities outside the major leagues. Yet, it does seem as if he entered professional baseball without graduating. He signed contracts to play with Wilmington in the Tri-State League in 1912–1913, and may also have played with them in the 1911 season. But here, too, there are no firm records.

In any case, Wyckoff was with the Athletics from the beginning of the 1913 season. The club received his contract in the mail on February 1, and he was effective in several spring training relief appearances, albeit against college and minor league clubs. On April 1, the young Bucknell recruit (the *Washington Post* called him a "student"[2]) pitched masterfully against the crosstown National League rival Phillies in one of the last tuneups of spring training. The *Boston Globe* described him as the star of the game, for shutting out the Phillies on six hits and two walks, and allowing only one batter to reach third base. He also went 2-for-3 at the plate, with a triple and double.[3] It is too bad that one of Wyckoff's finest performances in a major-league uniform should occur in an exhibition game.

As the season got underway, the Athletics eased him into things, but it was not pretty. On April 19, the Athletics' bats knocked 1912 Red Sox star Buck O'Brien out of the game in the first inning. But neither Eddie Plank nor Wyckoff was able to get the team past the fifth inning. Wyckoff entered the game in the fourth and struck out one batter, but allowed a hit and two walks to start the fifth, leaving the bases loaded and none out for Pennock, who allowed only one run to score and pitched the rest of the game to maintain the victory for Philadelphia.

Wyckoff did not make his first start until May 18, against the Indians, and was knocked off the mound in the second inning. Chief Bender came into the game in relief, rescuing the effort and winning the ballgame. Supposedly still fresh, Wyckoff was then slotted to start the next game, but he repeated his failures, getting hit hard, walking four and surrendering four hits in 2⅓ innings. Understandably, he was held out of the rotation until May 30.

After another disastrous start on June 4, Wyckoff found himself relegated to the bullpen, though he began to right his ship in that role, anchoring the Athletics' 12th straight victory on June 6. Several more ineffective and even incendiary relief appearances followed. The team's first-line starters were simply performing too consistently to allow the volatile youngster to take another turn in the rotation with the pennant on the line.

With the Athletics and Giants leading their respective leagues, the two teams staged an exhibition between their "second string" rookie teams. Wyckoff and Ferdie Schupp handled all the pitching duties for their teams, in a game that ended in the 11th inning in a 1–1 tie. Wyckoff struck out six and allowed only two walks.

The Athletics clinched the pennant by September 20, with a few games remaining on the schedule. Wyckoff finally made another start on September 24, but, the *New York Times* reported, he "was always in difficulty owing to his inability to get the ball over the plate, twelve passes being issued by him." Although he allowed nine hits and nine runs, he benefited from two double plays and held on for the whole game. On September 29, Walter Johnson made swift work of the Athletics' second-string lineup for his 36th victory, but missed in the report was that Wyckoff nearly matched him pitch for pitch, walking just one batter, allowing eight hits and allowing the game's sole run in the seventh on a force-out grounder.

On a frigid and windy October 3, the second-to-last day of the season, the Athletics played a doubleheader against the Yankees, with the first game a rocky World Series warmup for Plank and Bob Shawkey. The second game, called because of darkness in the sixth inning, featured Wyckoff and his typical wildness. He walked just two but tossed two wild pitches. He had completed his first year in the majors with seven starts and 10 relief appearances stretched over 61Đ innings, and with six other pitchers ahead of him in the Athletics' stable.

1914

Although he did not pitch as much as in the following year, one could argue that 1914 was Wyckoff's best in the majors. Connie Mack had not yet begun to disassemble the Athletics juggernaut that had won three championship flags in the previous three years, so the fact that Wyckoff started 20 games could be attributed to his potential to succeed, as well as to the typhoid fever that kept Jack Coombs out of action from early April 1913 until September 28, 1914. By the end of April, Wyckoff had entered the rotation on a regular basis. He began the season in the bullpen, continuing to show the wildness that plagued him the previous season. His first appearance, mopping up the losing end of a shutout, saw him walk two in just two-thirds of an inning. In his second appearance, though, he shut down the Red Sox on two hits over

back with eight unanswered runs, but in the bottom of the eighth, Wyckoff suddenly tired and surrendered four runs to tie the score. The game was called in order for the teams to catch a train, with the score tied and Plank again on the mound. Houck, a strong contributor to the 1913 Athletics' staff, soon jumped to the Federal League after giving up nine runs (five earned) in just 11 innings in Philadelphia.

Although completely ineffective in his first start of the season (he "was wild, and when he located the plate his curves were not puzzling," the *New York Times* reported), Wyckoff took full advantage in his next turn, on April 28, his second career matchup with Walter Johnson, outlasting Johnson, 2–1, on the strength of three errors by the Senators, including one on a fly ball by Wyckoff himself that brought in the winning run. His five strikeouts were one more than his opponent fanned and he showed remarkable control, walking but three, while scattering six hits.

In his fourth start, Wyckoff again mastered the Senators, 5–2, allowing no extra-base hits but nine singles and five walks, striking out but three. This start began a string of eight straight Wyckoff starts won by the A's. The next time out, on May 16, he held the White Sox to three hits and three walks. A week later, he was hit hard by the Tigers, especially by George Burns, who had three of the team's eight hits against him, including a home run, but he held on for the win. On May 29, the Athletics embarked on a marathon road trip that would keep them away from their home field until June 26. The team went a

Wyckoff with Philadelphia teammates, l-r: Orr, Pennock, Wyyckoff, Bush, Shawkey, Strunk. Photograph courtesy of MaryAnn Debbink.

five innings after entering the game in the third inning, walking only two. Despite allowed the game-tying run in the eighth inning (in a Patriots Day game lost when Eddie Plank imploded in the ninth), it was enough to earn him a place in the rotation, especially after Bob Shawkey exhausted himself the next day by throwing all 13 innings of a 1–1 game called by darkness.

On April 22, Wyckoff again bailed out an ineffective start by Byron Houck by entering the game in the fifth inning with the Athletics trailing 5–1. The Athletics roared

respectable 17–10 over this span, winning Wyckoff's first five starts. This is not to say that this was always to his credit. In the first game of the string, though he did not allow a hit, he was wild, walking five and lasting only $2\frac{1}{3}$ innings (Bush finished up and got the win. The next day, he was brought in relief into the second game of a doubleheader (the second in two days), and fared so much worse that he was the object of mockery by the *New York Times* columnist in his account of the game.[4] After he walked seven batters in $2\frac{1}{3}$ innings, one can understand the writer's contention that "Connie Mack made a mistake in not immediately isolating pitcher J. Weldon Wyckoff after his exhibition" in the game the day before and letting him "run loose among his players."

He regained in poise whatever he had not quite achieved in control, cruising to a 10–1 triumph over the powerful Red Sox in his next start, allowing six hits but, once again, seven walks. This he followed with a tight 5–4 victory against Detroit in which he walked no one. The win moved the Athletics from third place into a tie for first. He walked six on June 12, but again defeated his opponent handily. In his next start, on June 15, he again hurled a complete game, but walked eight. It was his last victory until late August.

His next five starts saw him spiral downward. Against the Browns, he walked only one, but he also lasted only one inning, allowing five hits and five runs.[5] In his next start, the Athletics lost to Walter Johnson by a tight 2–1 score, though Wyckoff managed to last only three innings before his wildness forced his removal. He took a 4–2 lead into the seventh on July 4 in a game hosting the Yankees, but tired quickly in that frame, allowed the Yanks to score four runs, and lost 7–5. In his next turn, July 9, he lasted but three innings and took the loss, then pitched in relief the next day, during an 8–8 tie called for darkness in the 11th inning, and once again was wild and ineffective. From then until late August, Wyckoff found himself banished to the bullpen. The Athletics clung to a slim, two-game lead, but were not ready to risk that margin on the fortunes of an increasingly unreliable pitcher.

By the next time Wyckoff was entrusted with a starting appearance, the Athletics had opened an 11-game lead. This time, finally, the young hurler made a quality showing, walking just one in a complete-game victory against the Tigers. He also struck out six, arguably his finest performance of the season. His reward? Two straight bullpen appearances as the "first string" hurlers began to receive their post-season tune-up. On September 8, he bested Walter Johnson again, this time as his teammates exploded for a seven-run fourth. In his remaining appearances, all with the pennant question settled, Wyckoff returned to his wild ways, walking eight in a 3–2 loss to the Tigers. He won his last start of the season, on October 1, a 3–1 mop-up affair over the Senators. He also pitched in the last game of the season, in relief, in a tune-up for the World Series.

Wyckoff did make the World Series roster that year and pitched in the first game against the Braves, mopping

Wyckoff. George Brace photo.

up for a battered Chief Bender with $3\frac{2}{3}$ innings of effective ball, with a striking amount of control. Entering the game in the sixth inning after Butch Schmidt had singled home Possum Whitted with the third run of the frame against Bender, Wyckoff walked Hank Gowdy, but then induced a fielder's choice and double play to get out of the jam. That first walk would be the only free pass he would issue that day, after being so profligate all season long. A leadoff single went for naught in the seventh, but, after getting Whitted to pop out to start the eighth, he allowed the next two batters to hit safely. The Braves, however, succeeded in plating but one run, and that on a steal of home by Schmidt, as Maranville struck out and Gowdy was caught stealing on the same play. The ninth inning was marked by three harmless groundouts. For the team, the game was a hopeless cause, a 7–1 Game One defeat in the process of being swept by the shocking Miracle Braves, a series that showed the serious chinks in the Athletics' armor and sparked the massive selloff that left the team dismantled and flailing for a generation. For Wyckoff, it was a sign that he could pitch himself out of tough jams, but it was his only career appearance in the Fall Classic.

1915

The 1915 season did not begin auspiciously, and it was easy to see how it would amount to Wyckoff's last full season in the big leagues, as well as his longest. He had always been wild, but the first several starts saw the problem compounded with interest. In his first start, a 9–1 loss to the Yankees on April 17, he surrendered five walks in just two innings, when he was lifted for a pinch hitter and a series of pitchers who fared just as badly. In his second start, he actually pitched long and well enough to get the win, despite surrendering eight walks. But, tiring in the eighth inning, he was lifted with two runners on and a 6–3 lead. The Red Sox came from behind in the ninth inning to hand the Athletics a loss.

On April 28, Wyckoff rose to the occasion of another duel with Walter Johnson. This time, though, he was done in by a rocky first inning, in which a hit, a sacrifice fly, a walk and an error led to the game's only run. The Athletics had a chance to score in the fifth but the Big Train this time got the best of them and handed Wyckoff his second loss of the season. Walks were once again the story, as Wyckoff surrendered six to just one by Johnson (though Wyckoff actually recorded one more strikeout than his opponent, five).

His first start in May saw a further decline into poor

form, as he was hit hard in a complete game loss to the Senators, in which he allowed just three walks but eight hits. By contrast, his first win of the season, on May 5 against the Yankees, occasioned some extraordinarily overblown purple prose, this time from the pen of the *New York Times* beat writer:

> *The main idea in the Yanks' defeat was a slim, modest youngster by the name of J. Weldon Wyckoff, who has been out of college such a short time that he still remembers his Latin and Greek.*
>
> *J. Weldon can do other things besides read Sanskrit. He can pitch. He can do more than that; he can pitch so well that it's next to impossible to hit him. The Yankees got three hits off Wyckoff. One of these slams was a three-bagger in the ninth by Doc Cook. Doc scored on a wild pitch. If J. Weldon had not taken it into his head to get wild at that moment, the Yankees would have been ignominiously kalsomined.*[6]

In mid-June Wyckoff strung together three straight impressive wins in which the Athletics provided him with plenty of run support. But he was being worked very hard. In a stretch of 42 games from April 28 to June 19, he started 14 times, sometimes on only two days' rest. He was pummeled in that June 19 game, and sat out the team's five-game homestand against New York, watching from the side as high-school recruit Bruno Haas walked 16 in a humiliating nightcap to one of two doubleheaders in the series (Haas would issue two walks per inning in a career that lasted six games).

Wyckoff rejoined the rotation on a road trip to Washington, but each start was worse than the one before: after losing 4–1 on June 26, he was shut out consecutively on June 29 and July 3, pummeled to the tune of 8–0 and 11–0. The rest of July was a rough month, with marginal respectability, but his team won only one of the seven games he started before July 31.

The high point of this long, hard, hopeless season was doubtless Wyckoff's 1–0 victory over the Cleveland Naps on July 31. The local press still thought vividly enough of his youth — he was still only 23, after all — to represent him as fresh out of college despite having weathered two tough previous campaigns with a much better team. Frustratingly, it was his only victory in a string of 14 starts stretching from June 11 to the end of the season, and it would prove the only shutout of Wyckoff's brief career.

1916

David Jordan attributes the sale of the 1915 "staff leader" of the Athletics to the Red Sox in 1916 to Connie Mack's general housecleaning of established players.[7] The statistics suggest different motivations. Wyckoff's performance in 1915 had only intermittently been good and, from the distance of history, could perhaps be seen as signaling only marginal value as emergency insurance to a contending club. And the *New York Times* reported his June 27 transfer to the Boston club as a simple release.[8]

Wyckoff's time in Philadelphia in 1916 had been a disaster, exemplified by a June 22 relief performance in which he hit a batter, gave up four walks, a hit, and a run in just two innings of a loss. But this had been typical. His first start of the season, on May 31, came in the second game of a doubleheader in New York, when he had already pitched to two batters in the first game (giving up a walk and a hit and held responsible when both scored). Although he pitched a complete game in this afternoon outing, it was an ugly, embarrassing affair. He walked "only" four, but struck out none, while allowing 10 hits and nine runs, five of which were earned, as the Yankees romped. Hugh High's fourth-inning home run was only the fifth home run Wyckoff allowed in his career, and it was the last. But he didn't get many more chances. A June 26 start was only his second of the season, on the road in Boston. The Athletics prevailed, 8–5, against an ineffective string of five pitchers. But Wyckoff lasted only three innings, and though he allowed no hits, he left with the score tied 2–2, having walked six batters. It was not his last appearance for Philly. The next night, he didn't walk any batters, but gave up two runs in 1⅔ innings. Then, during the week of July 29, he was sold to the Red Sox.[9]

With a set rotation of Carl Mays, Babe Ruth, Ernie Shore, Rube Foster, and Dutch Leonard, there was no hope that Wyckoff would earn a start; indeed no other pitcher started that year for the Red Sox after his arrival. He was lucky to find eight relief opportunities, and he averaged a little less than three innings per appearance. Indeed, he did not get into a game for over a week after the transaction, despite a string of four doubleheaders in a week and a 17-inning draw. His first appearance was in the second game on July 15, relieving the Babe in the seventh inning of a 17–4 romp. Ruth allowed only three singles in his six innings, but Wyckoff managed to surrender two runs. The next day, Vean Gregg was shipped to the International League, seeming to indicate more room for Wyckoff to get into games.

His next appearance was not for another two weeks, in the first game of a doubleheader against the Tigers on July 29. He came on in relief of an uncharacteristically ineffective Babe Ruth, who was hammered for three hits and three runs in one-third of an inning. But Wyckoff, while lasting longer into the game, was not much better, giving up eight hits and six runs in three innings, walking four. By the beginning of August, Gregg was back with the team and Wyckoff's role again was reduced. Boston was at this point in a desperate struggle with the White Sox, who went on a tear, took advantage of a Red Sox stumble against the visiting Browns and opened up a 1½-game lead. With their starting reliables performing at superhuman capacity, they simply could not take a chance on an uncertain pitcher who had not performed well all season. Wyckoff did not get into another game until August 16, when he was used as a pinch runner in the 14th inning of a 5–4 defeat of the White Sox.

By the time Wyckoff pitched again, it was August 26, and the Red Sox had opened up a five-game lead, this time over the Tigers. Once again, though, he failed. In relief of Mays, who had dueled Bill James for eight innings and allowed only one unearned run, Wyckoff gave up a ninth-inning triple to Ossie Vitt, who scored the game-winner on a Donie Bush sacrifice fly. Heading into the final month, the Red Sox fell into a slump, dropping 13 of 22 at one point and falling to third place. Wyckoff did pitch effectively for one inning in a loss on September 4.

Needless to say, he was left off the Red Sox' World Series roster. But, along with fellow Athletics import Herb Pennock, he was voted a half share of the purse. Vean Gregg was voted a three-quarters share, as was Heinie Wagner, despite playing in only six games.[10]

1917

Wyckoff barely made the Red Sox out of spring training in 1917, and was held out of games until May 14, when he was brought in to bail out Dutch Leonard, who was pulled out of a game against Cleveland after three innings with the Red Sox trailing 4–0. Weldon lasted five innings in this affair, but allowed four hits and three runs (just one earned), hit a batter, and walked four.

Although this ineffective performance left him sporting an impressive 1.80 ERA, his season in Boston was suddenly and literally cut short on May 16 when a piece of glass cut through his shoe and, according to the *Globe*, nearly severed his toe.[11] He did, however, recover sufficiently to pitch a half-season with the sixth-place Buffalo Bisons of the International League. There, Wyckoff possessed the best ERA on the staff in his 20 games (2.96), but was the least effective member in won-lost terms, going 6–11, and posting stats that were fully consistent with his Philadelphia years: 139 hits in 140 innings, but yielding a walk slightly more than once every two innings (73 total), and striking out far fewer than he walked (53 total).[12]

1918

After Wyckoff's moderate success in the International League, the Red Sox decided to give him another chance, and he returned his signed contract on February 28. Apparently, he was an envisioned as a replacement for Rube Foster, who had been traded to Cincinnati for Dave Shean (though Foster did not report).[13] Accounts of Wyckoff's activities in spring training depict an energy suited to one of the team's stars. Edward Martin of the *Globe* describes a March 19 workout where Wyckoff seemed to be trying to impress manager Ed Barrow. The description also shed light on why a fringe player like Wyckoff might have been

driven to burnout by a lack of consideration for his training regimen:

> Last evening "Ykee" made the assertion that he is full of the stuff. Command after command was shot at the Williamsport jitney man by the skipper at Majestic Park.
>
> He pitched in batting practice, shacked [sic] flies in the outfield, worked out in bunting practice and was near the head of the pack as they raced around the park.
>
> Once or twice it appeared as if there might be a short circuit or two, but never did "Ykee" threaten to burn out. A few times he looked appealingly toward the manager and admitted that he was tired when Ed inquired as to how he felt, but the best he could get out of the boss was a signal to keep hard at it.
>
> Manager Barrow is particularly interested in Weldon. There is a place for him on the pitching staff and the manager wants him to make good. Very few pitchers have any more stuff than Wyckoff. It is his control that is poor....
>
> In justice to Wyckoff...it should be said that there is nobody on this club that is working any harder....[14]

Wyckoff seemed to live up to the high expectations of Martin's article. He played very well in an exhibition match on April 1 in Little Rock against the Brooklyn Robins, and three days later, again vs. the Robins, this time in Austin, Texas, he not only pitched well but homered. On April 7, he played right field in Mobile and got the only hit of the game. It was as if he had been retooling as a double-threat player, perhaps inspired by the Babe's example.

But the promise of spring training came to naught. Although he appeared in an exhibition game after the start of the season against the Doherty Silk Sox, playing right field, batting leadoff, and hitting the first pitch of the game for a home run,[15] his only appearance of the regular season during the Red Sox' great 1918 run was on the short end of a 14–4 loss to Washington on May 8. The game was started by Joe Bush, who was ineffective. Wyckoff, in relief, did walk just one batter, and struck out two, but also allowed four hits and a run in just two innings in a mop-up role, a mediocre appearance but not the worst on his team that day. He went 0-for-1 at the plate.

Wyckoff hung on the active roster without being used until May 23, when the Red Sox released him to Minneapolis. Author Allan Wood opines that he "never truly fit in with the Red Sox. He exhibited tremendous accuracy in dropping bags of water from hotel windows, but was also the butt of many clubhouse pranks and was nicknamed 'Mr. Gloom.'"[16]

Wyckoff refused the demotion and returned, for the

moment, home to Pennsylvania. This refusal had fatal consequences for his career. His name appears on a list of players who had appealed for "reinstatement" as late as 1922. On March 10 of that year, Commissioner Kenesaw Mountain Landis issued his decisions about 11 players who had been suspended for various reasons. Landis's action restored Wyckoff to the active list for Boston.

The details of the dispute reveal the complicated story of a fringe player trying to salvage a modicum of self-respect under the reserve clause. Wyckoff had asked for half of his $1500 sale price in order to report to Minneapolis, and, when this request was denied, he asked for two months' salary (then $500), along with railroad fare and reimbursement for telephone and telegraph costs. This having been denied, on May 24, he telegraphed Toronto that he would join them for $400 per month. Toronto passed on this information to Jersey City, who asked and apparently received permission from Boston, and offered him $300 a month.[17]

It is difficult to reconstruct what happened next. He certainly did not record any statistics for Minneapolis, though he was purchased on June 19 by Jersey City of the International League. He appeared in one game for the Skeeters, on June 23, and seems to have pitched effectively. His line was a complete-game loss in which he gave up just seven hits and two walks and struck out seven.[18] That he never appeared in another game, despite such an auspicious beginning, could have been due to pressure from the major leagues, which a last-place club like Jersey City would have had no interest in fighting. We can speculate that the Red Sox publicly ignored his request to be declared a free agent, as well as his negotiations with International League clubs, and invoked the reserve clause to get him suspended when he refused the assignment. While the report about the commissioner's 1922 review gets some dates wrong (the 1918 refusal was backdated to 1917), the reason given for Wyckoff's reinstatement—"because

since 1916 he has engaged in no baseball activities"[19]—shows a charitable willingness to ignore basic facts about a fringe player's career. Since the rash of scandals in 1920 and after, Landis certainly had bigger fish to fry, and the reinstatement had no practical effect other than to clear Wyckoff's good name.

After his playing days, Wyckoff retired first to Williamsport, where he had maintained a residence throughout his playing career. There he continued to run the taxi (jitney) business inherited from his father and mentioned in Martin's 1918 spring training article. Yet the 1920 census reports that John Weldon, still just 28, recorded his occupation as "baseball player." He lived on West Fourth Street in Williamsport with his 29-year-old wife, Lena, and two children, John William Wyckoff, born in 1916, and Charles, born the year after.

During the next few years, John Weldon's life fell into some turmoil. He moved to Battle Creek, Michigan, where he performed warehouse and office work for the Postum (now Post) and Kellogg cereal companies and played on their company baseball teams. On May 12, 1924, he married Marie Therese Toomey of Shenandoah, Pennsylvania, implying, of course, that he and Lena were divorced. The staunchly Catholic Marie soon found herself cut off from her family, most likely because of objections to her marrying a divorced man. Marie and John Weldon moved

Wyckoff with the 1926 Sheboygan Chairmakers. Wyckoff is top row, third from the left. Photograph. Courtesy of MaryAnn Debbink.

to Sheboygan Falls, Wisconsin, in 1926 in order that he might join the Wisconsin outlaw baseball league. He played briefly with the Racine Horlicks before joining the Sheboygan Chairmakers, who won the league championship, and his play during the 1926 season earned "Wykie" (as he continued to go by his old nickname) induction into the Sheboygan County Baseball Hall of Fame. His son Joseph was also born in that year.

On April 8, 1927, he signed a contract for $450 per month to play with Sheboygan for that next season, but no record of his performance remains. Thenceforth, mention of Wyckoff's baseball career fades from family memory. His two surviving children, MaryAnn (born 1933, still living in Sheboygan Falls) and Jerome Francis (born 1935, now of Eagle River, though his children also continue to live in Sheboygan Falls) both report that baseball had become a painful subject for their father by the time they were old enough to talk to him about it. He felt bitter and ill-used, both because of the abuse his arm took during the 1915 season and his later treatment by the Red Sox organization. He had put much of his baseball memorabilia in storage in Chicago, where it was lost, and at one point he won a contest sponsored by the Red Sox that brought him back to Boston. He used the opportunity to try to confirm some aspects of his baseball career, but an employee turned him away from the team offices on the grounds that all record of his service to the Red Sox had been destroyed in a fire. It is possible that he was investigating his contract and details of his demotion to the minors, the matters that had gotten him temporarily banned from professional baseball.

He did provide the *Sheboygan County News* a 1942 interview in which he discussed his baseball career, confirming that he was often "pitted against some of the league's best pitchers" and remarking that he had faced and often mastered many of the biggest names in the sport but that, of all the batters he pitched to, the Senators' third baseman Eddie Morgan was the most difficult. "Eddie was small, he was short . . . he was awfully hard to pitch to, because of that and on top of it, he was shifty on his feet and could hit to any field."[20]

It seems that Wyckoff's marriage to Marie marked the birth of a brief fling as a baseball barnstormer, but it is also equally clear that it closed the door on the part of his life that included his major league career. Indeed, he was even more completely silent on the subject of his first family, awareness of which did not reach his daughter until 2005.

Into the 1950s he worked as a bartender at the Franklin Hotel, operated in Sheboygan Falls by Julius Heus. After Heus died, Wyckoff signed on as a machinist with the Kohler-Joa Company and also worked as a bartender at Gartzke's and Horn's taverns. On May 8, 1961, he died of a heart attack, aged 69, while working in his yard. He had had a gall bladder attack a few years before that had left him in a weakened condition.

In the end, Wyckoff enjoyed the career of a shooting star in three years with the Philadelphia Athletics and experienced the same highs and lows of his team during that time. When he was sold to the Red Sox during the next season, he was clearly damaged goods. However, he continued to impress management with his energy early in the next two seasons, before the rigors of the campaign would leave him depleted and unable to hold his own alongside the star players crowding the Red Sox dugout. He retired with a career record of 23–34 and a lifetime ERA of 3.55. But in 1915 he also sported the second highest single-season walk total of any American League pitcher of the Deadball Era.

Notes

1. Bill James and Rob Neyer. *The Neyer/James Guide to Pitchers*. New York: Simon and Schuster, 2004. p. 433.

2. *The Washington Post*, April 2, 1913.

3. *Boston Daily Globe*. April 2, 1913.

4. *New York Times*. May 31, 1914.

5. *New York Times*. June 16, 1914.

6. *New York Times*. May 6, 1915.

7. David M. Jordan. *The Athletics of Philadelphia: Connie Mack's White Elephants, 1901–1954*. Jefferson NC and London: McFarland Press, 1999, p. 76.

8. *New York Times*. June 28, 1916.

9. *The Sporting News*. July 6, 1916.

10. Frederick C. Lieb. *The Boston Red Sox*. New York; G.P. Putnam's Sons, 1947, p. 153.

11. *Boston Daily Globe*. May 18, 1917.

12. Marshall D. Wright. *The International League: Year-by-Year Statistics*, 1884–1953. Jefferson NC: McFarland, 2005, p. 202.

13. *The Sporting News*. April 11, 1918.

14. Edward F. Martin. *Boston Globe*. March 20, 1918.

15. Allan Wood. *Babe Ruth and the 1918 Red Sox*. San Jose: Writers Club Press, 2000, p. 39.

16. Wood, 117–118.

17. *The Sporting News*, October 24, 1918.

18. Wright, p. 211.

19. *Christian Science Monitor*. March 10, 1922.

20. Quoted in Scott Lewandowske. "Ex-major leauer featured in '20s teams." *Sheboygan Falls News*. Undated, possibly early 1990s.

EDWARD GRANT BARROW

Manager, 1918–1920 *by Dan Levitt*

Most famous for his wildly successful tenure in the New York Yankees front office from 1920 through 1945, Ed Barrow left his mark on the Deadball Era as well. Though he never played a game of professional baseball, the ubiquitous Barrow was a key participant in the careers of countless players and a major actor in many of the era's biggest controversies. The man who scouted Fred Clarke and Honus Wagner, moved Babe Ruth from the pitcher's mound to the outfield, and managed the Red Sox to their last world championship of the 20th century also experimented with night baseball as early as 1896, helped Harry Stevens get his lucrative concessions business off the ground, and led an unsuccessful campaign to form a third major league with teams from the International League and American Association. In his official capacities, he served as field manager for both major and minor league teams, owned several minor league franchises, and served as league president for the Atlantic League (1897–1899) and the International League (1911–1917).

Edward Barrow.

The family finally put down roots near Des Moines. At 16, Ed went to work as the mailing clerk for a local paper, and when later promoted to city circulator, Barrow found himself in charge of the newsboys. A large, strapping, generally good-natured but hot-tempered lad who had some ability as a boxer, Barrow surely had the right attributes for his new job. A baseball enthusiast as well, Barrow pitched on a town team, but his playing career quickly ended when he critically injured his arm pitching in a cold rain. His baseball spirit remained intact, however, and he soon organized and promoted his own town teams. After accepting a more senior position at another paper, Barrow discovered future Hall of Fame outfielder Fred Clarke among his newsboys and recruited him for his ballclub.

Hot-tempered and autocratic, over the years Barrow crossed swords with Kid Elberfeld, Frank Navin, Babe Ruth, and Carl Mays, among many others. Harry Frazee, owner of the Red Sox during Barrow's managerial tenure with the club, jokingly referred to his skipper as "Simon," after Simon Legree, the infamous slave-driver from *Uncle Tom's Cabin.* "Big, broad-shouldered, deep-chested, dark-haired and bushy-browed, [Barrow] had been through the rough-and-tumble days of baseball," Frank Graham later wrote. "Forceful, outspoken, afraid of nobody, he had been called upon many times to fight, and the record is that nobody ever licked him."

Edward Grant Barrow was born on May 10, 1868, in Springfield, Illinois, the first of four sons of Effie Ann Vinson-Heller and John Barrow. John and Effie met in Ohio after the Civil War, and the young couple decided to head west for the greener land-grant pastures of Nebraska; Edward's birth came during that arduous journey.

The Nebraska land the Barrows settled proved unproductive, and the family left for Iowa after six bleak years.

After a brief foray into the sale of cleaning products and time as a hotel clerk, in 1895 Barrow returned to baseball when he bought into the Wheeling franchise in the Inter-State League. At mid-season when the league collapsed Barrow moved his franchise into the Iron & Oil League. Baseball management now in his blood, Barrow acquired (with a partner) the Paterson, New Jersey franchise in the Atlantic League for 1896. Just after his acquisition of the Paterson club, Barrow signed the player he would later call the greatest of all-time, Honus Wagner. The following year, Barrow sold Wagner to the major league Louisville club for $2,100, a high price for the time.

The contentious Atlantic League elected Barrow as president for 1897, and for the next three years until the league folded after the 1899 season, Barrow oversaw the inter-owner squabbles, dealt with numerous player disputes, and managed the umpires. As league president during the Spanish-American War, he championed a number of marketing gimmicks to help keep the fan's interest: he brought in a woman, Lizzie Stroud (she played under last name Arlington) to pitch and heavyweight champions John L. Sullivan and James Jeffries to umpire. Another heavyweight, Jim Corbett, often played first base in exhibitions, mostly in 1897.

For 1900, Barrow purchased a one-quarter interest in the Toronto franchise in the Eastern League and became its manager. With little inherited talent, Barrow brought the club home fifth in his first year. Barrow acquired some better players for the next season, including hurler Nick Altrock, and finished second. Despite losing a number of players to the fledgling American League, Barrow's club captured the pennant in 1902.

With the tragic suicide of new skipper Win Mercer in January 1903, Detroit Tigers owner Sam Angus hired Barrow as manager on the recommendation of AL president Ban Johnson. Bolstered by two contract jumpers from the NL, pitcher Bill Donovan and outfielder Sam Crawford, Barrow brought the team in fifth, a 13-game improvement over the previous year. In one of the year's most notorious controversies, Barrow was forced to suspend star shortstop Kid Elberfeld in June after some outlandishly lackadaisical play. The St. Louis Browns were actively tampering with Elberfeld and encouraging him to maneuver for his release. The Giants, too, were likely interfering with the unhappy Elberfeld. Barrow claimed he would see Elberfeld out of baseball before sending him to one of these two teams, and charged "that in three of the last six games lost to St. Louis, Elberfeld made a muff fumble or wild throw at the moment of a critical stage." Ban Johnson intervened and engineered a trade of Elberfeld to the new AL franchise in New York.

After the season, Angus sold the franchise to William Yawkey after first offering it to Barrow and Frank Navin. The latter, soon promoted to secretary-treasurer, ingratiated himself with Yawkey, becoming his right-hand man. Barrow continued his effort to improve the club by adding several players that would contribute to the Tigers pennant four years later. Not surprisingly, however, Navin and Barrow, both young and ambitious, could not co-exist; with the Tigers at 32–46 Navin gladly accepted Barrow's resignation.

Following his stint in Detroit, Barrow began a two-year odyssey managing in the high minors. Montreal, in the Eastern League, recruited Barrow right after his resignation to come finish out the 1904 season as their manager. For 1905 he was hired by Indianapolis in the American Association, and 1906 found him back in Toronto. Disheartened with his baseball career after his first-ever last-place finish that year, Barrow left baseball to run Toronto's Windsor Hotel.

Four years later in 1910, Montreal offered Barrow the manager's post and a chance to get back into baseball. Barrow happily accepted, and after the season he was elected league president. In recognition of the two Canadian franchises, Barrow persuaded the Eastern League to change its name to the International League (IL) prior to the 1912 season.

In January 1912, Barrow married Fannie Taylor Briggs whom he had met in Toronto many years earlier. It was the second marriage for both and would last until Barrow's death many years later. Fannie brought her five-year-old daughter, Audrey, into the union, and Barrow raised her as his own. In his many autobiographical writings, Barrow never mentioned his first wife, whom he had married in 1898.

When the Federal League (FL) challenged Organized Baseball as a self-declared major league in 1914, the most severe hardship fell upon the high minors, particularly Barrow's IL, which lost numerous players to the upstart league. The FL also placed teams in the IL's two largest markets, Buffalo and Baltimore, significantly affecting attendance. To better position the IL for the struggle, Barrow tried to obtain major league status for his league or some eight-team amalgamation of the IL and the other affected high minor league, the American Association. Not surprisingly, nothing ever came of these efforts.

After holding the league together through the difficult 1914 season, 1915 proved even more challenging. The FL invaded Newark as well, and with Canada now fully engaged in the World War, the Toronto and Montreal franchises operated under wartime conditions. Before and during the season, moves and rumors of moves of IL franchises dominated league business. The financial strain forced the Jersey City and Newark (transferred to Harrisburg) owners to forfeit their franchises to the league, leaving Barrow to run both clubs until new owners could be found.

With the collapse of the FL after 1915, the IL received a brief respite in 1916. In 1917, however, America also entered the First World War, bringing financial hardship back to many of the beleaguered franchises. Barrow again battled to keep his league from folding, while at the same time striving to create a third major league of four IL and four AA franchises. After four extremely difficult years, a number of disagreements and bad feelings had developed between the authoritarian Barrow and several franchise owners, particularly those left out of the third major league scheme. When the owners voted to drastically cut his salary from $7,500 to $2,500, Barrow resigned. For 1918, he eagerly accepted the Boston Red Sox managerial post offered by owner Harry Frazee.

The Red Sox were less affected by war losses than most teams, and Barrow successfully guided the club to the pennant despite a showdown with his star player Babe Ruth in July. Earlier in the year, on the advice of outfielder Harry Hooper, Barrow had shifted Ruth to the outfield to take full advantage of his offensive potential. But when hurler Dutch Leonard left the team due to the war, Barrow looked to Ruth to pitch. Ruth begged off due to a sore wrist. The tension between the two erupted

THE RED SOX "DARK HORSE" MANAGER, WHOSE INDENTITY HAD THE FANS GUESSING, HAS NOW MATERIALIZED AS E. G. BARROW, BASEBALL EXPERT

Boston Post cartoon, February 13, 1918.

in July when Barrow chastised Ruth after swinging at a pitch after being given the take sign. When Ruth snapped back, the argument escalated, and Ruth left the club and returned to Baltimore, threatening to join a shipbuilding team. Ruth of course soon realized he'd gone too far and wanted to come back. Hooper and Frazee helped mediate and appease the furious, stubborn Barrow. The chastened Ruth ended up pitching a number of games down the stretch. Owing to complications from the war, in mid-year the season was shortened and adjusted to end on Labor Day, at which point the Sox found themselves 2½ games ahead of the Cleveland Indians. In the World Series, the Red Sox defeated the Chicago Cubs, four games to two.

Falling attendance and much lower receipts than anticipated from the World Series put additional financial burdens on Frazee. He now became a seller rather than buyer and sent three players to the Yankees for $25,000 prior to the 1919 season. During the year, Barrow became embroiled in two player controversies. The Babe spent the start of the season living the high life in Ruthian fashion beyond even his own standard. One morning on a tip, Barrow burst into Ruth's room at 6 A.M. right after the latter had snuck back in and caught Ruth hiding under the covers with his clothes on. The next morning in the clubhouse, Ruth confronted and threatened to punch Barrow for popping into his room. Barrow, well tired of Ruth's shenanigans, ordered the rest of the players onto the field and challenged Ruth to back up his threat. Ruth backed down, put on his uniform, and trotted out with the others. Barrow and Ruth eventually reached an unconventional detente: Ruth would leave a note for Barrow any time he returned past curfew with the exact time he came in.

The other hullabaloo began when star Boston pitcher Carl Mays refused to retake the mound after a throw by catcher Wally Schang to catch a base stealer grazed Mays' head. Barrow intended to suspend the dour Mays, until Frazee quickly quashed any suspension so as to possibly trade him. After listening to several offers, Frazee sold Mays to the Yankees for $40,000. AL President Johnson voided the sale and suspended Mays, arguing Frazee should have suspended him. In contrast to his Elberfeld machinations, Johnson now argued that a player should not be able force a favorable outcome through insubordination. The Yankee owners went to the courts, which upheld the sale. Boston finished the 1919 season tied for fifth, 20½ games back.

That offseason, when Frazee sold Ruth to the Yankees, Barrow grimly told him, "You ought to know you're making a mistake." Frazee tried to placate Barrow by promising him that he would get some players in return for Ruth, but Barrow snapped back, "There is nobody on that ball club that I want. This has to be a straight cash deal, and you'll have to announce it that way." Yankee owners Jacob Ruppert and Tillinghast L'Hommedieu Huston paid $100,000 — $25,000 down and three installments of $25,000 — and Ruppert agreed to personally lend Frazee $300,000 to be secured by a mortgage on Fenway Park.

Frazee desperately needed the money. When Frazee purchased the Red Sox in 1916, he and his partner paid Joseph Lannin $400,000 down and assumed $600,000 in debt and preferred stock, including a $262,000 note from Lannin. With the Federal League war over, Frazee assumed he could pay the interest and principal out of the team's cash flow. Attendance, though, collapsed in 1917 and 1918, and Frazee could not afford to carry both his ball club and his theater productions.

By the end of 1919, Frazee's financial situation had become particularly acute. The principal on Lannin's note was due, and Frazee was in the process of purchasing a theater in New York (the sale price of the theater is unavailable, but it cost $500,000 to build). Shortly after the Ruth sale, Frazee pleaded with the Yankee owners to help him borrow against the three $25,000 notes because he needed the money immediately. He further implored Ruppert to advance the funds from the promised mortgage loan quickly. With the money from the Ruth sale Frazee could meet his immediate financial obligations but showed little interest in reinvesting in his ball club.

The death of Yankee business manager Harry Sparrow during the 1920 season created an opportunity for the two sparing Yankee owners to bring in a strong experienced baseball man to run the team and thus help alleviate the friction between them. After a third-place Yankee finish in 1920, Huston and Ruppert plucked Barrow from Boston to run the baseball operation, technically as business manager, but practically in a *de facto* general manager-type role. While not technically a promotion,

Barrow must have been relieved to escape a deteriorating situation in Boston to join well-capitalized, competitive owners.

One of his first orders of business was to hire Red Sox coach Paul Krichell as a scout. Krichell would actually outlast Barrow as a Yankee, and along the way develop one of baseball's best scouting organizations. Barrow also quickly reassured manager Miller Huggins of his support despite Huston's known aversion to his diminutive skipper: "You're the manager, and you'll not be second guessed by me. Your job is to win; mine is to get you the players you need to win." And Barrow lived up to his half of the bargain: he found the necessary players and he did not interfere with his manager.

Forceful and competitive, yet optimistic by nature, Barrow actively sought to solidify his new club. At first this mainly involved going back to his old boss Frazee with Ruppert's money and acquiring the rest of Boston's stars. Yankee co-owner Ruppert was willing to spend money to acquire players when many other owners were not, despite the threat to his livelihood as a brewer from Prohibition. With his owners' encouragement, Barrow spent more, and more wisely, to build the Yankee dynasty.

In Barrow's first season at the Yankee helm, New York won its first pennant before losing to the Giants in the World Series. After the season, Ruth left on an offseason barnstorming tour in defiance of an old rule and Commissioner Landis's warning. Barrow needed to aggressively lobby the furious Commissioner to limit the Babe's suspension to the first 50 days of the 1922 season.

After the 1922 season, Barrow had to referee a disagreement between his two owners. Huston blamed manager Huggins for the World Series loss and wanted to fire him. Ruppert (and Barrow) supported Huggins, and Barrow helped instigate a relatively amicable solution: Ruppert would buy out Huston's interest in the franchise. When Ruppert purchased Huston's 50 percent ownership for $1.25 million, he allowed Barrow to buy a 10 percent interest in the club for around $300,000.

In 1923, the team opened Yankee Stadium, one of the great ballparks of American history. Several years earlier the New York Giants had informed the Yankees' owners that they were no longer welcome to remain as tenants in the Polo Grounds (the Giants stadium). Ruppert and Huston then initiated a site search for a new stadium. Business manager Barrow played a subsidiary but active role in this politically sensitive project.

Bolstered by the nucleus of the team Barrow had managed in Boston, the Yankees won their first World Championship in 1923. The Yankees' three straight pennants after Barrow joined the team foreshadowed the effectiveness of the Ruppert-Barrow team. The perfectionist Ruppert provided the capital and positive reinforcement to support Barrow's own completive desire and competence. Barrow proved able to impose his will on the Yankee front office to direct his team-building plans. And due to his good judgment, these were typically sound.

By 1925 the Yankees had fallen to seventh. Ruth's illness and antics made the year especially frustrating. Barrow began the season by extricating an incapacitated Ruth-he had succumbed to his world-famous "stomach ache"-through the window of a train car. Later in the year Huggins fined Ruth the then exorbitant sum of $5,000 after a confrontation regarding his off-field self-indulgence and tardiness to the ballpark. Ruth threatened to quit unless Huggins backed down, but Barrow stood behind his manager.

The team returned to the top of the AL in 1926 behind a number of young stars including future Hall of Famers Lou Gehrig, Earle Combs, and Tony Lazzeri. The world champion 1927 ball club is considered by many to be the greatest team of all-time. Ruth and Gehrig were at the top of their game, and the club boasted a crack pitching staff as well. The Yankees repeated in 1928 despite a summer charge from the Philadelphia A's.

Huggins died at the end of the 1929 season, and the club fell to second. At a game in May, two people died and many more were injured when fans tried to exit the right-field bleachers during a rainstorm. Barrow publicly defended the safety rules at Yankee Stadium and showed little sympathy for the trampled fans amid accusations that particular doors were improperly locked. After a drawn-out legal process, the Yankees were eventually found partially liable, but damages were reduced well below what the injured plaintiffs were seeking.

To replace Huggins, Barrow eventually settled for his third choice, former Yankee pitcher Bob Shawkey. After Shawkey brought the team home third, a frustrated Barrow jettisoned Shawkey in favor Joe McCarthy. McCarthy proved a brilliant choice and would go to win seven World Series with the Yankees.

By 1932, after paying $125,000 for minor leaguers Lyn Lary and Jimmie Reese, neither of whom turned into stars, the success of the Cardinals minor league operation, and changes to the player limit and option rules, the Yankees recognized that they needed to develop a farm system. Following the acquisition of the Newark International League franchise, the club hired another future Hall of Fame executive, George Weiss, to run it. Barrow actually wanted to hire Bob Connery of the St. Paul Saints with whom the Yankees had a long relationship, but Ruppert insisted on Weiss. Barrow and Weiss soon fell into a smooth working relationship and created one of baseball's most efficient farm systems. Krichell's wide network of scouts fed Weiss' well-run minor league clubs to produce some of the greatest teams in minor league history and several Hall of Fame ballplayers.

In McCarthy's second season, on the back of one last hurrah from Ruth and a typically great season by Gehrig, the Yankees again won the World Series. Over the next three seasons, however, the Yankees could not recapture the pennant. The clubhouse atmosphere was further eroded by an aging and dispirited Ruth. Frustrated by his declining skills and salary, Ruth desperately wanted to manage the Yankees, causing anxiety for McCarthy and a headache for Barrow. Barrow shrewdly engineered a move of Ruth to the Boston Braves, temporarily soothing Ruth and preventing the public relations nightmare of a disgruntled Ruth in New York.

Armed with a recommendation from his excellent scouts, in late 1934 Barrow took a chance on young west-coast star Joe DiMaggio despite a knee injury. The future Hall of Famer spent one final season in San Francisco before debuting with the Yankees in 1936. With DiMaggio on board and several other prospects emerging as well, the Yankees began another run of dominance as they won the next four World Series and seven of the next eight pennants.

Ed Barrow after being appointed Red Sox manager. Charles Conlon photograph. Courtesy of the Boston Red Sox.

During the Yankees string of titles, an incident in Chicago testified to the racism and race insensitivity in mainstream America. After a July game in 1938, Yankee outfielder Jake Powell was asked on the radio how he kept in shape over the winter. "Oh, that's easy, I'm a policeman," Powell replied, "and I beat N_____ over the head with my blackjack." When first publicized, the baseball establishment, the mainstream press, and Yankee management (including Barrow) were little exercised by this remark. The Black press, however, jumped on this egregious, racist remark and argued that Powell and his comments should be censored. Barrow tried to mitigate the fallout with the Yankees' Black fans by ordering Powell on an apology tour of Black newspapers and establishments. In a reflection of their growing clout, Landis suspended Powell for ten days. Unfortunately the lesson the baseball establishment and mainstream press learned form this sorry episode was simply that players should be more careful when speaking on the radio.

Ruppert died in 1939, and his will left the team (along with his other holdings) to a trust for the benefit of his two nieces and a young female friend. As expected, the trust named Barrow the new Yankees president; he had reached the pinnacle of his baseball career. His autonomy, particularly in financial matters, however, was limited by the estate tax requirement that tied up much of the team's capital.

After the 1939 season, Barrow further found himself hamstrung in his team building efforts because of a startling rule introduced by his American League rivals. He lacked the political skill necessary to counter the anti-Yankee sentiment, and at the winter meetings the league passed a rule prohibiting the league champion from making trades (unless the player(s) cleared waivers) until it was no longer the champion. Clearly (but not publicly) directed at the Yankees after their four straight pennants, the decree seemingly achieved its unspoken objective as the Tigers broke the Yankees streak and won the 1940 pennant.

Barrow's Yankees returned to the top in 1941 and continued to win during the first years of World War II with generally the same players (until they went into the military, of course) as during the late 1930s. But the replenishment of young stars slowed through this period. Naturally the war claimed healthy young men, but a couple other factors were at work as well. The push to the background of all non-military related activities during World War II leveled the economic playing field

Ed Barrow with Harry Hooper, spring training 1919. Courtesy of Michael Mumby.

in baseball. In addition, the Yankees were now run as a trust, not as wealthy sportsman's hobby, cutting into the franchise's financial flexibility.

In early 1945, the Yankees were sold to a triumvirate of Larry MacPhail, Del Webb, and Dan Topping. Barrow disliked the flashy MacPhail and tried to interest his hunting buddy and Boston owner Tom Yawkey in purchasing the club. The trust, however, needed money to pay its taxes, and the war-depressed sale price of only $2.8 million was well below the pre-war value estimate. Selling to an old rival and receiving no more for his interest than he originally paid 20 years earlier must have greatly annoyed Barrow. After the sale, the new ownership kicked Barrow upstairs with a title of chairman of the board, but it was a purely symbolic position.

Barrow's daughter Audrey lived an unhappy and unlucky life. She was first married in the mid 1920s and shortly thereafter she had two children, a girl and a boy. Unfortunately, thenceforth her life began to spiral downhill. In 1933, her husband committed suicide by running his car in a closed garage under the house. In the process, he nearly asphyxiated the two children as well. A young mother with two young children, Audrey fell back on her parents for financial support.

Ed Barrow in later years.
Courtesy of the *Boston Herald*.

In 1940, Audrey remarried an older man, but it didn't take, and less than three years later she moved out to Reno to get a Nevada divorce. Shortly thereafter she married the nephew of the late Jacob Ruppert. Her new husband promptly joined the air force and headed off to WWII, leaving Audrey and her two children in their new waterfront home not far from the Barrows. Sadly, this marriage didn't last either. In the late 1940's, Audrey tried marriage one more time and wedded an executive at a real estate agency. Tragically, in 1950 her fourth husband died at home from a heart ailment. A year later a despondent Audrey jumped (or fell) to her death from her 11th floor suite.

Barrow officially retired in 1947 but remained fairly active in baseball. He participated in several ceremonial events and served on the Hall of Fame old-timers committee, the body responsible for inducting players passed over by the baseball writers or excluded from their purview. Barrow survived a heart attack during the 1943 World Series, but in December 1953 at age 85 Barrow passed away after several years at home in ill health, just three months after his election to the Baseball Hall of Fame. He was buried in Kensico Cemetery in Valhalla, New York.

HARRY FRAZEE

Owner *by Glenn Stout*

When former Boston Red Sox owner Harry Frazee died on June 4, 1929, Red Sox president Bob Quinn ordered that the American flag at Fenway Park be flown at half staff in his memory. In the many obituaries that appeared in Boston newspapers at the time, most noted that during Frazee's tenure the Red Sox won a world championship in 1918, that Frazee sold Babe Ruth to the Yankees in 1919, sold the Red Sox to a consortium led by Bob Quinn in 1923, and that his musical *No, No, Nanette,* which reached Broadway in 1925, was one of the most successful shows of the era. Some made note of his many battles with American League president Ban Johnson and a few noted the "mystery" of Frazee's religion, but not a single obituary, published in Boston or elsewhere, drew any connection at all between the sale of Ruth and *No, No, Nanette,* treated Frazee as a pariah, or blamed Frazee

for the fact that the Red Sox had finished in last place the past four seasons.

Nevertheless Harry Frazee somehow became the most notorious owner in Red Sox history. The reason for that has little to do with the facts of his life and much more to do with the way the facts of history have been misused and overlooked.

Frazee owned the Boston Red Sox from November 1, 1916, to August 1, 1923. During his tenure the Red Sox finished in second place in 1917, won a world championship in 1918, finished sixth in 1919, fifth in 1920 and 1921, ended the season in last place in 1922, and were in last place when Frazee sold the club in 1923. Compared with the others who have owned the Red Sox, Frazee's performance was strictly middle of the pack — more successful than the reign of Tom Yawkey, his wife, the Yawkey

E. G. Barrow, Billy Sunday, and Babe Ruth at Red Sox spring training, Tampa, 1919.
Courtesy of Kerry Keene.

Foundation, and the syndicate headed by Bob Quinn that took over the team in 1923, and not as successful as those of Joseph Lannin or James McAleer. With one world championship followed by a slow demise, Frazee's record most resembles that of John I. Taylor, who owned the Red Sox from 1901 through 1911.

Frazee was born in Peoria, Illinois, on June 29, 1881. At the age of 16, he dropped out of high school and went to work at the Peoria Theater, learning the theater business from the ground up, then was hired as an advance agent for a traveling show.

His involvement with baseball began a few years later. After the Western Association ceased operations, Frazee reportedly booked the Peoria club on a successful barnstorming tour and learned a lesson of lasting value — baseball could be a lucrative business.

Turning his attention back to the theater, in 1901, Frazee produced his first successful show, a play called *Mahoney's Wedding*, which earned him a $14,000 profit. That attracted the attention of Cleveland outfielder Harry Bay, a school chum of Frazee's. Bay backed Frazee's next show, earned a 1,000% return on his investment, and Frazee was on his way. Over the next several years, Frazee produced a series of productions in and around Chicago, earning a small fortune. He then began to branch out, building Chicago's Cort Theater and earning money on that side of the business. At the age of 30, Frazee moved to New York and took aim on Broadway.

But Frazee remained interested in baseball. As early as 1909 he inquired about purchasing the Red Sox, and

in 1911, after his first Broadway production, *Madame Sherry*, ran for nearly eight months and earned Frazee $250,000, he made a bid to buy the Boston Braves. Over the next five years, as Frazee produced hit after hit — and, like any other producer, a few misses — he periodically made additional overtures about buying a major league team, and at various times was reported to be interested in both the Cubs and the Giants.

Meanwhile, he was printing money on Broadway. His shows *Ready Money, A Pair of Sixes, A Full House,* and *Nothing But the Truth* were huge hits that Frazee made even more profitable by breaking with convention and putting the productions on the road while the show was still a hit on Broadway. In 1913, he built the Longacre Theater — still in existence today — which he kept full with both his own productions and those of others. He was one of the most successful producers of his era. Nearly everything Frazee touched made money, and he continued to branch out, starting a real estate company and a brokerage business, managing professional wrestler Frank Gotch, and dabbling in the promotion of boxing. By 1916, he was a millionaire and knew everybody who was anybody, not just in New York, but all over the Northeast, including Boston.

[Note: Anyone interested in Frazee's theatrical career would do well to examine the Internet Broadway Database, www.ibdb.com, created and maintained by the Research Department of the League of American Theatres and Producers. The database includes a wealth of information about Frazee, the plays he produced, and the theaters he owned and leased. Even a cursory glace at this source makes it clear that the notion that Frazee was a failure who operated on a shoestring is pure fiction.]

One of Frazee's acquaintances was Red Sox owner Joseph Lannin. That was the beginning of Frazee's troubles, at least in regard to his lasting reputation in Boston. American League founder and president Ban Johnson ruled the American League with an iron hand and liked to decide who could and who couldn't own a franchise in his league, but his relationship with Lannin, once warm, had deteriorated. In October of 1916, Lannin decided to cash in on his championship team and he sold the club to

Frazee and a partner, Hugh Ward, an actor and theatrical entrepreneur, for $675,000, without Ban Johnson's permission. From the outset, Johnson disliked the fact that Frazee had crashed his private party. Like many in the game, Johnson looked at Frazee's New York-based theatrical background and assumed he was Jewish. In fact, he was Presbyterian, but Johnson and Frazee's other detractors sometimes referred to him in code, criticizing him for being too "New York," and referring to the "mystery" of his religion. Few observers missed the inference. Although Barney Dreyfuss owned the Pittsburgh franchise in the NL and another Jew, Andrew Freedman, had once owned the Giants, the American League would not have a Jewish owner from 1902 through 1946.

As soon as Johnson learned about the sale, he tried to get Lannin to back out of the deal, but it was too late. From the instant Frazee took over the Red Sox, he and Ban Johnson were at loggerheads.

Frazee announced he would "temporarily retire" from the theater, and did so for one season, 1917, staying more or less in the background as the Red Sox team finished in second place. But soon after the end of the season the United States entered the World War, putting the 1918 season at risk. No one in the game knew whether the government would allow major league baseball to continue during wartime.

In face of such uncertainty, most major league club owners retrenched and tried to shed salaries in the event the 1918 season was put on hold. Harry Frazee, however, saw opportunity in the crisis.

Philadelphia A's owner Connie Mack decided to break up his club and Ban Johnson steered Mack to Frazee, who he believed was the only man in baseball foolish enough to pay Mack the prices he wanted. On December 14, 1917, Frazee sent the A's $60,000 — what he accurately termed the "heaviest financial deal ever consummated in the history of baseball," and acquired catcher Wally Schang, pitcher Joe Bush, outfielder Amos Strunk, and a few prospects. A few weeks later, he picked up A's infielder Stuffy McInnis.

The Red Sox, already a solid contender, suddenly looked like a powerhouse, a fact not lost on the rest of the league. When the Yankees complained that they had never been allowed to bid on Mack's players, Johnson coerced Frazee into sending several players back to the A's to make the deal appear more equitable. Frazee then signed former International League president Ed Barrow to serve as manager and de facto general manager of the Red Sox. Everything was in place.

With both the draft and a "Work or Fight" order looming over the 1918 season, spring training opened in

uncertainty as many players took jobs in the war industry or joined the military to avoid the draft. Eventually, 124 major league players joined the service in 1918, leaving most rosters short. The Red Sox, however, flush with players from the A's and supplemented with minor leaguers, were less affected by the war than most teams. Still, some adjustments were necessary and a temporary lack of bodies in the spring led the club to play pitcher Babe Ruth at both first base and the outfield, where his batting prowess against war-ravaged pitching staffs proved to be a sensation.

The Red Sox began the season with their starting pitching intact and a solid lineup made even stronger by Ruth's occasional appearance. The club jumped out to a 12–3 start and didn't look back.

But in mid-May the government ruled that professional baseball was a "non-essential activity," meaning that players were supposed to go to work in the war industries or join the service. Ban Johnson tried to persuade the authorities to give the players a stay to allow the season to be completed, but Johnson made his argument on economic terms, offending the government and harming his cause. Johnson himself declared that the season was over "except for the cremation ceremonies."

Harry Frazee. Courtesy of the Boston Public Library.

Enter Harry Frazee. He had a major investment in the 1918 season and didn't want to see it wasted. With the blessing of a coalition of like-minded owners, he paid a personal visit to Secretary of War Newton Baker and convinced him that the season should continue, not because of economic reasons, but because it was good for the nation's morale. The move saved the season but Frazee's boldness embarrassed Johnson and relations between the two grew even colder.

The Red Sox, buoyed by Frazee's acquisitions, won the pennant, edging out the Indians by 2½ games, then took the World Series from the Cubs in six games. But the Series was marred by the threat of a player strike when players learned that the club owners had changed the distribution of Series money, seriously cutting into the players' take. In punishment, Ban Johnson refused to award Frazee's Red Sox their World Series medallions, the equivalent of today's World Series rings. All things Frazee, and Frazee-related, grated against Johnson.

When the war ended in November, baseball returned to normal. The Red Sox suddenly had more players than they needed and Barrow sold pitchers Ernie Shore and Dutch Leonard and outfielder Duffy Lewis to the New York Yankees. The Yankees, owned by Jacob Ruppert, were quickly becoming a Boston ally. Like Frazee, Ruppert disliked Johnson, who he felt had misled him by reneging on a promise to help him acquire players for the

Harry Frazee's New Year's resolution. January 1, 1918.
Boston Post cartoon.

Yankees. Meanwhile, the relationship between Johnson and Frazee deteriorated even further as the two clashed on a host of issues in the offseason and Frazee floated an idea that would have dumped Johnson and the three-man National Commission that ran baseball and installed former President William Howard Taft as the commissioner of baseball. The enmity between Johnson and Frazee was palpable. Johnson was determined to drive Frazee from the league and Frazee was determined to stay.

The Red Sox got off to a terrible start in 1919 as Babe Ruth, enamored with batting, balked at taking the mound. On June 1, he was barely hitting .200, Boston's pitching had collapsed, and the sixth-place club was already out of the pennant race. Although Ruth would eventually turn his season around and even agree to take the mound, the Red Sox's season was over and Ruth was much of the reason.

In mid-July, Boston pitcher Carl Mays walked off the mound in the middle of a game. Ban Johnson wanted Frazee to suspend him. Frazee balked and instead sold Mays to the Yankees. The deal sparked a political crisis in the league, which in response split into two factions — the Insurrectos, which included the Red Sox, White Sox and Yankees — and everyone else, the "Loyal Five." Johnson refused to recognize any game in which Mays appeared for New York and eventually withheld the money they were due after finishing third. For much of the next nine months, the biggest headlines in baseball weren't about the game on the field but about the courtroom battles between the Insurrectos and the Loyal Five, with Frazee and Johnson as the main protagonists.

In the meantime, Babe Ruth, who was already signed through 1920, wanted a new contract and a big raise after hitting a record 29 home runs in 1919. Frazee balked, for despite Ruth's raw numbers, Ruth was becoming a headache Frazee didn't need. He was staying out all night, had balked at pitching, and at the end of the season jumped the team without permission. The Yankees had been after Ruth, who always hit well at their home field, the Polo Grounds, for more than a year, and in December of 1919 approached Frazee again. Frazee consulted with Barrow and Barrow told him there wasn't a player he wanted from the third-place club. Frazee then agreed to a cash-only deal. On December 26, he sold Ruth to New York for $100,000 — $25,000 in cash and notes for the remainder in three installments.

That was Frazee's great crime, which over time spawned the so-called "Curse of the Bambino," the notion that a cash-starved Harry Frazee sold Ruth, accepted a mortgage on Fenway Park from New York as part of the same deal, then sold his other Red Sox stars, destroying his baseball team to finance his play *No, No, Nanette*, earning Frazee the lasting enmity of Boston fans, leading to the creation of the Yankee dynasty, the subsequent demise of the Red Sox, and a championship drought that did not end until 2004.

All that, however, was still years away. At the time Ruth was sold, no lynch mobs formed in Boston. Public opinion over the Ruth deal, in fact, was split in both Boston and New York. Although some, like uber fan Mike McGreevey of Boston's Royal Rooters, bemoaned the loss of a talent like Ruth, others, such as former player Hugh Duffy and ex-manager Bill Carrigan, felt the Red Sox, who despite Ruth had finished sixth in 1919, would be better off without him. Many New York observers, such as New York Giants manager John McGraw, believed the Yankees were taking a considerable gamble. No one knew that Ruth would go on to hit 665 more home runs, and the notion that Ruth or anyone else ever could seemed as likely as sending a rocket to the moon.

Frazee immediately explained his reasons for dealing Ruth, which included his salary demands, his disruptive influence on the team, and the fact that he had jumped the club at the end of the 1919 season. Nowhere was it suggested that Frazee was broke or in any kind of financial difficulty whatsoever. He was, most certainly, not broke, either in 1919 or at any other time since he ran away from home at age 16. In fact, from 1911 through 1922, he never went more than a year between producing a Broadway hit, a remarkable record. His first play after returning to the theater in 1917, *Ladies First*, ran for 164 performances and was equally successful on the road. Three weeks before the Ruth deal, on December 3, 1919, his play *My Lady Friends* opened on Broadway and was an instant hit, eventually running for more than 200 performances.

Such successes were extremely lucrative. Frazee's Broadway shows played in theaters that held nearly 1,000 spectators. Ticket prices generally ranged from $1.00 up to $5.00 or more for choice seats. In contrast, at the same time you could see a game in the Fenway Park bleachers for 25 cents. One successful show, running for 200 or more performances, grossed roughly as much as the Red Sox did in an entire season at the time (from 1915 through 1924, the Red Sox home attendance averaged nearly 400,000 fans annually). Taking into account Frazee's income from his many other enterprises, from his theaters, and from the touring shows that he produced it is clear that the Red Sox were a relatively minor part of Frazee's financial portfolio.

Frazee also did not use the proceeds of the sale to finance *No, No Nanette*, either directly or indirectly. All evidence suggests that he kept his theater operation completely separate from his sporting interests. In addition, *Nanette*, a musical adaptation of his successful production *My Lady Friends*, was not produced until more than three years after the Ruth sale, in 1923, and did not reach Broadway until 1925, when it became one of the most lucrative musicals of the era.

Despite this timeline problem, in 2003 historian Eric Rauchway propagated the notion, since aped by several other writers who have written that since *Nanette* was spun off from *My Lady Friends*, which predated the Ruth sale, Frazee *must* have used the proceeds of the Ruth deal to finance *Nanette*. This act of mental gymnastics conveniently ignores the fact that *My Lady Friends* was profitable on its own (and, in fact, even toured overseas), that in 1921 Frazee's play *Dulcy*, written by George S. Kaufman, ran for 241 performances (at the time Frazee's second most successful production ever), that in March of 1920 Frazee made a bid to sponsor a fight between Jack Dempsey and black champion Harry Wills for $350,000, and that in September of 1920 Frazee was financially secure enough to purchase the Wallack Theater (likely with the proceeds of his 1919 sale of the Longacre Theater). He renamed the theater the Frazee and, like the Longacre, it never sat empty for more than a few weeks.

Frazee announced that he planned to use the proceeds of the Ruth sale to rebuild his team, and even made noise about acquiring Joe Jackson from the White Sox, but before he was able to do so he became embroiled in two legal fights that combined to make his task nearly impossible. On February 1, the Yankees filed a half-million-dollar lawsuit against Ban Johnson, and a few days later Joseph Lannin, in a dispute with Frazee over which owner was responsible for making a $30,000 payment to the Federal League as part of major league baseball's 1916 legal settlement with that failed enterprise, went to court and slapped a lien on Frazee's "material assets," which legally prevented him from making any trades. This came as no surprise to Frazee. The previous November, the dispute had led Frazee to purposely withhold an installment due Lannin on his purchase of the team.

Although Frazee and Lannin reached a settlement in May, by then the 1920 season was already under way. The result of the lawsuit against Johnson left Frazee and the other Insurrectos virtually frozen out by the Loyal Five, a situation soon made worse by the fact that the White Sox would soon be hamstrung by the emerging Black Sox scandal. Apart from waiver claims, the Yankees became Boston's only willing partner in trades, and vice versa.

But what about that mortgage on Fenway Park? Actually, that wasn't part of the Ruth deal at all. Frazee did not own Fenway Park at the time of the Ruth sale. As papers held by the University of Texas indicate, when the Taylor family sold the Red Sox to James McAleer, they kept Fenway Park. Frazee rented it from the Taylors for $30,000 annually until purchasing it outright on May 3, 1920. Three weeks later, on May 25, Jacob Ruppert of the Yankees gave him a $300,000 mortgage on the property.

So why did Frazee buy the park and why then did Ruppert take out a mortgage on the property? At the time, as part of Johnson's ongoing battle with both Frazee and Ruppert, Ban Johnson had persuaded New York Giants owner Charles Stoneham to cancel the Yankees' lease of the Polo Grounds. That would have left the Yankees homeless, allowing Johnson to force a sale. The AL president even promised Stoneham that he could select the Yankees' new owner. It was an ingenious plot, but Frazee's acquisition of Fenway and the subsequent mortgage thwarted Johnson's and Stoneham's plans. Frazee's acquisition of Fenway may even have been at Ruppert's behest. It served both Frazee and Ruppert — the mortgage on the ballpark gave Frazee access to some cash for his trouble, but, more importantly, gave the Yankees leverage if Stoneham and Johnson followed through with their threat. They had a place to play if necessary — Fenway Park. While any attempt to do so would have certainly sparked a legal challenge from Johnson, the league president wasn't doing very well in his legal fight with the Insurrectos in the New York courts, where Ruppert and Frazee enjoyed a home court advantage — New York Supreme Court Justice Robert Wagner, who had considered the Yankees lawsuit, later represented Frazee in his 1923 divorce from his first wife, Elsie Clisbee. It was likely no accident that as soon as Ruppert acquired Fenway, Stoneham and Johnson abandoned their threat.

Babe Ruth, of course, flourished in New York, hitting a record 54 home runs and leading the Yankees to a second-place finish in 1920. Meanwhile the Red Sox, without Ruth, still managed to move up one spot in the standings, to fifth place.

At the end of the season, after Ban Johnson ruled against the Red Sox in an illegal arrangement Ed Barrow had made with a minor league team, costing Boston prospect and eventual Hall of Famer Pie Traynor. Frazee allowed Barrow to leave the Red Sox and join the Yankees. Over the next few seasons, the two clubs made a series of trades, most of which in the long run worked out to New York's favor and were later used as evidence of Frazee's incompetence.

Fair enough, but one must also note that at the time the deals were made, in both public opinion and statistical terms, the deals were roughly equitable. The press in both New York and Boston was split on virtually every deal between the two clubs through 1922. In 2002 at the convention for the Society for American Baseball Research, SABR member Steven Steinberg gave a graphic presentation that analyzed the deals according to Bill James' "Win Shares" system and concluded that there was no great imbalance at the time the trades were made. Steinberg has since published his findings. Over time, of course, many of the deals did, in fact, work out to New York's benefit, but

Scout Billy Murray, Harry H. Frazee and Ed Barrow in the Red Sox dugout. Courtesy of the Boston Public Library.

as several promising players acquired by Boston during this time, such as pitchers Hank Thormhalen and Allen Russell, suffered serious injuries, while players like Herb Pennock and Waite Hoyt, who had been awful in Boston, suddenly flourished in New York.

Neither did the Red Sox instantly become a last-place team. They got off to a quick start in 1920 before falling back, and in 1921 the 70–70 Red Sox were in fourth place before stumbling over the final days of the season to finish in sixth place as the Yankees won their first pennant. Johnson was still politicking for Frazee's ouster, and for the first time, Frazee, tired of fighting, admitted that he was thinking of selling.

Then, in September, Henry Ford's virulently anti-Semitic nationally distributed weekly newspaper, the *Dearborn Independent*, slandered Frazee in a series of articles that falsely identified him as being Jewish. One article, in particular, excoriated Frazee, attacking him for promoting boxing matches featuring "Negro" fighters, for encouraging "sensuousness" in the theater, for his undermining of Ban Johnson, and for the demise of the Red Sox.

"Baseball was about as much of a sport to Frazee as selling tickets to a merry-go-round would be," opined the *Independent*. "He wanted to put his team across as if they were May Watson's girly girly burlesquers. Baseball was to

be 'promoted' as Jewish managers promote Coney Island." The *Independent* also asserted that when Frazee bought the Red Sox, "another club was placed under the smothering influences of the 'chosen race.'" The article concluded that baseball's essential problem was that Frazee and other Jews were "scavengers [that] have come along to reduce [baseball] to garbage. But there is no doubt anywhere, among either friends or critics of baseball, that the root cause of the present condition is due to Jewish influence.... If baseball is to be saved, it must be taken out of their hands."

From this point forward, almost to the present day, the facts of Frazee's life and career became ever more distorted. The "curse" and virtually all that came to be attached to it came into being after the series of articles appeared in the *Independent*.

In 1922, the Red Sox again got off to another decent start. On June 24, after beating the Yankees four straight, they trailed the Yankees by only 6½ games. But a month later, after the team collapsed in July, Frazee made a truly bad trade, sending Joe Dugan to New York and receiving little in return. The Red Sox tumbled to a last-place finish as the Yankees won another pennant. Ironically enough, however, the last-place Sox were the only team in the league to win the season series against New York, beating the Yankees 13 times in 22 games.

Attendance tumbled and at the end of the season Frazee announced his intention to sell the team. Thereafter he gave his full attention to the theater, even buying Boston's Arlington Theater. After protracted negotiations, on August 1, 1923, Frazee finally sold the Red Sox to a group financed by bottle manufacturer Palmer Winslow and fronted by Bob Quinn for one million dollars, $350,000 more than Frazee and his partner had originally paid for the team. Under Quinn, the Red Sox rapidly got worse. When Winslow died in 1926, Quinn, who had no financial resources whatsoever, took over. From 1924 through 1932, the Red Sox avoided last place only twice — barely — before Tom Yawkey purchased the team in 1933.

Meanwhile, Harry Frazee continued to flourish. After his divorce he married actress Margaret Boyd. He brought *No, No, Nanette* to the stage in Detroit in 1923 and spent the next two years tinkering with the production before finally taking over as director in 1925. The show opened on Broadway on September 16, 1925, and was a sensation, touring the world and over the next few years earning Frazee more than four million dollars.

Frazee was in his glory, one of Broadway's giants, a man who knew everyone and everybody, a confidant of New York Mayor Jimmy Walker, a mover and shaker of the first order in New York politics and culture. A measure of Frazee's stature is that when Charles Lindbergh returned to America for a tickertape parade in New York after his flight across the Atlantic, he spent the night at the home of Harry Frazee.

Frazee's good fortune, however, did not last for long. For two decades he'd been the life of the party and it began to have an effect. He developed Bright's disease, a kidney ailment exacerbated by alcoholism, and died on June 4, 1929, leaving an estate of nearly $1.3 million.

Harry Frazee should have passed into history as just another name in Boston's ownership roster, for at the time of his death no one blamed Frazee for much of anything, and certainly not for the ongoing fate of the franchise. From the time of his death through World War II, Frazee's name was rarely mentioned in regard to the Red Sox and he seemed destined to become a footnote in the history of the franchise, much like previous owners John I. Taylor, James McAleer, and Joe Lannin, all of whom won at least one championship but were little examined afterwards.

But in 1947, baseball writer Fred Lieb published the first narrative history of the team, *The Boston Red Sox*. Lieb, whose writing career began with the *New York Press* in 1911, was a longtime supporter of Ban Johnson. And unbeknownst to most of the people in baseball, Lieb was also an avowed occultist whose two books on the subject demonstrated pronounced anti-Semitic beliefs. In his Red Sox book, Lieb turned Frazee into a caricature with overtly Jewish overtone, as a money-grubbing skinflint who sold the Red Sox out to line his own pocket. In so doing, Lieb laid the groundwork and provided much of the misinformation that others later cobbled together to create "the curse." For the next 50 years, virtually every printed discussion of Frazee took its cue from Lieb, repeating and enhancing his many inaccuracies.

Yet Frazee did not really become known to contemporary fans until 1986, when the Red Sox lost the World Series to Mets. To this point no one had ever assigned any kind of curse to Frazee's sale of Ruth. But the excruciating nature of Boston's defeat in Game Six called for an explanation and sent fans and sportswriters alike scurrying for some kind of precedent, something that could explain what had just happened. They found it in Fred Lieb's book. First John Carroll in the *San Francisco Chronicle* and then George Vecsey of the *New York Times* made mention of such a notion, the first time the idea ever appeared in print. In Carroll's story, the notion appeared in a quote from SABR president Gene Sunnen, while Vecsey wrote an entire column entitled "Babe Ruth Curse Strikes Again" around the idea.

Still, the idea had little traction until 1990, when Dan Shaughnessy published *The Curse of the Bambino*. That book, taking its cues from Lieb, gave both Frazee and Ruth a central role in Red Sox history that neither had ever had before. The book rescued Harry Frazee from obscurity, and a generation of Red Sox fans found the perfect patsy to explain how one team could go so long without winning a championship. As the author wrote in 2004 in an article on the subject for ESPN.com, the "Curse" fit Boston, a parochial place that always goes after the new guy, the outsider, perfectly. It made everyone an insider. Just as Boston's Brahmins once blamed the Irish for Boston's ills and Irish blamed the Yankees and Southie blamed busing and the *Boston Globe*, the "Curse" gave Red Sox fans someone to blame, that rat bastard Harry Frazee. He was perfect for the role: dead and a New Yorker, a patsy no one knew and who couldn't fight back.

The Curse was narcotic. The Curse explained everything. The Curse made everybody an expert. The Curse worked. "See, it was somebody else's fault after all."

Somebody became Harry Frazee.

1918 Boston Red Sox—Day by Day

by Allan Wood and Bill Nowlin

Opening Day 1918. Detail from *Boston Post* sports page cartoon.

April 15—Boston 7, Philadelphia 1—Babe Ruth made his third consecutive Opening Day start for the Red Sox—and won for the third consecutive time. Ruth gave up a run in the top of the second, but Boston scored twice in the home half and went on to win before a Fenway Park crowd of 7,180. Ruth finished with a complete-game four-hitter—and drove in three runs. Right fielder Harry Hooper hit two doubles.

April 16—Boston 1, Philadelphia 0—Carl Mays one-upped Ruth, taking a no-hitter into the eighth inning. However, after Red Sox second baseman Dave Shean knocked down Joe Dugan's line drive, he slipped on the edge of the infield grass and could not make a throw. The play was ruled a single, costing Mays the no-no and a $100 bonus. In the bottom of the ninth, Stuffy McInnis doubled off Scott Perry, advanced to third on a fielder's choice, and scored on Everett Scott's single for a Boston victory.

April 17—Boston 5, Philadelphia 4—The Red Sox rallied in the bottom of the ninth for the second day in a row.

Philadelphia led 4–2 when McInnis singled and George Whiteman walked. Scott bunted, and an error on the throw brought in one run. Pinch-hitter Babe Ruth was walked intentionally, loading the bases, before another pinch-hitter, Wally Schang, won the game with a two-run single. Or as the *Globe* put it: "This gent of all jobs lambasted the agate right on the proboscis."

April 18—The fourth game of the Red Sox/Athletics series was rained out.

April 19—Boston 2, New York 1 / Boston 9, New York 5—The Red Sox swept a doubleheader from the visiting Yankees. Bullet Joe Bush recorded his first win for the Red Sox with a four-hitter in the morning game while a five-run fifth—and five Yankee errors—helped Ruth prevail in the afternoon affair. In the sixth inning of the second game, Everett Scott scored from second base on Ruth's sacrifice fly to deep right field.

April 20—Boston 4, New York 3—The Red Sox won again, starting a season 6–0 for the first time in team history.

The deciding run came in the eigshth inning when Harry Hooper doubled, was bunted to third, and scored on Dick Hoblitzell's squeeze bunt. Dave Shean contributed two doubles and the Red Sox turned four double plays.

April 21—No game scheduled in Boston on the Sunday.

April 22—New York 11, Boston 4—Lefty George Mogridge continued to be a Red Sox nemesis—he pitched a no-hitter against Boston in 1917—but it was the Yankees bats that handed the Red Sox their first loss of the season. The Sox got off to a 2–0 lead, but neither Dutch Leonard nor Sam Jones could hold New York back, as the Yankees pounded out 13 hits. Boston didn't get a safe hit out of the infield until the ninth inning.

April 23—Boston 1, New York 0—Hank Thormahlen, the Yankees' rookie left-hander, was two outs away from a no-hitter when Amos Strunk singled, scooted to third on Babe Ruth's pinch-hit single, and scored when George Whiteman's fly ball was dropped by left fielder Ping Bodie. Joe Bush finished with a three-hitter and helped himself by picking three Yankees off base; Bodie was caught twice, including at second with the bases loaded in the sixth inning.

April 24—Philadelphia 3, Boston 0—The Red Sox, after a 7–1 homestand, headed to Philadelphia and proceeded to drop the first game of the series (and the Athletics' home opener at Shibe Park) when George Burns clubbed a three-run homer off Babe Ruth in the eighth inning. Red Sox captain Dick Hoblitzell, batting a woeful .036, was dropped from his clean-up spot to sixth in the order.

April 25—Boston 6, Philadelphia 1 –The Red Sox scored once each in the first three frames, helped out by Willie Adams's seven walks in the first two innings. Former Athletics Amos Strunk (4-for-5) and Stuffy McInnis (three hits) led the offense. The game started later than usual—4:00 P.M.—in an attempt to boost attendance. The crowd was approximately 2,000. It was twilight by the time Carl Mays recorded the final out.

April 26—Boston 2, Philadelphia 1—Scott Perry held the Red Sox without a hit until the seventh inning. That's when Strunk singled, was bunted to second, stole third, and came home on a wild pitch. Dick Hoblitzell doubled and a fumbled ball allowed him to score on Everett Scott's single. Sox starter Dutch Leonard had a rocky game—he allowed seven hits and walked 10 A's—and was saved more than once by strong infield defense. Three times a Philadelphia runner tried to go from first to third on a single and each time was gunned down. The A's left 11 men on base.

April 27—Boston 4, Philadelphia 1—The series became a nightmare for Philadelphia as once again former Athletics won the game for Boston. Joe Bush scattered seven hits and allowed only one run while pitching his third straight complete game, while Stuffy McInnis (two RBIs), Wally Schang (one), and Amos Strunk (one) drove in the Red Sox runs.

April 28—Exhibition: Boston 7, Bridgeport 0—Sunday baseball was against the law in most eastern cities, so a bunch of Red Sox traveled to Connecticut for an exhibition game. Sam Jones pitched a complete game and Babe Ruth played a few innings at first base. Red Sox pitcher Dick McCabe, who had yet to appear in a game for Boston this season, started for Bridgeport, where he had begun his professional career.

April 29—Back in Boston, the day's game was called off because of cold and rain. Harry Frazee told the *Herald and Journal* that he had recently rejected a $100,000 offer for pitcher Babe Ruth: "I might as well sell the franchise and the whole club as sell Ruth. It is ridiculous to talk about it. Ruth is our big ace. He's the most talked of, most sought for, most colorful ball player in the game." Frazee did not name the team, but the newspaper assumed it was either the Yankees or White Sox.

April 30—Boston 8, Washington 1—Babe Ruth allowed a single on his first pitch of the game, but that was the only hit the Senators could muster for six innings. Ruth earned accolades for his fielding off the mound, pouncing on one bunt and starting a bases-loaded double play on another ball. Ruth finished with a five-hitter, giving Boston an 11–2 record in April. The Chicago White Sox finished the month in second place at 5–2, having had several postponements in the first two weeks of the season.

May 1—Washington 5, Boston 0—Senators ace Walter Johnson shut out the Red Sox on four hits (three of them by Harry Hooper) before a Fenway crowd of 2,169. The Senators scored all five runs off Carl Mays in the fourth inning. Boston manager Ed Barrow let Mays work his way out of the inning and go the distance.

May 2—Boston 8, Washington 1—Harry Hooper had three hits in a game for the second day in a row (three doubles, boosting his average to .396) and Dutch Leonard pitched his first solid game of the season, scattering five hits. The Red Sox left for New York without outfielder George Whiteman, who had a bad cold and fever and was told to stay home.

May 3—New York 3, Boston 2 (11 innings)—Boston took a quick 2–0 lead at the Polo Grounds in upper Manhattan, but the Yankees battled back, eventually winning in

11 innings. The Yankees loaded the bases with none out in the bottom of the 10th, when Bush fielded a line drive with his pitching hand. He was able to start a double play, but was clearly in pain. He convinced Barrow to let him stay in the game, but then allowed three straight hits and the winning run in the following inning.

May 4—New York 5, Boston 4—It was rumored that Yankees manager Miller Huggins, knowing that Babe Ruth had been out all night before his start, told his players to run Ruth ragged in the field. Whether true or not, Babe fielded a whopping 13 chances on the mound, and his two throwing errors helped the Yankees win. At the plate, Ruth hit a two-run homer and a double, driving in three of Boston's four runs.

May 5—Exhibition: Boston 3, Doherty Silk Sox 1—The Red Sox played another Sunday exhibition—this time in Clifton, New Jersey against the Doherty Silk Sox, the top semipro team in the state. Dick McCabe again pitched—this time for Boston; two other Red Sox pitchers started in the outfield: Sam Jones (CF) and Weldon Wyckoff (RF), who led off and homered on the first pitch of the game.

Back in Boston, at the Tremont Temple, Rev. Dr. Cortland Myers denounced Sunday entertainment in his sermon, entitled "Even During These War Days Has Sodom And Gomorrah Anything on Boston in the Way of Pagan Amusements?" The Reverend Doctor proclaimed, "The moving picture is a source of tremendous peril to the coming generation.... Most of the things seen on the screen are not fit for human eyes to see.... They say they must be realistic, and it is better to show the young sin as it really is.... Modern dances come from the animal and savage world. Savage music and savage motion is what the young people who indulge in these dances go through.... Statistics show that the majority of young women who go astray do so through the modern dance."

May 6—New York 10, Boston 3—The Yankees finished a three-game sweep by pounding Carl Mays and Sam Jones. This game was historic because Babe Ruth played first base and batted sixth. It was the first time Ruth had started a game at a position other than pitcher and the first time he batted anywhere in the lineup other than ninth. Ruth belted another two-run home run. Paul Shannon of the *Boston Post* began his game story: "Babe Ruth still remains the hitting idol of the Polo Grounds." The *Boston Globe* compared Ruth to former Red Sox pitcher Smoky Joe Wood, then an outfielder for Cleveland: "Ruth's batting, could it be turned to advantage every day, would help the club a lot. Just now it's not likely that Barrow will use Ruth except as an emergency regular, but the Babe's work yesterday suggests that the

fzuture holds much in store for him." Harry Hooper hit safely in his seventh straight game, raising his average to .410.

May 7—Washington 7, Boston 2—The Red Sox moved on to the nation's capital and lost again, this time to Walter Johnson. Ruth again played first base, but was now hitting in the cleanup spot. He hit a home run for the third game in a row, tying Ray Caldwell's major league record. Ruth's blast landed far beyond the right field fence, and scared a stray dog. Ruth's reputation as a power hitter was growing and he was given a loud ovation from the Griffith Stadium crowd as he trotted around the bases.

May 8—Washington 14, Boston 4—The Red Sox held a 4–0 lead after four innings, but then the roof fell in. Joe Bush, Carl Mays, and Weldon Wyckoff bore the brunt of the beating administered during an eight-run fifth inning and a five-run sixth that crushed any hopes of a Red Sox win.

May 9—Washington 4, Boston 3 (10 innings)—The Red Sox fell out of first place with their sixth consecutive loss. Cleveland (11–8) edged ahead of Boston (12–9). Ruth was the starting pitcher and batted fourth. He went 5-for-5 with a single, a triple, and three doubles—one more hit than the rest of the lineup combined. It gave him the top batting average in the American League: .500 (16-for-32). Ruth was also thrown out trying to steal third base with one out in the top of the 10th. In the bottom half, Ruth gave up two singles, a walk, and a sacrifice fly that gave the Senators a win.

May 10—Boston 4, St. Louis 1—After losing six in a row on the road, the Red Sox were happy to get back to Boston. Carl Mays dispatched the Browns and Babe Ruth made his debut in left field. Coming back to the dugout at the end of an inning, Ruth complained that it was "lonesome in the outfield. It's hard to keep awake with nothing to do." Babe went 0-for-3, snapping his 10-game hitting streak.

May 11—St. Louis 4, Boston 2—Ruth was back at first base as Fenway had its second-best crowd of the young season: 7,046. Babe hit a double and two singles and played exceptionally well in the infield. However, an error by catcher Wally Schang on a play at the plate in the eighth helped open the gates for three St. Louis runs. Boston lost an opportunity to get back into first place as Washington beat Cleveland 1–0; Walter Johnson pitched a five-hitter, tripled, and scored the game's only run.

May 12—No Sunday game, but Chicago beat Cleveland 1–0 in a five inning, rain-shortened contest, putting the Red Sox back on top of the standings.

May 13—Boston 7, St. Louis 5 –Manager Ed Barrow continued tinkering with his lineup. He gave Ruth the day off, moved Stuffy McInnis back to his usual position of first base, and started rookie Fred Thomas at third base. McInnis had played third base early in his career before becoming a star first baseman in Philadelphia and he admitted that his time at third this season had negatively affected his hitting. However, he was batting .284, not all that bad. Joe Bush wasn't at his best for Boston, allowing nine hits and seven walks. Everett Scott and Amos Strunk each had three hits.

May 14—Wet grounds caused a cancellation of the game against the Browns. Boston held a slim half-game lead over both the Yankees and Indians. According to a report from Washington, first baseman Dick Hoblitzell, nursing a sore elbow, was nominated by President Woodrow Wilson to be a first lieutenant in the Army Dental Corps.

May 15—Boston 5, Detroit 4—Ty Cobb and the Tigers rolled into Boston. The *Boston Post* termed the Tigers the "most bitter antagonists that the Red Sox have fought against during the past four seasons." In the first game of the series, Detroit scored three times in the third inning, but the Red Sox clawed back, scoring single runs in the fourth, fifth, and sixth, and finally won the game in the bottom of the ninth. With one out, Wally Schang walked and Everett Scott singled. Dick Hoblitzell's single tied the game at 4–4. Then, after Ruth (back in the #9 spot) was walked to load the bases, Harry Hooper singled over Bobby Veach's head in right field to win the game. Cobb went 0-for-4, hitting nothing out of the infield off of Ruth, who allowed only three outs to the outfield.

May 16—Boston 7, Detroit 2—Tigers pitcher Bill James was driven from the mound in a six-run third inning and the Red Sox won with ease. Carl Mays allowed only four singles, two by Ty Cobb. Harry Hooper hit an inside-the-park home run during the big rally, one of only two home runs hit at Fenway Park during the entire 1918 season. At 16–10, Boston led the Yankees in the AL by 1½ games.

May 17—Boston 11, Detroit 8—It was a "biff, bang affair" with 23 hits and 21 runs. The Red Sox had their 7–0 lead cut to 7–5, then they upped it to 10–5 before Detroit came back within two, 10–8. Dutch Leonard walked seven, but still went the distance; he also got three hits and drove in three runs. Everyone in the Red Sox lineup had a hit except for Babe Ruth, though the Big Fellow recorded two assists from left field.

May 18—Boston 3, Detroit 1—Weekend temperatures in the high 80s helped bring more than 10,000 fans to Fenway on Saturday to watch the Red Sox rally in the seventh. Amos Strunk doubled in Joe Bush and Harry

Hooper, snapping a 1–1 tie. Bush held the Tigers at bay, finishing a four-game Boston sweep.

May 19—No game on Sunday. Babe Ruth enjoyed a picnic with his wife Helen.

May 20—Boston 11, Cleveland 1—Babe Ruth (on his day to pitch) showed up at Fenway Park with a fever and was sent to the hospital. His illness was reported as tonsillitis and he was expected to be out of action for a week. In

Carl Mays beans Tris Speaker on May 20.
Detail from *Boston Post* sports page cartoon.

his absence, the Red Sox racked up 16 hits and walloped the Indians. A seven-run fifth inning was highlighted by three triples—from Carl Mays, Fred Thomas, and Everett Scott. Late in the game, Mays beaned former Boston teammate Tris Speaker and the two men got into a heated shouting match.

May 21—Cleveland 6, Boston 5—Dutch Leonard continued his dismal season, allowing 12 hits and walking six. In eight starts covering 65.1 innings, Leonard had surrendered 71 hits and 27 walks. The Red Sox scored all of their runs in the bottom of the fifth.

May 22—The game was rained out, giving the short-handed Red Sox pitching rotation a day to rest.

May 23—Cleveland 1, Boston 0—The day began with ominous news as the United States Army announced a "work or fight" draft regulation. All able-bodied men were expected to either enlist or find employment in essential war-related work by July 1. One group affected by the order was people "engaged and occupied in connection with games, sports and amusements." Baseball players between the ages of 18–30 would be affected if the order was strictly enforced—approximately 75% of every team's roster—but a formal decision would not be made until specific cases were brought by local draft boards after the July 1 deadline.

The *Boston Herald and Journal* reported that there is "little chance that Uncle Sam will disrupt big league baseball.... The players represent big investments involved in the two big leagues. They are entitled to the same treatment that is accorded the stars of the theatre [who would be exempt from the order].... To deprive baseball of its stars means depriving many thousands of out-of-door amusements which parallels the recreation and fun derived from attending the theatre.... There is no chance in any event of the big leagues closing their gates."

On the diamond, Guy Morton threw a one-hitter at the Red Sox. Amos Strunk had the team's lone hit in the seventh inning, what the *Post* called "a cheap Texas leaguer" just beyond second baseman Ray Chapman's reach into right field. Cleveland scored in the fourth when Bobby Roth's hit took an unexpected bounce off the big left-field wall, eluding George Whiteman. The *Globe* complained that Whiteman usually played too deep and that balls hit off the wall bounce by him quickly and roll back towards the infield.

May 24—Boston 5, Chicago 4—The defending World Series champion White Sox were welcomed to Boston by Joe Bush, who limited them to seven hits while driving in three runs himself, including a "sweet single to center" in the bottom of the ninth that gave the Red Sox the walkoff victory. The Red Sox scored four times in what the papers called their "lucky fifth inning" (16 runs in the last four games).

May 25—Boston 3, Chicago 2 (10 innings)—Chicago's Lefty Williams, who had pitched an 18-inning duel against Washington's Walter Johnson 10 days earlier—both hurlers went the distance in a game that lasted 2:47, hooked up with Carl Mays for another tight game. With one out in the bottom of the 10th, Wally Schang doubled to left center. Mays lined out to shortstop and Harry Hooper was walked intentionally. Dave Shean (who had been a weak 0-for-3) drove a double over Nemo Leibold's head in left field to win the game.

May 26—Babe Ruth was discharged from the Massachusetts Eye and Ear Infirmary, but was expected to take a few more days to get back in form. The Red Sox planned to play this day (Sunday)—and donate the gate receipts to the Red Cross, but Police Commissioner Stephen O'Meara maintained that it would be in violation of the law. The game was rescheduled for Monday.

May 27—Chicago 6, Boston 4—Dutch Leonard lost to Ed Cicotte, despite twice being staked to two-run leads. Babe Ruth attended the game in civilian clothes and received a huge cheer. Because the charity game was played on a weekday, instead of an estimated $50,000 in gate receipts, the Red Sox collected no more than $6,000. The Yankees beat Cleveland and crept to within 1½ games of Boston.

May 28—Boston 1, Chicago 0—Joe Bush's combination of pitching and batting led to a Red Sox win. Bush tossed a one-hitter (Happy Felsch singled in the first inning) and drove in the day's only run. Fred Thomas had three of Boston's five hits. Ed Cicotte, who lasted only one inning in the previous game, returned to start for the second day in a row.

Before the game, Harry Frazee revealed which team had made the huge offer for Babe Ruth about one month earlier. He also indicated the offer was for far more money. "I see that there have been some skeptical remarks about the offer of $150,000 I received for the baseball services of Babe Ruth. Well, they're all wrong. Col. Ruppert of the New York Yankees asked me if I would sell the Babe for $150,000 and I told the colonel I would not. I think the New York man showed good judgment in making such a big offer. Ruth already is mighty popular in New York, and just think what he would mean to the Yankees if he were playing for them everyday and hitting those long ones at the leftfield bleachers and the rightfield grandstand!"

May 29—Boston 4, Washington 2; Boston 3, Washington 0—The Senators came into a very cold Fenway Park and dropped the first game to Carl Mays. The Red Sox broke a 2–2 tie with three straight singles (and an outfield error) with two outs in the seventh. In the second game, Sam Jones outpitched Walter Johnson (who came into the game with a 40-inning scoreless streak).

May 30—Boston 9, Washington 1; Washington 4, Boston 0—Dutch Leonard cruised in the first game of the Memorial Day doubleheader in what was described as "arctic" weather. Everett Scott doubled three times and drove in five runs. Strapped for pitchers, Ed Barrow handed the ball in the second game to Dick McCabe, who made his first major league start. He pitched eight good innings, but Boston managed nothing against Washington's Doc Ayers. Babe Ruth pinch-hit in the late innings of the second game.

May 31—No game scheduled. The Red Sox "hit the western trail" at 2 PM for a 17-game western road trip. They had finished their homestand with a 13–5 record and, at 25–14, Boston began June two games ahead of the Yankees and four games ahead of the Indians.

June 1—Detroit 4, Boston 3 (13 innings)—The Tigers jumped on Joe Bush for three runs in the first—not the way the Red Sox wanted to start the road trip—but Boston picked up single runs in the fourth, seventh, and ninth innings and sent the game into extras. Carl Mays took the mound at Navin Field (later renamed Tiger Stadium) in relief once the Red Sox tied the game and managed to escape a bases-loaded, nobody-out jam in the bottom of the ninth. Mays pitched into the 13th, when Harry Heilmann's liner sailed well over Amos Strunk's head in center field, bringing in the winning run. The two teams engaged in their usual bench jockeying, with the umpires stepping in several times and warning both sides.

June 2—Detroit 4, Boston 3—A big crowd of 14,000 turned out, hoping to see more on-field fireworks, but long-time enemies Ty Cobb and Carl Mays shook hands in a pre-arranged display behind the plate before the game, and both teams behaved themselves. Babe Ruth returned to the mound for the first time since his illness, but was rusty, issuing two bases-loaded walks. He also hit a homer, his fourth of the season—double the number he'd hit in all of 1917.

June 3—Boston 5, Detroit 0—Dutch Leonard's rollercoaster season continued. At times looking like an overmatched amateur on the hill, this time out Leonard threw a no-hitter (the second of his career). His only blemish was a first-inning walk to Bobby Veach. Babe Ruth started in center field, as Amos Strunk had twisted his ankle while heading to the dressing room after the previous game. Ruth hit his fifth home run of the year.

June 4—Boston 7, Detroit 6—Carl Mays went the distance and prevailed when the Red Sox scored three runs in the top of the ninth. Babe Ruth played center field again and hit yet another home run. After the game, the Red Sox headed to Cleveland by boat.

June 5—Cleveland 5, Boston 4 (10 innings)—Babe Ruth homered for the fourth consecutive game—a new major league record. While the *Herald and Journal* headline screamed: "Babe Ruth Establishes World's Record Of Four Home Runs In Four Successive Days," the *Post* made no mention of the record at all, only noting that Ruth "kept up his home-run crusade by driving out the longest home run of the season." The *Globe*'s headline: "Ruth's Fourth Homer in Four Days Goes to Waste." The Indians won the game in extra innings, when, after a missed

bunt attempt, Boston catcher Wally Schang threw down to third base in an attempt to pick off Bobby Roth. The throw hit Roth and rolled away, allowing him to score.

June 6—Boston 1, Cleveland 0—Another extra-inning affair in Cleveland, and this time Sam Jones (five-hitter) beat Stan Coveleskie (three-hitter). Jones got the nod after Babe Ruth told Ed Barrow that pitching and playing the outfield was too exhausting and pitching had become a chore (Ruth had also lost three of his last four starts). The Red Sox scored in the 10th without a hit. After Harry Hooper walked, Dave Shean bunted, but Coveleskie threw too late to second and both runners were safe. Amos Strunk then dropped a bunt down the third base line, and again Coveleskie was too late to get a force, this time at third. Ruth hit a hard drive to shortstop and while Strunk was forced at second, Hooper was able to score.

June 7—Cleveland 14, Boston 7—It was a disaster of a game. Six Red Sox pitchers (including Babe Ruth, who came in from left field in relief) combined to issue 11 walks. The Indians collected 13 hits, stole seven bases, and pulled off a triple steal. Despite having a 4–0 lead in the first inning, Dutch Leonard was knocked out of the box during a six-run third.

June 8—Cleveland 3, Boston 1—Carl Mays had beaten Cleveland in 13 of his last 15 starts against them over the last two years. But not this day. Guy Morton defeated the Sox again, dropping them into second place. Boston was a lackluster 16–16 in its last 32 games.

June 9—Boston 2, Cleveland 0—The Red Sox moved back into first place as Dutch Leonard shut out the Indians. Each of Leonard's two singles sent a teammate to third base, where he was promptly knocked in by Harry Hooper. Cleveland had runners on base in each of the last six innings, but wound up stranding 10 men. The umpires were accosted after the game by irate fans (though controversial calls had gone against both teams) and mounted policemen had to disperse the crowd to get the umpires to safety.

Back in Boston, in one of many instances of anti-Germany sentiment stoked by the Great War, former Mayor John "Honey Fitz" Fitzgerald (John F. Kennedy's maternal grandfather) called for a massive book burning on the Fourth of July. "Every German book in the Boston schools should be gathered together on Boston Common on the Fourth of July and bonfired.... Measures like this will make [Germany] understand that nobody cares to love or associate with a race whose leadership employs the means lowest and most demonical to accomplish its ends. We in America have been too timid...too tolerant."

June 10—Boston 1, Chicago 0—The White Sox managed

only two hits off of Joe Bush. The Red Sox got a mere three hits off Frank Shellenback, but one of them was a fourth-inning triple by Dave Shean, who then scored the game's lone run on a passed ball. Red Sox pitchers had not allowed a run in 22 innings. Dick Hoblitzell left for the Army Dental Corps at Camp Oglethorpe in Georgia. Harry Hooper was named the team's new captain.

June 11—Chicago 4, Boston 1—Lefty Williams was scheduled to start for the White Sox, but before the game, he and second-string catcher Byrd Lynn told manager Pants Rowland they were planning on joining former teammate Joe Jackson at the Bethlehem Shipyards in Pennsylvania. The players say they would play for a few more days, but White Sox owner Charles Comiskey told them to leave the club immediately. Red Faber, a hero of the 1917 World Series, was scheduled to leave the team for the Navy that evening, but when he heard what had happened, he asked for his uniform back and took the mound. For Boston, Sam Jones pitched seven innings.

June 12—Boston 7, Chicago 0—Carl Mays threw a three-hitter and did not allow any White Sox runner to reach third base. Harry Hooper went 4-for-5 with a triple, a stolen base, and two runs scored. Amos Strunk, George Whiteman, and Everett Scott each had two hits. Mays tripled in Boston's first run in the second inning.

As draft-age men comply with the government's "work-or-fight" order, attendance at afternoon games begins to plummet. In Detroit, a crowd of only 300 showed up for the A's-Tigers game.

June 13—Boston 6, Chicago 0—Dutch Leonard pitched his third straight shutout and the reigning World Champion White Sox were blanked for the third time in four days.

June 14—St. Louis 5, Boston 4—Joe Bush was trying to preserve a 4–3 lead with two outs in the bottom of the ninth when Browns pinch-hitter Pete Johns socked his only triple of the year and knocked in two runs to win the game. Johns's hit was even more impressive considering that he took over at the plate after pitcher Allen Sothoron had fallen behind 0–2. Since their dynamite 12–3

start, Boston had gone only 20–18. The Sox held a slim 1½-game lead over the Yankees.

June 15—Boston 8, St. Louis 4—Babe Ruth drove in five runs, the crowning blow a three-run homer in the seventh. The Browns pitched to Ruth despite loud cries from the crowd calling for an intentional walk. It was Babe's eighth home run of the year.

Ruth's five RBIs won the June 15 ballgame. Detail from *Boston Post* sports page cartoon.

June 16—St Louis 2, Boston 1—It was a pitcher's duel between Dutch Leonard (on two days rest) and Urban Shocker until the Browns won the game in the bottom of the ninth. Ernie Johnson was on first base with one out. He took off for second and Schang's throw skipped by Dave Shean and rolled into center field. Johnson dashed for third. Fred Thomas took the throw from the outfield and tried to tag Johnson, but he had already rounded third base and was sprinting home. Thomas's throw to the plate was late and Johnson slid across with the winning run. Four of the Red Sox's five hits were doubles. Babe Ruth filled in at first base for Stuffy McInnis.

The *New York Times* reported that if the "work-or-fight" order was applied to professional baseball, one proposal would combine the American and National leagues into one eight-team league with players both under and over draft age. A majority of owners were said to favor continuing the season, even with a poorer quality of play.

June 17—Boston 8, St. Louis 0—Carl Mays shut out the Browns on four hits as the temperature hovered near 100 degrees. Babe Ruth had been walked intentionally in his final three plate appearances the day before, so Barrow shuffled his lineup, moving Wally Schang into the fifth spot after the Babe. The Browns still avoided Ruth, putting him on base in his first two times up—a string of five consecutive free passes. By the late innings, even the St. Louis fans had tired of this and began yelling to let Ruth hit. In the eighth inning, Babe banged a double off the wall in right-center and drove in Boston's final two runs.

June 18—No game, as the Red Sox traveled back to Boston. They ended the road trip with a 9–8 record, though four of the eight losses were by only one run. Seven of the nine wins were shutouts. Boston started the trip two games ahead of the Yankees and, nearly three weeks later, were still 1½ games ahead. Their season road record stood at 12–15.

June 19—Philadelphia 5, Boston 0—The Red Sox left the heat of the midwest and returned to chilly Boston (61 degrees) and their bats were equally cold against A's rookie Robert Geary. Dave Shean had stomach trouble and stayed home, so Frank Truesdale played second base. Joe Bush was effective in all but the sixth inning, when Philadelphia bunched three hits, two walks, and two Red Sox errors, and scored four times. Dutch Leonard received word that his California draft board had reclassified him into Class 1. Not wanting to be drafted, Leonard had spoken with management at Quincy's Fore River Shipyard about a possible position.

June 20—Philadelphia 2, Boston 0 / Boston 3, Philadelphia 0—The Red Sox were shut out for the second game in a row, as Philadelphia's Vean Gregg allowed only three infield hits. The only two runs off Sam Jones both came in the top of the ninth when "Tillie Walker massaged the apple sweetly with this shillaleh, driving it over the garden wall in left." In other words, he hit a homer. According to the papers, it was only the 15th time a home run had been hit over Fenway's big wall since the park opened seven years earlier—and Walker was the only player to have done it twice. The tables were turned in the second game, as Dutch Leonard was dominant before leaving in the sixth after a line drive hit his pitching hand. Vince Molyneaux finished out the game and received credit for the win—the only win of his major league career.

Right-hander Lore Bader, who had pitched in 15 games for Boston in 1917 and had been recently discharged from the Charlestown Navy Yard because of a bad knee, worked out with the Sox before the first game. For most of June, Babe Ruth had been arguing with manager Ed Barrow about whether or not he was going to pitch. Despite the team's need for pitching, Ruth said he saw himself as an outfielder only. He also started wearing a leather strap on his left wrist, saying he had recently hurt it sliding into second base. Barrow was highly skeptical

WITH 2 OUT AND THE BASES FILLED—"BABE" RUTH TRIPLED (CLEANING THE BASES THEN SCORED HIMSELF ON A WILD THROW MAKING 4 RUNS IN THE 4TH INNING—

Ruth's three-bagger helped the Sox to a 13–0 whitewash of the Athletics, June 21. Detail from *Boston Post* sports page cartoon.

and told Ruth firmly that he would be starting against the Yankees on June 24th.

June 21—Boston 13, Philadelphia 0—Carl Mays tossed his third straight shutout and his second one-hitter of the season. Mays had only himself to blame for the fifth-inning hit, a little nubber in between home plate and the mound. The *Globe* reported that Wally Schang could easily have made the play himself, but Mays pounced on the ball and his throw to first was too late to nip Jake Munch. Because of a depleted roster, A's manager Connie Mack had to play several men out of position and Philadelphia ended up committing seven errors.

June 22—The game against Philadelphia was rained out. National League president John Heydler said that his league would finish the 1918 schedule with amateur players, if necessary, relying "on local pride and [the] tolerance of the public during the process of developing such playing talent."

June 23—The Red Sox were off on Sunday and an exhibition game in Connecticut was cancelled due to cold. Dutch Leonard did not travel with the team to New York. Shortstop Everett Scott was reclassified from Class 4 to Class 1A by his draft board in Bluffton, Indiana. Scott, married with a young son, appealed the decision.

June 24—New York 3, Boston 2—Babe Ruth was adamant that his left wrist still hurt, so he rode the bench and Joe Bush took the hill. Bush had a 2–1 lead in the bottom of the ninth, but a walk to the leadoff batter and a single puts runners at first and third. A sacrifice fly tied the game and then Wally Pipp belted the ball into the right-field stands. Under the rules at that time, it was not recorded as a home run because there was a runner on first and as soon as that man scored, the game was over. Pipp's hit was reported by some as a double and others as a triple.

June 25—Boston 7, New York 3—With the help of Sam Jones's pitching, the Red Sox held onto first place. Ruth, subbing in center field for Amos Strunk, and Fred Thomas each hit homers (it was the only one of the year for Thomas), while Harry Hooper and Dave Shean each tripled.

The Red Sox purchased the contracts of three players from the New Orleans Pelicans—Walter Barbare, Red Bluhm, and Jack Stansbury—who were told to join the Red Sox once the Southern Association season was over at week's end.

June 26—New York 3, Boston 1—Slim Love threw a three-hitter and his two-run double off Carl Mays in the second inning spelled defeat for the Red Sox. Boston scored in the ninth when Babe Ruth doubled (it missed clearing the fence by inches—and was the first game all year in New York that Ruth did not homer). Stuffy McInnis drove in Ruth from second base. Three innings earlier, Ruth had clubbed a long foul ball that struck the back of an upper grandstand seat next to a napping fan. The *New York Times* reported the fan "stayed awake for the rest of the game, and kept one eye on Ruth."

June 27—New York 7, Boston 5—The Yankees took over first place, .583 to .578, after winning the third of four games from the Red Sox. Joe Bush started for the second time in four days. The *Globe* wrote that "Bush had the better of Mogridge and but for costly errors both of commission and omission should have come through an easy winner." The Red Sox nearly doubled the Yankees' hit total (17–9). Sam Agnew got himself picked off third base. He also made one of Boston's five errors, but Shean's two errors were more costly. It wasn't a good day.

June 28—Washington 3, Boston 1—The Red Sox continued their losing ways in Washington, managing only one hit off Harry Harper: a seventh-inning homer by Babe Ruth, who again refused to pitch. Lore Bader threw a six-hitter, though he had control problems as well, walking five Senators.

June 29—Boston 3, Washington 1—The Red Sox turned the previous day's score around and won, scoring twice in the eighth and adding an insurance run in the ninth. They also left 14 men on base. Sam Jones started for Boston and Joe Bush finished up. At the end of the day, New York (36–26), Boston (38–28), and Cleveland (39–29) were in a three-way tie for first place.

June 30—Boston 3, Washington 1 (10 innings)—It was a pitchers' duel: Carl Mays against Walter Johnson. A constant drizzle forced three delays in the game. Johnson wasn't at his best, giving up a total of 11 hits, but only one run. Mays retired the first 16 Senators, but Washington tied the game in the bottom of the ninth. In the top of the 10th, Babe Ruth hit "the longest home run ever made" at Griffith Stadium, to deep right-center field. Mays allowed a one-out single in the bottom half of the 10th, but struck out the side for the win. In the last 15 years, only three American League players had hit as many as 11 home runs in a season; each of them finished with 12. Ruth had now already clubbed 11 (every one of them hit on the road) by the end of June.

July 1—No game. With the win on the final day of June, the Red Sox entered July having claimed first place again with a record of 39–28, a half-game ahead of second-place New York. The Indians were only 1½ games behind and the Senators (thanks to losing two straight to the Sox) were four games back.

July 2—Washington 3, Boston 0—After a heated dugout argument with manager Ed Barrow over a possible missed sign and a strikeout, Babe Ruth quit the team and went back to his father's house in Baltimore. The Sox traveled to Philadelphia without him. In addition, third baseman Fred Thomas received his draft notice and headed home to Wisconsin for his physical exam. Harry Harper's shutout was the least of Boston's troubles.

July 3—Philadelphia 6, Boston 0—Another day, another whitewash. This time, it was Vean Gregg, with a four-hitter. Jack Stansbury played center field as Ruth was AWOL. Red Bluhm made his only major league appearance as a pinch-hitter. Speaking from Baltimore, Babe Ruth told the *Globe* he had not jumped the team, but did plan on playing for the Chester Shipbuilding Company team in Pennsylvania to keep active until things simmered down between him and Ed Barrow. Carl Mays was informed that he was now in Class 1A and could expect a call-up. Everett Scott was still awaiting news of his draft board appeal. Dave Shean was out of action with an infected foot, so 37-year-old coach Heinie Wagner (who hadn't played the infield on a regular basis since 1913) filled in at second base. Amos Strunk returned to the lineup, but he was mired in a dismal 8-for-73 slump.

July 4—Boston 11, Philadelphia 9; Philadelphia 2, Boston 1 (11 innings)—Heinie Wagner, dispatched to collect Babe Ruth from Baltimore, returned with the Big Fellow at 2 A.M. Ruth had soured on playing for Chester when he learned they wanted him to pitch. At the ballpark, Barrow refused to speak to Ruth, and Ruth took off his uniform, shouting that he was quitting again. Other players talked him out of it, but Ruth sat out the first game; he played center field in the second. The score in the nightcap was 1–1 in the 11th inning, but Philadelphia had the bases loaded with one out. Ruth caught a fly ball and fired it home. His throw was off the mark, but Red Shannon, the runner coming from third, missed the plate. While catcher Wally Schang fumbled for the ball, Shannon scrambled back and touched the dish.

The Cleveland Indians swept a doubleheader from the Browns and moved into first place. Dutch Leonard (now pitching for the Fore River Shipyard) struck out 18 Bethlehem Steel Company batters in a Steel League game, winning 2–0.

July 5—Boston 4, Philadelphia 3 (10 innings)—After long conversations with Barrow and Harry Frazee, Ruth took the mound for his first start since June 2. He won the game, allowing seven hits and four walks (and two Philly runs in the bottom of the ninth that sent the game into extra innings). Ruth also scored the winning run, despite an 0-for-3 day. With two outs and no one on in the top of the 10th, Ruth walked and scored when Stuffy McInnis tripled to right field. The *Boston Post* reported that the Red Sox "pitching staff is fairly shot to pieces, the infield is badly crippled and there is no help in sight." No one could imagine the team was about to go on its hottest streak of the season.

July 6—Boston 5, Cleveland 4—The Red Sox returned home to host the first-place Indians. The *Globe*: "Our own Mr. G. Babe Ruth, the widely known, buxom and blushing matinee idol, recently featured in Peck's Bad Boy and the Prodigal Son, crashed into the calcium again against Cleveland." Ruth began the day on the bench, with Walter Barbare getting the start in left field. Trailing 4–2 in the sixth, George Whiteman doubled into the left-field corner and Everett Scott singled to center. The Fenway fans had been yelling all day for Ruth to make an appearance and when he walked out of the dugout swinging several bats, ready to pinch-hit for Barbare, they went nuts. The Colossus of Clouters (as the *Herald and Journal* dubbed him) looked at two balls and a strike before tripling to right field, tying the game. When shortstop Bill Wambsganss's relay from the outfield sailed over third baseman Joe Evans's head, Ruth strutted home with the go-ahead run.

In September 1918, *The Sporting News* looked back and said that this error changed the complexion of the pennant race. That's probably an exaggeration, as Boston held a half-game lead and would play 53 more games, but the Red Sox would stay in first place for the rest of the season.

July 7—No game. There was talk of Ray Collins coming out of retirement in Vermont to pitch for the Sox, or Ernie Shore being allowed to leave ensign school in Wakefield for a home start or two. Talking about the pennant race, Ed Barrow said he believes Boston will finish on top, but will be challenged by the Indians and Senators, but not the Yankees. "I am not afraid of the New York club. I never yet have seen a team of sluggers win a pennant. Have you? I am much more inclined to fear a team possessed of good pitchers and tight fielding."

July 8—Boston 1, Cleveland 0 (10 innings) / Cleveland 4, Boston 3—In the 10th inning of the first game, with Amos Strunk on first base, Ruth delivered a "mighty crash into the right field bleachers" which "landed more than two-thirds of the way up the bleachers." That's up in what is now considered Ted Williams "red seat" territory.

The Red Sox took over first place on July 6. Detail from *Boston Post* sports page cartoon.

With Strunk on first, Ruth hit one into the bleachers, but under the rules of the day was only credited with a triple and one RBI for a 1–0 win in the 10th inning. Detail from *Boston Post* sports page cartoon.

However, it showed up in the box score as a triple, since Strunk needed only three bases to score the winning run. Sam Jones and Stan Coveleskie dueled in game one—and it was Guy Morton and Carl Mays in the second game. Morton held the Sox to three hits. Cleveland scored the go-ahead run in the top of the ninth on a triple and a wild pitch.

July 9—Boston 1, Cleveland 0 (12 innings)—For the second time in three games, the Red Sox and Indians battled through nine scoreless innings. Catcher Wally Mayer, who usually did nothing more than warm up pitchers in the bullpen, was the hero, cracking a single to left that scored Frank Truesdale. Mayer drove in only five runs in 1918, but this one was a game-winner.

July 10—Boston 2, Cleveland 0 (5 innings, rain)—Babe Ruth's triple to Duffy's Cliff in left field drove in Amos Strunk, and then George Whiteman brought Ruth home. It was the third time in five games that a Ruth triple led to a Red Sox win. Lore Bader got the rain-shortened victory. For the rest of the year, each Monday was designated Soldiers and Sailors Day at Fenway Park, with uniformed servicemen admitted free of charge. Boston led the AL by 2½ games over both Cleveland and New York.

July 11—Boston 4, Chicago 0 -The Red Sox pitching staff won its third consecutive shutout. Carl Mays was magnificent, allowing only four hits, two of them in the final inning. The White Sox tried pitching Babe Ruth low and away, so the Colossus simply smacked three doubles to the opposite field. He also recorded an astonishing 20 putouts at first base, the final two coming on a ninth-inning, game-ending, unassisted double play with the bases

loaded! Cleveland and New York began a series in New York. The Indians took the opener 1–0 behind Stan Coveleskie's three-hitter.

July 12—Boston 6, Chicago 3 (7 innings, rain)—Babe Ruth continued his torrid hitting, with two more triples and a double, as Boston won for the seventh time in eight games. Sam Jones picked up the win in a game called after seven innings due to pouring rain. A *Herald and Journal* sportswriter commented: "The more I see of Babe and his heroic hitting, the more he seems a figure out of mythology or from the fairy land of more modern writers. He hits like no man ever has, truly the master man of maulers . . ." In seven games from July 6–12, Ruth went 11–23, with two singles, four doubles, and five triples.

July 13—Chicago 5, Boston 0—Lefty Reb Russell baffled the Red Sox with a steady diet of curves and slowballs. For Boston, Joe Bush was battered for 12 hits. Babe Ruth went 0-for-4 and committed an error at first base. The Yankees beat Cleveland and closed to within 2½ games of the Sox.

July 14—No game. A group of Red Sox pitchers and scrubs traveled to Woonsocket, Rhode Island, where playing under the name of "Woonsocket," they beat Queen Quality of Jamaica Plain, 5–2. Pitcher Joe Bush played center field and batted fourth, while Red Bluhm played first base, pitcher Dick McCabe played right field, and Horace Ford, who had been working out with the Red Sox, but did not sign with them (he debuted with the Boston Braves in 1919), was at shortstop. Vince Molyneaux pitched.

July 15—Boston 3, Chicago 1—Carl Mays threw a five-hitter, allowing only two balls to be hit beyond the infield all afternoon. The Red Sox outfield recorded no putouts, no assists, and no errors. Ruth hit a couple of singles.

July 16—Boston 2, St. Louis 1—Boston scored in the second inning when Ruth tripled and Whiteman singled. The Browns tied the game in the top of the ninth, but in the bottom half, Dave Shean singled and took second on Amos Strunk's sacrifice. St. Louis walked Ruth, but didn't expect the double steal that Ruth initiated. Catcher Les Nunamaker's throw to third went wild and Shean was able to pick himself up and run home with the winner. There were a couple of injuries: Boston catcher Sam Agnew lost a fingernail to a foul tip and left the game in the sixth, and Sam Jones's line drive broke St. Louis second baseman Joe Gedeon's wrist.

July 17—Boston 7, St. Louis 0 / Boston 4, St. Louis 0 (5innings)—Joe Bush shut out St. Louis in the first game of a twinbill; Red Sox pitching had now allowed only two runs over four games. Bush went 3-for-4 at the plate, with a triple. Babe Ruth left the first game in the eighth inning so he could warm up and pitch the second contest (only his second start since June 2). Boston led 2–0 in that game as rain clouds moved into the area. The Browns started stalling, hoping the game would get called, but umpire Tom Connolly pushed it along and the Sox won when it was called with the Browns batting in the top of the sixth. Ruth hit two doubles.

July 18—St. Louis 6, Boston 3—The Browns batted around in the fifth inning and took the final game of the four-game set, avoiding a sweep. Lore Bader (six innings, 10 hits, five runs) and Vince Molyneaux pitched for Boston. Babe Ruth had both of his knees x-rayed (he was banged up during the recent White Sox series). Everett Scott's eye was swollen from an insect bite he'd suffered a few days earlier.

July 19—Boston 5, Detroit 0—Ty Cobb missed the train and was not available for this game. Carl Mays won his 16th game of the season, holding the Tigers to three hits. The Red Sox scored three times in the first inning and twice more in the eighth. Frazee signed former Tigers pitcher Jean Dubuc, and released both Bluhm and Molyneaux to the Jersey City ballclub.

Secretary of War Baker made his decision: professional baseball was *not* an essential occupation under the "work-or-fight" order. He stated: "I am of the opinion that the 'work or fight' regulation question should not be changed, but rather, that the scope of its provisions should be so enlarged as to include other classes of persons whose professional occupation is solely that of entertaining." Without consulting any of the American League club owners, league president Ban Johnson announced that the season would end in two days. Harry Frazee proposed holding the World Series after 100 games of the season had been played. The Red Sox had played 86 games by this point.

July 20—Boston 5, Detroit 1—Faced with the possibility of the end of professional baseball until the end of the war, a season-high crowd of 13,515 came out to Fenway Park. The Tigers scored first, but Harry Hooper's third-inning triple tied the game. In the fifth, Hooper drove in the go-ahead run and Boston scored three times. They added another run in the eighth. Sam Jones got the win. Catcher Wally Mayer received his draft notice and left the team the following day for South Carolina. Wally Schang received a telegram before the game, suspending him for a fracas he'd been in on July 17. It was perhaps the shortest suspension on record—100 minutes long—as another telegram arrived after the game, lifting the suspension.

July 21—No game, but the morning's newspapers carried the news that A.L. president Ban Johnson had ordered all ballparks to close down after July 22 for the duration of the war. Ed Barrow, speaking on behalf of Harry Frazee, said Boston "does not propose to abide by that arbitrary ruling," adding that he had no idea why Johnson issued his edict. Barrow said that at least New York, Washington, and Philadelphia felt the same way. Johnson urged all the players to join in the war effort, but Barrow and others weren't sure that War Secretary Baker's comments required an immediate end to the season. During the day, after learning that many owners, including Frazee, were going to simply ignore him, Johnson amended his earlier remarks, saying that clubs could keep playing until further notice.

July 22—Boston 1, Detroit 0 (10 innings) / Boston 3, Detroit 0—What better way to end a homestand than with two shutouts—1–0 (Joe Bush) and 3–0 (Carl Mays)—giving the Red Sox a 14–3 record. Many fans feared it would be the last time they'd see Babe Ruth, Ty Cobb, and others, with no clear end of the war in sight. Bill James pitched for the Tigers and the first game was scoreless after nine innings. In the bottom of the 10th, Bush walked, took third on Harry Hooper's single, and scored on Tigers right-fielder Frank Walker's errant throw to second base. Hooper had a 3-for-3 day with two walks. In the second game, the Red Sox scored one in the first, two in the second, and then coasted as Mays fired a four-hitter.

July 23—No game. Unofficial temperatures of 102 (Boston Common) and 103 (Harvard Square) are reported in Boston. The Red Sox hold their largest lead of the season—6½ games over Cleveland, 7½ over New York, and 8 over Washington. Ed Barrow departed Boston with a 20-man Red Sox team; infielder Eusebio Gonzalez joined the ballclub as the train headed west.

July 24—No game. The Red Sox arrived in Chicago, where pitcher Jean Dubuc and catcher Wally Mayer meet the team at the train station (It turned out that Mayer's draft board was not ready to send him to camp).

July 25—Chicago 4, Boston 2—The road trip began at Comiskey Park, with both clubs unsure from day to day whether that day's game would be their last. Carl Mays got the ball—for the second consecutive game—as he had pitched the last game of the homestand on the 22nd. Junkballer Reb Russell baffled the Red Sox hitters once again.

July 26—Chicago 7, Boston 2—The White Sox scored five times in the third inning to take a commanding lead. An announcement was made in the fifth inning that Secretary Baker has said baseball players would now have until September 1 to comply with the "work-or-fight" order. Baseball's request for an extension until October 15 was denied. Contrary to common belief, the government did not order baseball to shut down in 1918. A letter from the White House around this time clearly stated that there was "no necessity at all for stopping or curtailing" the major league schedule. The owners were more than welcome to carry on with rosters comprised of men either below or over draft age. Later in this game, two Red Sox made their major league debuts: shortstop Eusebio Gonzalez and pitcher Walt Kinney. Gonzalez, born in Cuba and not subject to US military service, tripled in his first at-bat.

July 27—Boston 6, Chicago 4—Joe Bush's seventh-inning double sparked a three-run rally as the Red Sox came from behind to beat the White Sox.

July 28—Chicago 8, Boston 0—Reb Russell returned on two days rest and silenced the Red Sox yet again. No Boston runner reached third base. Carl Mays, also working on two days rest, took the loss.

July 29—Boston 3, St. Louis 2—Babe Ruth was fairly ordered by manager Ed Barrow to pitch because Mays, Jones and Bush were all exhausted. Ruth had pitched only twice in two months—a total of 14 innings—but he was about to became the hot pitcher on the club. He would make nine more starts until the end of the season and complete eight of them, picking up more wins than any other Red Sox hurler. He threw a four-hitter on this day, mixing up a good fastball and curve. He batted cleanup and tripled.

July 30—Boston 11, St. Louis 4—A Sportsman's Park crowd of only 750 watched the Red Sox rout the Browns. Harry Hooper was 2-for-4 at the plate and scored three times. Amos Strunk singled, doubled, and tripled. Babe Ruth had three singles. Sam Jones walked seven batters and did not record a strike out, but had no trouble pocketing the win. As Boston batted in the top of the sixth, about 20 gamblers were arrested and marched out of the park. Left-handed pitcher William Pertica, formerly of the Los Angeles club in the Pacific Coast League, joined the Sox.

July 31—Boston 8, St Louis 4—Joe Bush was the hero of the day, pitching a complete game win (striking out seven) and going 4-for-4 at the plate, with two doubles, two runs scored, and three RBIs. St. Louis tied the game in the bottom of the eighth on George Sisler's first home run of the season, but Boston got four runs in the top of the ninth. That rally was highlighted by Stuffy McInnis's triple, a double from Bush, and two Browns errors.

Boston finished July with a record of 20–9. Bush and Carl Mays each pitched three shutouts and all three of Babe Ruth's starts were complete games. In a 13-day stretch—July 8–20—Sam Jones won four games. The overall Red Sox record of 59–37 (.615) gave them a 4½-game lead over Cleveland.

August 1—Boston 2, St. Louis 1—The Sox completed a four-game sweep in St. Louis. Ruth pitched a beauty, allowing only five hits. Boston scored once in the first and once in the eighth. The Browns run came in the bottom of the ninth, and with the tying run on third base, Ruth got Tim Hendryx looking at a full-count fastball for a game-ending strikeout. In the National League, Jim Vaughn of the Cubs allowed only a second-inning single to the Giants and extended Chicago's lead over New York to 4½ games.

August 2—Cleveland 6, Boston 3—Holding a 5½-game lead over the Indians, the Red Sox began an important four-game weekend series at League Park in Cleveland, including a Sunday doubleheader on Sunday. Carl Mays allowed only six hits, but he also threw two wild pitches and was burned by an error from catcher Wally Schang. Boston welcomed another outfielder to the team: Oakland's Hack Miller, from the Pacific Coast League.

August 3—Cleveland 5, Boston 1—Sam Jones had limited Cleveland to only one run in his last 29 innings against them, but he couldn't sustain that success. The game was knotted 1–1 when the Indians scored four times in the fifth, thanks to two-run doubles from both Ray Chapman and Tris Speaker. Jim Bagby held the Red Sox in check, allowing no base runners over the final four innings. Boston's lead shrank to 3½ games.

All of the AL owners were also in Cleveland on this day, deciding when to end the regular season. There were early indications that the magnates would vote to end the season on August 17 or 20 and be able to complete the World Series before the September 1 "work-or-fight" cutoff. However, Pittsburgh Pirates owner Barney Dreyfuss, attending as the National League's representative, would not agree to any closing date earlier than September 2. The AL finally agreed—and planned to have the World Series begin a day or two later (perhaps the men on the two pennant-winners could get an extension to September 15).

The decision to cut the September games out of the schedule worked in the Red Sox's favor. They would have spent almost the entire month of September on the road—where they were a below-.500 team. Their eventual split for the season was 49–21 at home and 26–30 on the road.

August 4—Boston 2, Cleveland 1 (12 innings) / Cleveland 2, Boston 0 (6 innings)—The Red Sox rebounded nicely in the first game of the Sunday twin bill before a huge crowd of 20,000. Babe Ruth pitched all 12 innings, allowing only four hits (two in the third and two in the eighth) and one run. In 10 of the 12 innings, Ruth retired the Indians in order. Boston took a quick 1–0 lead in the first inning. With two outs and a runner on second, Guy Morton decided to put Ruth on intentionally after reaching a full count. But his 3–2 pitch was too close to the strike zone and Ruth pounced, lining an RBI single. Cleveland tied the game in the eighth inning. In the 12th, Boston's third baseman George Cochran reached first on a force play, stole second, and scored on Wally Mayer's single. The second game was called due to rain right after the Indians scored two runs in the bottom of the sixth.

August 5—No game. The Red Sox, still hanging on to a 3½-game lead over Cleveland, traveled to Detroit. In the National League, the Cubs took four of five games from the Giants and boosted their lead to 6½ games. The *New York Times* quipped: "If there is a world's series in New York next month, it will have to be at checkers or pinochle."

August 6—Boston 7, Detroit 5 (10 innings)—The game day temperature at Navin Field was reported at 114 degrees, as Carl Mays and the Red Sox won a wild one. After seven innings, the Tigers led 4–1, but Boston rallied for three runs in the eighth to tie the game and then won it with three more in the 10th as Detroit reliever Rudy Kallio walked two Boston batters and committed two errors.

August 7—Detroit 11, Boston 8—The *Globe* reported that Joe Bush was "kicked around like an Ozark hound dog," as 11 Tigers batted in the first inning; six of them scored. Boston rallied in the sixth, scoring four times and closing the gap to 8–6, but they ended that inning with the bases loaded.

August 8—Boston 4, Detroit 1—It was Boston's turn to strike in the opening inning. Harry Hooper walked, Dave Shean sacrificed, and Amos Strunk walked. The Detroit fans yelled for Babe Ruth to do something big, and Ruth tried to comply. He swung mightily at three pitches and missed them all, but doubles from Stuffy McInnis and Hack Miller brought in three runs. On the mound, Ruth scattered seven hits, bearing down only when runners were on base, conserving his energy in the intense heat.

August 9—No game. The Red Sox headed home to face the Yankees. Two new players joined the team: catcher Norman McNeil (who would not make his debut until 1919) and infielder Jack Coffey.

August 10—New York 5, Boston 1; New York 4, Boston 1—Joe Bush battled in the first game. He fanned 10 and the score was tied 1–1 after nine innings, but the Yankees broke through with four runs in the 10th inning. Bush

seemed to have escaped trouble, getting two outs with a man on first, but then Bill Lamar doubled to deep center and Frank Baker was walked intentionally to set up a force at any base. Del Pratt singled up the middle and Jack Fournier cracked a double over Amos Strunk's head in center to clear the bases. The Red Sox went down 1–2–3 in their half of the 10th as their nemesis George Mogridge got his fifth win against them this season.

In the second inning of the second game, Yankee Ham Hyatt was credited with an inside-the-park home run when the ball went through a hole under the right field fence. After the game, Ed Barrow said: "The grounds keeper says he didn't know there was a hole in the fence. You can gamble it is plugged up now all right. But what I want someone to tell me is why did that ball have to find that particular hole in a close series like this?... If I were superstitious, I would say that the Yankees have a jinx on us.... If we don't win the pennant now after our good start we ought to be run out of baseball on a fence rail."

August 11—No game. In Cleveland, the Indians rallied for four runs in the bottom of the ninth to win 6–5 and salvage a split of their Sunday doubleheader against the White Sox. Boston's lead was now down to three games.

August 12—New York 2, Boston 1—The Yankees took the third game of the series, beating Babe Ruth and sweeping the Red Sox. It was yet another lefty that befuddled the Red Sox—Hank Robinson, making his first American League appearance now that the Southern Association season was over. The *Boston Post* called Robinson "a National League discard who gets a renewed lease of big league life simply because of the draft." Of the three Boston hits, two of them were infield singles. In Cleveland, Guy Morton two-hit the White Sox and the Indians' 11–2 win cut the Red Sox's lead to two games.

August 13—No game. Ed Barrow: "Washington is the team I am watching every day. I never have felt that the Cleveland team was dangerous. The Senators have some great pitchers and finish up at home."

August 14—Boston 5, Chicago 3—Chicago came to Fenway and started lefty Reb Russell, who had shut out the Red Sox in each of his last two starts against them. Sam Jones hadn't pitched for 11 days and was a bit rusty, walking five and hitting a batter. Boston tied the game at 2–2 in the third and scored three more times in the sixth. Hack Miller singled and scored on Everett Scott's triple. Scott himself came across when the outfield relay throw was wild. Another error and singles by Sam Agnew and Jones brought home the last run. Cleveland beat the Yankees 7–2 at the Polo Grounds.

August 15—Chicago 6, Boston 2—The Red Sox scored

two runs in the first, but Chicago came right back with three in the top of the second and Jack Quinn blanked Boston the rest of the way. It was the eighth loss for the Red Sox in their last 12 games. Boston batters tried to be more aggressive at the plate, often swinging on 0-1 and 1-2 counts. Carl Mays, who expected to be called into military service in the next 10 days, took the loss. Fortunately, the Yankees beat Cleveland 3–2, keeping Boston's lead at two games.

August 16—Boston 2, Chicago 0—Boston scored once in the first and once in the second and Joe Bush threw a very efficient shutout. The game lasted a mere 75 minutes. The Red Sox then readied themselves to host the Indians, their only real threat for the pennant. Cleveland routed the Yankees 12–4 in New York to remain two games behind the Red Sox.

August 17—Boston 4, Cleveland 2—Babe Ruth faced the second-place Indians before a Saturday crowd at Fenway Park of more than 15,000. Boston held a 2–1 lead when Ruth came to the plate in the bottom of the eighth with runners on second and third. There was no way the Indians were going to pitch to the Babe in that situation, so they walked him intentionally (for the second time in the game). Stuffy McInnis then whacked a first-pitch double, driving in two insurance runs.

August 18—No game. The Red Sox traveled south to play a Sunday exhibition game against the New Haven Colonials. Babe Ruth played first base and batted fourth. The *Boston Post*: "In the 8th, Ruth made the longest home run ever seen at the Lighthouse grounds. The ball was knocked over the bathing pavilion in right field, something never before accomplished." New Haven won the game, 4–3. Wally Pipp, who had recently left the Yankees for aviation school, and former major leaguer Neal Ball were both in New Haven's lineup.

August 19—Boston 6, Cleveland 0—Sam Jones tossed his best game of the year—a two-hitter that gave Red Sox a four-game lead with 14 games left to play. Harry Hooper recorded eight putouts in center field. Ruth was walked intentionally two more times. Hooper, Amos Strunk, Everett Scott, and Stuffy McInnis all received notices from their draft boards that their period of exemption for performing war-related work will be extended to September 15, which would cover the duration of the World Series.

August 20—Cleveland 8, Boston 4—Ruth tried to come back on two days' rest, but allowed 13 hits in seven innings. A three-run fifth inning for Cleveland—helped by Boston outfielders losing two balls in the sun—put the game out of reach. For the Sox, Ruth was walked intentionally in the first inning and McInnis drove in a

run—making it three games in a row that Stuffy had come through after a Ruth BBI. The Cubs held a 9½-game lead in the National League and roughly 20 players wrote to their local draft boards asking for permission to play past the September 1 deadline.

August 21—Boston 4, St. Louis 1—Boston managed only four hits off Allen Sothoron, but Carl Mays was able to win his 19th game of the season. Jack Coffey hit a home run to center field for Boston—the only one of his career.

August 22—St. Louis 1, Boston 0—Dave Davenport shut out the Red Sox and Joe Bush was once again a hard-luck loser. When the team owners decided to end the regular season once month earlier that originally scheduled, they also conspired to deny their players the rest of their season salaries. Every owner "released" every player from his contract with 10 days' notice—which counting backwards from the new end of the season, would be approximately this day. These mass releases meant that every major league player was a free agent, and could theoretically offer his services to the highest bidder, but the owners colluded not to tamper with any other team's players. As Connie Mack later admitted: "It was only natural that we should enter into an agreement to protect our interests." Several players, including Brooklyn's Jake Daubert and Washington's Burt Shotton, took their clubs to court.

The War Department announced that the World Series will be played. The government also acknowledged that American soldiers in France were keenly interested in the results and with only two clubs playing, the number of men given two-week exemptions from the "work-or-fight" order would be minimal.

August 23—Boston 6, St. Louis 5—Amos Strunk was on first with one out in the bottom of the ninth of a 5–5 tie. After a wild pitch moved Strunk to second, Babe Ruth was walked intentionally. With Stuffy McInnis at the plate, Ruth and Strunk attempted a double steal. St. Louis catcher Hank Severeid's throw to third was high, and sailed into left field. Strunk never slowed down, rounding third and scoring the winning run.

August 24—Boston 3, St. Louis 1—All of the day's runs were scored in the second inning as the Red Sox finally beat a left-handed pitcher: Lefty Leifield. Babe Ruth pitched and won, though he also wrenched his leg as he stole home on the front end of another double steal. He was cheered as he limped out to the mound to start the third inning. (Ruth stole home 10 times in his career.) Washington shut out Cleveland, so the Red Sox upped their lead to a more comfortable four games.

August 25—No game. Sometime during the night of the 24th, Babe Ruth's father got into a fist fight with his brother-in-law outside of his Baltimore saloon. George Ruth Sr. was knocked down, struck his head on the curb, and later died of a fractured skull. He was 45 years old.

The National Commission announced that the first three World Series games will be played in Chicago, beginning on Wednesday, September 4. The remaining games would be played (most likely) in Boston. The 3–4 schedule was intended to save money on rail travel, but it also meant that there would no games on either Saturday and Sunday—the teams would leave Chicago on Friday evening after Game Three and arrive in Boston on Sunday night for Monday's Game Four—thus depriving the participants of sizeable gate receipts.

August 26—Detroit 6, Boston 3—Carl Mays had a disappointing outing, allowing 11 hits and losing to the visiting Tigers. Babe Ruth was not in the lineup and he left after the game to attend his father's funeral in Baltimore. Ty Cobb showed up late and took over in center field in the third inning. Cobb hit an inside-the-park home run in the eighth when new left fielder Hack Miller played the hit poorly and fell down. Mays, who was never pleased when his fielders made errors behind him, bawled out Miller from the mound.

August 27—Detroit 2, Boston 1—Joe Bush struck out 13 Tigers—a season-high for any Boston pitcher—but once again, he received no run support. Bush ended August with a 1–6 record, but four of his six losses were by scores of 2–0, 1–0, 2–1, and 1–0. The Indians won, narrowing the Red Sox's lead to 2½ games with seven games remaining. Cleveland's Tris Speaker was ejected from the game and suspended for punching umpire Tom Connolly.

August 28—Boston 3, Detroit 0—Sam Jones followed up his two-hitter against Cleveland on the 19th with a three-hitter against the Tigers. Harry Hooper went 3-for-3, with two doubles and a triple. Philadelphia beat Cleveland 1–0, effectively ending the Indians' chances at catching the Red Sox.

August 29—No game. Tris Speaker's suspension and absence from the Cleveland lineup is thought of as the final nail in the coffin for the Indians' pennant chances, but this is not true. After Speaker slugged Connolly, the Indians never lost ground to Boston: they remained 2½ games out. The Indians did lose on August 28 (falling three games out), but after a rainout on August 29, they won their last four games, sweeping the Tigers in a doubleheader on August 30 and winning single games against the White Sox on August 31 and September 1. Speaker

missed the game on the 28th, but he never served his suspension. He was in the starting lineup for all four Cleveland victories.

August 30—Boston 12, Philadelphia 0 / Boston 4, Philadelphia 1—The Red Sox had three doubleheaders scheduled for the final three days of the season, not an ideal situation for a team who would then play the World Series. Carl Mays pitched both ends of this twin bill at Shibe Park, both of them complete nine-inning wins. He finished the season with 21 wins, earning a $1,500 bonus. With an 8–0 lead after three innings in the opener, Mays pitched a more relaxed game and told Barrow he felt strong enough to pitch the second game, too—and tossed a four-hitter. These two wins began a streak of 23 consecutive victories over Philadelphia for Mays, a streak that ran more than five years—until October 1923.

August 31—Boston 6, Philadelphia 1 / Philadelphia 1, Boston 0—Not to be outdone by Mays's iron-man performance the day before, Philadelphia's Mule Watson threw two complete games against the Red Sox. Watson faced Babe Ruth in the first game, but Ruth's three-hitter clinched the pennant for Boston. Watson allowed only one hit in the second game, a single by catcher Sam Agnew.

September 1—No game. Pitchers Carl Mays and Joe Bush, and catcher Sam Agnew left for Pittsburgh to scout the Chicago Cubs in preparation for the World Series. After watching the Cubs-Pirates series, they met up with their teammates in Chicago on September 3.

September 2—Boston 3, New York 2; New York 4, Boston 3—Sam Jones beat the Yankees in the first game, but George Mogridge did the Red Sox in yet again, winning his sixth game against Boston in 1918. Harry Hooper and Everett Scott finished out the season having played in all 126 Red Sox games.

Final American League Standings

	W	L	PCT.	GB
BOSTON RED SOX	75	51	.595	–
CLEVELAND INDIANS	73	54	.575	2.5
WASHINGTON SENATORS	72	56	.563	4.0
NEW YORK YANKEES	60	63	.488	13.5
ST. LOUIS BROWNS	58	64	.475	15.0
CHICAGO WHITE SOX	57	67	.460	17.0
DETROIT TIGERS	55	71	.437	20.0
PHILADELPHIA ATHLETICS	52	76	.406	24.0

Winning a Championship

by Bill Nowlin

Winning a championship involves a large number of ingredients coming together in just the right fashion and at the right time. 1918 was an unusual season in that it was truncated by war and the timing of the truncation was not known until shortly before it occurred. Because teams played the season without knowing how many games they would play, or whether there would be a World Series at season's end, many of the usual strategies involved in conducting a 154-game campaign didn't apply. When the regular season ended, the Red Sox had played 126 games (while Washington and Philadelphia had both played 130, and the Browns had only played 123).

As we see in perusing the many individual biographies, and in considering the timeline, Ed Barrow and Harry Frazee were wheeling and dealing throughout the entire season. Players were called off to war; others signed up for war-related work to preempt conscription. Unusual for the era, there were 10 players who only appeared in six or fewer games for the Red Sox.

Using earned run average as a rough measure of a pitching staff's performance, the Red Sox (2.31) were distinctly better than most teams, second in the American League to the Washington Senators (2.14). In third place was Cleveland with a 2.64.

The Red Sox allowed the fewest runs (with 381, they were the only team under 400) and the fewest earned runs (287—Washington, with 292, was the only other team under 300). Boston's 105 complete games overshadowed the last-place Athletics, who had 80.

A full 26 of the Red Sox's games (more than 20% of the schedule and more than 1/3 of the team's wins) were shutouts. Only two other teams reached double digits in shutouts. Eight of Boston's shutouts were by a 1–0 score. And, if that wasn't remarkable enough, Bullet Joe Bush won five of those eight 1–0 shutouts. Sad Sam Jones won two and Carl Mays won one. Bush's five 1–0 shutouts set a major league record; the final two of them were extra-inning affairs: July 9 (12 innings) and July 22 (10 innings). Bush led the Red Sox starters with a 2.11 ERA, but poor run support gave him a year-end record of only 15-15.

Carl Mays led the league with 30 complete games—his eight shutouts also led the league. Bush was second with seven shutouts.

In addition to the eight 1–0 shutouts, the Red Sox won 16 additional games by a margin of just one run.

It was pitching where the Sox excelled. It certainly wasn't batting. The team batting average was .249, the same as Detroit (who finished in seventh place, 20 games out of first place). The only team with a lower average was Philadelphia at .243. The team ranked more or less in the middle of the pack in on-base percentage and slugging average, and even in runs batted in (four teams had an equal or higher number of RBIs, and three teams a lower number).

The 15 home runs hit by the team as a whole was still a smaller total than Philadelphia's 22 and New York's 20. Interestingly, the Red Sox had the fewest at-bats of any team—the only team with fewer than 4000 at-bats—but that's a function of winning so many home games in which they led after 8½. There were 38 games in which the Red Sox never needed to bat in the bottom of the ninth. There were 11 additional games in which the Red Sox won in a walkoff and thus made fewer than three outs in the bottom of the final inning, whatever inning that might be. Of these, twice the winning run scored before they made any outs, six times there was only one out, and three times there were only two.

The Red Sox were the best fielding team in the league overall with a .971 fielding percentage, and concomitantly the fewest errors (the number of errors per team ranged from their 152 up to 228—an average of more than one per game was typical during an era where fields were still rougher and gloves more primitive than those of today.) The two positions at which they were strongest were at first base and shortstop; they led the league in fielding at both positions. They were weakest at catcher; Boston catchers were tied for the lowest fielding percentage at that position. Carl Mays recorded 122 assists, still the most ever for a Red Sox pitcher. It was a record he'd built on two years in a row: in 1916, he set the record with 117 and in 1917 he had 118 assists.

It was friendly Fenway for the 1918 Red Sox. They were 49–21 at home, for an outstanding .700 winning percentage at Fenway Park. They were 26–30 on the road. Note that because of the truncated schedule, the Red Sox ended up playing 70 games at home and only 56 on the road (they would have spent much of September on the road). Playing 55% of their games at home favored their chances of success. Even with all the one-run games they played (several of which were on the road), they outscored their opponents 272–165 in Boston.

Against the second-place Indians and the third-place Senators, the Red Sox played .500 ball overall. They beat up on the Browns (14-5) and the Athletics (13-5), and had a losing record against only one team (they were 6–11 against the Yankees, who finished a distant fourth in the standings).

Of the 26 shutout victories, 18 were at home and eight on the road. The shutouts were mostly clustered in two months, June and July, with nine in each month, with only four prior to June 1 and four after July 31. Boston was shut out 12 times.

The Red Sox jumped out to an 11–2 start in April and really never looked back. They were 0–6 on the road in May, swept by New York and then by Washington on a six-game road trip, but the experience obviously didn't sink them. There were only 12 days throughout the season when they were not in first place. On nine of those days, they trailed by percentage points. On one day, they were a half game behind the leader. On only two days (June 28 and July 4) were they as much as one game behind. After July 5, they were never out of first place, despite playing .500 ball (16–16) in their last 32 games. The race was never a foregone conclusion, though, as Cleveland ended the season only 2½ games out and Washington was four games behind.

1918 World Series
Boston Red Sox – Chicago Cubs

by Allan Wood

The Chicago Cubs won the 1918 National League pennant by 10½ games and were solid favorites to win the World Series against the Boston Red Sox.

Hugh Fullerton, a sportswriter for the *New York Evening World*, looked at the Cubs–Red Sox match-up using a personal statistical formula—"Position Strength"—which included "hitting, waiting out pitchers, long-distance hitting, getting hit by pitched ball, speed" and defense.

Fullerton calculated "each man's value and then figure[d] how his values, both in attack and defense, will be affected by the opposing team." Fullerton concluded that the margin was "too small to indicate any marked superiority for either team," but in his final analysis, he believed the Cubs would prevail in six games.

Many other writers agreed, including Henry Edwards of the *Cleveland Plain Dealer*, Thomas Rice of the *Brooklyn Eagle*, Bill Phelson of *Baseball Magazine*, and George S. Robbins of the *Chicago Daily News*. New York syndicated writer Joe Vila gave the Cubs an edge because of its left-handed pitchers and the "yowling, heartless rooters" at Comiskey Park. (Cubs owner Charles Weeghman had decided to use Comiskey Park, which had a greater seating capacity.)

However, Philadelphia Athletics manager Connie Mack thought the schedule (three games in Chicago and the remaining contests at Fenway Park) gave Boston an edge. Eddie Hurley of the *Boston Evening Record* said the Red Sox "are the better defensive club" but questioned whether the team could score enough runs to win. Burt Whitman of the *Herald and Journal* said Boston would win in six games: "On paper, the Cubs figure 'to beat' the Red Sox ... [but] this series will not be played on a typewriter."

1918 World Series program. Courtesy of National Baseball Hall of Fame Library.

The Cubs had finished the regular season with a better record than Boston (84–45 to 75–51) and a superior team batting average (.265 to .249), on-base percentage (.325 to .322), and slugging percentage (.342 to .327). The Cubs had also scored more runs (538 to 474).

Rookie shortstop Charlie Hollocher led the National League in hits (161) and total bases (202), was second in on-base percentage (.379), third in stolen bases (26), and fourth in runs scored (72) and batting average (.316). He was the only Chicago regular to hit over .300.

Les Mann, Chicago's 24-year-old left fielder, hit .288 and reached personal bests in doubles, stolen bases and walks. Center fielder Dode Paskert, at age 37, had his best season since 1912, batting .286 and finishing with 125 runs produced (RBI + runs scored—HR), second behind George Burns of the Giants (127).

Chicago's team ERA was lower than Boston's (2.18 to 2.31), although the Red Sox led the majors with 26 shutouts (the Cubs had 23). Both teams had the lowest opponents' batting average in their respective leagues, Boston at .231 and Chicago at .239.

Chicago would rely heavily on its top left-handed pitchers, Jim Vaughn and Lefty Tyler. The Red Sox were 11–18 in games started by lefties.

Vaughn led the National League in wins (22), shutouts (8), ERA (1.74), strikeouts (148), and lowest opponents' batting average (.208)—the best season of his 10-year career. And while he had a hard fastball and good control, Vaughn also carried a reputation of buckling in important games.

The ERAs of the four Red Sox starters were all between 2.11 and 2.25. Joe Bush had the lowest ERA on the staff, but bad luck and poor run support left him with a

15–15 record. In the season's last month, Bush had gone 1–6; four of those losses were by scores of 2–0, 1–0, 2–1, and 1–0.

In the 15 years since the National and American Leagues had begun playing a post-season series, a team from either Boston or Chicago had been involved 11 times, but never during the same year.

Thursday, September 5—
Comiskey Park, Chicago
Game One—Babe Ruth v. Jim Vaughn

RED SOX   000 100 000—1 5 0
CUBS   000 000 000—0 6 0

Rain had pushed the start of the series ahead one day. The National Commission's original schedule had included no weekend games, which puzzled the players on both teams, but now, thanks to the postponement, Game Three would be played on Saturday.

Early rumors were that either Carl Mays or Joe Bush would start for Boston, but manager Ed Barrow went with Ruth in the opener. This was Ruth's second World Series start. In Game Two of the 1916 series, he beat Brooklyn 2–1, pitching all 14 innings (still the longest World Series game by innings).

Babe had been batting in the cleanup spot since early May, but for the World Series, Barrow put him back down at the bottom of the order.

Ruth got two quick outs in the bottom of the first, before Les Mann singled and stole second. Dode Paskert followed with a single and Fred Merkle walked. With the bases loaded, Ruth got Charlie Pick to fly out to George Whiteman in left-center field.

Whiteman opened the top of the second with a single and was bunted to second by Stuffy McInnis, but Everett Scott and Fred Thomas couldn't advance him.

Ruth retired the bottom three of the Chicago order in the second and worked around a leadoff single in the third.

Vaughn had control problems early on, going to full counts on several Boston batters and allowing a hit in each of the first three innings. He began the fourth by walking Dave Shean. Amos Strunk attempted to sacrifice him to second, but popped up the first pitch to Vaughn.

Whiteman singled to left—Cubs shortstop Charlie Hollocher seemed out of position—and Shean moved up to second. With McInnis at the plate, Barrow called for a hit-and-run. Stuffy smacked Vaughn's 1-0 pitch to left field. The ball rolled slowly on the soggy grass and Les Mann's hurried throw to the plate was not in time.

With a 1–0 lead, Ruth settled into a rhythm, retiring the Cubs in order in the fourth and getting two quick outs in the fifth before hitting Max Flack with a pitch. Hollocher flew out to center to end that inning.

Paskert and Merkle both singled with one out in the bottom of the sixth, and Barrow told Sam Jones and Joe

Bush to start loosening up. Charlie Pick moved the runners up to second and third with a ground ball to first base and when Ruth started Charlie Deal off with two balls, the Chicago crowd started to make some noise.

Ruth battled back and Deal fouled off three straight pitches before swinging at what was probably ball four and flying out to Whiteman in left center.

Both teams went down in order in the seventh and eighth innings. The Red Sox tried to get an insurance run in the ninth when Shean lead off with a walk. Strunk sacrificed him to second, but Whiteman struck out and after McInnis was intentionally walked, Everett Scott grounded back to the mound.

Ruth retired the first two batters in the bottom of the ninth—Merkle flew to left and pinch-hitter Bob O'Farrell popped to third—but Deal reached on an infield single. Bill McCabe pinch-ran. Cubs catcher Bill Killefer swatted the ball to deep right field. Harry Hooper caught it on the run and Boston had taken Game One.

It was the first shutout in a World Series opener since 1905, and only the second 1–0 World Series game in 13 years. Coupled with his victory in 1916, Ruth had now pitched 22 1/3 consecutive scoreless World Series innings. Christy Mathewson's record of 28 innings was within reach in his next start.

Shean reached base three times (two singles and a walk) for Boston and scored the game's only run. Whiteman singled twice, and made five catches in left field, three of which were tough chances on a windy afternoon. Ruth went 0-for-3, lining out to center and striking out twice.

The crowd of only 19,274 was roughly 13,000 fewer fans than had attended the first game of the 1917 Series, which had also been played at Comiskey Park.

Friday, September 6—
Comiskey Park, Chicago
Game Two—Joe Bush v. Lefty Tyler

RED SOX   000 000 001 — 1 6 1
CUBS   030 000 00X—3 7 1

Ed Barrow went with Bullet Joe Bush in the second game, figuring that Carl Mays's submarine delivery would baffle the Cubs and either put Boston up by three games or break a Series tie.

The weather was perfect—clear skies, 70 degrees—but the turnout was only slightly larger than the day before—a crowd of 20,040. One sportswriter counted fewer than 100 women in attendance, quite low for a World Series game.

Bush and Tyler had faced each other in Game Three of the 1914 World Series at Fenway Park, Tyler for the Boston Braves and Bush for the Philadelphia Athletics. In that game, Bush's 12th-inning error allowed the Braves' winning run. Seven players from that Series were in uniform today, including Mann, Charlie Deal, Stuffy

McInnis, Wally Schang, and Amos Strunk. Cubs manager Fred Mitchell had been the Braves' manager in 1914.

Facing another lefty, Barrow again started George Whiteman in left field, which left Babe Ruth was on the bench.

There had been some heckling in the opener, but things got much more intense in Game Two. In the first inning, when lead-off batter Harry Hooper tried to steal second base, Dave Shean stepped across the plate, bumping catcher Bill Killefer's right arm with his bat. Shean was called out on strikes and Hooper ruled out on Shean's interference. In the bottom of the first, the Cubs believed Amos Strunk intentionally dropped a popup in shallow center to force speedy Charlie Hollocher at second base, leaving a slower runner on first.

Bush had trouble controlling his fastball, so he relied more on his curve, which was not his best pitch. He walked Fred Merkle to start the second inning, then gave up a bunt single to Charlie Pick. After Charlie Deal popped out, Killefer drilled a first-pitch double down the right field line, scoring Merkle. With the Red Sox infield playing on the grass, Tyler grounded a ball up the middle. Shortstop Everett Scott dove to his left, but it scooted past him. Pick scored and Killefer rounded third. Strunk's throw home was too late to get Killefer, so Sox catcher Sam Agnew came forward towards the mound, got the ball on one hop and fired to second. Scott slammed a hard tag on Tyler.

Otto Knabe, the Cubs' first base coach, had been yelling at Bush throughout the three-run rally. Knabe had also baited Babe Ruth the previous day. At the end of the second inning, as the Red Sox left the field trailing 3–0, Heinie Wagner walked across the infield to take his spot in the third base coaching box; he met Knabe going in the same direction, towards the Cubs dugout. It is not clear exactly what was said, but both men started cursing. Wagner pointed to the alleyway leading to the Cubs clubhouse—challenging Knabe to a fight.

Once the men were in the Cubs dugout, Wagner grabbed Knabe's arm and tried dragging him along the floor. Knabe quickly subdued Wagner, and Jim Vaughn apparently knocked Wagner down before he, Knabe, Claude Hendrix, and a few others started punching. Wagner later claimed Knabe had also kicked him while he was on his back. "I wouldn't mind it if I was hit with a fist," he later said.

When Wagner finally emerged from the dugout, his hair was a mess, his face pale and bruised, the back of his uniform torn and muddy. The umpires did not get involved. Afterwards, third base umpire Hank O'Day, who had been close to the Cubs dugout, said he hadn't seen or heard anything.

Ticket to Game Two of the World Series.

After this incident, Bush began pitching almost exclusively inside—*way* inside. After Hollocher grounded out, Bush buzzed a fastball near Mann's head. Mann cursed Bush, then pushed a bunt up the first base line. Stuffy McInnis made the play unassisted, but when Bush dashed off the mound to cover the bag, he tried tripping Mann on his way to first. Then Bush made the next batter, Dode Paskert, duck away from a beanball before retiring him on an infield pop-up.

Tyler walked the Red Sox leadoff batter in each of the first three innings, but the Red Sox were unable to exploit his lack of control. They didn't force him to throw strikes, swinging early in the count and chasing poor pitches.

Chicago had an opportunity to widen its lead in the sixth when Hollocher tripled into the right field corner. With the infield in, Hollocher could not score when Mann grounded out. Agnew tried to pick off Hollocher, but his throw got under Fred Thomas's glove. Thomas deliberately tangled himself up with Hollocher, so the runner couldn't get up and advance. Already in a foul mood, the crowd howled at Thomas.

Hollocher broke for home when Dode Paskert chopped a grounder to short. It was a foolish play, perhaps borne of frustration, as Scott's throw to Agnew was in plenty of time for the out.

Boston had very little luck against Tyler. Over the course of 20 batters, from the second inning to the end of the seventh, the Red Sox managed only one hit. In the eighth, Wally Schang pinch-hit for Agnew and singled. After Bush flew out, Hooper singled to right. Schang tried to go to third, but Max Flack made a perfect one-hop throw to Charlie Deal and Schang was cut down. It was a crucial mistake—instead of runners at first and second and one out, Boston had a man at first and two outs. Shean bounced to first and the threat vanished.

With the Red Sox down to their last three outs, Amos Strunk led off the ninth with a triple over Flack's head in right. Whiteman followed with another triple, this one over Paskert's head in center. Chicago's lead was now 3–1 and the potential tying run (Stuffy McInnis) was at the plate.

Cubs manager Fred Mitchell had Phil Douglas and Claude Hendrix in the bullpen, but he stayed with Tyler. Instead of squeezing the runner home, McInnis swung away. He tapped a weak grounder right back to Tyler, who checked the runner and threw McInnis out. Tyler then walked Everett Scott.

Barrow thought about sending Babe Ruth up as a pinch-hitter, but opted for another pitcher: Jean Dubuc, who batted right-handed. It was an odd choice. If Barrow was intent on having a pitcher at the plate, Carl Mays, whose .357 on-base percentage was fourth best on the team, would have been a wiser choice.

Dubuc fell behind in the count 1-2, then fouled off four consecutive pitches before swinging and missing a curve about a foot off the plate. Schang was next, and Ruth waited on the dugout steps, black bat in hand, ready to hit for Bush if Schang could keep the inning alive.

Considering how hard Tyler had worked to get Dubuc, Schang should have looked at a few pitches. But he swung at the first one he saw, and popped it up. Hollocher moved a few steps to his right, made the catch, and ran quickly off the field, disappearing into the dugout with the baseball still in his glove. The Series was tied at one game apiece.

For the Red Sox, it was a game of missed opportunities. Boston's leadoff batter had reached base in five of the first eight innings. The Boston sportswriters were dumbfounded by Barrow's ninth-inning strategy. Eddie Hurley of the *Boston Evening Record* thought letting Ruth watch the entire inning from the bench was "nothing but criminal."

Saturday, September 7—
Comiskey Park, Chicago
Game Three—Carl Mays v. Jim Vaughn

| RED SOX | 000 200 000—2 7 0 |
| CUBS | 000 010 000—1 7 1 |

The Red Sox were convinced that spitballer Claude Hendrix would pitch for Chicago, so they were shocked when Jim Vaughn came back to pitch on one day's rest. The fans were also surprised, and they gave Vaughn a standing ovation as he walked to the mound. (Another Cubs lefty on the hill also meant Babe Ruth remained on the bench.)

A light rain started to fall in the top of the second inning. Home plate umpire Bill Klem saw no reason to pause the game, and it drizzled off and on all afternoon.

Boston drew first blood with one out in the fourth inning. Vaughn worked Whiteman inside and hit him in the back. McInnis tried to hit-and-run on the first pitch, but fouled it off. When he swung and missed the next pitch, Whiteman was trapped off the bag. Catcher Bill Killefer hesitated for a moment before throwing to first baseman Fred Merkle, and that slight pause allowed Whiteman to dive back safely.

Vaughn's 0-2 pitch was high and inside and McInnis punched it into left field. Schang followed with a single to center; Whiteman scored and McInnis raced to third.

Ed Barrow was not a fan of the suicide squeeze, but with Scott, a good bunter, at the plate, the play was on. Scott dropped the first pitch right in front of the plate—a beautiful bunt—too far out towards the mound for catcher Bill Killefer to field it. Vaughn grabbed it, but when he tuned to throw to first, he saw that Merkle also had run

in on the bunt and second baseman Charlie Pick hadn't covered first. McInnis scored and Boston led, 2–0.

Thomas followed with a single to right field, his first hit of the Series. Heinie Wagner wanted Schang to stop at third, which would have loaded the bases and kept Vaughn on the ropes, but Schang ran through the stop sign. Max Flack's throw was perfect and Schang was easily tagged out. Mays lined out to center field and Vaughn escaped with minimal damage.

Carl Mays was well-rested—he hadn't pitched since his back-to-back wins against Philadelphia a week earlier—and he was nearly perfect. After walking the first hitter he faced, Mays set down 10 in a row, breezing through the third inning on only five pitches.

Facing Mays for the second time, however, the Cubs had a better read on his delivery and hit him hard. Les Mann doubled with one out in the fourth. Paskert whacked a fly ball to deep left center that looked like it might carry into the bleachers. Whiteman sprinted back, until he was literally against the wall—and grabbed the ball with a leap at the fence.

After his near-disastrous fourth inning, Vaughn was untouchable. He kept the ball in the infield in both the fifth and sixth innings, and at one point retired 13 Red Sox batters in a row. Meanwhile, his teammates repeatedly threatened to come back against Mays.

Charlie Pick's fifth-inning grounder slipped under Everett Scott's glove and slowly rolled into center field. By the time Amos Strunk got it back to the infield, Pick was on second. One out later, Killefer banged a single off Scott's bare hand into left. Whiteman charged in, but there was no play to make. Pick scored, cutting Boston's lead to 2–1. Killefer, perhaps thinking the Red Sox defense was unnerved, broke for second on Mays's 2–0 pitch to Flack. Schang's throw was low, but Scott dug it out of the dirt and put the tag on Killefer's foot as he slid into the bag.

Mann and Paskert both singled with two outs in the sixth, but were stranded when Merkle struck out swinging. With one out in the seventh, Deal reached on an infield hit to third. All of Chicago's six hits had come within the last 14 batters—nearly every other Cub was reaching base. Mays battled back: Killefer bounced back to the mound and Vaughn flew to left.

In the eighth, Mays retired the top of the Cubs lineup in order and got the first two batters in the bottom of the ninth. Facing the daunting prospect of needing to win three games at Fenway Park, Chicago tried to rally.

Charlie Pick was safe on an infield hit to second. Left-handed hitter Turner Barber pinch-hit for Deal. Mays's first offering was ball one. On the next pitch, Pick sprinted to second. Wally Schang's throw was right on the money—but Shean bobbled it. Pick made a great slide and the Cubs were still alive.

Runner retreats toward third base on a bunt to the pitcher (runner on first advancing to second).
Courtesy of the Boston Public Library.

Barber smacked a line drive that landed about six inches foul down the third base line, then Schang set up outside. But Mays threw too far outside. The ball glanced off Schang's mitt and rolled a few yards to his left behind the plate. As Pick ran to third, Schang fired a throw to Fred Thomas. Pick and the baseball arrived at almost the same time. Umpire George Hildebrand began calling Pick out, then saw Thomas hadn't held onto the ball. He spread his arms: "Safe!"

Thomas and Pick were tangled in the dirt. Pick had overslid the bag and was on his stomach, trying to crawl back and touch the base with his hand. Thomas was yelling at Hildebrand, arguing that Pick had kicked the ball out of his glove. Cubs manager Fred Mitchell, coaching at third base, shouted at Pick to run home.

The ball had stopped rolling about 20 feet away in foul territory. Pick took off. Thomas finally ran over and grabbed the ball. He had no time to set himself, but his throw was straight and true. Pick slid in, spikes high, and Schang tagged him in the ribs a foot or two from the plate. The game was over—and the crowd exhaled a huge, collective groan. The Cubs had come close, but Boston's razor-thin victory gave them a 2–1 lead in the Series, with all remaining games at Fenway Park.

Sunday, September 8— Traveling from Chicago to Boston

Before the 1918 season began, the National Commission decided to allow the top four teams in each league to share some of the gate receipts of the first four World Series games. This decision, coupled with low attendance and reduced ticket prices, meant that the shares for the winning and losing teams could be 75% smaller than they had been in 1917.

During the train ride to Boston, players on both teams discussed whether anything could be done. Some felt the Commission was deliberately exploiting them and wanted to abandon the series immediately. Eventually, the players came up with two proposals: either guarantee shares of $1,500 and $1,000 or postpone the revenue-sharing plan until after the War. Harry Hooper and Dave Shean of the Red Sox and Les Mann and Bill Killefer of the Cubs tried meeting with Commissioner August Herrmann on Sunday afternoon, but he refused to see them, saying that he couldn't make any official decisions without the other commissioners present. Herrmann and the players agreed to meet in Boston on Monday morning.

Game Four, ninth inning: Wortman's sacrifice Fred Merkle was caught off third base when Sox first baseman McInnis fired the ball to Thomas at third. Courtesy of the Boston Public Library.

Monday, September 9— Fenway Park, Boston
Game Four: Lefty Tyler v. Babe Ruth

CUBS	000 000 020—2 7 1
RED SOX	000 200 01X—3 4 0

On Monday morning, the full Commission refused to speak to the players, saying they needed to know what the actual revenues from the fourth game would be, and suggested getting together after that afternoon's game.

Game Four was the Red Sox's first World Series game in Fenway Park since 1912. Their home games in 1915 and 1916 had been played at Braves Field, which had a larger seating capacity.

Babe Ruth took the mound with yellow iodine stains visible on his left hand. He had injured his pitching hand the night before fooling around with fellow pitcher Walt Kinney on the train. Ruth was trying to break Christy Mathewson's record of 28 consecutive scoreless World Series innings (his streak was at $22^1/_3$).

Left fielder George Whiteman was again batting cleanup and Ruth was hitting sixth. Babe had been in the sixth spot only once before all season—back on May 6, the day he debuted at first base. Barrow gave no explanation for the switch.

It was obvious from the first inning that Ruth had difficulty getting the proper spin on his curveball. Chicago put men on base in each of the first three innings, but was turned back by Ruth's gutsy pitching and Boston's airtight infield.

The game was scoreless in the fourth when Tyler walked Dave Shean. With right-handed hitters George Whiteman and Stuffy McInnis coming up, Amos Strunk tried to bunt. After two failed attempts, he lined out to center field. Shean took advantage of Tyler's leisurely windup and stole second without a throw. The Fenway crowd stomped its feet in unison, clamoring for a run. Tyler couldn't find the strike zone and walked Whiteman. The roar increased as Claude Hendrix came out of the third-base dugout and began warming up.

McInnis hit the ball right back at Tyler. The pitcher grabbed it, then paused for a split second before throwing to Deal at third base and forcing Shean. His slight delay meant the relay to first was late. Boston now had runners at first and second with two outs—and Babe Ruth was up.

Tyler looked over at his dugout, waiting for a sign from his manager. Should he walk Ruth intentionally, loading the bases for Everett Scott (who was 1-for-11 in the Series)? Should he pitch to Ruth? Was Hendrix coming in?

All summer long, Ruth had been walked in situations like this, often as early as the first inning. Ruth hadn't faced Tyler in Game Two and he had yet to hit safely in a World Series game, wearing an 0-for-10 collar dating back to 1915.

Mitchell decided Tyler should pitch carefully to Ruth, and hope the Big Fellow would chase a bad ball. Max Flack was at normal depth in right field; he had been much deeper on Ruth in the second inning, but Babe had grounded out, and now he stayed where he was.

Tyler's first three pitches were low and outside, well off the plate. Ruth was patient and everyone could see this was an "unintentional intentional walk." Then Tyler slipped a slow curve on the inside corner. Ruth took a big swing and missed, spinning nearly all the way around.

Ruth thought Tyler's next pitch was too high and a bit outside. He tossed his bat aside and started jogging to first. "Strike two!" Brick Owens yelled above the din. Ruth glared at Owens and kicked the dirt.

Killefer called for a curveball—Tyler's strongest pitch and Ruth's weakest—but the lefty came back with another fastball, and this time it remained belt high. Ruth pulverized it, sending it screaming into right field. Flack took a half-step forward, not seeing the ball clearly until it rose out of the shade of the grandstand. By that time, it was too late. He turned, ran back towards the bleachers. It was a triple, and Whiteman and McInnis scored easily. Boston led 2–0.

Everett Scott tried twice to squeeze Ruth home before flying to center for the third out. The Fenway crowd never stopped roaring as Ruth ran back to the dugout, grabbed his mitt, and returned to the mound.

Ruth began losing his control in the sixth inning --the iodine on his finger was rubbing off on the ball, causing it to sail—and it was only Boston's strong infield that saved his lead. Tyler walked to start the inning. Flack grounded straight back to Ruth. He turned and fired to second base, but it was a poor throw that got by Scott. Shean, however, was positioned only a few feet behind the base. He was on his knees when he gloved Ruth's errant toss, then crawled on his stomach in the dirt, tagging the bag with his mitt just ahead of Tyler's foot.

The next two Cubs grounded out and it was official: Ruth had set a new World Series record of $28\frac{1}{3}$ consecutive scoreless innings.

But in the seventh, Ruth's control got worse, as he walked Fred Merkle and Rollie Zeider with one out. Joe Bush began warming up. Pinch-hitter Bob O'Farrell hit the ball hard up the middle. Scott raced over, scooped it up, and flipped to Shean, who fired to first for an inning-ending double play.

After Ruth's triple, Tyler retired the next seven Boston hitters and prayed his teammates would rally. Killefer walked to open the eighth, Ruth's third walk to his last four batters, his fourth free pass in two innings. Bush, still warming up, was joined by Carl Mays.

Claude Hendrix, a right-handed hitting pitcher, batted for Tyler. Hendrix had hit .264 in 1918, with three triples and three home runs. Mitchell's move paid off when Hendrix singled to left. Killefer stopped at second. Flack bunted the first pitch foul, then Ruth threw one in the dirt. It skipped past Agnew's glove for a wild pitch, and the Cubs had men at second and third.

The Cubs bench was heckling Ruth from the dugout and anxious Red Sox fans were poised on the edge

of their seats. Flack bounced the next pitch to first and McInnis gloved it along the line and tagged Flack for the first out. Hendrix must have thought Killefer broke from third on the play because he was halfway to third before he realized his mistake. Everett Scott yelled for the ball, but Hendrix was able to get back to second.

Cubs manager Mitchell noticed the gaffe and even though he had wanted Hendrix to pitch the eighth inning, he yanked him and sent in Bill McCabe as a pinch-runner at second.

Charlie Hollocher, slumping at 1-for-13 in the Series, hit a sharp ground ball to Shean. The second baseman might have had a shot at Killefer at home, but he opted for the sure out at first. Killefer scored and Boston's lead was 2–1. Les Mann singled to left and McCabe's run tied the game at 2–2. Ruth avoided further trouble when Paskert grounded out to third. Ruth's scoreless innings record ended at $29\frac{2}{3}$.

When the Red Sox batted in their half of the eighth, they faced a right-handed pitcher—Phil Douglas—for the first time in the Series. Wally Schang, a switch-hitter batting for Sam Agnew, singled to center and took second on a passed ball. Harry Hooper bunted to the third base side of the infield. Douglas's throw to first was wild and sailed down the right field line. Schang scored to give Boston a 3–2 lead. Douglas then retired the next three hitters: Shean flew out to left, Strunk flew out to center, and Whiteman grounded to third.

In the top of the ninth, Ruth was three outs away from his second victory in the Series, but he was clearly out of gas. When Merkle singled to left and Zeider walked, Barrow decided he had seen enough. Barrow double-switched, bringing in Bush to pitch and sending Ruth (who would bat second in the bottom of the ninth inning, if necessary) out to left field.

Bush's first batter was Chuck Wortman, who bunted. McInnis raced in from first and fired the ball to third. Merkle was forced by about 30 feet. Next, Turner Barber came up to hit for Killefer. Barber lined the ball on the ground towards Scott. The sure-handed shortstop flipped the ball to Shean, who threw to first for a game-ending double play. Bush had saved the win for Ruth, and the Red Sox were one victory away from their fifth World Series title.

Tyler pitched a much better game than Ruth, allowing only three hits in seven innings, but had no luck or support. Babe gave up seven hits and six walks, and threw one wild pitch, but the game had been a litany of missed opportunities by the Cubs. Much of Chicago's inability to bring those runners home could be chalked up to the phenomenal play of Everett Scott. The Deacon handled 11 chances flawlessly, several of which robbed the Cubs of hits up the middle. Scott also started two double plays in the final three innings.

The outlook for the Cubs was grim, but back in the

1903 World Series, Boston had trailed Pittsburgh 3–1 before winning four games in a row. However, that had been a best-of-nine series—no team had come back from a 3–1 deficit in a seven-game series.

That evening, Harry Hooper, Everett Scott, Les Mann, and Bill Killefer went to the Copley Plaza Hotel to meet with the National Commission. However, they were told the commissioners had stood them up and gone to the theater instead.

Tuesday, September 10—
Fenway Park, Boston
Game Five: Jim Vaughn v. Sam Jones

CUBS	001 000 020—3 7 0
RED SOX	000 000 000—0 5 0

The players were finally able to meet with the National Commission on Tuesday morning, but the discussion was fruitless. The commissioners promised to render a final decision after the game, but the players knew if the Red Sox won, the Series would be over and any leverage they held would be gone. So they decided to wait in their locker rooms until a decision was announced. When two of the commissioners showed up at Fenway drunk and in no shape to discuss financial matters, the players again had a choice to make. With nearly 25,000 fans waiting in the stands, they decided to play the game.

Because of the delay, the game began one hour late. Sam Jones hadn't pitched in eight days and was a little rusty (or perhaps nervous). Max Flack walked on four pitches to start the game and Charlie Hollocher followed with a hard-hit single up the middle. Carl Mays began warming up.

Les Mann bunted the runners to second and third. The Red Sox infield played back, willing to concede an early run. Dode Paskert's sinking liner to left was caught on the run by George Whiteman. Without stopping to set himself, Whiteman fired the ball to Dave Shean at second base. Hollocher, thinking the ball would drop for a hit, had taken off for third base and was doubled up for the inning's third out with Flack still 20 feet from the plate.

After pitching complete game losses in the first and third games, Jim Vaughn was once again on the hill. After a leadoff single by Harry Hooper, Vaughn retired seven batters in a row.

In the third, Hollocher walked on four pitches. He took a long lead off first, daring Sam Agnew to try and pick him off. It worked—the Boston catcher called for a pitchout, McInnis took the throw from Agnew and turned towards the bag—but he swiped at nothing but air. Hollocher was safe at second with a stolen base.

Mann followed with a double into the left field corner, scoring Hollocher and giving Chicago a 1–0 lead. After 21 innings in the series, Jim Vaughn was finally pitching with a lead.

It was a dull first three innings for the home fans:

Hooper's first-inning single and Jones's walk in the third was the extent of the Red Sox offense. The Fenway crowd cheered as Amos Strunk led off the fourth inning with a double to deep right. But the rally fizzled when Whiteman popped up a bunt attempt and McInnis lined into a double play to first base, with Strunk being doubled off second.

In the fifth, Vaughn was likely tiring: he was pitching his 23rd inning in six days. The Red Sox began hitting him hard, but for all their line drives, Boston came up empty.

Jones pitched well through five innings, having allowed only two hits and one run. In the sixth, Hollocher singled and Paskert walked. Merkle singled to left, but George Whiteman was able to gun Hollocher out at the plate to keep the score at 1–0.

Babe Ruth came out to coach first base in the bottom of the seventh, and the crowd roared, hoping his presence on the field might spark a rally. With one out, Whiteman singled, but another double play, the third turned by the Cubs in the last four innings, killed any hope of a run.

Flack drew his second walk of the game in the eighth and Hollocher dropped down a perfect bunt. Jones and Fred Thomas watched the ball roll slowly along the third base chalk line. It struck a small rock, veered in about three inches and stopped. It was Hollocher's third hit of the game, and with minimal effort Chicago had runners at first and second with nobody out.

Carl Mays and Jean Dubuc were busy in the bullpen as Jones retired Mann on a pop-up. Paskert whacked a double off the wall in left-center and two runs scored.

Scott, Thomas, and pinch-hitter Wally Schang went down in order in the eighth. With one inning left for the Red Sox, trailing 3–0, Hack Miller batted for Jones. He smashed the ball to deep left. Mann ran up the embankment, then slipped and fell. But even though he was sitting on the slope, he managed to catch the ball in his lap. It was a tough break for their team, but the Red Sox fans applauded the unlikely play.

Hooper popped to short left field. It looked like it would drop for a hit, but Hollocher, his hands outstretched, raced back and grabbed it. Instead of a double and a single, Boston was instead down to its last out.

Shean singled into the shortstop hole, but Vaughn zipped three pitches past Strunk for his fourth strikeout and the final out of the game.

Wednesday, September 11—
Fenway Park, Boston
Game Six: Lefty Tyler v. Carl Mays

CUBS	000 100 000—1 3 2
RED SOX	002 000 00X—2 5 0

The players' committee met with Harry Frazee, Charles Weeghman, and several shareholders of both clubs shortly before 11:00 A.M. There were rumors that the owners promised the players a little more money from the gate receipts, but nothing was confirmed.

A morning temperature of 48 degrees and rumors that the sixth game would not be played had left Fenway Park half full.

Barrow selected Carl Mays to pitch, telling Joe Bush that he'd start the seventh game, if it was necessary. Fred Mitchell sent Lefty Tyler back to the Fenway mound and so George Whiteman was in left field and Babe Ruth was on the bench.

Mays was in peak form and retired the first four Cubs on ground balls. Charlie Pick singled, but Mays picked him off first base. Eight of the first nine outs were recorded by the Boston infield.

Tyler faltered in the bottom of the third when he walked Mays on four pitches. After Harry Hooper bunted Mays to second, Tyler walked Dave Shean. Amos Strunk fouled off four pitches before grounding out, putting runners at second and third with two outs. Whiteman's line drive to right field should have been the final out of the inning, but the ball caromed off Max Flack's glove for an error. Both Mays and Shean scored easily to give the Red Sox a 2–0 lead.

Flack tried to atone for his error by singling up the middle to start the fourth inning. With one out, Mays hit Les Mann in the leg with a pitch. Catcher Wally Schang recorded a crucial out when he picked Mann off first base. Mays walked Paskert and Flack stole third on ball four. Fred singled to left, scoring Flack and cutting Boston's lead to 2–1. Pick followed with a hard drive to short right field, very similar to Whiteman's liner to Flack. Harry Hooper raced in and grabbed it for the final out.

After his stumble in the fourth, Mays regained control and kept the ball down in the strike zone and the Chicago batters hit ground ball after ground ball after ground ball.

In the fifth, Deal and Killefer grounded back to the mound. In the sixth, Mays speared a hot shot headed up the middle and threw to Shean for a force play. The other Red Sox were just as sure-handed. McInnis robbed Hollocher of a hit in the fifth and Schang threw Mann out at second to end the sixth. Fred Thomas knocked down Merkle's smash in the seventh with his bare hand, recovered the ball in foul territory, and fired a strike across the infield to McInnis.

Cubs manager Fred Mitchell went to his bench in the eighth. Turner Barber lined the ball over shortstop. From the third base dugout, the Cubs could see that the sinking liner was going to drop in front of Whiteman for a single. But just as the ball was about to hit the ground, Whiteman dove forward, stuck his glove out in front of him and snagged the ball a few inches off the grass.

He landed head first and turned a full somersault, bouncing back to his feet with the ball securely in both hands. Whiteman was staggering a bit, but he was also grinning. He tossed the ball in to Everett Scott, who whipped it around the infield. The Fenway crowd leapt to its feet and hollered for a full three minutes.

The next batter, pinch-hitter Bob O'Farrell, popped up to short left field. There was no way Whiteman could reach this one—but Scott glided out and made a difficult catch look almost routine. At that point, with two outs, Whiteman jogged in to the Red Sox bench, rubbing his sore neck. As he crossed the infield, the crowd rose to its feet and applauded again. He was replaced by Babe Ruth.

Mitchell's third pinch-hitter of the inning, Bill McCabe, lifted a foul ball near the third base stands. Scott caught that one, too, and the inning was over.

The first three hitters in Chicago's lineup were due up in the ninth and Mays retired them without incident. Flack fouled out to third, Hollocher hit a routine fly to left (when the fans roared, Ruth took a graceful bow), and Mann grounded out to second.

With a 2–1 win, the Red Sox were World Series champions for the third time in four years, and the first franchise to win five World Series titles.

Carl Mays faced only three batters over the 27-man minimum. Chicago hit the ball out of the infield only twice in the last five innings and no Cub reached second base.

Max Flack was immediately compared to Fred Snodgrass, who dropped a routine fly ball that helped the Red Sox beat the New York Giants in the 10th inning of the final game of the 1912 World Series.

Many of the post-game wrap-ups concentrated on how lucky the Red Sox had been.

The *Washington Post*: "The Red Sox have often been called the luckiest ball club in the world. They lived up to their reputation again today." Hugh Fullerton also believed "the best team did not win" and that if the Series were played over again, "the majority of the experts who have watched all of the games would wager on Chicago."

Fred Mitchell was more magnanimous. "All the glory that goes with winning the world championship belongs to Boston. The pitching on both sides was the best in years. It was a tough series to lose. The scores of the games prove that.... I'm not trying to detract anything from the Red Sox. They are a great team and proved it. But I'd like to play the series over again if such a thing were possible.... I shall always contend that with an even break, we would have won. That's all I have to say on the subject."

The Red Sox batted only .186 in the series and slugged .233. The Cubs were not much better, batting .210, though Chicago did score 10 runs to Boston's nine.

Wally Schang led the Red Sox with a .444 average (4-for-9). Both Whiteman and McInnis hit .250 (5-for-20). For Chicago, Charlie Pick was 7-for-18, .389. Merkle, Mann, and Flack each had five hits.

Each team used only four pitchers. For the Cubs, Vaughn and Tyler pitched 50 of their team's 52 innings.

The winning shares turned out to be $1,108.45 per player, the lowest amount ever awarded to the World Series champions. The Cubs' losing share was $671 per player.

1918 World Series Most Valuable Player

by Bill Nowlin

If an official MVP had been chosen for the 1918 World Series, the laurels would almost certainly have been placed on the brow of Red Sox outfielder George Whiteman. And what a way to wrap up his time in the majors: the 35-year-old's last big league game was the clinching game of the 1918 Series.

This is not revisionist history. A number of writers who covered the Series nominated Whiteman at the time for the honor. The *Washington Post*, for instance, offered as the subhead for its story on the sixth game: "Whiteman Hero of Contest." J. V. Fitz Gerald of the *Post* declared that Whiteman "won the 1918 world's baseball championship for the Red Sox."

Before the World Series, the up-and-down Mr. Whiteman had only 258 major league at-bats—12 in 1907 with the Red Sox, 32 more in 1913 with the New York Yankees, and 214 in 1918, again with the Red Sox. But when it came to the Series against the Chicago Cubs, manager Ed Barrow had him start in left field and bat cleanup in all six games. "Whitey" hit .250 with five hits in 20 at-bats, and scored two runs—unimpressive totals by today's standards, perhaps, but this wasn't a World Series noted for offense. Of all the batters with at least 10 at-bats, Whiteman's batting average, hits, and runs scored all tied for his team's lead.

Although Whiteman was the lone member of the Red Sox team to commit an error in the World Series, it was an inconsequential one. He contributed a number of key defensive plays (such as banging into the left-field bleacher wall in Chicago and robbing Dode Paskert of a long extra-base hit in Game Three) that helped hold the Cubs to their grand total of 10 runs scored over six games. The Red Sox scored only nine runs—but the Red Sox prevailed.

One way or another, Whiteman was involved in the rallies that brought in eight of the Red Sox's nine runs. It was his "sizzling line drive" in the third inning (dropped for an error by Cubs right fielder Max Flack) that drove in both of Boston's two runs in the clinching Game Six.

Whiteman's final moment of glory came on defense, in the top of the eighth, when he made —again according to the *Post*—"one of the most sensational catches ever seen on a ball field to take a sure triple and possible home run from Turner Barber." Whiteman wrenched his neck with his somersaulting catch and had to leave the game, but he did so to "one of the greatest ovations that has ever been accorded a world's series player. Whiteman is the hero of the 1918 championship struggles."

Hugh Fullerton's nationally syndicated column ran in the *Atlanta Constitution* under the headline "Whiteman, Once Adjudged Failure, Becomes Star." He termed Whiteman "the active principal in all four of the Red Sox victories."

One could also make an MVP case for pitchers Carl Mays and Babe Ruth. Mays pitched complete game victories in Games Three and Six. In 18 innings, Mays allowed only 10 hits and three walks. The Cubs scored one run in each of his two starts which, of course, gave him an earned run average of 1.00.

Like Mays, Ruth was 2–0 on the mound, though with a slightly higher ERA and—with seven walks – somewhat less dominant (he was lucky to have allowed only two runs). Ruth was the only player on the team to have more than one run batted in; his triple in Game Four drove in two. It was Ruth who took Whiteman's place in left after Whitey had hurt his neck. Prior to that, the only games in which Ruth played were those in which he pitched. It was Whiteman who played in each and every game and seemed to be a central figure in most of the plays that mattered.

In post-Series remarks, the often-passed-over George Whiteman said, "They all want to talk to me now. It came late but I got my chance at last.... I have been on several pennant winning teams in the minors. But somehow or other I never seemed to land in the majors.... I never seemed to get the publicity that some fellows get.... If it hadn't been for this season, no one would ever have heard of George Whiteman, I suppose. And there you are. I don't know how many other players there have been in the minors that no one ever heard of either, who might have delivered the goods if they had had a chance. It's a hard game, professional baseball, and on one can tell me that you don't have to have luck as well as ability to rise very far in it. But while I think that I should have had a chance a long time ago, I am satisfied. I had had my day, brief as it is. I am certainly better off than hundreds of other fellows who never had their day at all."

The final ball from the 1918 World Series, caught by Fred Thomas and retained by his son Warren. Courtesy of Sportsworld USA and Phil Castinetti.

The Years that Followed

by Bill Nowlin

After 1918, the Red Sox began to slip—and stumbled badly, winning less than half their games in 1919 and finishing in sixth place, 20½ games behind the league-leading Chicago White Sox, whose World Series performance soon resulted in that year's team forever being branded the "Black Sox" when it was revealed that eight players had conspired with gamblers to lose the World Series to the Cincinnati Reds.

The 1920s were a decade of unmitigated disaster for the Red Sox. It was hardly an improvement that the team finished fifth in 1920; they were 25½ games behind the first-place Indians. From 1922 through 1930, only once did they manage to escape last place, and that was by only one-half game.

It's a wonder baseball ever recovered in Boston, that fans were willing to wait out the Harry Frazee/Bob Quinn years until Tom Yawkey purchased the team in 1933. Yawkey's main contribution was his wealth, and that money bought in a lot of great players (Jimmie Foxx, Lefty Grove, and more) and financed a strong farm system that brought players such as Bobby Doerr, Ted Williams, and Johnny Pesky to Fenway Park. It still took a dozen years for a Yawkey team to secure a pennant in 1946 and it would be a full 86 years before the Red Sox reclaimed the title of World Champions.

It was a long time in coming. By that time, the very year of their last championship had become a singsong taunt—"nine-teen eight-teen"—that rained down on Red Sox fans from Yankees partisans not shy about crowing over their own team's successes and their rival's disappointments, which were legion.

Then came 2004. Did the Red Sox stage the greatest comeback in baseball history or did the Yankees pull the biggest choke in American sports history? For happy/delirious Red Sox fans, it was both!

Now 1918 becomes a year worthy of a little more appreciation, a look at a distant day that shaped the psyche of many of today's Red Sox rooters.

General References

Many biographers drew on the same sources while researching their articles. The listing which follows presents sources which were used by multiple authors. Readers should assume that most authors used several of these references in preparing their work.

We will also present a listing of special references, which will typically be unique to the biographies in question and listed alphabetically by player. When these sources are included within the text or in endnotes to a given article, we will not repeat them again in the list of special references.

Books

Lee, Bill. *The Baseball Necrology, The Post-Baseball Lives and Deaths of Over 7,600 Major League Players and Others* (Jefferson NC: McFarland & Company, 2003)

Stout, Glenn and Richard A. Johnson. *Red Sox Century, The Definitive History of Baseball's Most Storied Franchise* (Boston: Houghton Mifflin Company, 2004)

Thorn, John and Peter Palmer, eds., with Michael Gershman. *Total Baseball* (4th edition), *The Official Encyclopedia of Major League Baseball* (Viking Press/Penguin Group, 1995)

Waterman, Ty and Springer, Mel. *The Year the Red Sox Won the Series* (Boston: Northeastern University Press, 1999)

Wood, Allan. *Babe Ruth and the 1918 Red Sox* (Lincoln, NE: Writers Club Press, 2000)

Periodicals

Atlanta Constitution
Boston Globe
Boston Herald and Journal
Boston Post
Chicago Tribune
Christian Science Monitor
Los Angeles Times
New York Times
The Sporting News
Washington Post

Websites

The SABR Online Encyclopedia, available to SABR members at www.sabr.org

www.baseball-almanac.com
www.baseballlibrary.com
www.baseball-reference.com
www.retrosheet.org
www.1918redsox.com

Many authors also consulted United States Census records and recently made available World War I draft registration records. Most authors used minor league statistical data prepared by SABR member Ray Nemec.

Special References

Agnew, Sam

"Sam Agnew, Batterymate for Ruth on Red Sox, Dies: He Caught Both of Babe's Hill Victories Over Cubs in World Series of 1918," *The Sporting News*, August 1, 1951, p. 30.

Several clippings from Sam Agnew's Hall of Fame newspaper clipping file. Some have neither a title nor an author, but they include clippings from March 7, 1919, and July 29, 1937. Others from the file include:

"Troy Agnew Gives Brother Job," February 4, 1937.

"Sam Agnew Buys Meridian," December 21, 1939.

"Agnew's New Deal Includes New Moniker for Meridian," February 1, 1940.

"Sam Agnew Wants to Place Meridian Franchise in Florida," October 24, 1940.

Bader, King

In addition to news items from some of the general references, *Providence Evening Bulletin, Syracuse Herald, Fitchburg Sentinel, Daily Kennebec Journal,* and the *LeRoy Reporter.* The Bader scrapbook assembled by Bill Perrin at the National Baseball Hall of Fame proved a treasure trove of information. Also helpful were Bill Nowlin, Dick Thompson, Tim Wiles, and Claudette Burke of the Baseball Hall of Fame, and Brad Bisbing of the Buffalo Bisons.

Barbare, Walter

Barbare's player file at the National Baseball Hall of Fame file, including minor league data, his obituary, and the letter from Franklin Rostock to August Herrmann.

Communications from Arlene Marcley of the Shoeless Joe Jackson Museum, Greenville.

Bluhm, Red

Harvey Bluhm's player file at the A. Bartlett Giamatti Research Center, National Baseball Hall of Fame, contains copies of scrapbook pages. The pages have newspaper clippings with pictures and stories of Bluhm's baseball career. Unfortunately, most of the clippings have no attribution. Thanks to Derby Gisclair for his help with the details of Red Bluhm Day.

Bush, Bullet Joe

Neft, David S. and Richard M. Cohen, *The World Series,* St. Martin's Press, 1990

Cole, Milton and Jim Kaplan, *The Boston Red Sox,* World Publications Group Inc., JG Press, 2005

Gentile, Derek, *The Complete Boston Red Sox,* Black Dog & Leventhal Publishers Inc., 2004

Chadwick, Bruce and David M. Spindel, *Boston Red Sox: Memories and Memorabilia of New England's Team,* Abbeville Press, 1991

Okrent, Daniel, and Harris Lewine, eds., with historical text by David Nemec. *The Ultimate Baseball Book,* Houghton Mifflin Co., 1988

Wolff, Miles and Lloyd Johnson, *Encyclopedia of Minor League Baseball,* Baseball America, Inc., 1993

Lane, F.C., "The Yankees' Pitching Ace," *Baseball Magazine,* February 1923, p. 395–396

Bush, "Bullet Joe," with Carroll S. Slick, "On the Mound," *Saturday Evening Post,* June 8, 1929, p. 10

Bush, "Bullet Joe," with Carroll S. Slick, "At Bat," *Saturday Evening Post,* June 22, 1929, p. 40

Bush, "Bullet Joe," with Carroll S. Slick, "Breaking In," *Saturday Evening Post,* August 24, 1929, p. 38

Bush, "Bullet Joe," with Carroll S. Slick, "The Lost Arts in Baseball," *Saturday Evening Post,* April 5, 1930, p. 54

Nack, William, "Lost in History," *Sports Illustrated,* August 15, 1996, p. 74–85

Tholkes, Robert (SABR member) of Columbia Heights, Minn., contributed research information on a young Joe Bush from his review of local papers, the *Brainerd Dispatch* and *Daily Missoulian.*

Van Essen, John of Fridley, Minn., 3rd-great grandson to Joe Bush's maternal grandparents [Van Essen's great-grandmother was Bush's cousin], contributed extensive family genealogy and census detail on the Bush family.

Crow Wing County Historical Society, 320 Laurel Street, Brainerd, Minn., 56401.

Cochran, George

E-mail correspondence with John Hall, 2006–07

E-mail correspondence with Michelle Hansford, 2006

In addition to news items from some of the general references:

Decatur Daily Review, Decatur IL, 1911

Topeka Daily Capital, Topeka KS, 1912–16

Hutchinson Daily News, Hutchinson KS, 1917

Toledo Times, 1918

Carthage, Missouri City Directories 1900–1927

Coffey, Jack

The author gives special thanks to Patrice M. Kane, Head, Archives and Special Collections at the Fordham University Library. Ms. Kane kindly donated her time and resources, providing the author with invaluable information about Jack Coffey.

In addition to news items from some of the general references:

Fordham Ram

Hartford Courant
New York Mirror
New York World-Telegram and Sun

Dubuc, Jean

Buffalo Bisons Historical Page.

Burlington Free Press, June 29, 2006 and online edition, October 19, 2006.

Dubuc scrapbooks in the National Baseball Hall of Fame Library, Cooperstown NY.

"Flaws in the Diamond" University of Massachusetts, October 15, 1975.

Lane. F. C. "Slow Ball Wizard"

Correspondence from Bob O'Leary, December 31, 2006.

University of Notre Dame website.

Thanks for research assistance by Cappy Gagnon and Bob O'Leary.

Gonzalez, Eusebio

Thanks to: Peter Bjarkman, Orestes "Tico" Chavez, Ryan Christoff, Tim Conway, Ayla Demiray, Barrie Public Library, Matt De Waelsche, Ian Gilchrist, Gary Goldberg-O'Maxfield, Roberto Gonzalez Echeverria, Kevin Hill, Calobe Jackson, Tom Kayser, David King, Kit Krieger, Sean Lahman, Geddy Lee, Cesar Lopez, Conrado Marrero, Ralph Maya, Ray Nemec, Eddy Martin Sanchez, Luz Perez del Alba Bardaji, Frank Saucier, David Skinner, Noe Torres, John Virant, Tim Wiles, Nick Wilson, and Robyn Zuck

A more exhaustively-detailed biography of Eusebio Gonzalez appears on SABR's BioProject site, at the following link: http://bioproj.sabr.org. Those wishing more information might enjoy the voyage taken while researching this largely unknown ballplayer. It is, perhaps, instructional as to how much can be gleaned about one of our most obscure Red Sox.

Hoblitzell, Dick

The author wishes to thank Connie (Hoblitzell) Michael for her extensive help with this biography, and Bill Nowlin for putting him in touch with Connie. The other major source was Dick Hoblitzell's clippings file from the National Baseball Hall of Fame. An earlier and much shorter version of this biography appears in the SABR book *Deadball Stars of the National League.*

Hooper, Harry

This biography is drawn from Paul Zingg's book *Harry Hooper: An American Baseball Life* (Urbana: University of Illinois Press, 1993).

Jones, Sam

Interviews by Alex Edelman with Ronald Turner (June 25, 2007); Sandra Jones Taylor (August 12, 2007, and e-mail correspondence); and George Jones (June 29, 2007).

Clippings from *The Spirit of Democracy* newspaper, Woodsfield, OH, and the *Monroe County Beacon.*

Lieb, Frederick G., *The Boston Red Sox* (New York: G.P. Putman & Sons 1947, republished Carbondale & Edwardsville: Southern Illinois University Press, 2003)

Schlemmer, Bill. "A Fella Named Jones," *The Erie Daily Times* (Erie, Pennsylvania), October 20, 1950.

Bullard, Jim, "All Time Great Baseball Player Recalls 22 Years in Big Leagues," *Martins Ferry Times-Leader,* Martins Ferry, Ohio (date unknown).

Kinney, Walt

E-mail correspondence in 2007 with, and documents provided by Kinney's niece Marjorie Kinney Sherrill; her father was Walt's older brother Carl Kinney.

Leonard, Hubert "Dutch"

The Leonard file at the National Baseball Hall of Fame

Alexander, Charles. *Ty Cobb* (NY: Oxford University Press, 1984)

Ginsburg, Dan. *The Fix Is in: A History of Baseball Gambling and Game Fixing Scandals* (Jefferson NC: McFarland, 2004)

Stump, Al. *Cobb: A Biography* (NY: Algonquin Books, 1996)

Mayer, Wally

Gillette, Gary, and Pete Palmer. *The 2005 ESPN Baseball Encyclopedia.* (New York: Sterling, 2005)

Lowry, Philip. *Green Cathedrals* (NY: Walker & Company, 2006)

Neft, David S., Richard Cohen and Michael Neft. *The Sports Encyclopedia: Baseball 2004.* 24th Edition. (NY: St. Martin's Griffin, 2004)

Ritter, Lawrence. *Lost Ballparks, A Celebration of Baseball's Legendary Fields* (NY: Penguin Books, 1992)

Roberts, Randy, editor. *The Rock, the Curse and the Hub, A Random History of Boston Sports,* (Cambridge MA: Harvard University Press, 2003)

Thornley, Stew. *On to Nicollet: The Glory and Fame of the Minneapolis Millers* (Minneapolis: Nodin Press, 1988)

Doyle, Patric, "Wally Mayer," Old-Time Data

Hamann, Rex, "Workhorse Catchers of the American Association," *The American Association Almanac, A Baseball History Journal,* 1902–1952, Volume 1, Number 4, February, 2003

Minnesota Department of Health, Division of Vital Statistics, Certificate of Death 1951–5739, Walter Mayer.

Baseball Magazine
Minneapolis Morning Tribune
Minneapolis Star

www.stewthornley.net/millers
www.baseballfever.com
www.minorleaguebaseball.com
Special thanks to Stew Thornley and Rex Hamann.

Mays, Carl

Nowlin, Bill, *Mr. Red Sox: The Johnny Pesky Story* (Cambridge MA: Rounder Books, 2004)

Sowell, Mike, *The Pitch That Killed* (New York: MacMillan, 1989)

Lane, F.C., "Carl Mays' Cynical Definition of Pitching Efficiency," *Baseball Magazine*, August 1928.

McCabe, Dick

Minor League Baseball Stars Volume II: Career Records of Players and Managers Compiled by the Society for American Baseball Research

www.village.mamaroneck.ny.us

In addition to news items from some of the general references: *Buffalo News, Fitchburg Daily Sentinel, Fresno Bee, Galveston Daily News, Modesto Evening News, Oakland Tribune, Port Arthur News, Reno Evening Gazette, San Mateo Times and Daily News Leader, Syracuse Herald, Van Nuys News, Woodland Daily Democrat.*

McInnis, Stuffy

The Baseball Encyclopedia (New York: The Macmillan Co., 1969)

Baseball: The Biographical Encyclopedia (Sport Media Publishing, Inc., 2003)

Baseball Hall of Fame Library clippings file on Stuffy McInnis

Douskey, Franz, "Smoky Joe Wood's Last Interview," *National Pastime*, No. 27, p. 69 (2007)

Garland, Joe, "'That's the Stuff!' They Said," *North Shore Magazine*, March 4, 1972, p. 3.

Honig, Donald, *The Greatest First Basemen of All Time* (New York: Crown Publishers, 1988)

Karst, Gene & Jones, Martin J. Jr., *Who's Who in Professional Baseball* (New York: Arlington House Publishers 1973)

Lieb, Frederick G., *The Boston Red Sox* (New York: G.P. Putman & Sons 1947, republished Carbondale & Edwardsville: Southern Illinois University Press, 2003)

Lieb, Frederick G., *Connie Mack—the Grand Old Man of Baseball* (New York: G.P. Putnam & Sons, 1945)

McInnis, Stuffy, "My Fifth World's Series," *Baseball Magazine*, Oct. 1918 at p.470.

Murphy, Jeremiah V., "The Tale of Stuffy McInnis' 1921 Error," *Boston Globe*, Feb. 21, 1993, at p.2 North Weekly

Philadelphia Athletics 1910 Championship Season Souvenir Program, as excerpted by the Philadelphia Athletics Historical Society at www.philadelphiaathletics .org

Parsons, Roy, "Stuffy is Gone, but His Legend Will Live Forever," *Gloucester Daily Times*, Feb. 17, 1960, p. 1.

Porter, David L. ed, *Biographical Dictionary of American Sports* (New York: Greenwood Press 1987)

Romanowski, Jerome G., *The Mackmen* (self-published 1979)

Shatzkin, Mike, ed., *The Ballplayers* (New York: William Morrow & Co. 1990)

Smith, Ira L., *Baseball's Famous First Basemen* (New York: A.S. Barnes & Co. 1956)

Stang, Mark, *Athletics Album — A Photo History of the Philadelphia Athletics* (Wilmington, Ohio: Orange Frazer Press 2006)

Miller, Hack

Ahrens, Art. "Cub Strongman," *The National Pastime*, Vol. 10, 1990.

———. "Would You Believe, 49 Runs in One Game," *Baseball Digest*, December 1974.

Grimm, Charlie, with Ed Prell. *Grimm's Baseball Tales: Jolly Cholly's Story* (Notre Dame, Indiana: Diamond Communications, 1983). Originally published under the title *Jolly Cholly's Story: Baseball, I Love You!* (Henry Regnery Company, 1968).

Hoie, Bob. "Determining Batting Champions," *SABR Minor League Newsletter*, June 2002.

Johnson, Lloyd, and Miles Wolff, editors. *The Encyclopedia of Minor League Baseball* (Durham, North Carolina: Baseball America, 1993).

Lane, F.C. *Batting: One Thousand Expert Opinions on Every Conceivable Angle of Batting Science* (New York City: Baseball Magazine Co., 1925). 68.

———. "The Importance of Physical Strength in Baseball," *Baseball Magazine*, September 1925.

Richter, Francis C., editor. *Reach Official Base Ball Guide* (Philadelphia: A.S. Reach, 1916).

Spalding, John. "Hack Miller," in *Pacific Coast League Stars: One hundred of the best, 1903 to 1957* (Manhattan, Kansas: Ag Press, 1994).

Waggoner, Glenn, Kathleen Moloney, Hugh Howard. *Spitters, Beanballs, and the Incredible Shrinking Strike Zone* (Chicago: Triumph Books, revised edition, 2000).

Who's Who in Baseball (New York: Baseball Magazine Company, issues 1920–28).

In addition to news items from some of the general references:

Dallas Morning News
Danville (Illinois) Commercial-News
Houston Chronicle
Houston Press
Minneapolis Tribune
Oakland Tribune.

Molyneaux, Vince

Thanks to Jon Dunkle, Tom Darro, Marty Friedrich, Brian Engelhardt, Ed Washuta, Ray Nemec, Greg Spira, Grace Bounty and the Stamford Historical Society, Craig Fuller, Steve Steinberg, Maurice Bouchard, and the Cambridge Public Library.

Pertica, Bill

Thanks to Kelly Sagert, Bob Hoie, Dick Beverage, Rod Nelson, Walter Kephart, Calvin Bohn, and Jim Buckley.

Ruth, George Herman "Babe"

Creamer, Robert W. *Babe: The Legend Comes To Life* (New York: Simon and Schuster, 1974)

Montville, Leigh. *The Big Bam: The Life and Times of Babe Ruth* (New York: Doubleday, 2006)

Smelser, Marshall. *The Life That Ruth Built* (New York: Random House, 1975)

Stout, Glenn and Richard A. Johnson. *Yankees Century: 100 Years of New York Yankees Baseball* (Boston: Houghton Mifflin Company, 2002)

Wagenheim, Kal. *Babe Ruth: His Life and Legend* (New York: Praeger Publishers, 1974)

Schang, Wally

Hirshberg, Al. *Baseball's Greatest Catchers* (New York: GP Putnam's Sons, 1966)

Jordan, David M. *The Athletics of Philadelphia* (Jefferson, North Carolina: McFarland & Co., 1999)

James, Bill. *The New Bill James Historical Abstract (The Classic – Completed Revised Edition)* (New York: Simon & Schuster, 2001)

Shatzkin, Mike. *The Ballplayers, Baseball's Ultimate Biographical Reference.* (New York: The Idea Logical Press, 1991)

Sargent, Jim. "Walter "Wally" Schang, the Greatest Forgotten Catcher: 1913–1931," *Oldtyme Baseball News*, Volume 6 – Issue 2, 7–11.

Kashatus, B. *Connie Mack's '29 Triumph.* (Jefferson, North Carolina: McFarland & Co., 1999)

Scott, Everett

All sources are indicated in the endnotes in Scott's biography.

Shean, Dave

Martin Donell Kohout, *Hal Chase: The Defiant Life and Turbulent Times of Baseball's Biggest Crook* (Jefferson NC: McFarland and Company, 2001)

Interviews with Dave Shean's daughter-in-law Helen Shean and his grandchildren Leslie Flanagan and Henry Shean in 2004

In addition to news items from some of the general references: *The Arlington Advocate, Arlington High School Clarion, Providence Journal.*

Stansbury, Jack

Creamer, Robert W. *Babe: The Legend Comes to Life* (New York: Simon and Schuster, 1974)

Cummins, George Wyckoff. *History of Warren County, New Jersey* (New York: Lewis Historical Publishing Company, 1911)

Hoppel, Joe. *The Series* (St. Louis: *The Sporting News*, 1988)

Kennedy, David M. *Over Here: The First World War and American Society* (New York: Oxford University Press, 1980)

Seymour, Harold. *Baseball: The Golden Age* (New York: Oxford University Press, 1971)

Simon, Tom, ed. *Deadball Stars of the National League* (Washington DC: SABR and Brassey's, Inc., 2004)

Wright, Marshall D. *The American Association: Year-by-Year Statistics for the Baseball Minor League, 1902–1952* (Jefferson, NC: McFarland & Company, 1997)

Wright, Marshall D. *The Southern Association in Baseball, 1885–1961* (Jefferson, NC: McFarland & Company, 2002)

Wright, Marshall D. *The Texas League in Baseball, 1888–1958* (Jefferson, NC: McFarland & Company, 2004)

Zieger, Robert H. *America's Great War: World War I and the American Experience* (Lanham, MD: Rowman & Littlefield Publishers, Inc., 2000)

E-mail correspondence with Jane Stansbury Miller (grandniece), May 30, 2007

In addition to news items from some of the general references:

Galveston Daily News
Indianapolis Star
Sporting Life
www.americanassociationalmanac.com
heritagequestonline.com.
newspaperarchive.com
theoldaa.wordpress.com
tsha.utexas.edu/handbook/online/articles/BB/hdb2.html

Strunk, Amos

Unattributed clippings from Strunk's file at the National Baseball Hall of Fame.

Dell, John. "Whatever Happened to Amos Strunk?" *Philadelphia Inquirer*, June 25, 1973.

Kofoed, J.C. "The Fable of the Flying Feet: Amos Strunk, Star Outfielder of the Athletics, and How Speed Has Been the Watchword of His Career" *Baseball Magazine*. August 1916. Volume 17, Number 4, pages 33–35.

Williams, Edgar. "Obituaries: Amos Strunk, 89, outfielder for pennant-winning Athletics." *Philadelphia Inquirer*, July 26, 1979.

Yeutter, Frank, "Incident in Life of A's Old Timer:

Amos Strunk Won Baseball Fame After 'Jumping' S. Carolina Team" *Bulletin*, March 3, 1958.

Thomas, Fred

Interview with Fred Thomas, circa 1973. Tape provided by Warren Thomas.

Interview with Warren Thomas, August 17, 2007

In addition to news items from some of the general references:

Topeka (Kansas) Daily Capital

Rice Lake (Wisconsin) Chronograph, January 16, 1986

www.townofmukwonago.us

www.fredthomasresort.com

Truesdale, Frank

Baseball Encyclopedia (New York: Barnes & Noble Books, 2004)

http://www.southernnewmexico.com/Articles/Southwest/Grant/SantaRita-Thetownthatvani.html

http://www.ghosttowns.com/states/nm/gamerco.html

http://www.legendsofamerica.com/HC-McKinley-County2.html

SABR members Howard W. Henry and Davis O. Barker supplied useful information about Frank Truesdale's minor league career in Buffalo and Texas

Wagner, Charles Francis "Heinie"

All sources are indicated in the endnotes in Wagner's biography.

Whiteman, George

In addition to news items from some of the general references is the *Decatur Review*.

Wyckoff, J. Weldon

Interview with MaryAnn Debbink on October 17, 2007.

Interview with Jerome Wyckoff on October 17, 2007.

Jordan, David M. *The Athletics of Philadelphia: Connie Mack's White Elephants, 1901–1954.* Jefferson NC and London: McFarland Press, 1999.

Lieb, Frederick C. *The Boston Red Sox*. New York; G.P. Putnam's Sons, 1947.

Wood, Allen. *Babe Ruth and the 1918 Red Sox*. San Jose: Writers Club Press, 2000.

Marshall D. Wright. *The International League: Year-by-Year Statistics*, 1884–1953, Jefferson, NC: McFarland, 2005.

Barrow, Edward Grant

The information for Ed Barrow's entry was consolidated from Dan Levitt's book *Ed Barrow: The Bulldog Who Built the Yankees First Dynasty* (University of Nebraska Press, 2008). Please contact the press at: http://www.nebraskapress.unl.edu.

Frazee, Harry

Impossible Dreams: A Red Sox Collection. Edited by Glenn Stout. Houghton Mifflin, 2003. Contains several primary source articles relating to Harry Frazee's tenure in Boston.

Yankees Century. Text by Glenn Stout, photographs selected and edited by Richard A. Johnson. (Boston, Houghton Mifflin, 2002). Updates the story detailed in *Red Sox Century.*

"A 'Curse' Born of Hate," ESPN.com, October 3, 2004. The anti-Semitic roots of the so-called 'Curse of the Bambino.' Originally appeared in *Boston Baseball*, September 2004. Reprinted in the *Elysian Fields Quarterly*, vol. 22 #4, 2005.

Link: http://sports.espn.go.com/mlb/playoffs2004/news/story?page=Curse041005

When the Yankees Nearly Moved to Boston," ESPN.com, July 18, 2002. Untold story of how the New York Yankees nearly moved to Boston in 1920.

Link: http://espn.go.com/mlb/s/2002/0718/1407265.html

Stout, Glenn. "1918," *Boston Magazine*, October 1987.

Stout, Glenn "The Last Champions," *NEW ENGLAND SPORT*, July 1993.

Steinberg, Steve. *The Yankees and the Red Sox: The Curse of the . . . Hurlers?*

Baseball Research Journal, No. 35.

Ibdb.com. The Internet Broadway Database, contains a wealth of information about Frazee as a producer and theater owner, as well as detailed information on his shows.

Acknowledgements

This book about the 1918 Red Sox team grew out of a project of the Boston chapter of the Society for American Baseball Research (SABR). Chapter member David Southwick conceived of a publication to honor the 30th anniversary of the 1975 Boston Red Sox team that won the American League pennant and took the quest for a world championship to the seventh game of the 1975 World Series. That work was published by Rounder Books as *'75: The Red Sox Team That Saved Baseball.* It was edited by Bill Nowlin and Cecilia Tan. In 2007, Rounder published *The 1967 Impossible Dream Red Sox: Pandemonium on the Field* (edited by Bill Nowlin and Dan Desrochers), a book that drew on the collective efforts of more than 60 members of SABR, as well as contributions of photography from the *Boston Herald* and the Boston Red Sox and numerous others.

When Boston Still Had the Babe: The 1918 World Series Champion Red Sox is the work of an even 30 SABR members who contributed a biography or editing work, as well as many other SABR members who helped out here or there in one way or another.

The series of books featuring great Red Sox teams of the past is intended to be followed by another 2008 book featuring both of Boston's major league teams during the 1948 season. *Spahn, Sain, and Teddy Ballgame: Boston's (almost) Perfect Baseball Summer of 1948* is edited by Bill Nowlin with Mark Armour, Bob Brady, Len Levin, and Saul Wisnia. The book includes biographies of every player on the 1948 Boston Braves and every player on the 1948 Boston Red Sox.

Future volumes in the series are in production, with the next intended to be a book on the 1939 Red Sox.

We want to thank Ty Waterman for generously loaning all of the graphics that he assembled for use in his own book: *The Year the Red Sox Won the Series* by Ty Waterman and Mel Springer (Boston: Northeastern University Press, 1999)

Additional thanks are due:
Phil Castinetti
Dan Desrochers
S. Derby Gisclair
Tom Kayser
Cord Scott
Aaron Schmidt, Boston Public Library
Alan Thibeault, *Boston Herald*

page 210 is blank

Contributors

Ron Anderson grew up in the Boston area and is a consummate Red Sox and baseball fan. Ron attributes his love for the game to his father who played ball in the Boston City Park League, and who got him started in a life of baseball. He was a contributing writer to the *'75: The Red Sox Team That Saved Baseball, The 1967 Impossible Dream Red Sox: Pandemonium On The Field,* and he is currently working on a biography of former Red Sox standout George Scott. He is now retired and lives with his wife Gail, in Plymouth, Mass.

Mark Armour grew up in Connecticut but now writes about baseball from his home in Oregon. He is the co-author of *Paths to Glory,* editor of *Rain Check,* the director of SABR's Baseball Biography Project, a contributor to many websites and SABR journals, and, most importantly, Maya and Drew's father.

Ray Birch lives in North Kingstown, R.I. He is a retired school teacher; he co-taught a class on baseball. He has been a member of SABR since 2000. He wrote the article about Rick Burleson for the SABR book on the 1975 Red Sox, and the articles about George Thomas and Joe Foy for the SABR book on the 1967 Red Sox. Ray is a life-long Red Sox fan, who attended his first game at Fenway Park in 1961, just missing seeing the great Ted Williams play. He also was at the game at Fenway Park in July, 1967 against the Orioles where the Red Sox turned a triple play, and Game Seven of the 1975 World Series, thanks to Carlton Fisk's homer in Game Six.

Maurice Bouchard, who lives in Shrewsbury, Mass., with his wife Kim, has been a baseball fan since Sandy Koufax struck out Bob Allison for the final out of the 1965 World Series. Bouchard, who grew up in upstate New York, was originally a Yankees fan but George Steinbrenner cured him of that. Since 1987, he has rooted for the Old Towne Team. He has two children, Ian and Gina, both of whom are inveterate Red Sox fans. Bouchard has been a member of SABR since 1999.

Tony Bunting writes about baseball in the early decades of the 20th century. His article on the 1906 Chicago Cubs and White Sox recently appeared in *108* magazine, and he contributed two biographies (Earl Moore and Branch Rickey) to SABR's *Deadball Stars of the American League.* An employee of the Art Institute of Chicago, Bunting lives on the Windy City's northwest side, a 45-minute jaunt from Wrigley Field.

Jon Daly is a life-long resident of the Greater Hartford area. His father introduced him to baseball and the Red Sox during the 1975 season. Because he was a young lad at the time, he expected the Red Sox to play in the World Series every year. Boy, was he wrong! In his free time, he works in the financial service industry. Jon has been a SABR member since 2001.

Aaron Davis was born and raised in the San Francisco Bay Area, where he still resides. Despite the imploring of family and friends, Mr. Davis developed a severe case of being a Yankee fan at a very early age, which he has thus far been unable to kick. He lives with his wife and bulldogs, and is a practicing attorney with a love of baseball history, particularly the Deadball Era.

Nicole DiCicco is a Mets fan (thanks to Gary Carter) who grew up and still resides in enemy territory Philadelphia. Even though never a hometown rooter, she always appreciated and was mesmerized as a child watching Steve Carlton pitch at Veterans Stadium and coincidentally attended Phillies games with Carlton's spot in the pitching rotation. She is a baseball fan first, Mets fan second. She was a contributor of the bio on George Stacey Davis in the 2007 publication *Deadball Stars of the American League.* As a result of the research, she found an error on Davis' Hall of Fame Plaque that led to the Hall's president correcting the plaque. Contributor to Babe Ruth's great-grandson's website www.baberuthcentral.com

Alex Edelman is a recent graduate of Maimonides School, in Brookline, Mass., where he lives — just blocks from Fenway Park. Besides his baseball and music writing, Alex is also a established stand-up comedian, and tours all over the country. In 2005, Alex's Essay, "Paradise Found," about the 2004 Playoffs, was honored with a Will McDonough Sportswriting Award from the New England Sports Museum. In 2006, Alex was selected to the Middlebury College's New England Young Writers Conference in Middlebury, Vt., where he was taught by one of his favorite writers, Alexander Wolff from *Sports Illustrated.*

Rob Edelman teaches film history at the University at Albany and is a Contributing Editor of *Leonard Maltin's Movie Guide.* He is the author of *Great Baseball Films* and *Baseball on the Web;* has published essays in *Base Ball: A Journal of the Early Game, Baseball in the Classroom,* and *Baseball and American Culture: Across the Diamond;* and has written an essay that appears on the DVD compilation *Reel Baseball: Baseball Films From the Silent Era, 1899-1926.* He also is the co-author of *Matthau: A Life* and *Meet the Mertzes,* a double biography of *I Love Lucy's* William Frawley and Vivian Vance.

James E. Elfers. As a lifelong Phillies fan he knows what pain is. A member of SABR since 1986 James Elfers is the author of *The Tour to End All Tours: the story of major league Baseball's 1913-1914 World Tour*, an around-the-world baseball tour which included Boston's Tris Speaker playing as a temporary member of the Chicago White Sox. He works as a Library Assistant at the University of Delaware.

A native of Middlebury, Vermont, and a SABR member since 2001, **Michael Foster** is a Senior Lecturer at Curry College in Milton, MA, and a Librarian Media Specialist with Saint Raphael Academy in Pawtucket, RI. When he's not prowling around the Boston Public Library looking for information on Boston American League deadball stars, he can usually be found playing baseball with his wife Sarah and children, Maggie and Griffin, behind their home in Hopkinton, Mass.

Don Geiszler grew up as a Met fan through the '60s. He became a mild Red Sox fan during the '67 Series, rooting against the hated Cardinals. He has a shrine to Bill Buckner in his basement (actually it's just a picture of the play.) He was able to make his first Fenway visit this past summer and left his initials on the fabulous Green Monster. Don is a director for a major financial institution in NYC and has been a SABR member for many years. Contributions include biographies in *Deadball Stars of the American League* and *Deadball Stars of the National League*.

Joanne Hulbert is a co-chair of the SABR Boston chapter and is also co-chair of the SABR Arts committee. She regrets, despite spending countless hours accumulating 19th century and dead ball era poetry, and although finding poetry for all the other players on the 1918 Red Sox team, she has yet to find a masterpiece dedicated to Charles "Heinie" Wagner, truly an unsung hero. She has not given up the quest.

David Jones grew up in Annapolis, Maryland, as a fan of the Baltimore Orioles, and now makes his home with his wife and daughter in upstate New York. The editor of the 2007 SABR publication *Deadball Stars of the American League*, Jones is also the author of *Joe DiMaggio: A Biography*, published by Greenwood Press in 2004. A doctoral student in African history at the University at Albany, David is currently researching the history of Namibia's struggle for independence from South African rule.

Craig Lammers is both a SABR member and Country/Bluegrass Music Director at WBGU radio in Bowling Green, Ohio. He's currently working on a Deadball era history of minor league baseball in Ohio. Craig is a member of the Wood County Infirmary Inmates Vintage Base Ball team. A catcher, his speed has been compared to an ice wagon going backward.

Len Levin has had a love affair with the Red Sox — with all the joy and heartbreak that entails — since the mid-1940s, when he saw Dave Ferriss shut out the Yankees in his very first game at Fenway Park (the heartbreak: The leadoff Yankee in the second game of the twin bill hit a home run and the Sox were trounced.) He has done extensive research on Babe Ruth's brief stay with the Providence Grays in 1914, when the Babe pitched the Grays to the International League pennant. A former copy desk chief at the *Providence Journal*, he keeps a hand in the newspaper profession by working part time at the *Patriot Ledger* in Quincy, Mass., and conducting workshops for copy editors. He is married and has two daughters.

Dan Levitt is the author of *Ed Barrow: The Bulldog Who Built the Yankees First Dynasty* (University of Nebraska Press, 2008) and co-author with Mark Armour of *Paths to Glory: How Great Baseball Teams Got That Way*, which won the Sporting News-SABR Baseball Research Award. He lives in Minneapolis with wife and two boys.

Les Masterson is a managing editor at HCPro, a healthcare communications company based in Marblehead, Mass. As a journalist, he won numerous awards for his newspaper writing and editing from the New England Press Association and Massachusetts Press Association. He is also a rarity — a New York Mets fan who was born and raised in the shadows of Boston. He and his wife, Danielle, live in Malden, Mass., with their black Lab, Jake.

John McMurray is Chair of the Society for American Baseball Research's Deadball Era Committee. He contributed to SABR's 2006 book *Deadball Stars of the American League* and is a past chair of SABR's Ritter Award subcommittee, which annually presents an award to the best book on Deadball Era baseball published during the year prior. He has contributed many interview-based player profiles to *Baseball Digest* in recent years.

Bill Nowlin is national Vice President of SABR and the author of nearly 20 Red Sox-related books. Bill is also co-founder of Rounder Records of Massachusetts. He's traveled to more than 100 countries, but says there's no place like Fenway Park.

E. A. (Betsy) Reed came by her devotion to the Red Sox honestly. A product of New England, she learned to keep a perfect scorebook listening to the '75 Sox, and also learned the emotional investment required to be a true member of the Red Sox Nation. Currently living in Henderson, Nevada, she is also first cousin to Doug Pappas, founder of SABR's Business of Baseball Committee, and the namesake for the award that recognizes the best oral research presentation at SABR's annual convention.

C. Paul Rogers III is the co-author with boyhood hero Robin Roberts of *The Whiz Kids and the 1950 Pennant* and with Bill Werber of *Memories of a Ballplayer: Bill Werber and Baseball in the 1930s*, among other writings on baseball history. He is also editor of a new "Sport in American Life" series to be published by the SMU Press. He has been a Phillies fan since his boyhood in Casper, Wyoming, and feels like he has endured each of the Phils' 10,000 losses personally. His real job is as a law professor and former dean at the SMU School of Law in Dallas, Texas, where he writes about antitrust law when he cannot find an excuse to read or write about baseball.

Tom Simon founded SABR's Deadball Era Committee and its Gardner-Waterman (Vermont) Chapter, but lately he serves as breadwinner, husband to Carolyn, and father to three-year-old Nolan and six-month-old Calista.

Doug Skipper is a marketing research, customer satisfaction and public opinion consultant from Apple Valley, Minn., who reads and writes about baseball, and engages in father-daughter dancing. A SABR member since 1982, he researched and wrote four biographies for *Deadball Stars of the American League*, and a profile of Norm Siebern for *The 1967 Impossible Dream Red Sox: "Pandemonium on the Field."* Doug and his wife Kathy have two daughters, MacKenzie and Shannon. He has followed the Red Sox from afar since his grandfather escorted him and his two brothers to see their first major league game, on Thursday, August 3, 1967 at Fenway Park (a 5–3 win).

Mike Sowell grew up in Houston but became a Red Sox fan at age nine when he got his first baseball card: a 1957 Tom Brewer. He still pulls for the Red Sox, along with his hometown Houston Astros and his adopted Cleveland Indians, so he knows what suffering is all about. He is the author of *The Pitch That Killed, July 2, 1903* and *One Pitch Away*, and has been a member of SABR since 1985. He now is an associate professor of journalism at Oklahoma State University in Stillwater, Oklahoma, where he lives with his wife, Ellen, and his dogs, all named for former baseball greats.

Glenn Stout has been series editor of The Best American Sports Writing since its inception and is the author and editor of more than sixty books, including *Red Sox Century, Yankees Century, Nine Months at Ground Zero*, and *The Cubs: The Complete Story of Chicago Cubs Baseball*. He lives in Vermont.

A native of Cohasset, Mass., **Christopher Williams** is a music historian who lives in northwest Ohio with his wife and four cats. He grew up in the Boston area, where he experienced the frustrations of the great and disappointing Red Sox teams of the 1970s, and has been an avid baseball fan ever since. His interests in historical baseball date from childhood, and were reawakened in graduate school with the aid of some similarly-minded music graduate students at Berkeley. He has taught music history at Case Western Reserve University, the Cleveland Institute of Music, the University of Alberta, the University of Salzburg, and Bowling Green State University, has published and presented scholarly work on 20th-century music and the music of turn-of-the-century Vienna and Germany's Weimar Republic, and was a contributing writer to *Deadball Stars of the American League*. He has been a SABR member since 2003.

Allan Wood is the author of *Babe Ruth and the 1918 Red Sox*. He also writes the blog "The Joy of Sox." Allan has been writing professionally since age 16, first as a sportswriter for the Burlington (Vt.) *Free Press*, then as a freelance music critic in New York City for eight years. His writing has appeared in numerous publications, including *Baseball America, Rolling Stone*, and *Newsday*. He has contributed to two SABR books: *Deadball Stars of the American League* and *Deadball Stars of the National League*. He currently lives in Ontario, Canada.

Paul Zingg came to the Red Sox through Harry Hooper and a lifelong loathing of the Yankees. He even forgives Harry and his teammates for defeating his beloved National League Giants in the 1912 World Series. His baseball books include a biography of Hooper (*Harry Hooper: An American Baseball Life*) and a history of the old Pacific Coast League (*Runs, Hits, and an Era: The Pacific Coast League, 1903-1958*). He is the president of California State University, Chico, home of a perennial participant in the NCAA Division-II World Series.